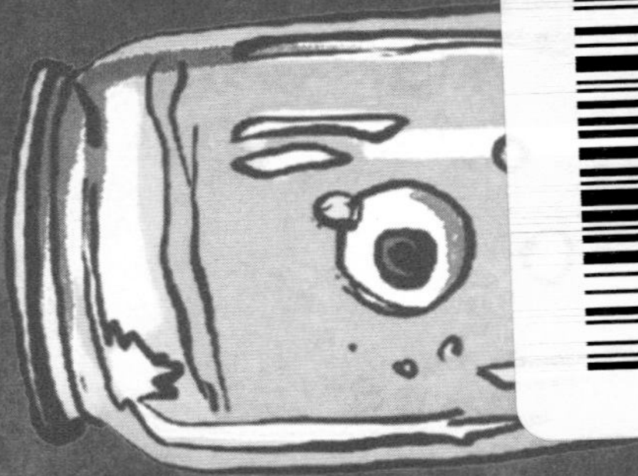

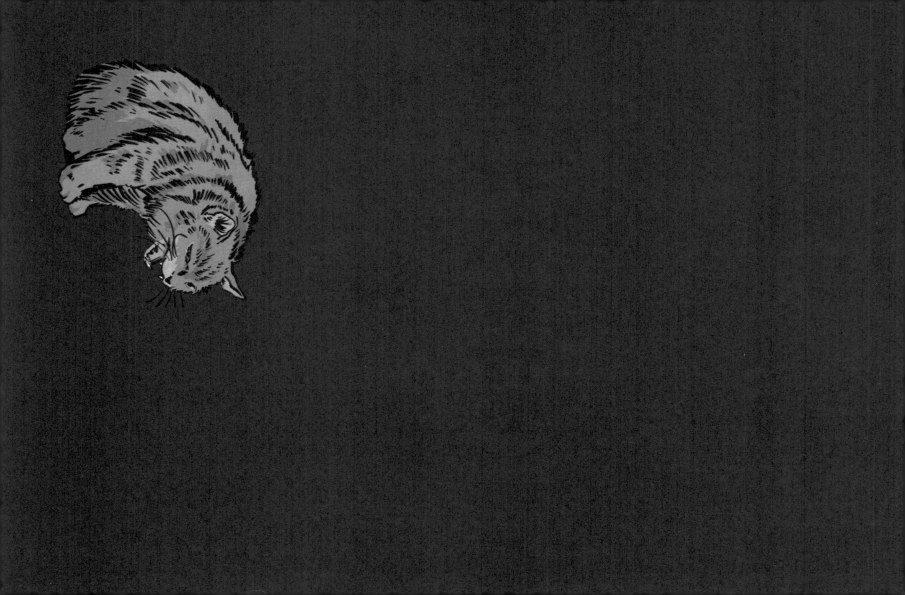

THE KEEPER

BY Tananarive Due AND Steven Barnes

ILLUSTRATED BY Marco Finnegan

Abrams ComicArts Megascope · New York

MEGASCOPE Curator: John Jennings
Editor: Charlotte Greenbaum
Editorial Assistant: Lauren White-Jackson
Designer: Marie Oishi
Managing Editor: Andrea Miller
Production Manager: Alison Gervais
Colorist: Alexandria Batchelor
Lettering: Dave Sharpe

Library of Congress Control Number
2022932920

ISBN 978-1-4197-5155-4

Text © 2022 Tananarive Due and Steven Barnes
Illustrations © 2022 Marco Finnegan

Published in 2022 by Abrams ComicArts®,
an imprint of ABRAMS. All rights reserved.
No portion of this book may be reproduced,
stored in a retrieval system, or transmitted in any
form or by any means, mechanical, electronic,
photocopying, recording, or otherwise, without
written permission from the publisher.

Printed and bound in China
10 9 8 7 6 5 4 3 2 1

Abrams ComicArts books are available at
special discounts when purchased in quantity
for premiums and promotions as well as
fundraising or educational use. Special editions
can also be created to specification. For details,
contact specialsales@abramsbooks.com or
the address below.

ABRAMS The Art of Books
195 Broadway, New York, NY 10007
abramsbooks.com

Abrams ComicArts® is a registered
trademark of Harry N. Abrams, Inc.

MEGASCOPE™ is a trademark of
John Jennings and Harry N. Abrams, Inc.

MEGASCOPE is dedicated to show-
casing speculative and non-fiction
works by and about people of color,
with a focus on science fiction, fantasy,
horror, history, and stories of magical
realism. The megascope is a fictional
device imagined by W. E. B. Du Bois
that can peer through time and space
into other realities. This magical
invention represents the idea that so
much of our collective past has not
seen the light of day, and that there
is so much history that we have yet
to discover. MEGASCOPE will serve as
a lens through which we can broaden
our view of history, the present, and
the future, and as a method by which
previously unheard voices can find
their way to an ever-growing diverse
audience.

MEGASCOPE ADVISORY BOARD

Frederick Luis
Aldama

Kinitra Brooks

Stanford Carpenter

Julian Chambliss

JC Cloutier

Rachelle Cruz

Damian Duffy

Henry Louis Gates Jr.

Frances Gateward

Jonathan Gray

D. Fox Harrell

Kathleen McClancy

Susana Morris

Adilifu Nama

Ricardo Padilla

Darieck Scott

Matt Silady

Sherryl Vint

Rebecca Wanzo

Deborah Whaley

Qiana Whitted

Daniel Yezbick

To Great-Grandmother Lydia and Grandmother
Lucille for teaching me about past generations—
and to Nicki Barnes and Jason Due-Barnes for
leading us into the future.

—TD

To my grandmothers Lula and Muddy.
I wish I could have shown you my children.
But at least I can show my children a
grandmother's heart.

—SB

For Ashlyn. Thank you for the inspiration.
I love you.

—MF

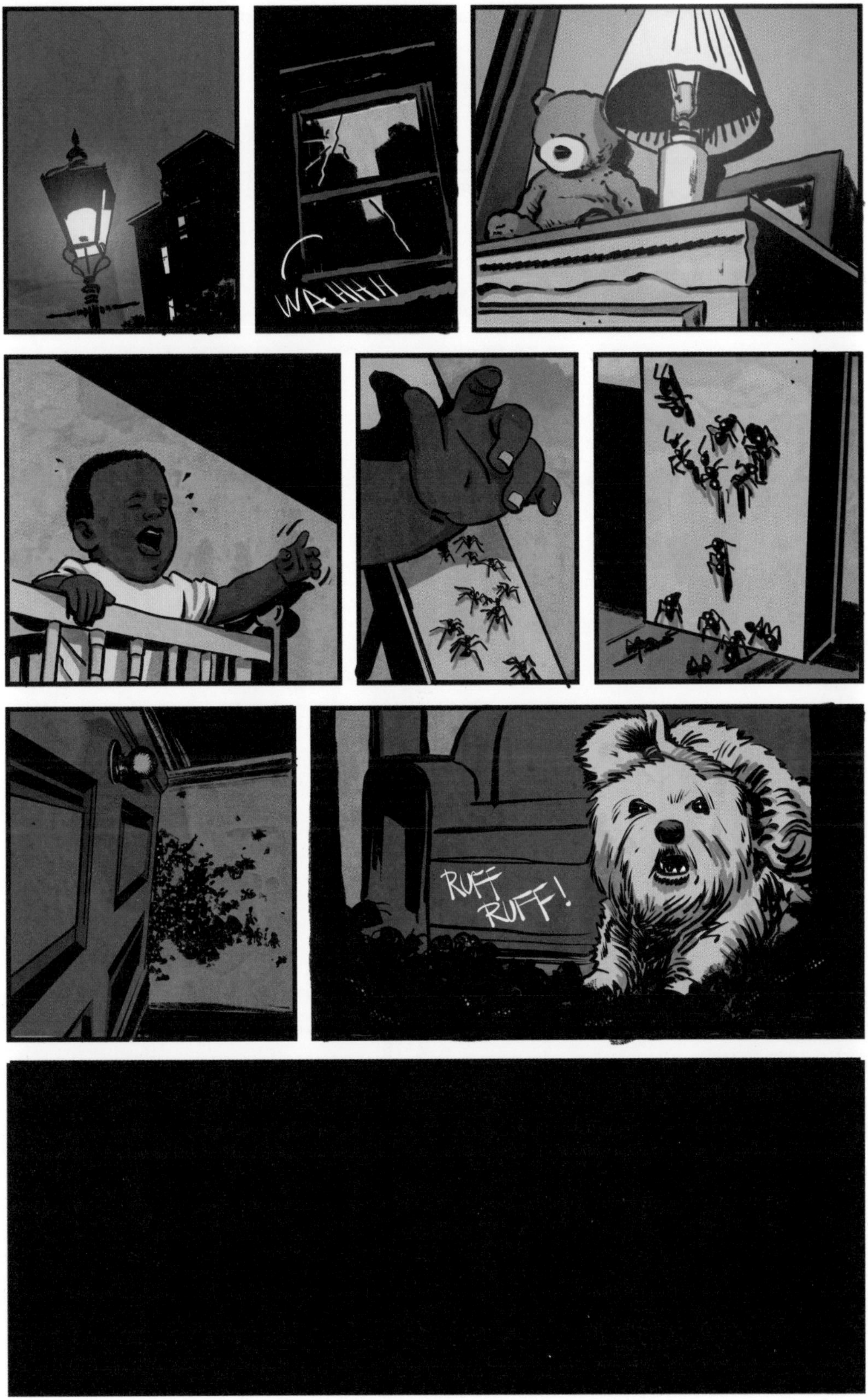
WAHHH
RUFF RUFF!

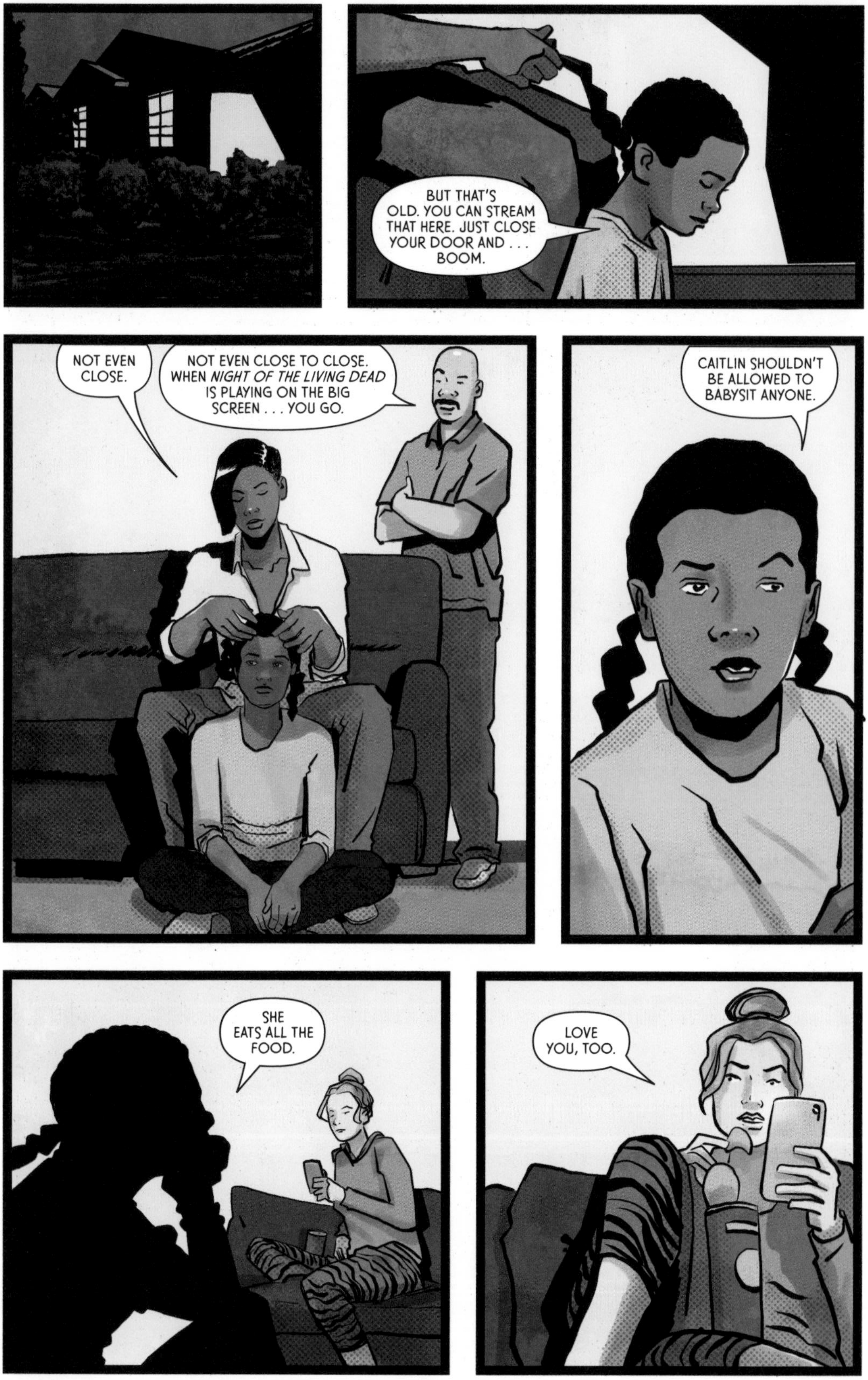
BUT THAT'S OLD. YOU CAN STREAM THAT HERE. JUST CLOSE YOUR DOOR AND . . . BOOM.
NOT EVEN CLOSE.
NOT EVEN CLOSE TO CLOSE. WHEN *NIGHT OF THE LIVING DEAD* IS PLAYING ON THE BIG SCREEN . . . YOU GO.
CAITLIN SHOULDN'T BE ALLOWED TO BABYSIT ANYONE.
SHE EATS ALL THE FOOD.
LOVE YOU, TOO.

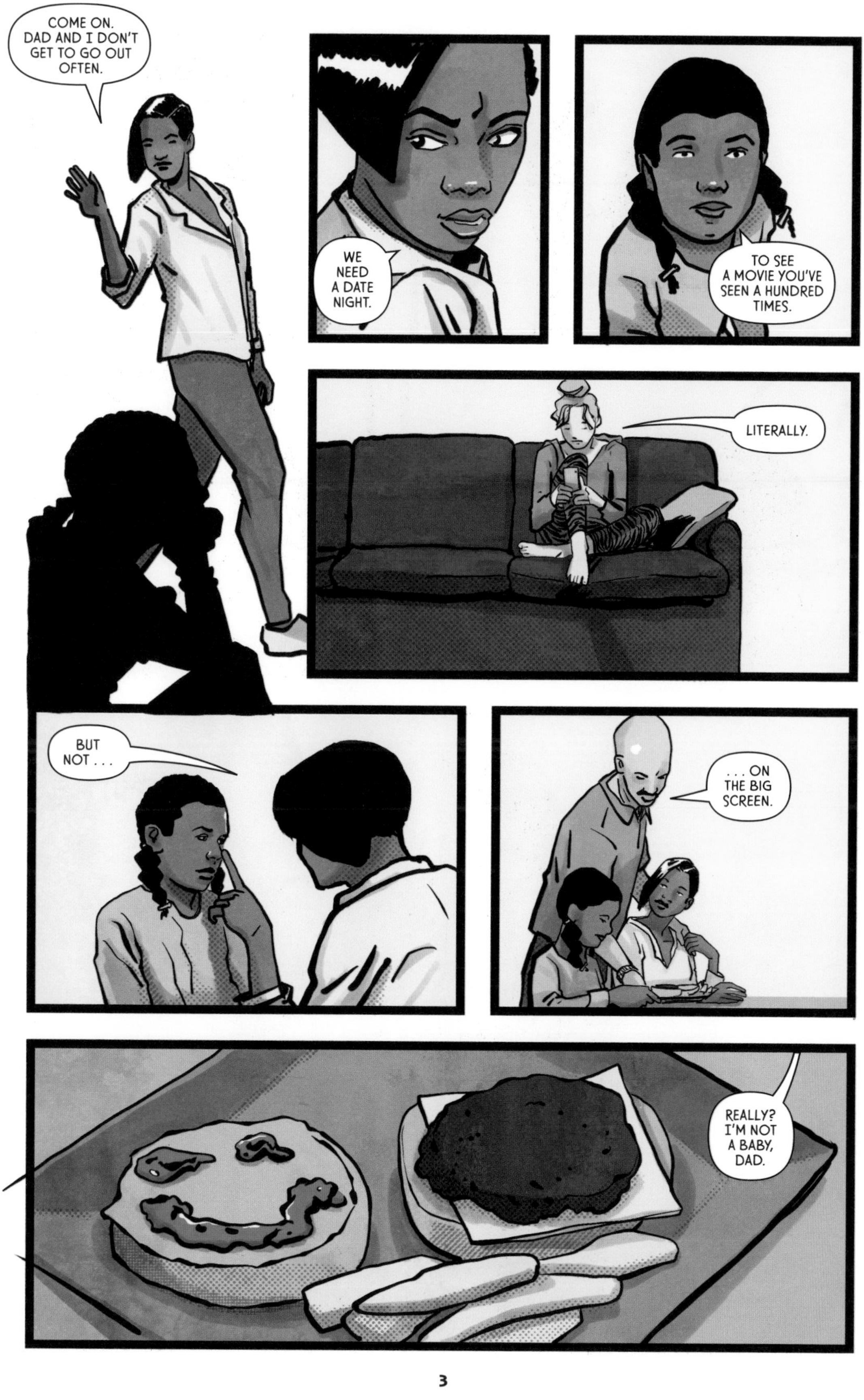
COME ON. DAD AND I DON'T GET TO GO OUT OFTEN.
WE NEED A DATE NIGHT.
TO SEE A MOVIE YOU'VE SEEN A HUNDRED TIMES.
LITERALLY.
BUT NOT . . .
. . . ON THE BIG SCREEN.
REALLY? I'M NOT A BABY, DAD.

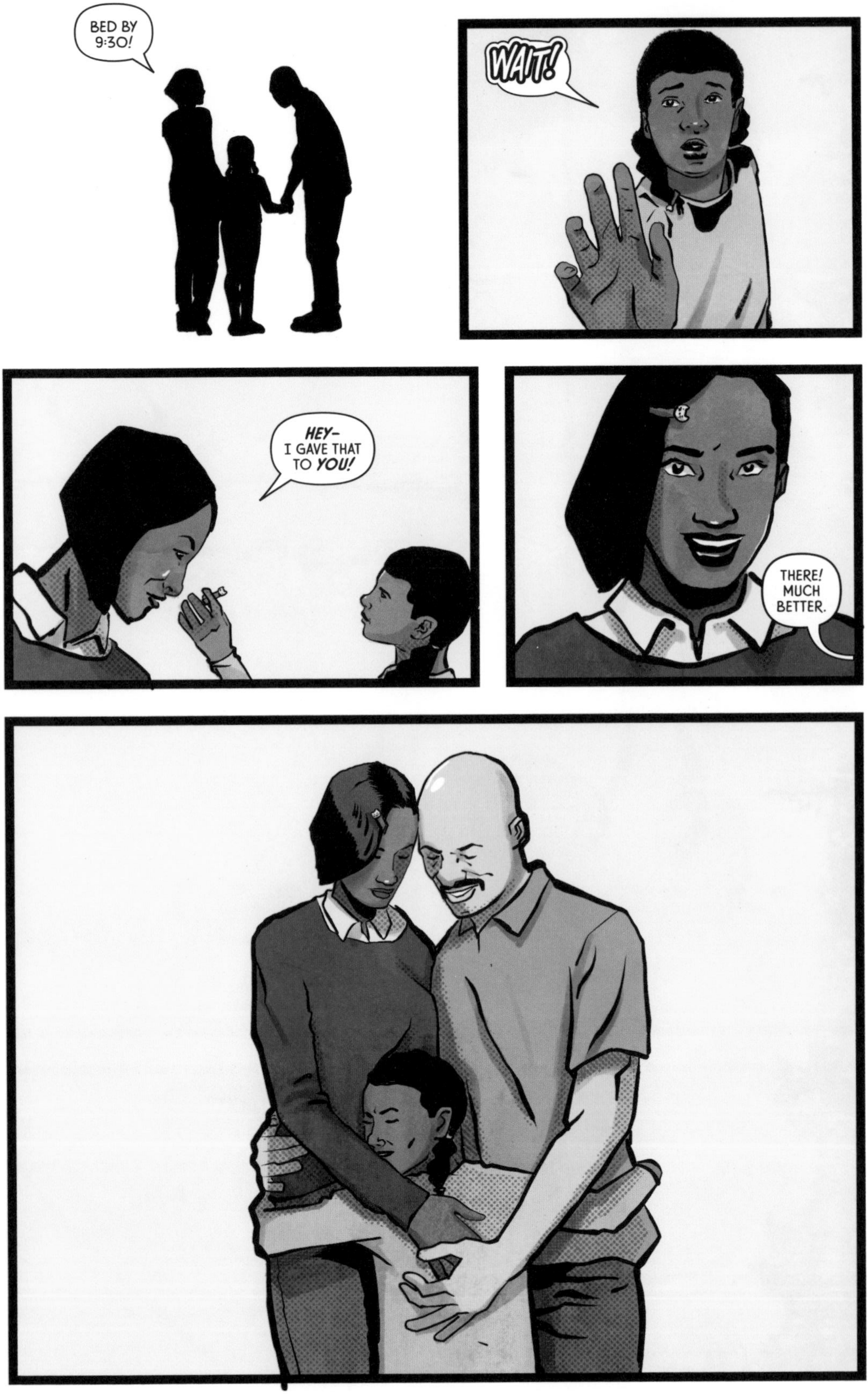
BED BY 9:30!
WAIT!
HEY– I GAVE THAT TO *YOU!*
THERE! MUCH BETTER.

Klik

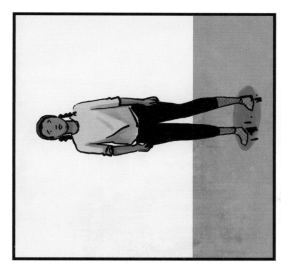

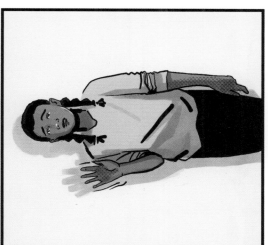

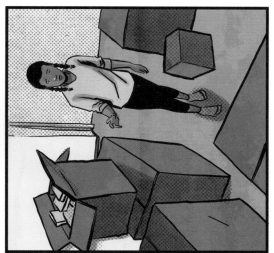

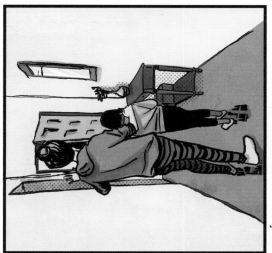

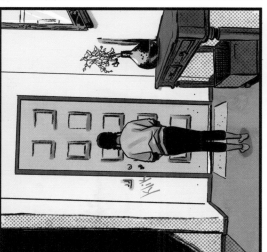

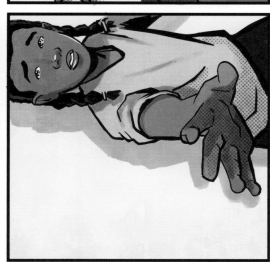

WAIT . . . THIS WASN'T HERE. WHAT HAPPENED TO . . . ?

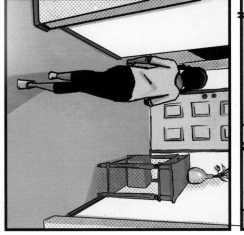

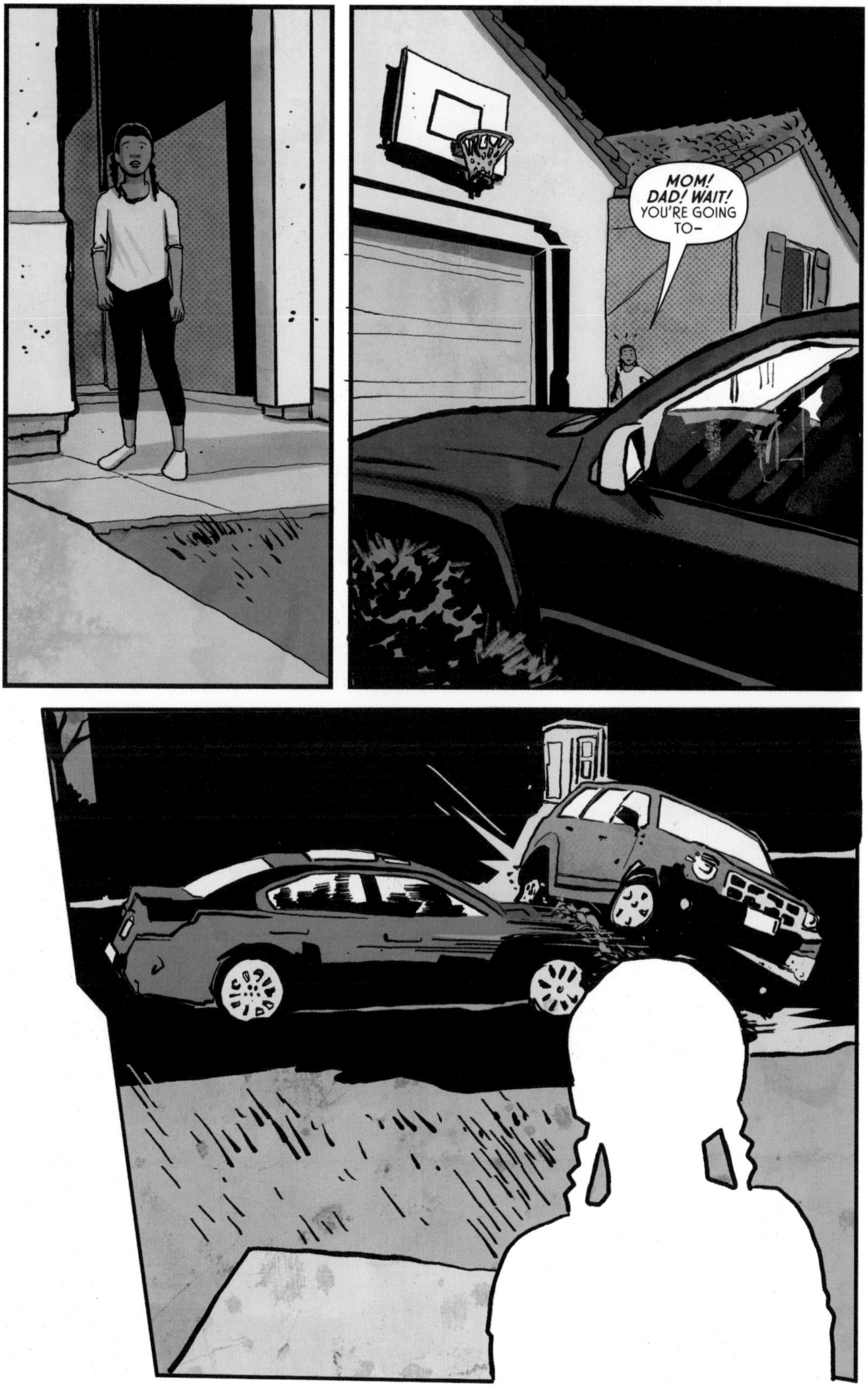
MOM! DAD! WAIT! YOU'RE GOING TO–

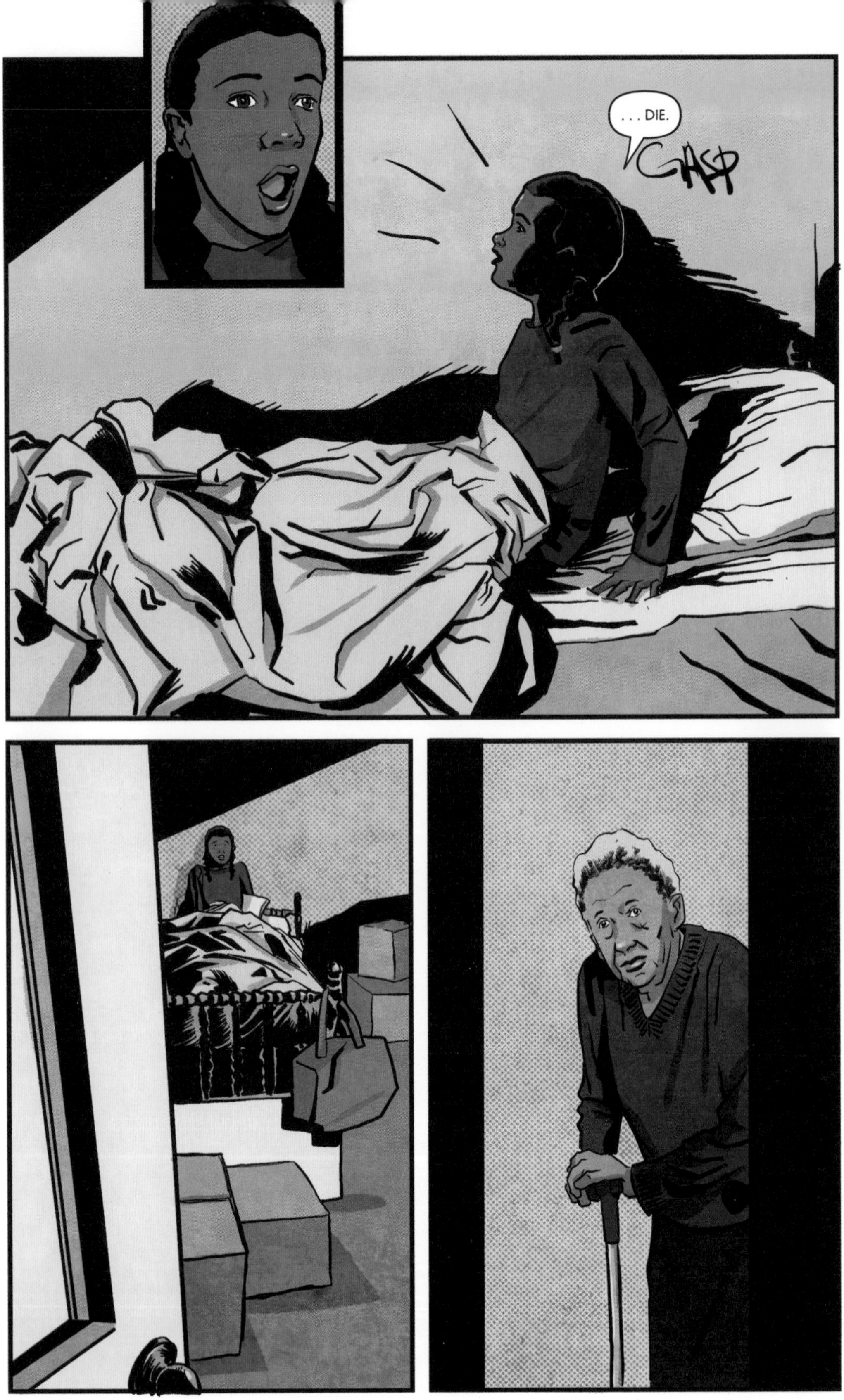
. . . DIE.
GASP

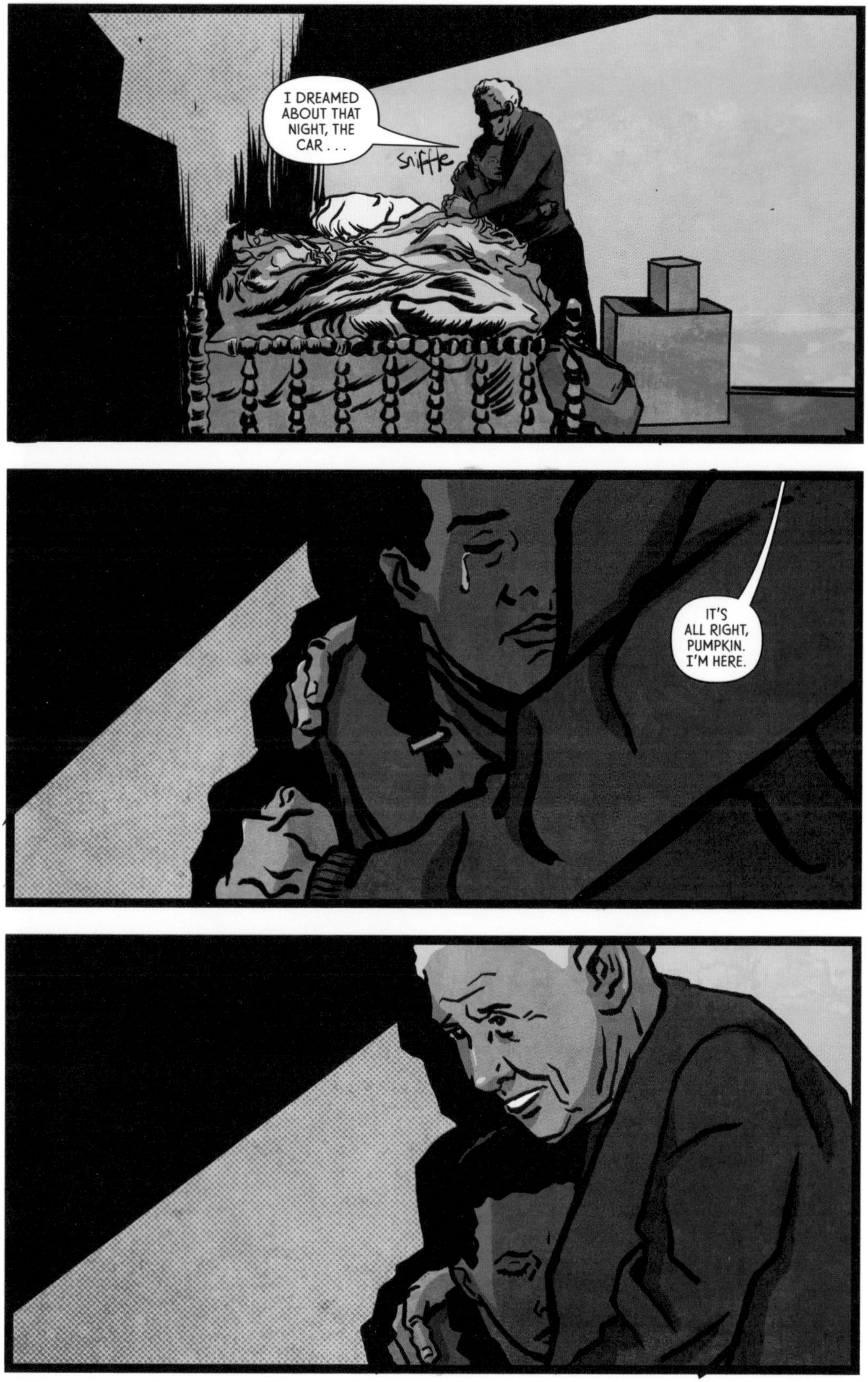
I DREAMED ABOUT THAT NIGHT, THE CAR . . .
sniffle
IT'S ALL RIGHT, PUMPKIN. I'M HERE.

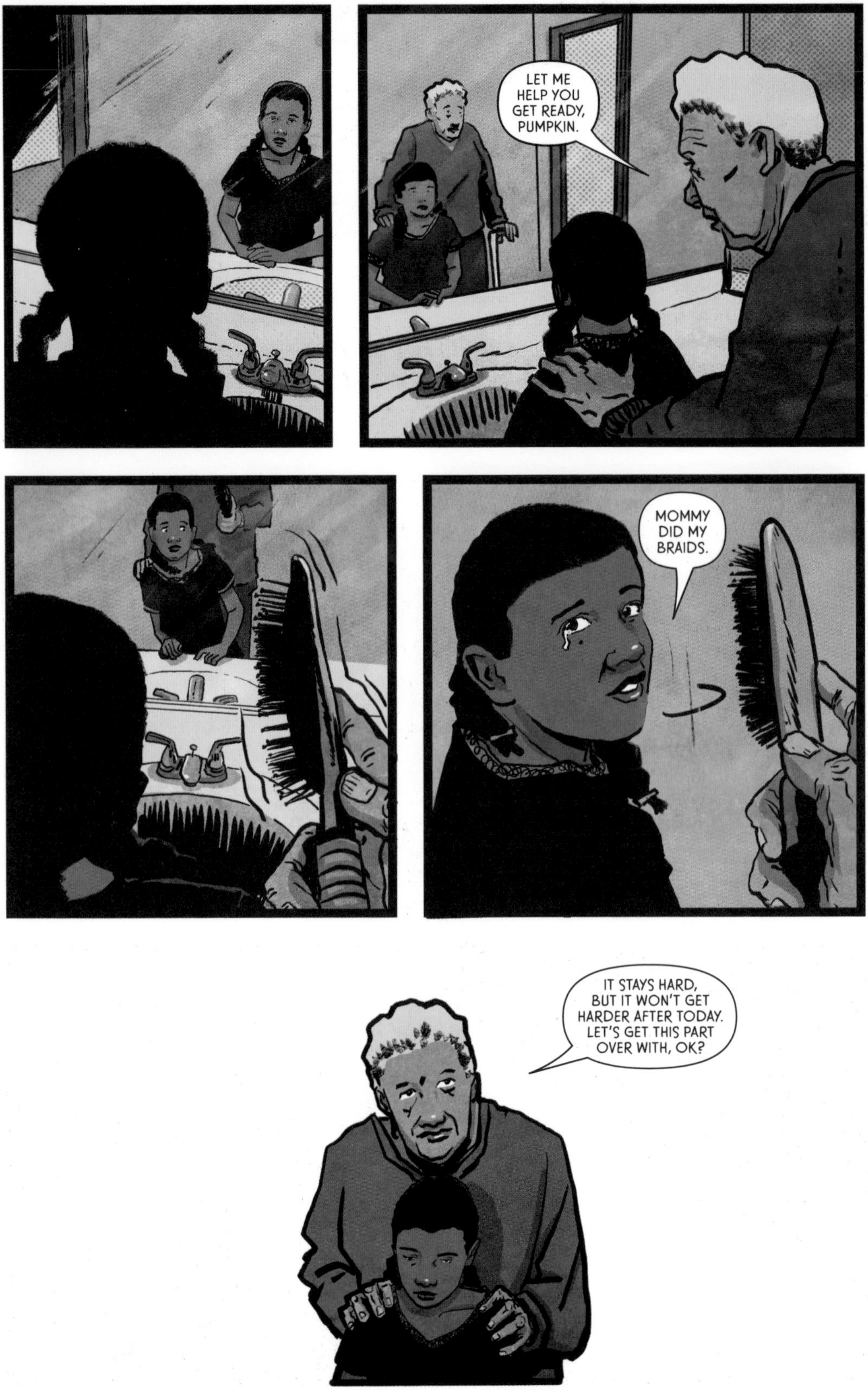
LET ME HELP YOU GET READY, PUMPKIN.
MOMMY DID MY BRAIDS.
IT STAYS HARD, BUT IT WON'T GET HARDER AFTER TODAY. LET'S GET THIS PART OVER WITH, OK?

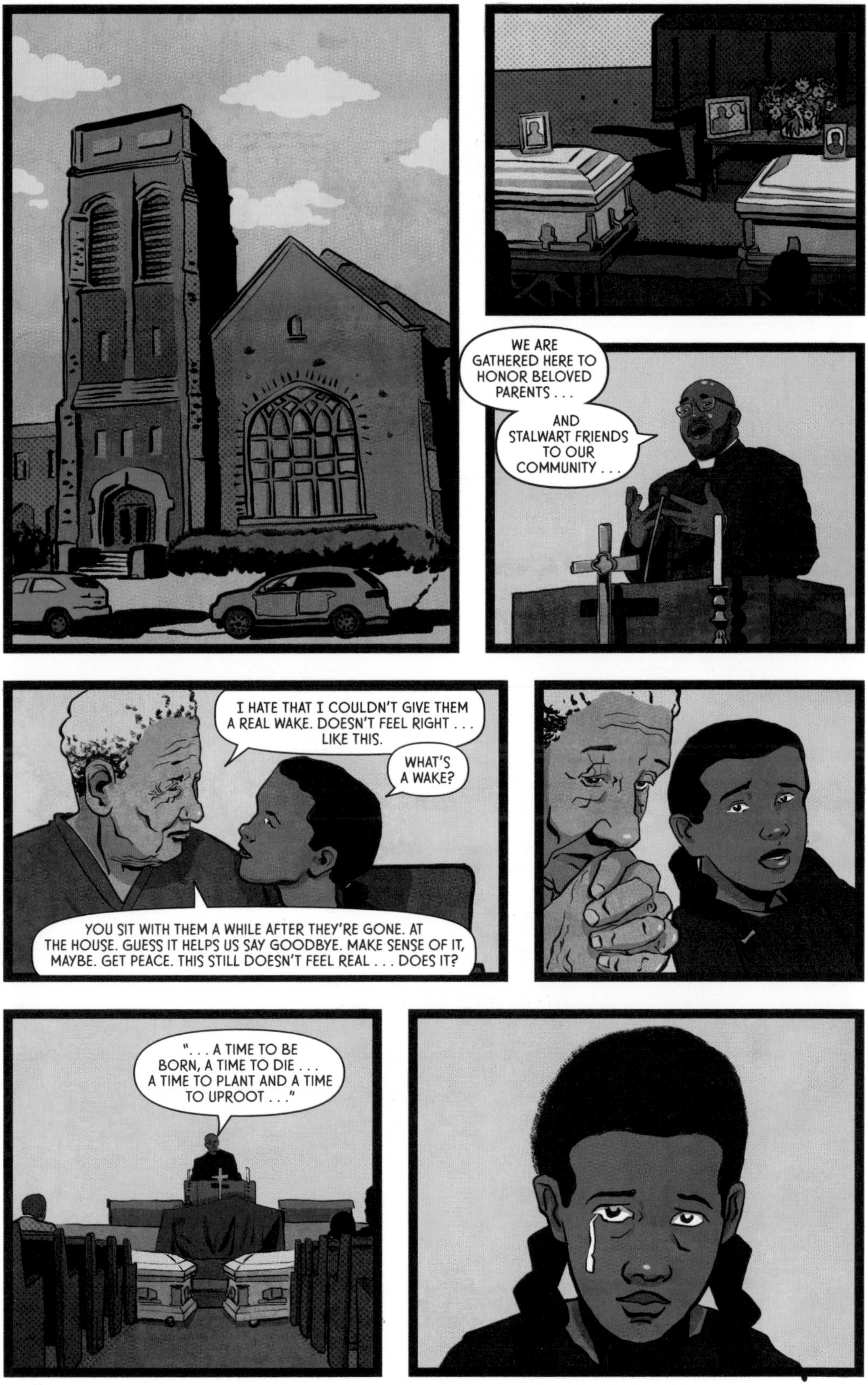
WE ARE GATHERED HERE TO HONOR BELOVED PARENTS . . .
AND STALWART FRIENDS TO OUR COMMUNITY . . .
I HATE THAT I COULDN'T GIVE THEM A REAL WAKE. DOESN'T FEEL RIGHT . . . LIKE THIS.
WHAT'S A WAKE?
YOU SIT WITH THEM A WHILE AFTER THEY'RE GONE. AT THE HOUSE. GUESS IT HELPS US SAY GOODBYE. MAKE SENSE OF IT, MAYBE. GET PEACE. THIS STILL DOESN'T FEEL REAL . . . DOES IT?
". . . A TIME TO BE BORN, A TIME TO DIE . . . A TIME TO PLANT AND A TIME TO UPROOT . . ."

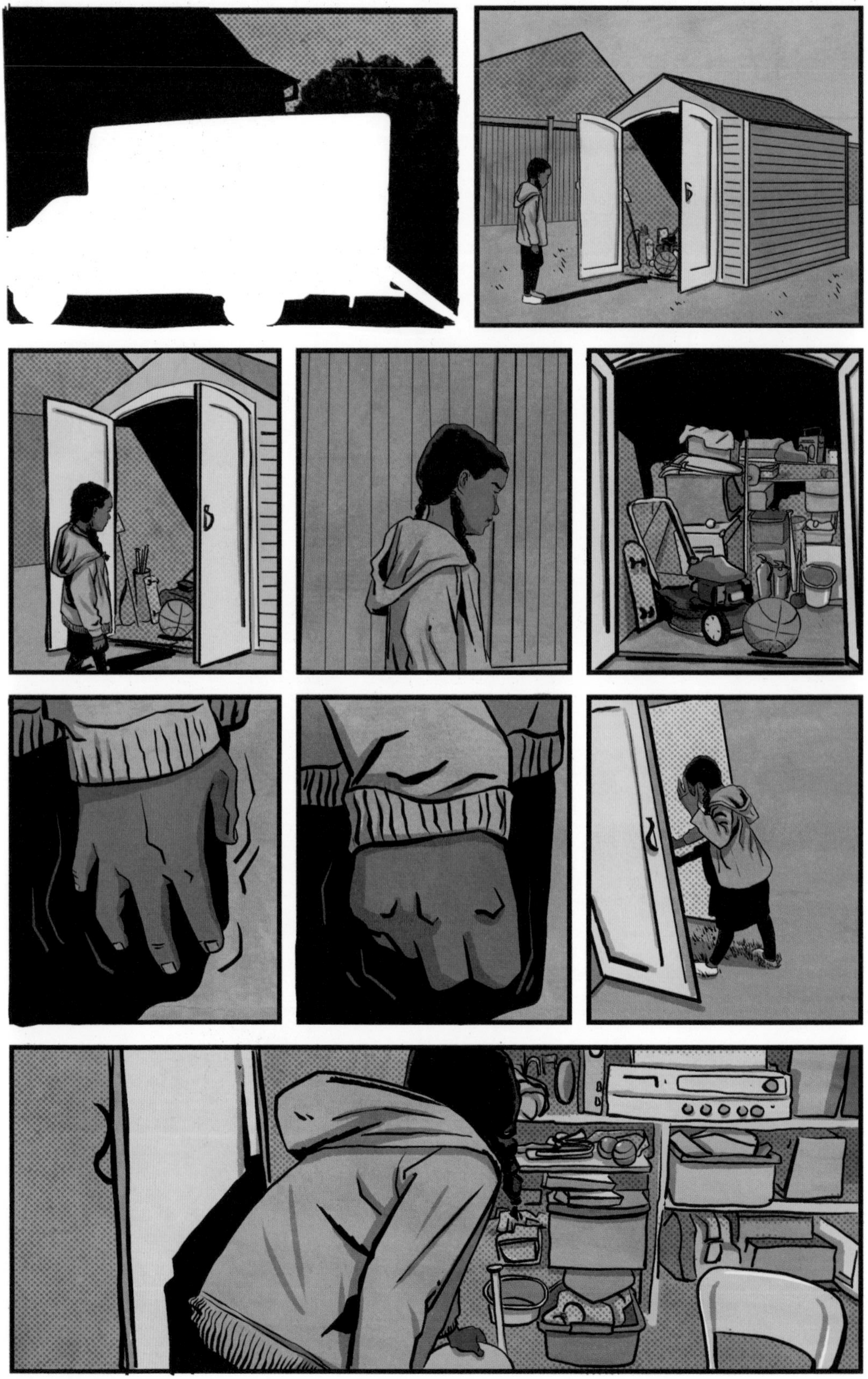

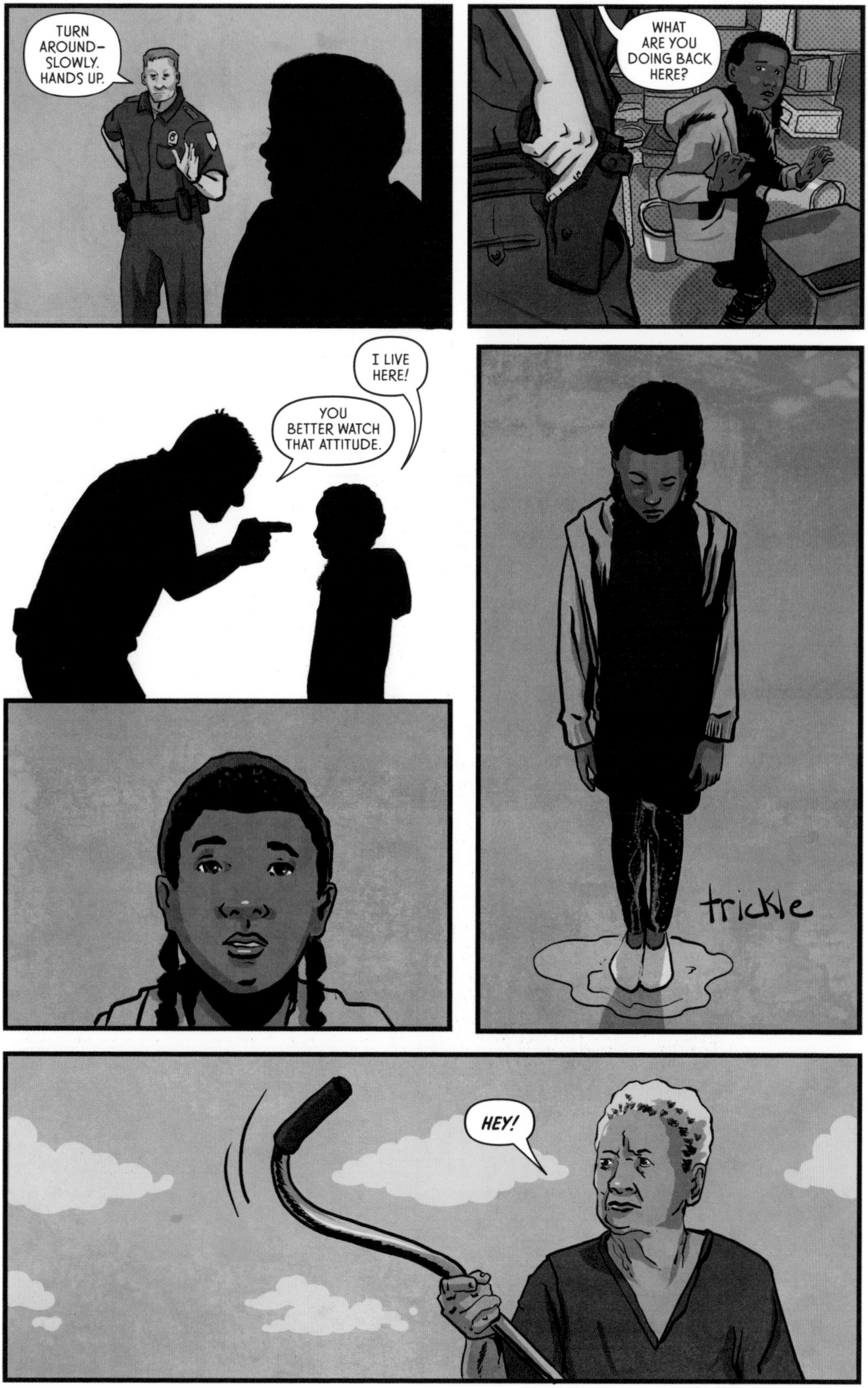
TURN AROUND– SLOWLY. HANDS UP.
WHAT ARE YOU DOING BACK HERE?
I LIVE HERE!
YOU BETTER WATCH THAT ATTITUDE.
trickle
HEY!

WHAT THE GODDAMN HELL IS THIS? DO YOU KNOW WHAT SHE'S BEEN THROUGH? YOU OUGHT TO BE 'SHAMED.
MA'AM, CALM DOWN. A NEIGHBOR CALLED THE POLICE—
YOU NEVER WANTED THEM HERE, DID YOU? THEY OUGHTA CALLED THE COPS ON ***YOU***—SPITEFUL-ASS HEIFER.
SORRY, "SEE SOMETHING, SAY SOMETHING . . ."
SEE A BITCH, SLAP A BITCH.

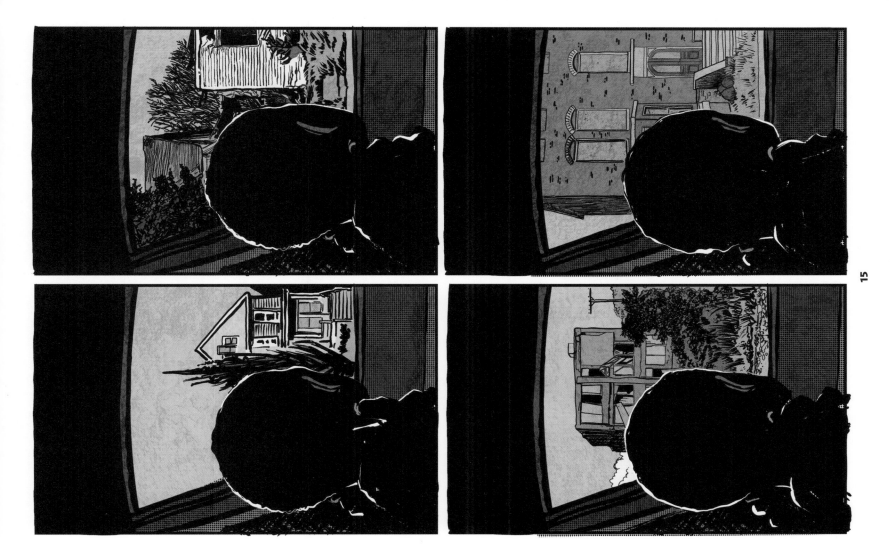

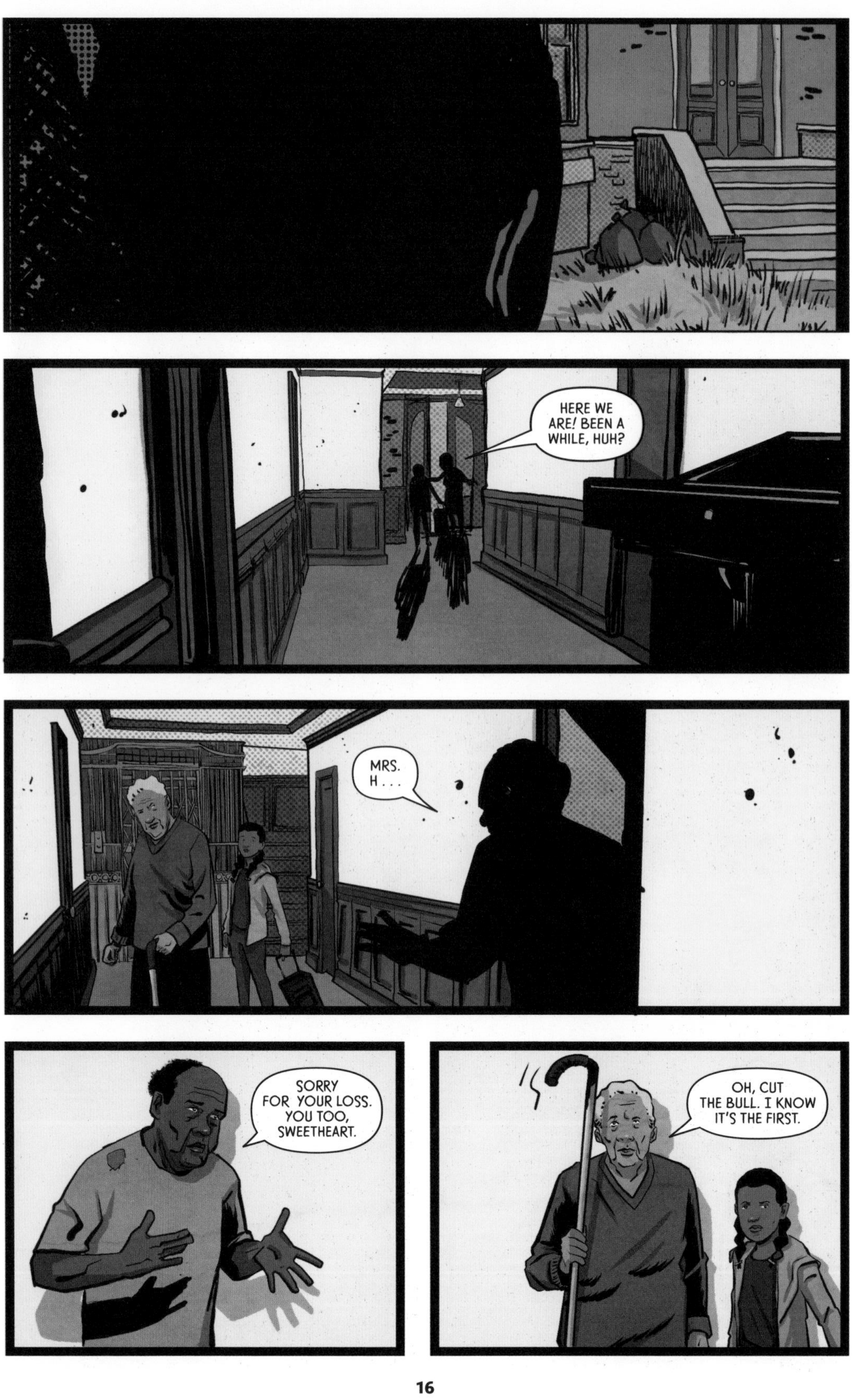
HERE WE ARE! BEEN A WHILE, HUH?
MRS. H . . .
SORRY FOR YOUR LOSS. YOU TOO, SWEETHEART.
OH, CUT THE BULL. I KNOW IT'S THE FIRST.

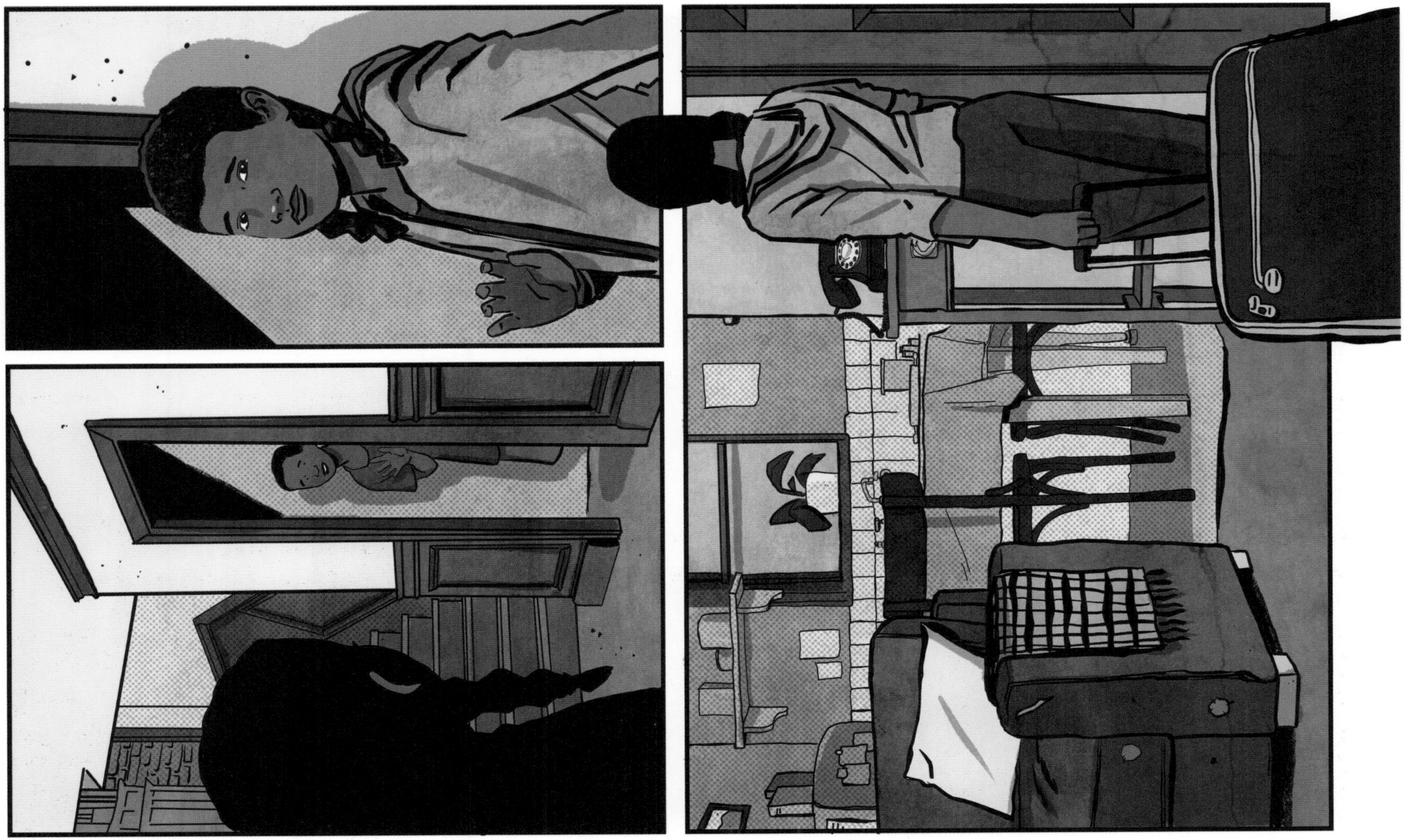

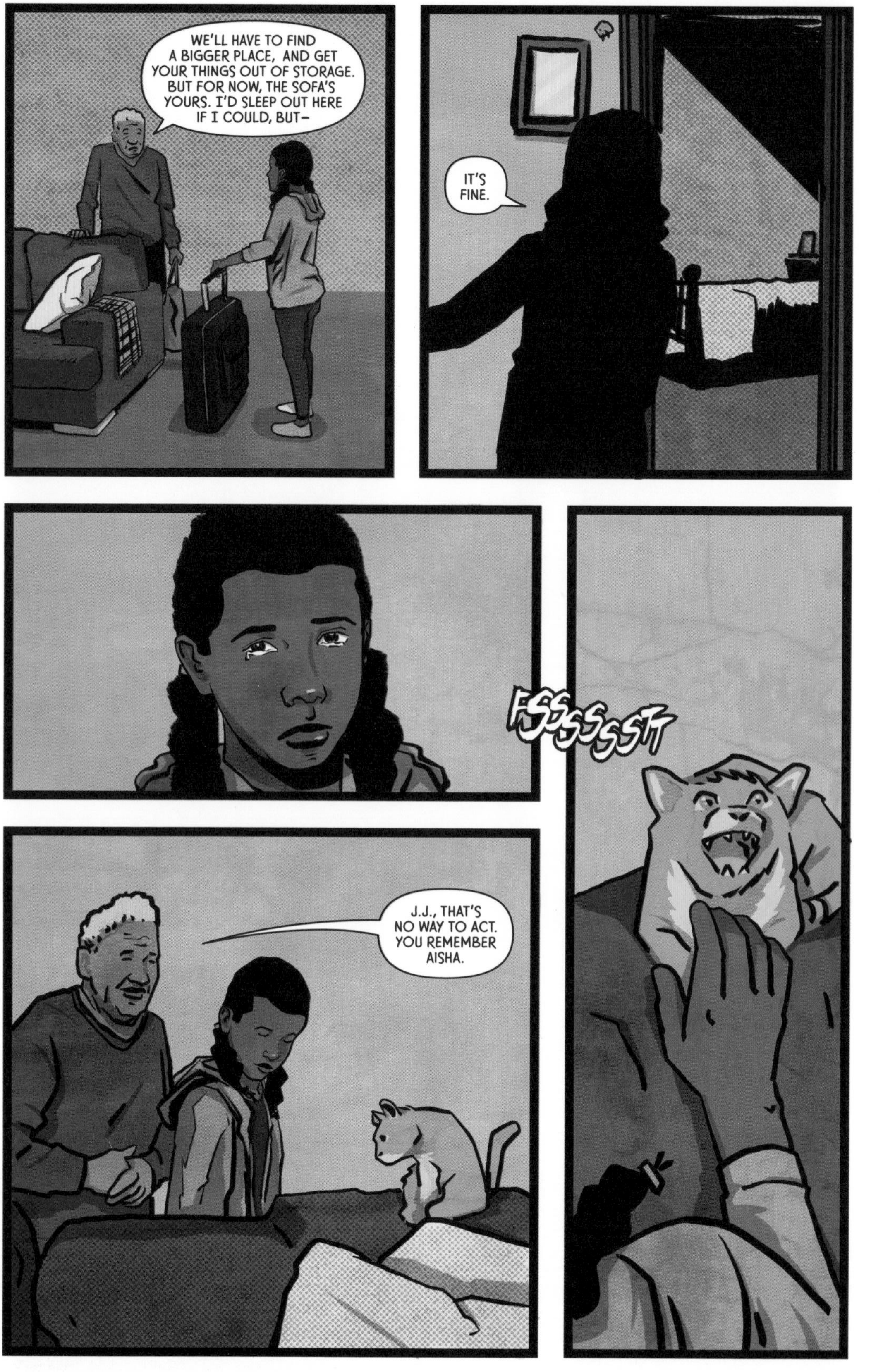
WE'LL HAVE TO FIND A BIGGER PLACE, AND GET YOUR THINGS OUT OF STORAGE. BUT FOR NOW, THE SOFA'S YOURS. I'D SLEEP OUT HERE IF I COULD, BUT–
IT'S FINE.
FSSSSSST
J.J., THAT'S NO WAY TO ACT. YOU REMEMBER AISHA.

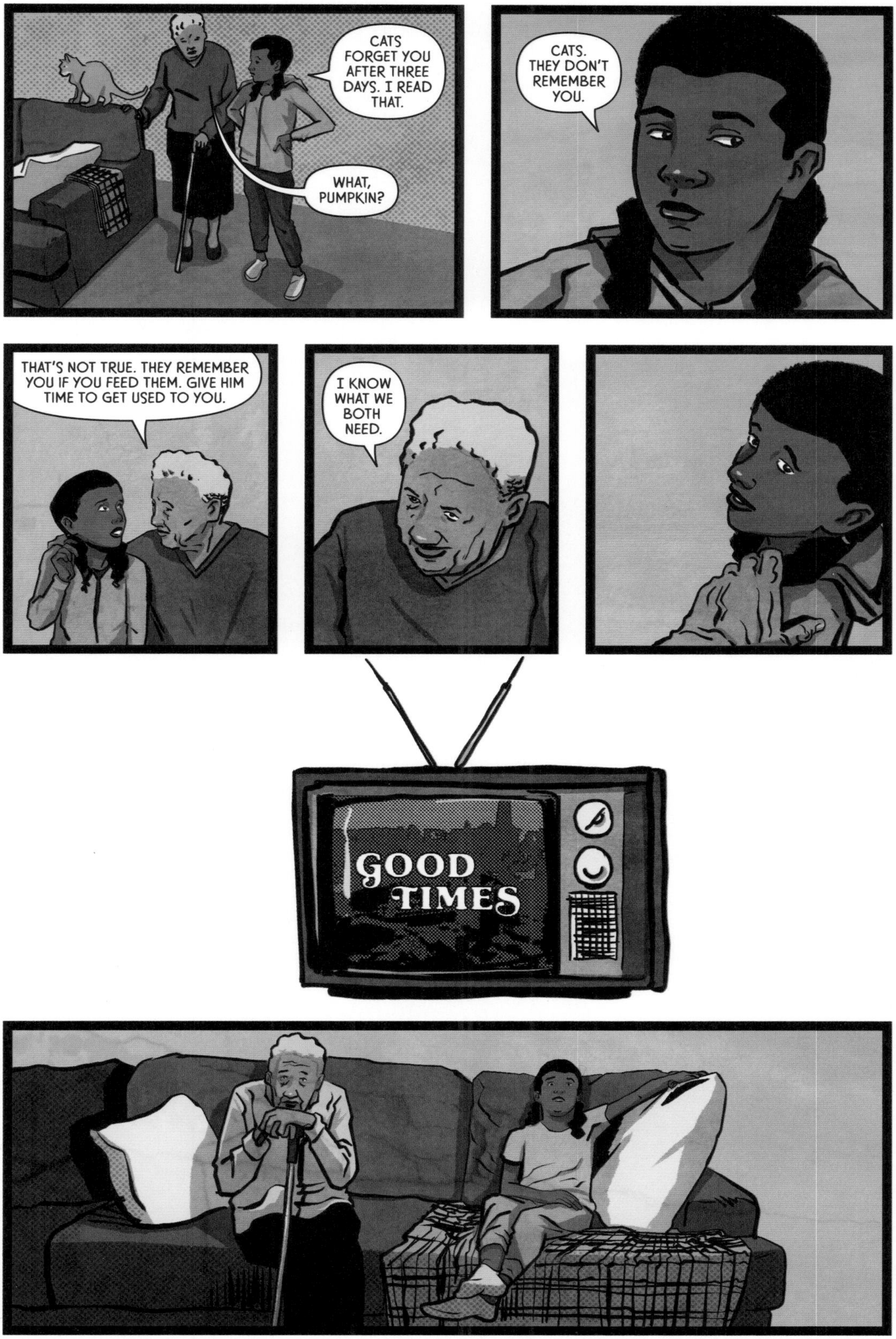
CATS FORGET YOU AFTER THREE DAYS. I READ THAT.
WHAT, PUMPKIN?
CATS. THEY DON'T REMEMBER YOU.
THAT'S NOT TRUE. THEY REMEMBER YOU IF YOU FEED THEM. GIVE HIM TIME TO GET USED TO YOU.
I KNOW WHAT WE BOTH NEED.
GOOD TIMES

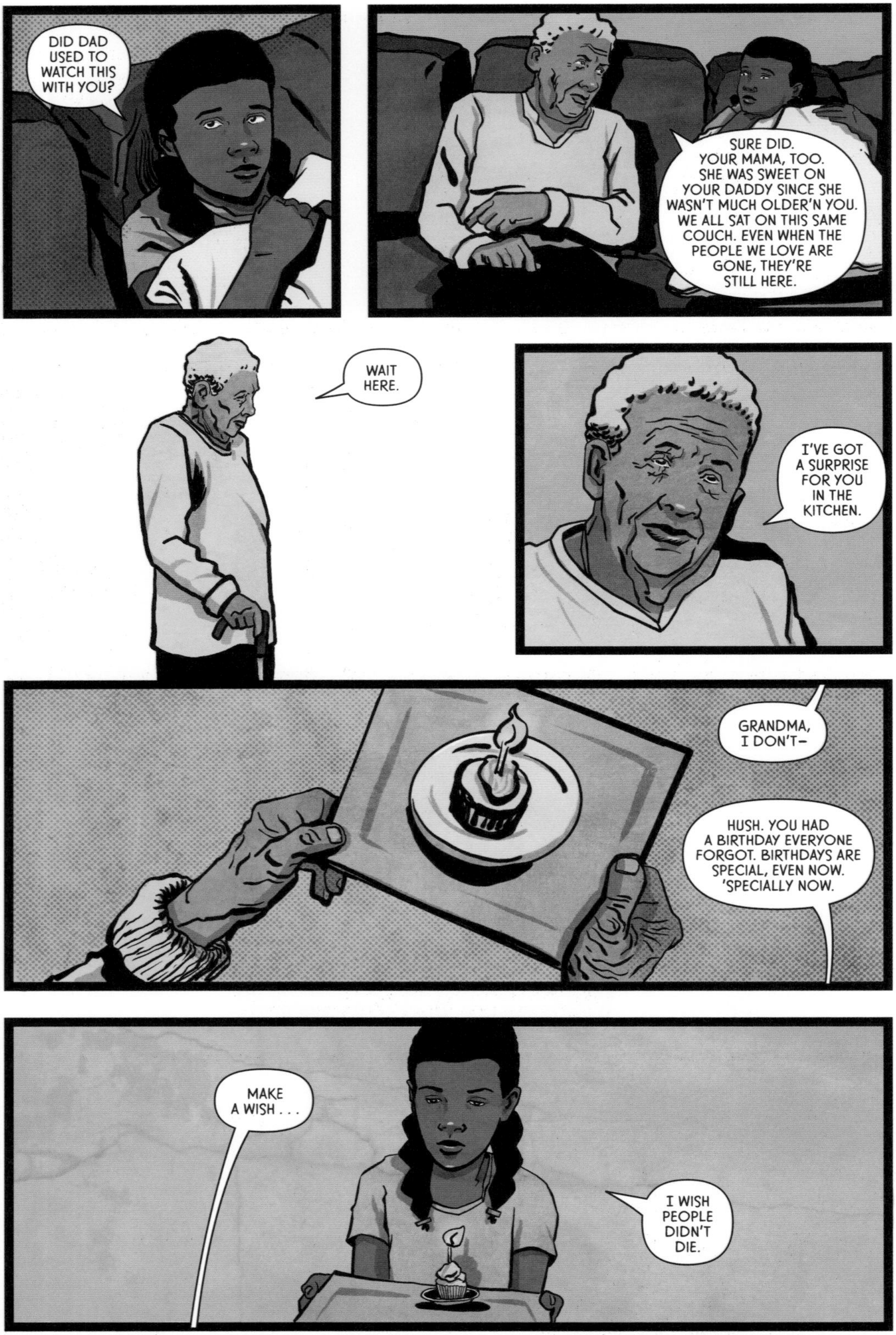
DID DAD USED TO WATCH THIS WITH YOU?
SURE DID. YOUR MAMA, TOO. SHE WAS SWEET ON YOUR DADDY SINCE SHE WASN'T MUCH OLDER'N YOU. WE ALL SAT ON THIS SAME COUCH. EVEN WHEN THE PEOPLE WE LOVE ARE GONE, THEY'RE STILL HERE.
WAIT HERE.
I'VE GOT A SURPRISE FOR YOU IN THE KITCHEN.
GRANDMA, I DON'T–
HUSH. YOU HAD A BIRTHDAY EVERYONE FORGOT. BIRTHDAYS ARE SPECIAL, EVEN NOW. 'SPECIALLY NOW.
MAKE A WISH . . .
I WISH PEOPLE DIDN'T DIE.

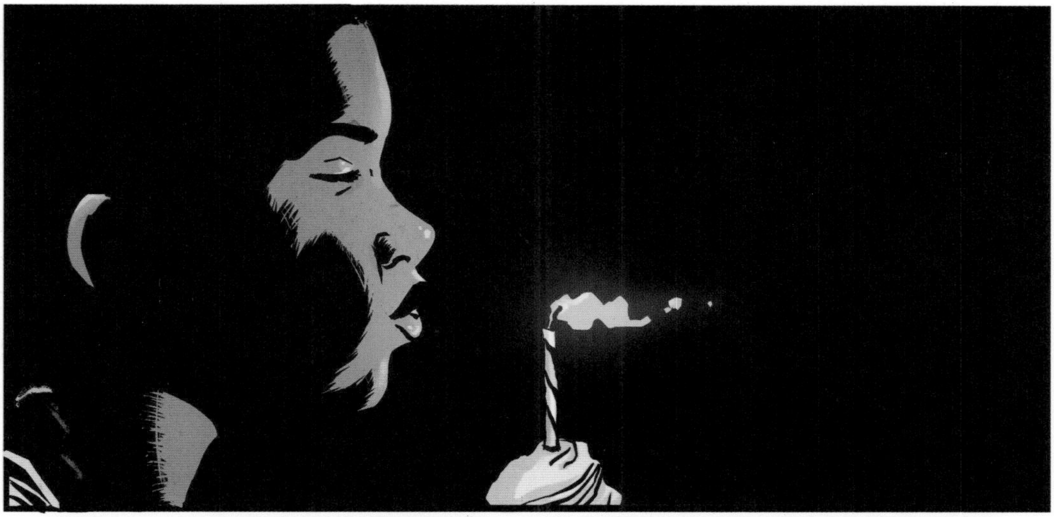
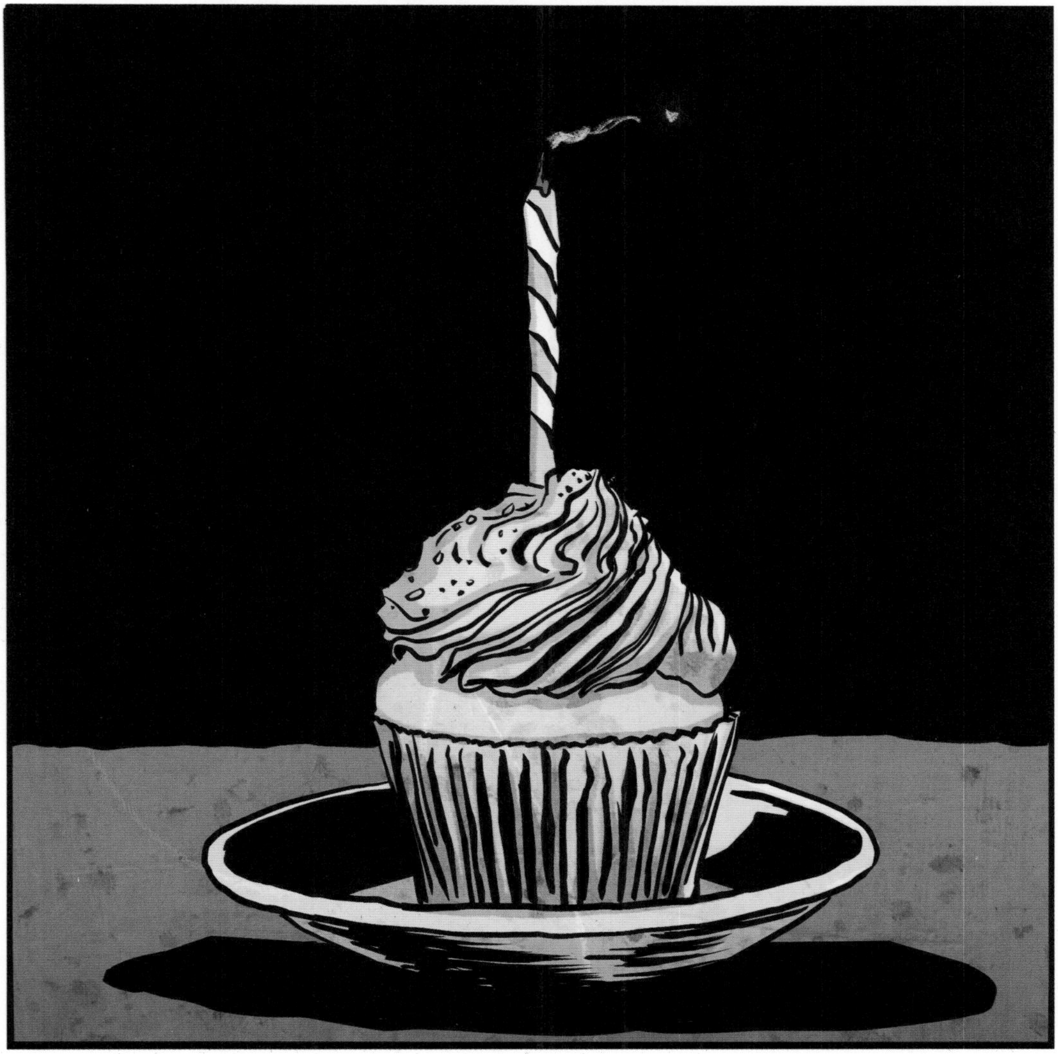

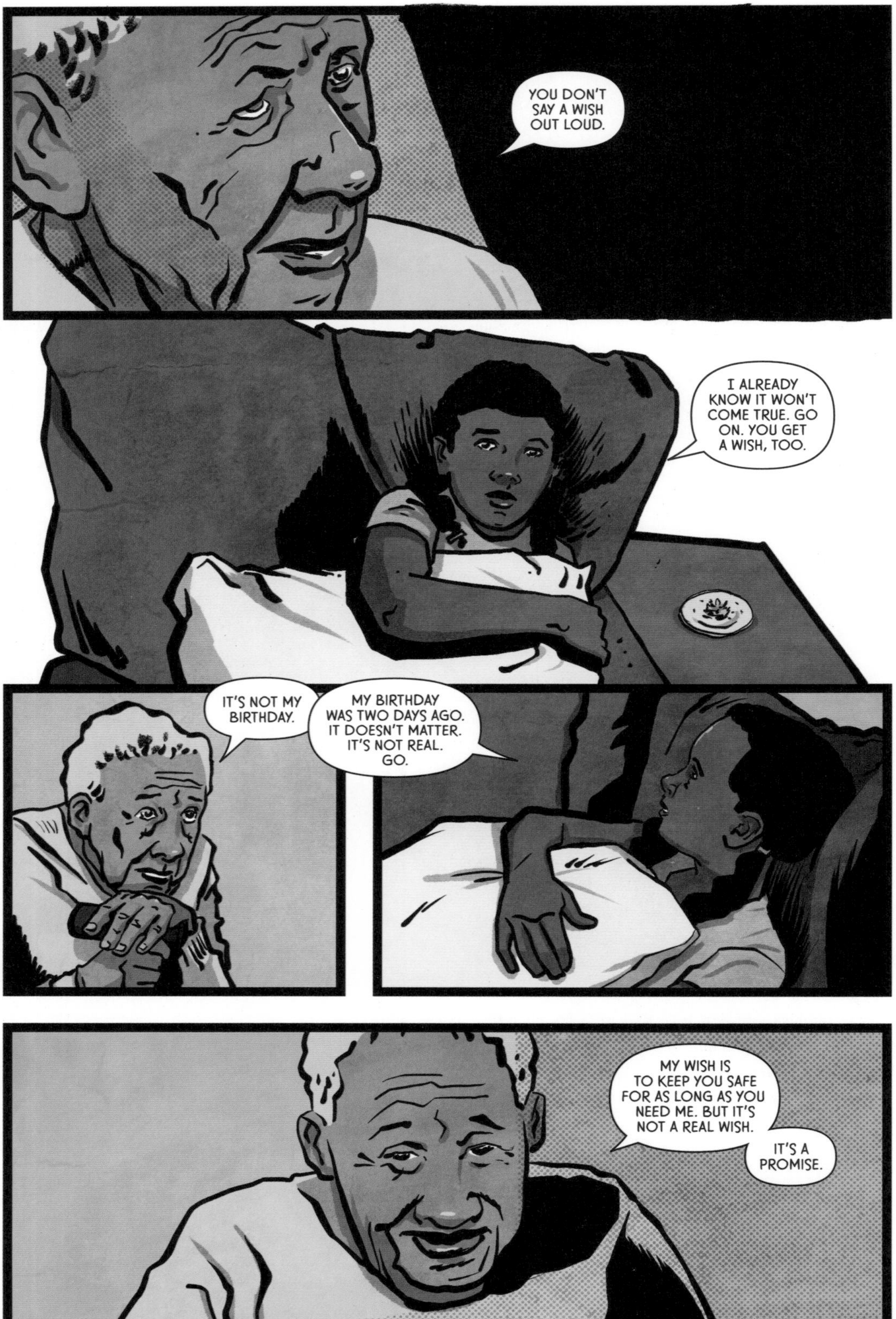
YOU DON'T SAY A WISH OUT LOUD.
I ALREADY KNOW IT WON'T COME TRUE. GO ON. YOU GET A WISH, TOO.
IT'S NOT MY BIRTHDAY.
MY BIRTHDAY WAS TWO DAYS AGO. IT DOESN'T MATTER. IT'S NOT REAL. GO.
MY WISH IS TO KEEP YOU SAFE FOR AS LONG AS YOU NEED ME. BUT IT'S NOT A REAL WISH.
IT'S A PROMISE.

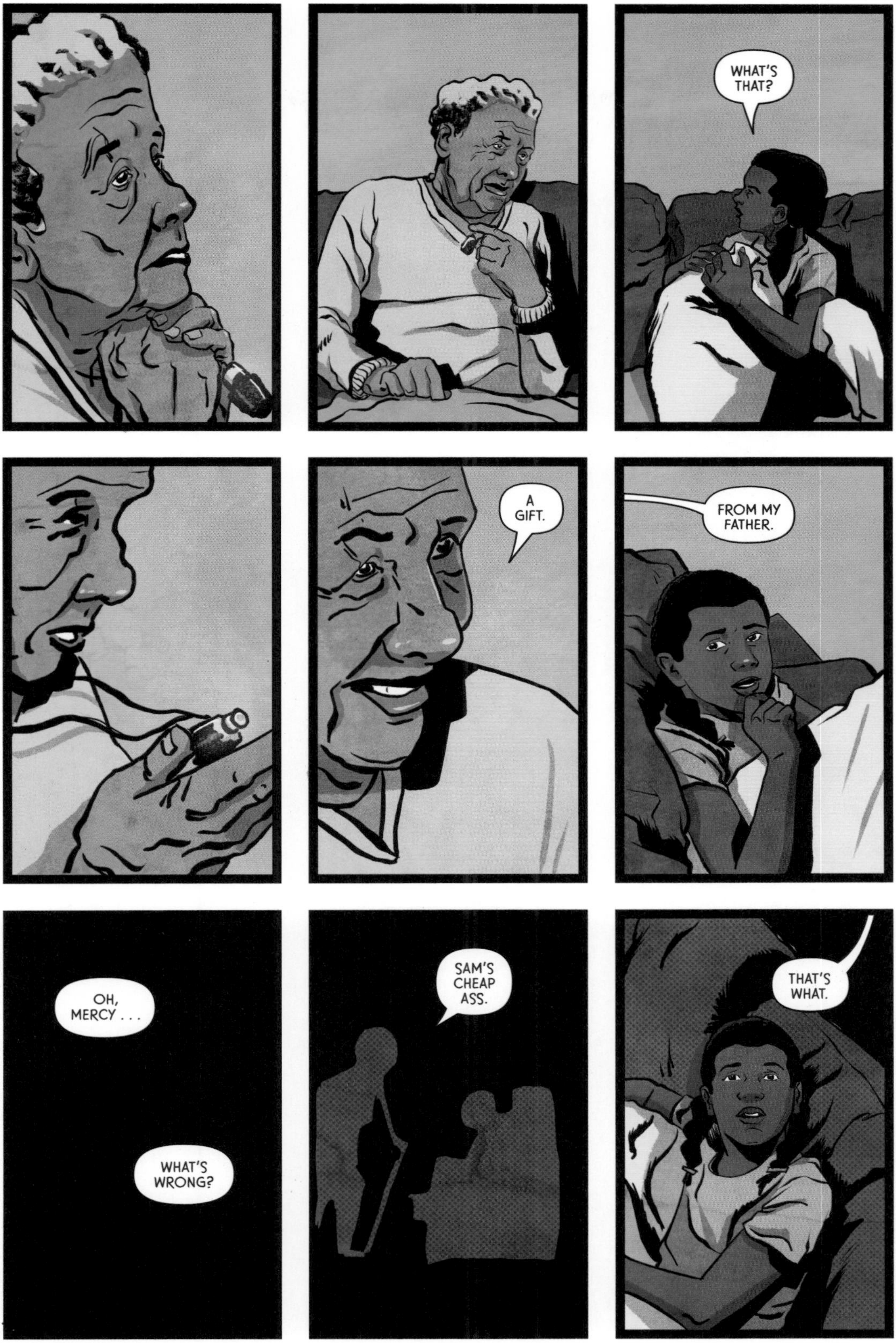
WHAT'S THAT?
A GIFT.
FROM MY FATHER.
OH, MERCY . . .
WHAT'S WRONG?
SAM'S CHEAP ASS.
THAT'S WHAT.

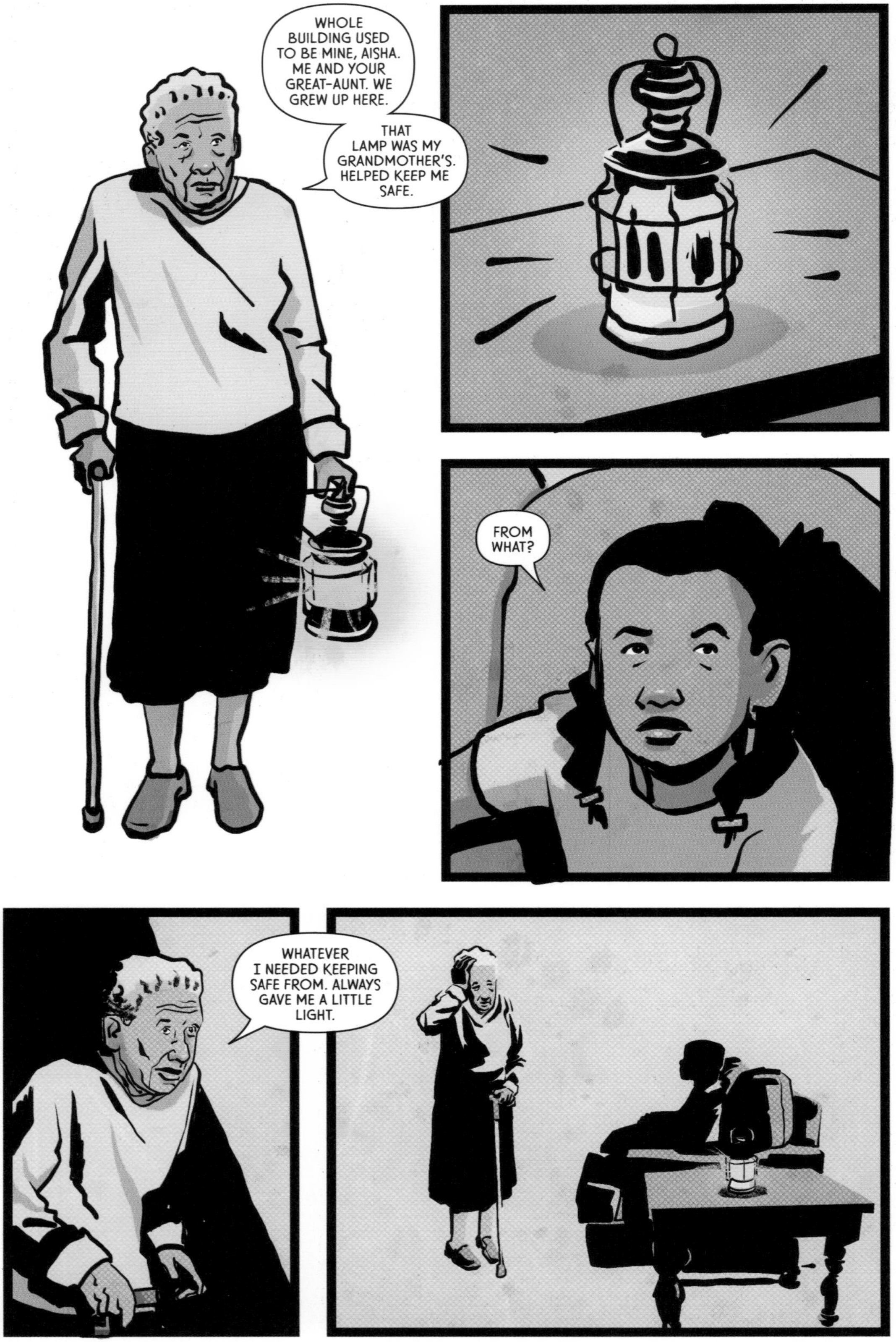
WHOLE BUILDING USED TO BE MINE, AISHA. ME AND YOUR GREAT-AUNT. WE GREW UP HERE.
THAT LAMP WAS MY GRANDMOTHER'S. HELPED KEEP ME SAFE.
FROM WHAT?
WHATEVER I NEEDED KEEPING SAFE FROM. ALWAYS GAVE ME A LITTLE LIGHT.

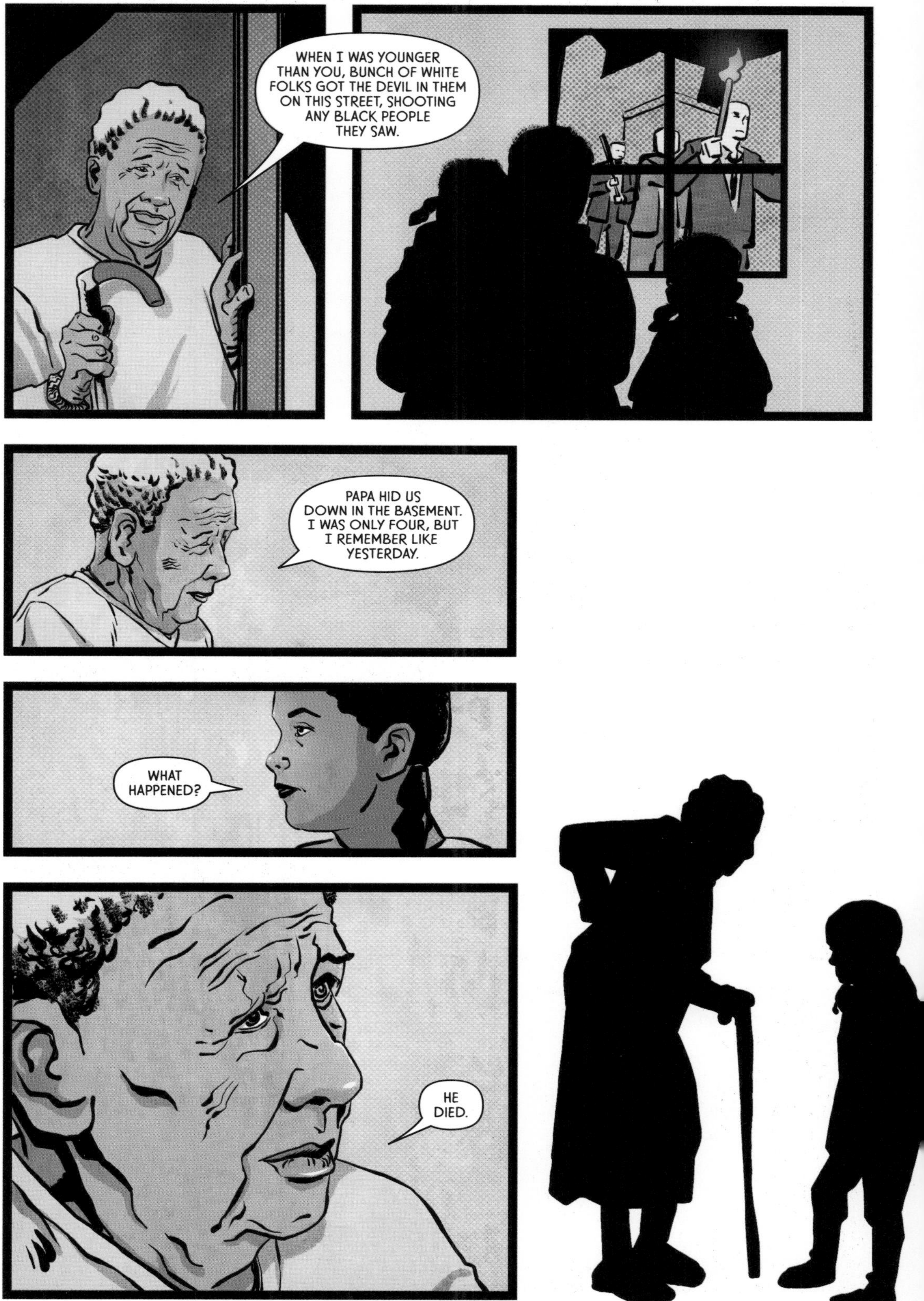
WHEN I WAS YOUNGER THAN YOU, BUNCH OF WHITE FOLKS GOT THE DEVIL IN THEM ON THIS STREET, SHOOTING ANY BLACK PEOPLE THEY SAW.
PAPA HID US DOWN IN THE BASEMENT. I WAS ONLY FOUR, BUT I REMEMBER LIKE YESTERDAY.
WHAT HAPPENED?
HE DIED.

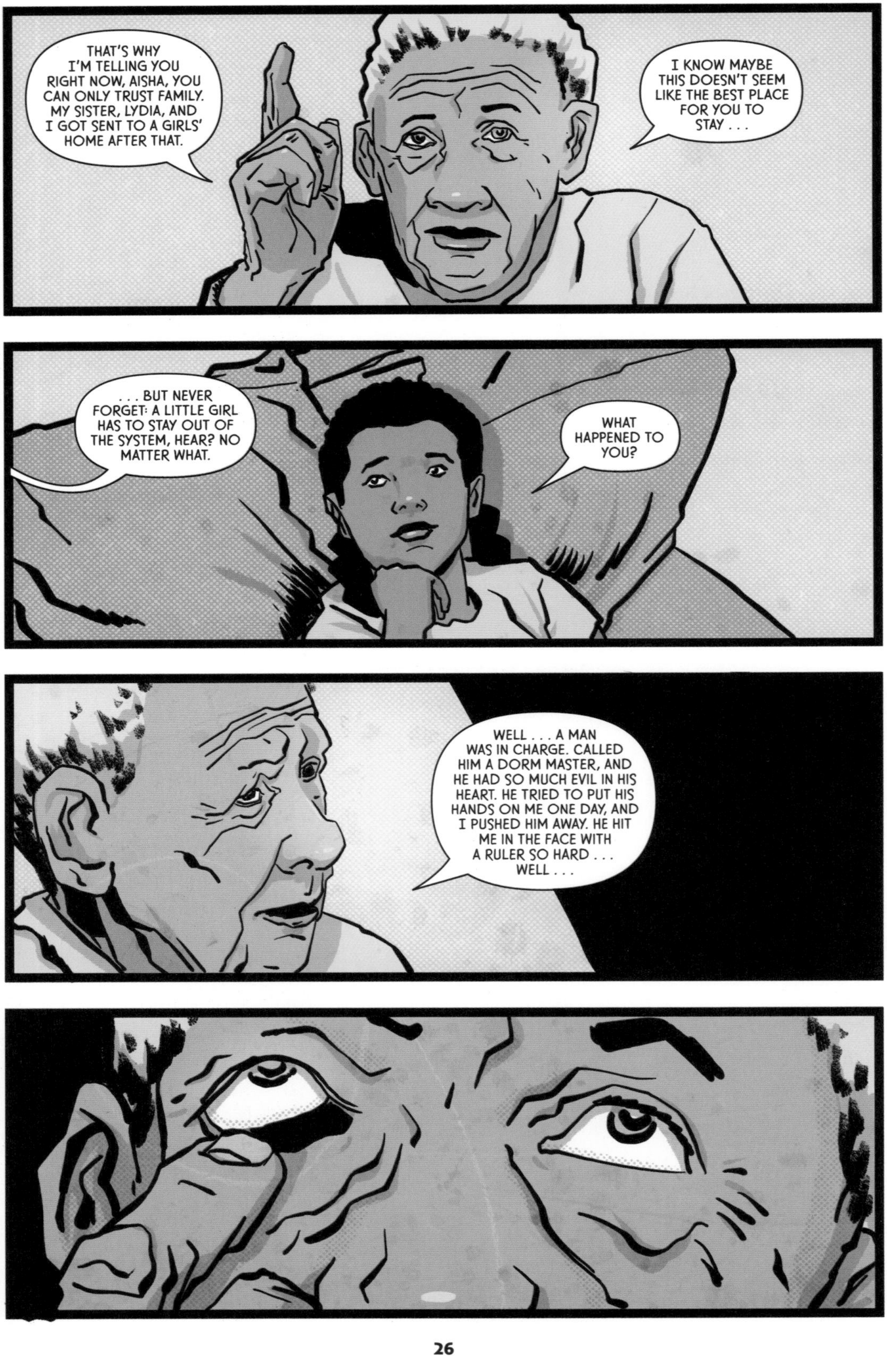
THAT'S WHY I'M TELLING YOU RIGHT NOW, AISHA, YOU CAN ONLY TRUST FAMILY. MY SISTER, LYDIA, AND I GOT SENT TO A GIRLS' HOME AFTER THAT.
I KNOW MAYBE THIS DOESN'T SEEM LIKE THE BEST PLACE FOR YOU TO STAY . . .
. . . BUT NEVER FORGET: A LITTLE GIRL HAS TO STAY OUT OF THE SYSTEM, HEAR? NO MATTER WHAT.
WHAT HAPPENED TO YOU?
WELL . . . A MAN WAS IN CHARGE. CALLED HIM A DORM MASTER, AND HE HAD SO MUCH EVIL IN HIS HEART. HE TRIED TO PUT HIS HANDS ON ME ONE DAY, AND I PUSHED HIM AWAY. HE HIT ME IN THE FACE WITH A RULER SO HARD . . . WELL . . .

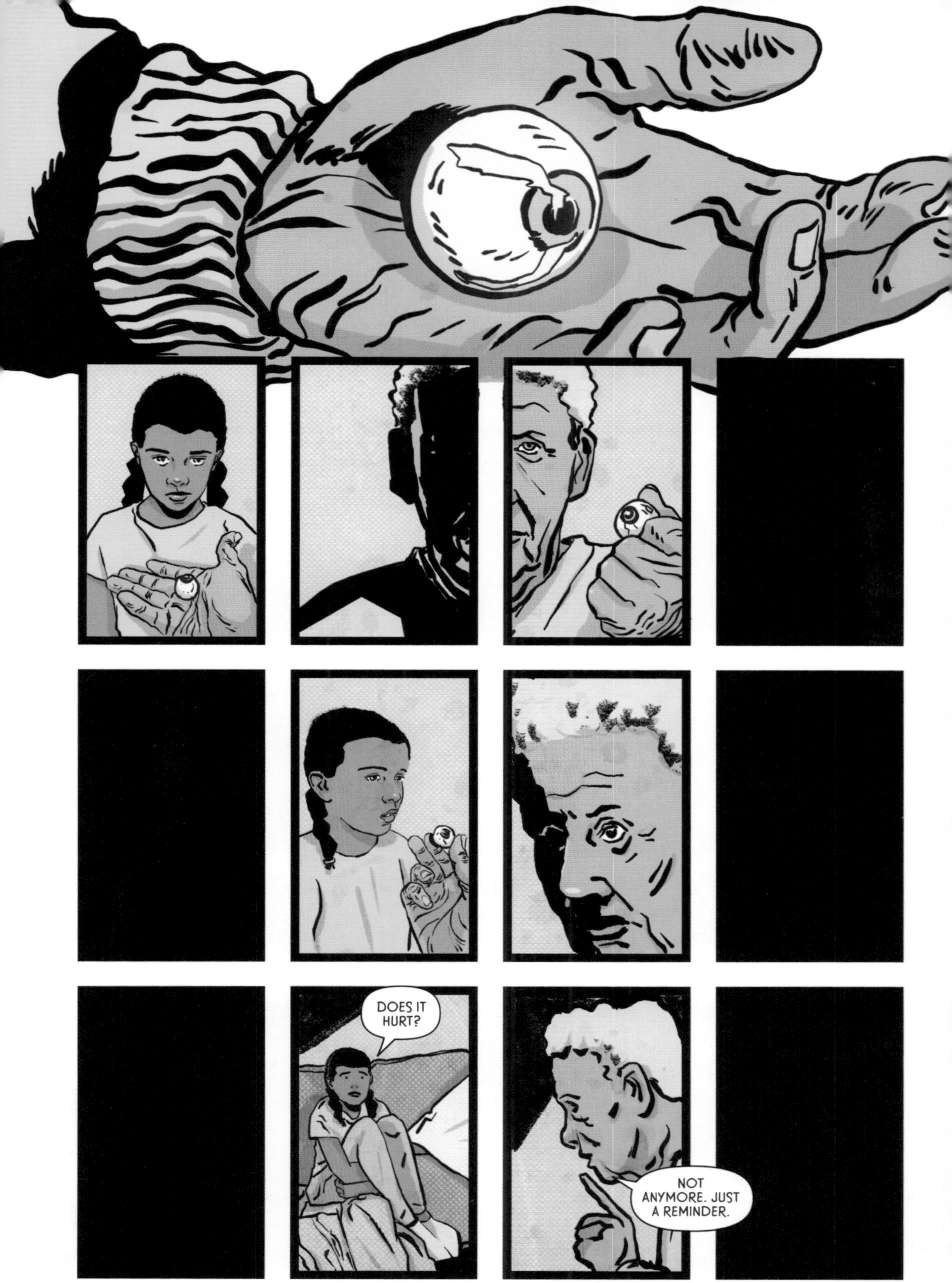
DOES IT HURT?
NOT ANYMORE. JUST A REMINDER.

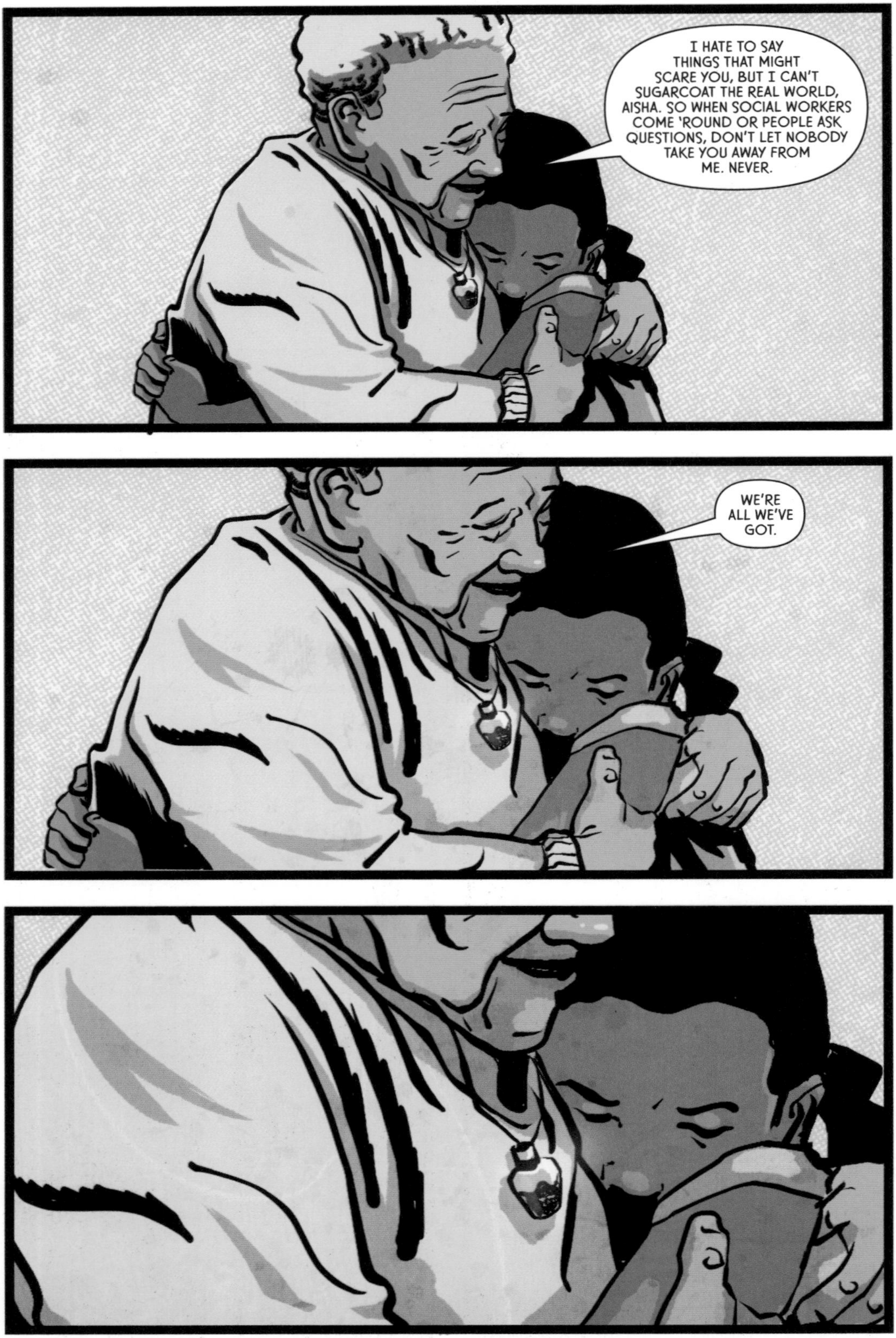
I HATE TO SAY THINGS THAT MIGHT SCARE YOU, BUT I CAN'T SUGARCOAT THE REAL WORLD, AISHA. SO WHEN SOCIAL WORKERS COME 'ROUND OR PEOPLE ASK QUESTIONS, DON'T LET NOBODY TAKE YOU AWAY FROM ME. NEVER.
WE'RE ALL WE'VE GOT.

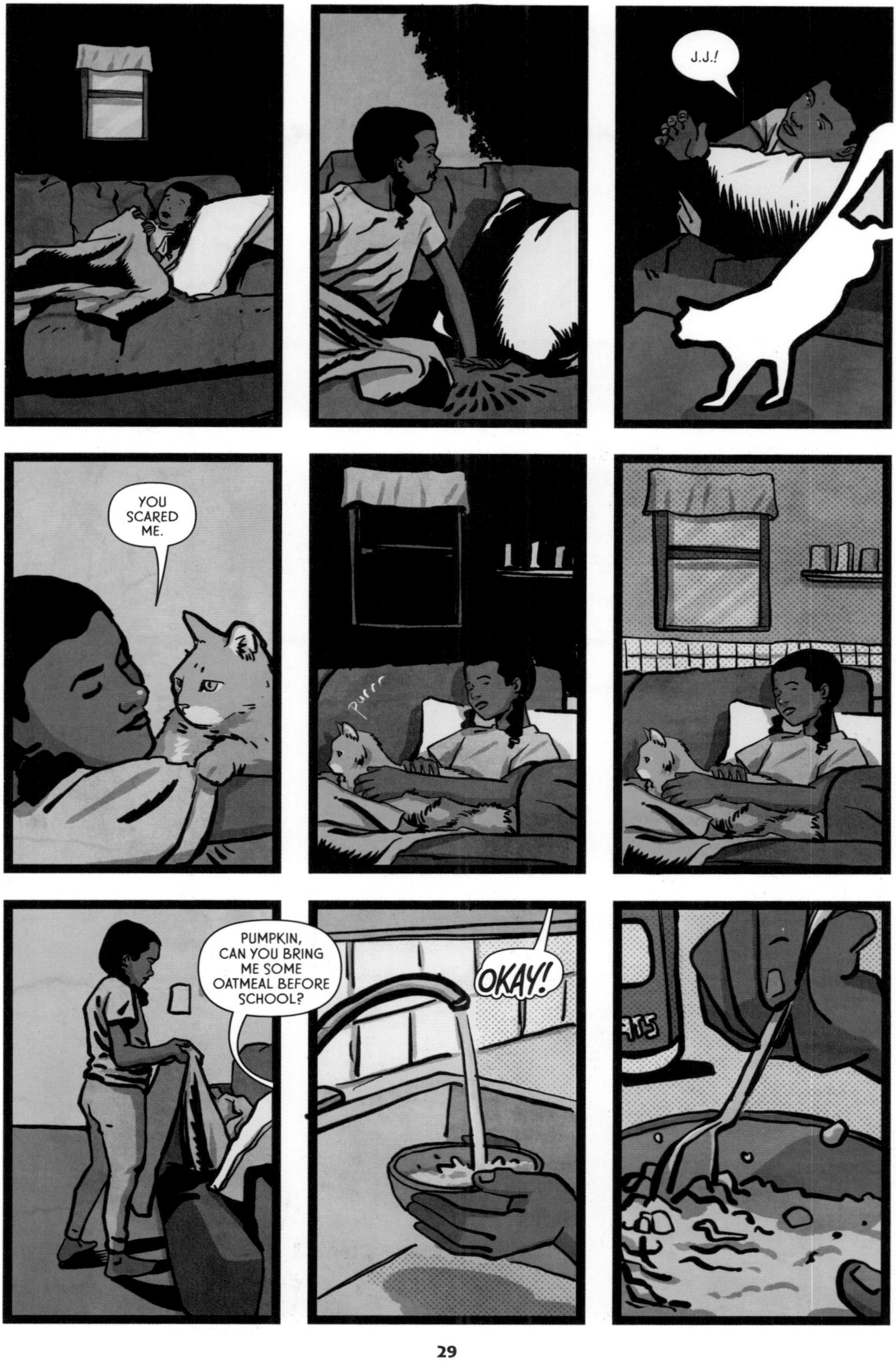
J.J.!
YOU SCARED ME.
purrr
PUMPKIN, CAN YOU BRING ME SOME OATMEAL BEFORE SCHOOL?
OKAY!

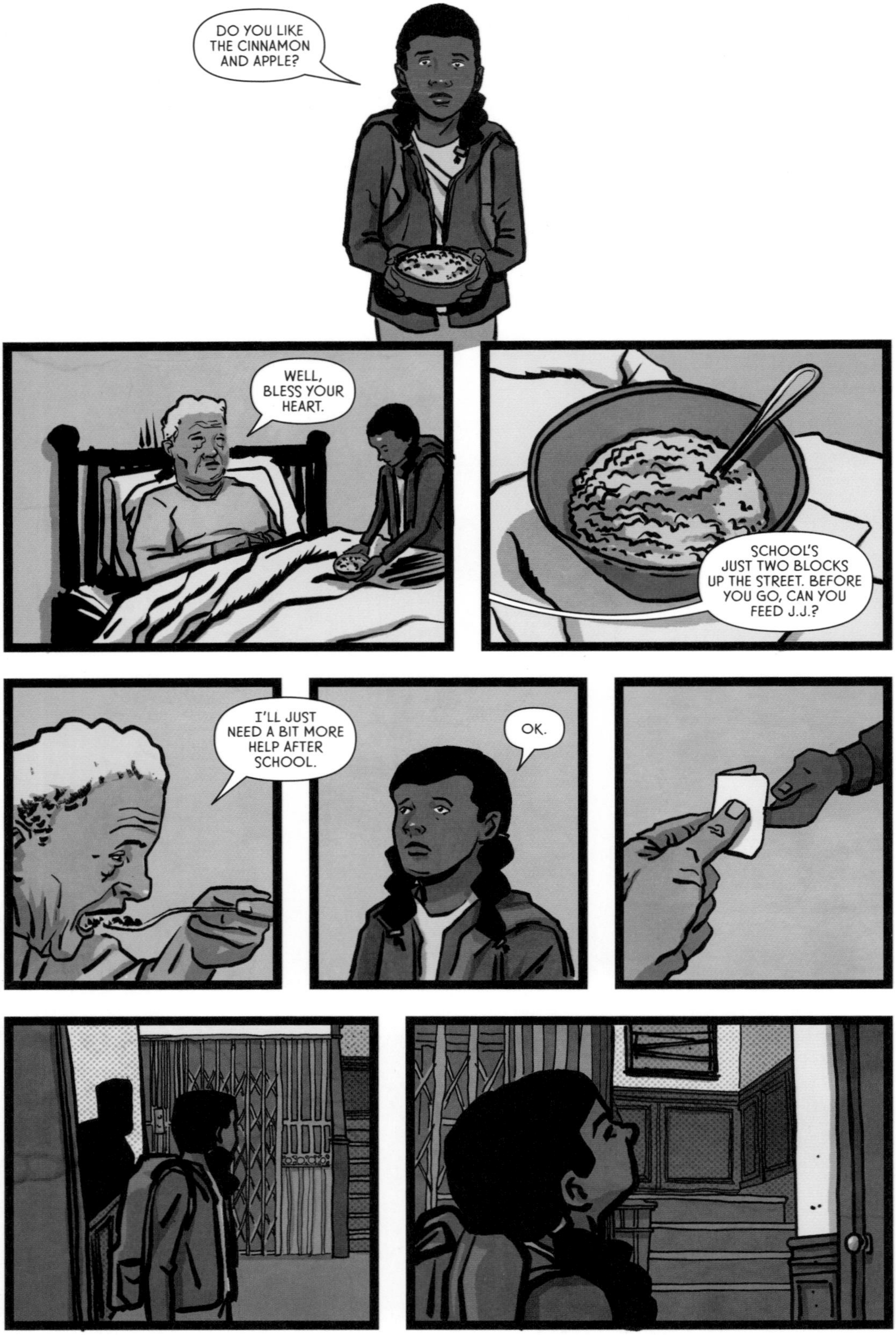
DO YOU LIKE THE CINNAMON AND APPLE?
WELL, BLESS YOUR HEART.
SCHOOL'S JUST TWO BLOCKS UP THE STREET. BEFORE YOU GO, CAN YOU FEED J.J.?
I'LL JUST NEED A BIT MORE HELP AFTER SCHOOL.
OK.

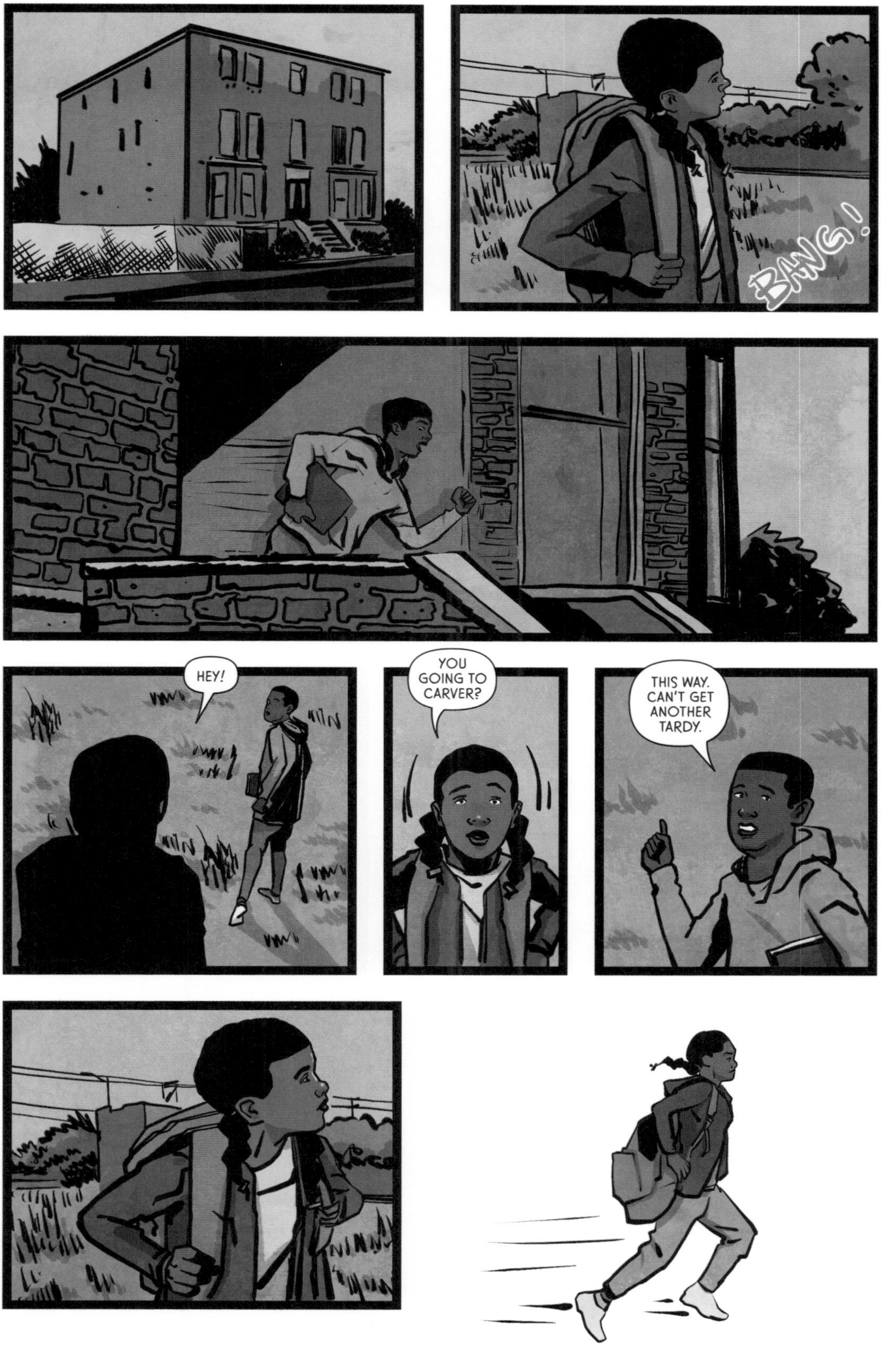
BANG!
HEY!
YOU GOING TO CARVER?
THIS WAY. CAN'T GET ANOTHER TARDY.

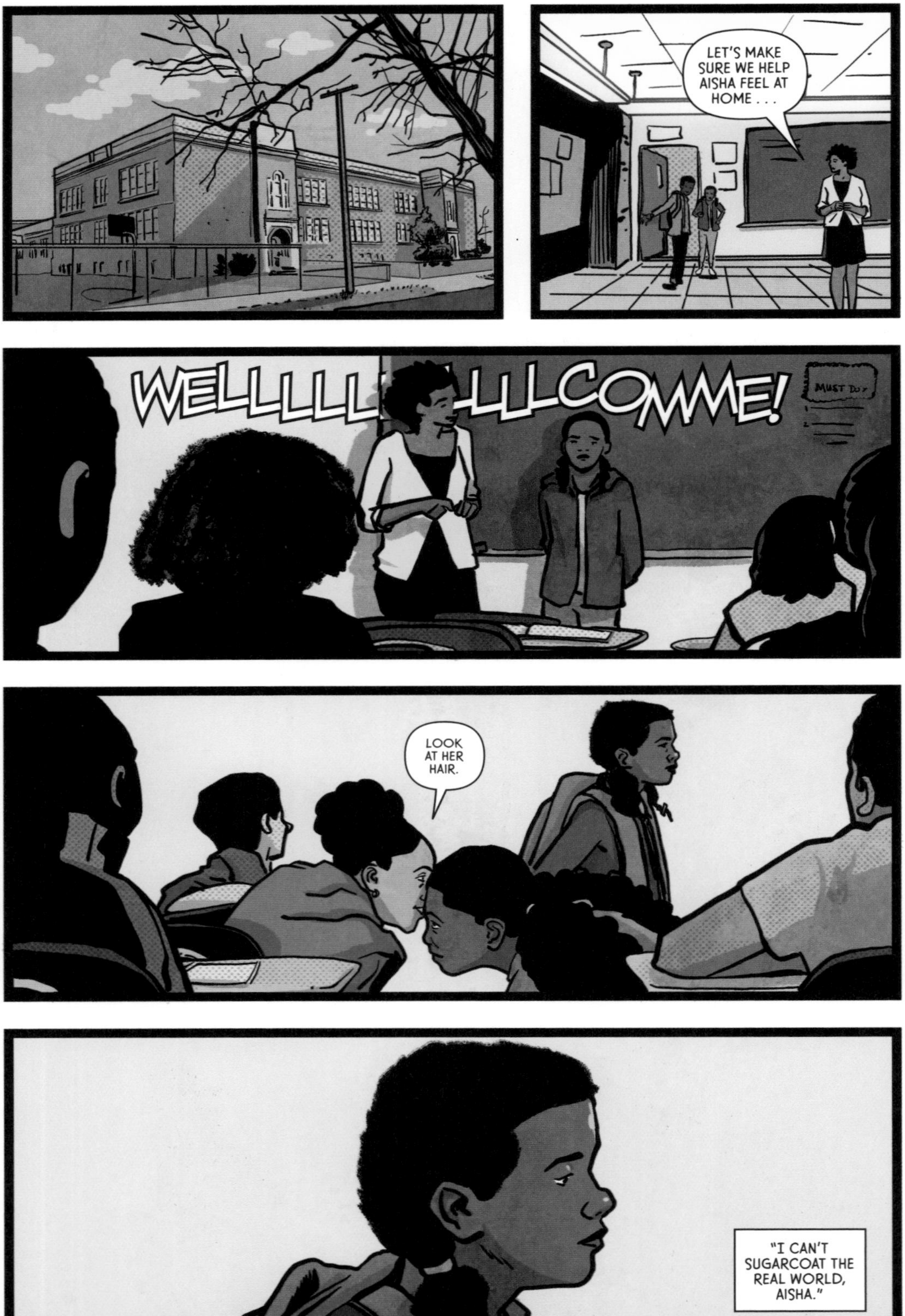
LET'S MAKE SURE WE HELP AISHA FEEL AT HOME . . .
WELLLLLLLLLLCOMME!
MUST DO:
LOOK AT HER HAIR.
"I CAN'T SUGARCOAT THE REAL WORLD, AISHA."

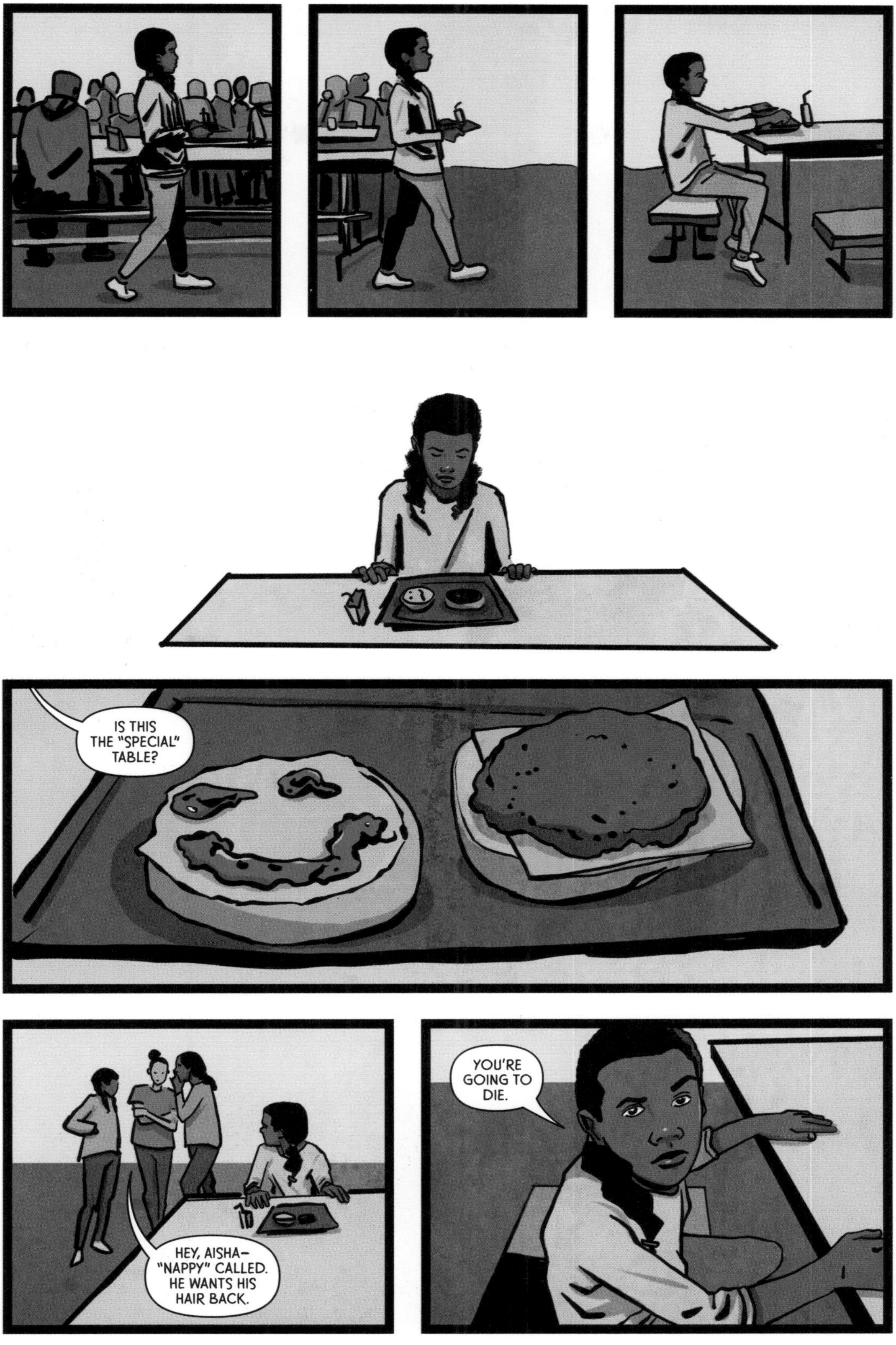
IS THIS THE "SPECIAL" TABLE?
HEY, AISHA—"NAPPY" CALLED. HE WANTS HIS HAIR BACK.
YOU'RE GOING TO DIE.

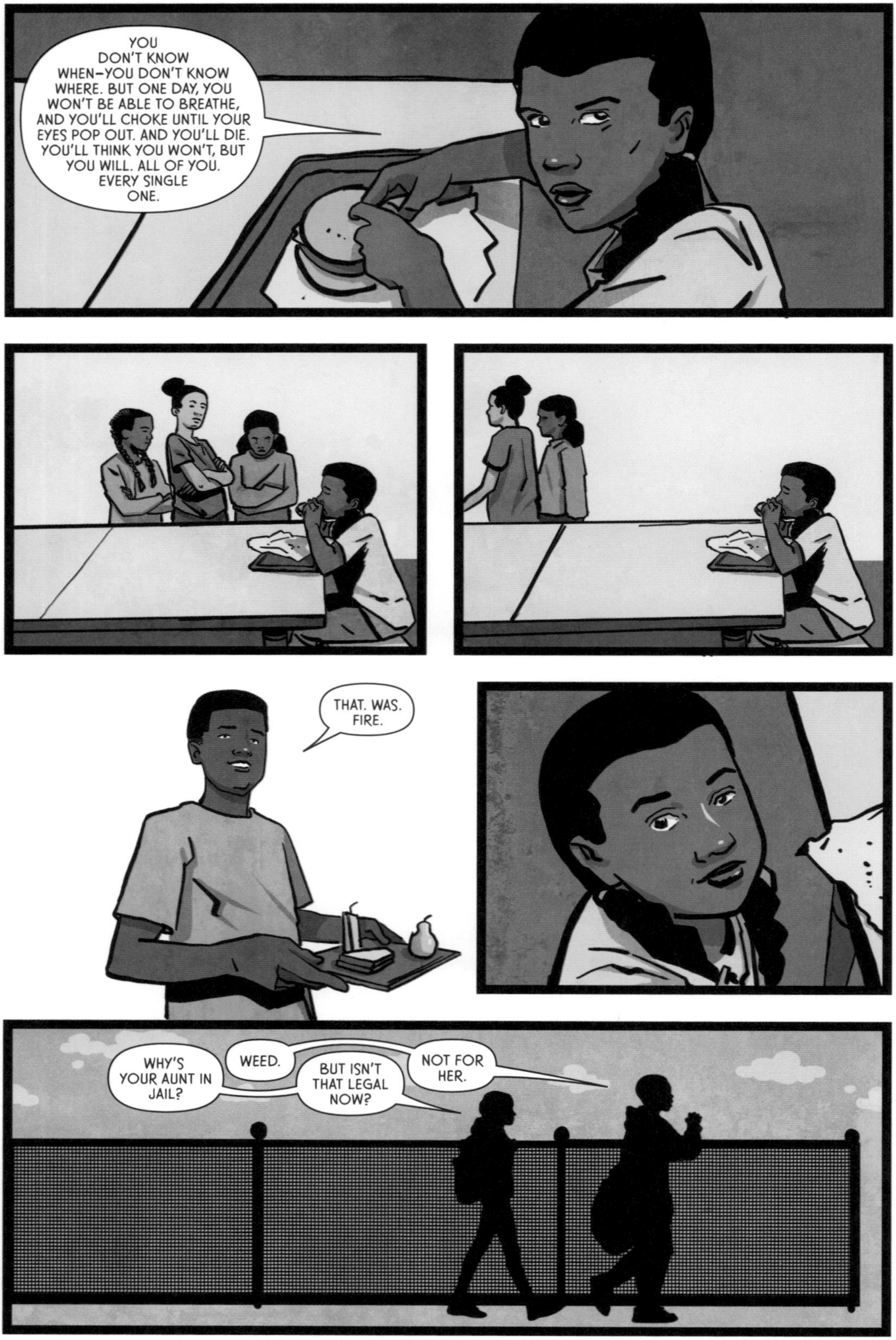
YOU DON'T KNOW WHEN—YOU DON'T KNOW WHERE. BUT ONE DAY, YOU WON'T BE ABLE TO BREATHE, AND YOU'LL CHOKE UNTIL YOUR EYES POP OUT. AND YOU'LL DIE. YOU'LL THINK YOU WON'T, BUT YOU WILL. ALL OF YOU. EVERY SINGLE ONE.
THAT. WAS. FIRE.
WHY'S YOUR AUNT IN JAIL?
WEED.
BUT ISN'T THAT LEGAL NOW?
NOT FOR HER.

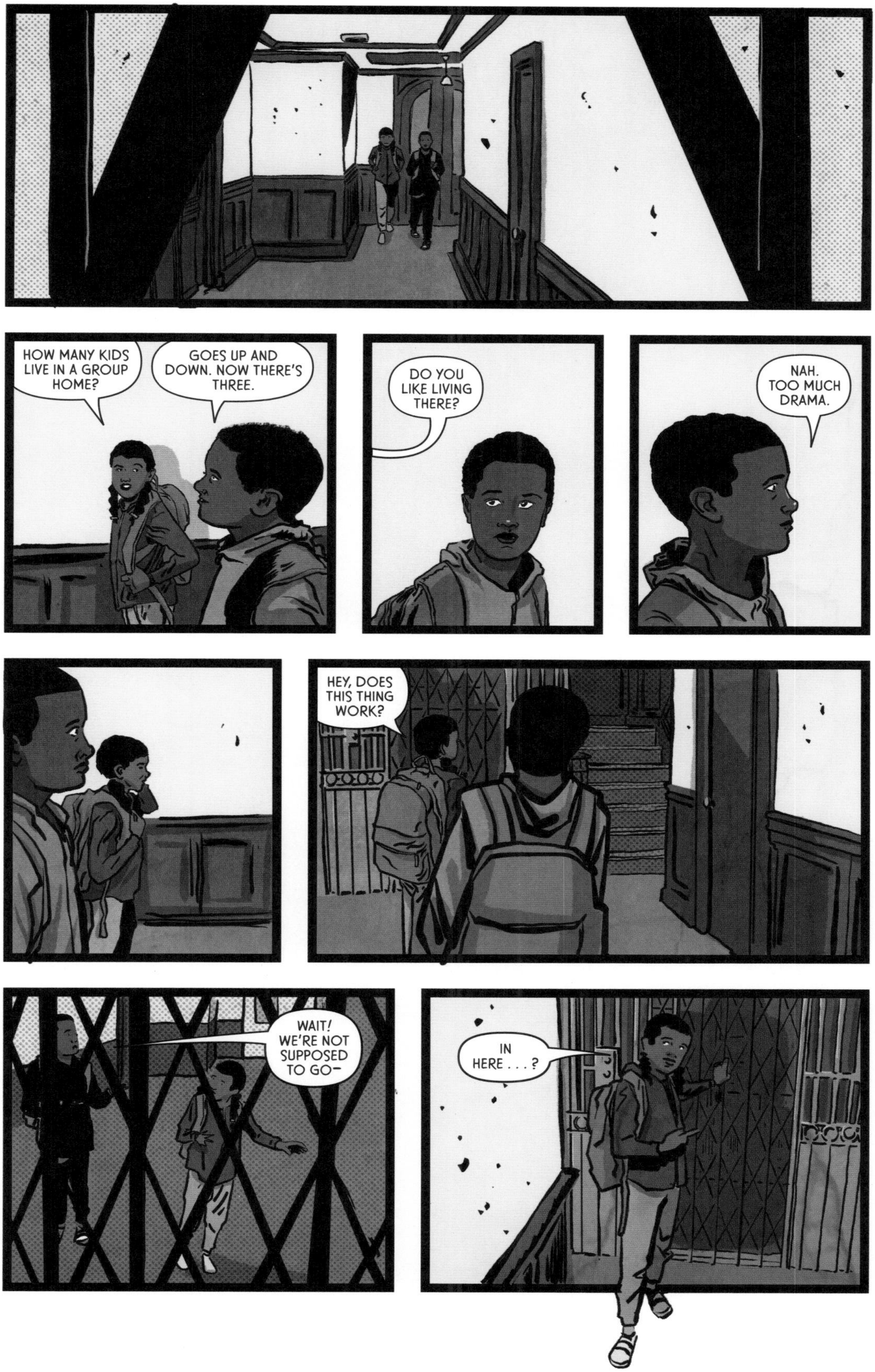
HOW MANY KIDS LIVE IN A GROUP HOME?
GOES UP AND DOWN. NOW THERE'S THREE.
DO YOU LIKE LIVING THERE?
NAH. TOO MUCH DRAMA.
HEY, DOES THIS THING WORK?
WAIT! WE'RE NOT SUPPOSED TO GO–
IN HERE . . . ?

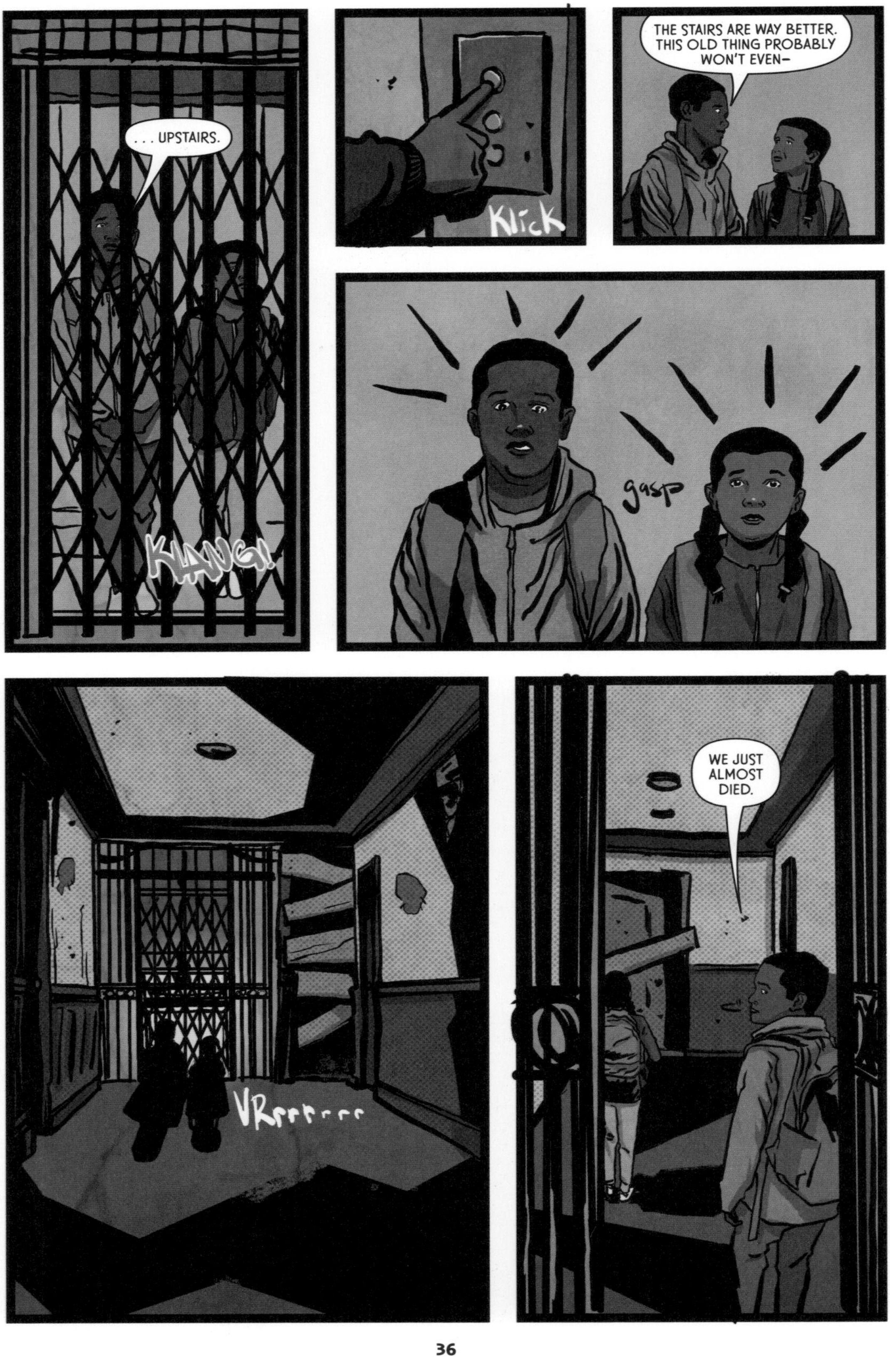
. . . UPSTAIRS.
KLANG!
Klick
THE STAIRS ARE WAY BETTER. THIS OLD THING PROBABLY WON'T EVEN—
gasp
VRrrrrrr
WE JUST ALMOST DIED.

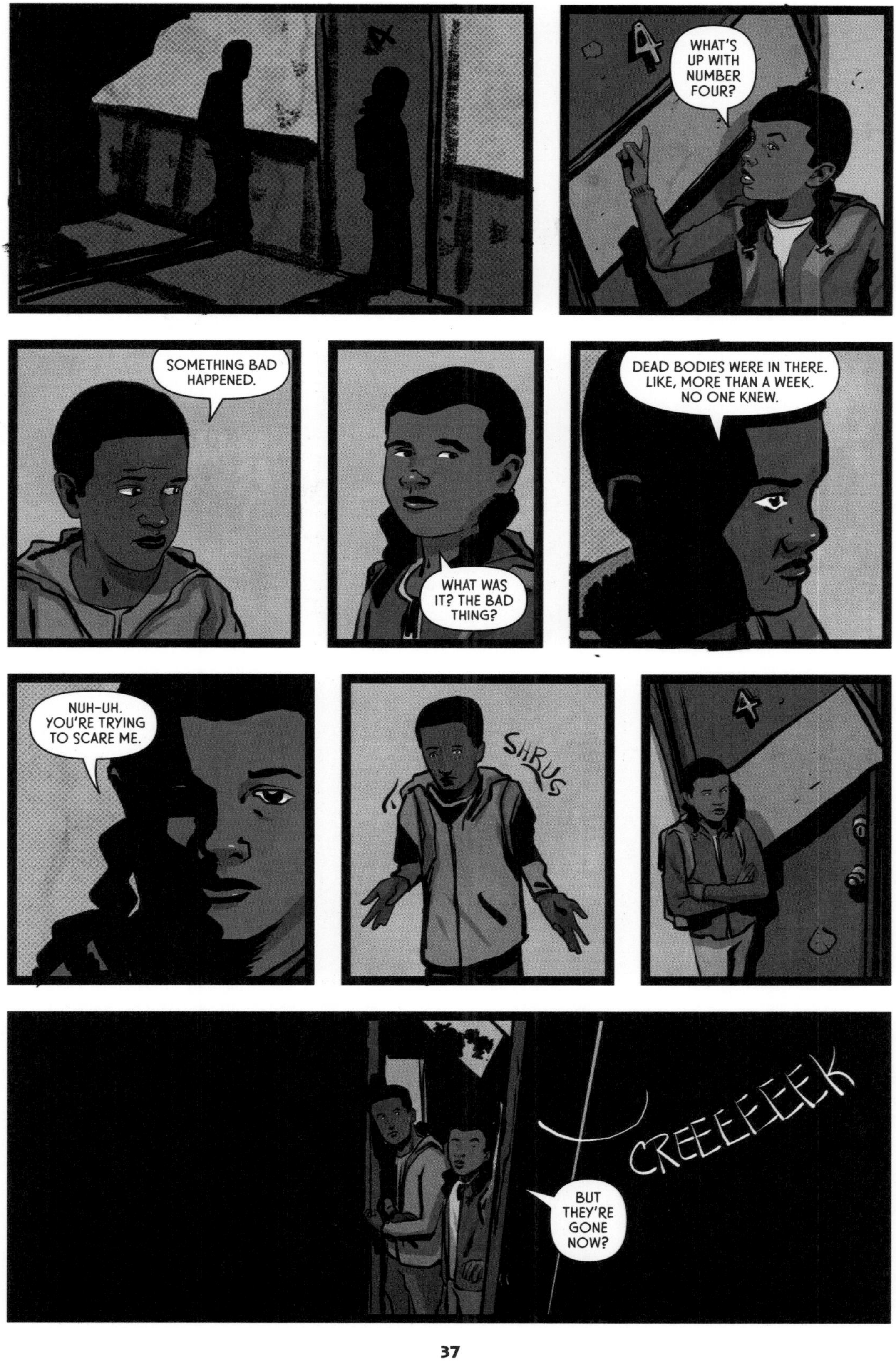
WHAT'S UP WITH NUMBER FOUR?
SOMETHING BAD HAPPENED.
WHAT WAS IT? THE BAD THING?
DEAD BODIES WERE IN THERE. LIKE, MORE THAN A WEEK. NO ONE KNEW.
NUH-UH. YOU'RE TRYING TO SCARE ME.
SHRUG
CREEEEEEK
BUT THEY'RE GONE NOW?

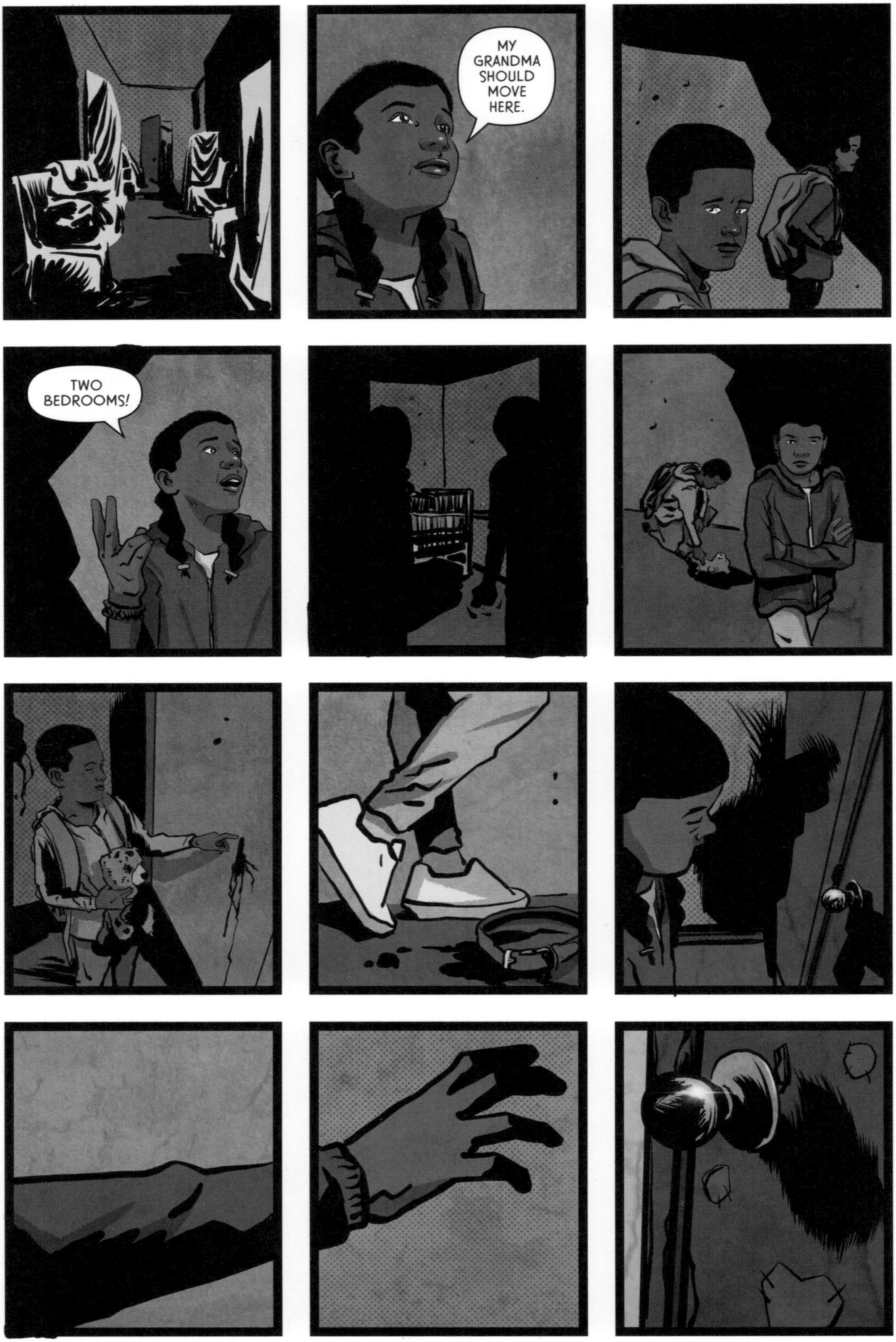
MY GRANDMA SHOULD MOVE HERE.
TWO BEDROOMS!

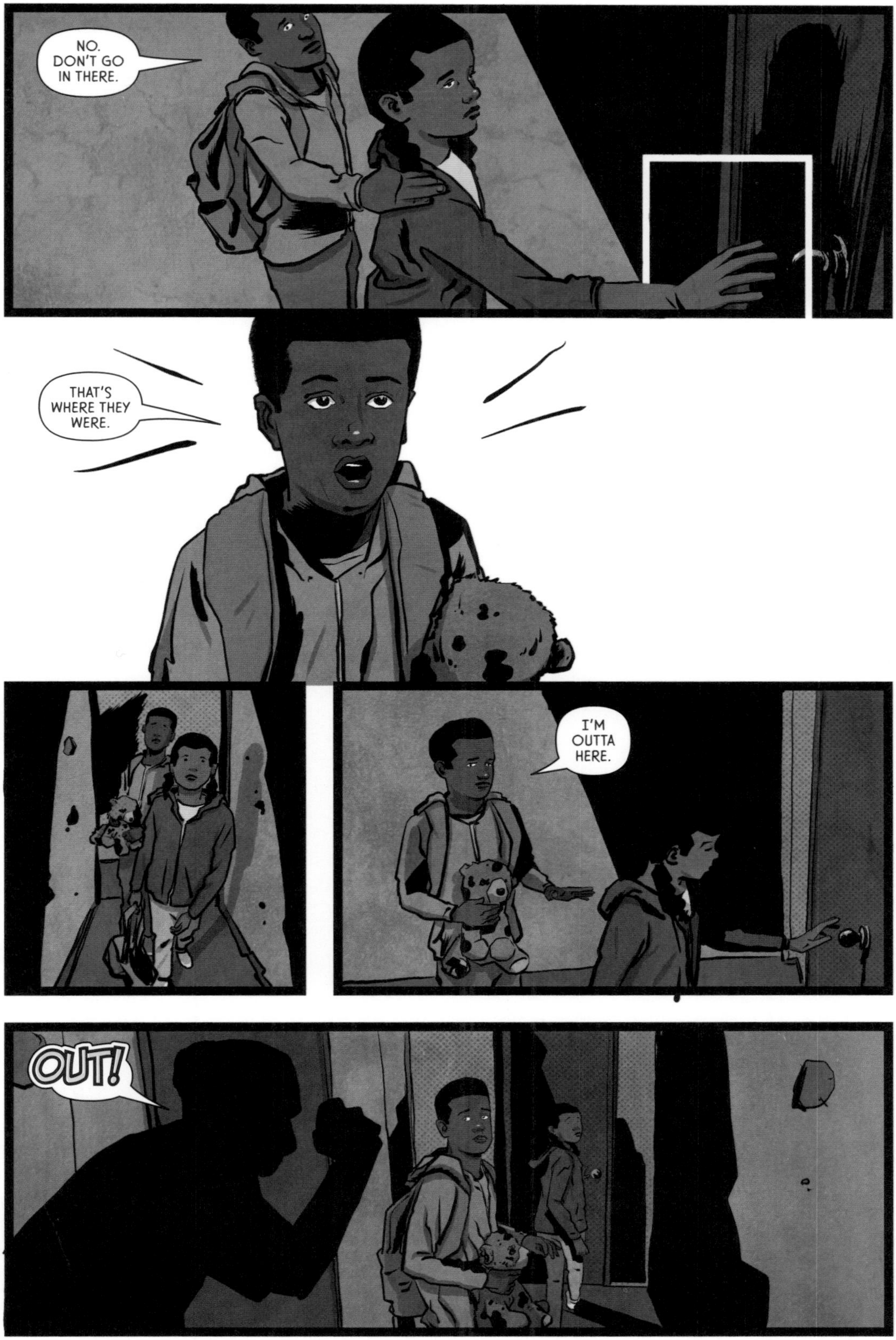
NO. DON'T GO IN THERE.
THAT'S WHERE THEY WERE.
I'M OUTTA HERE.
OUT!

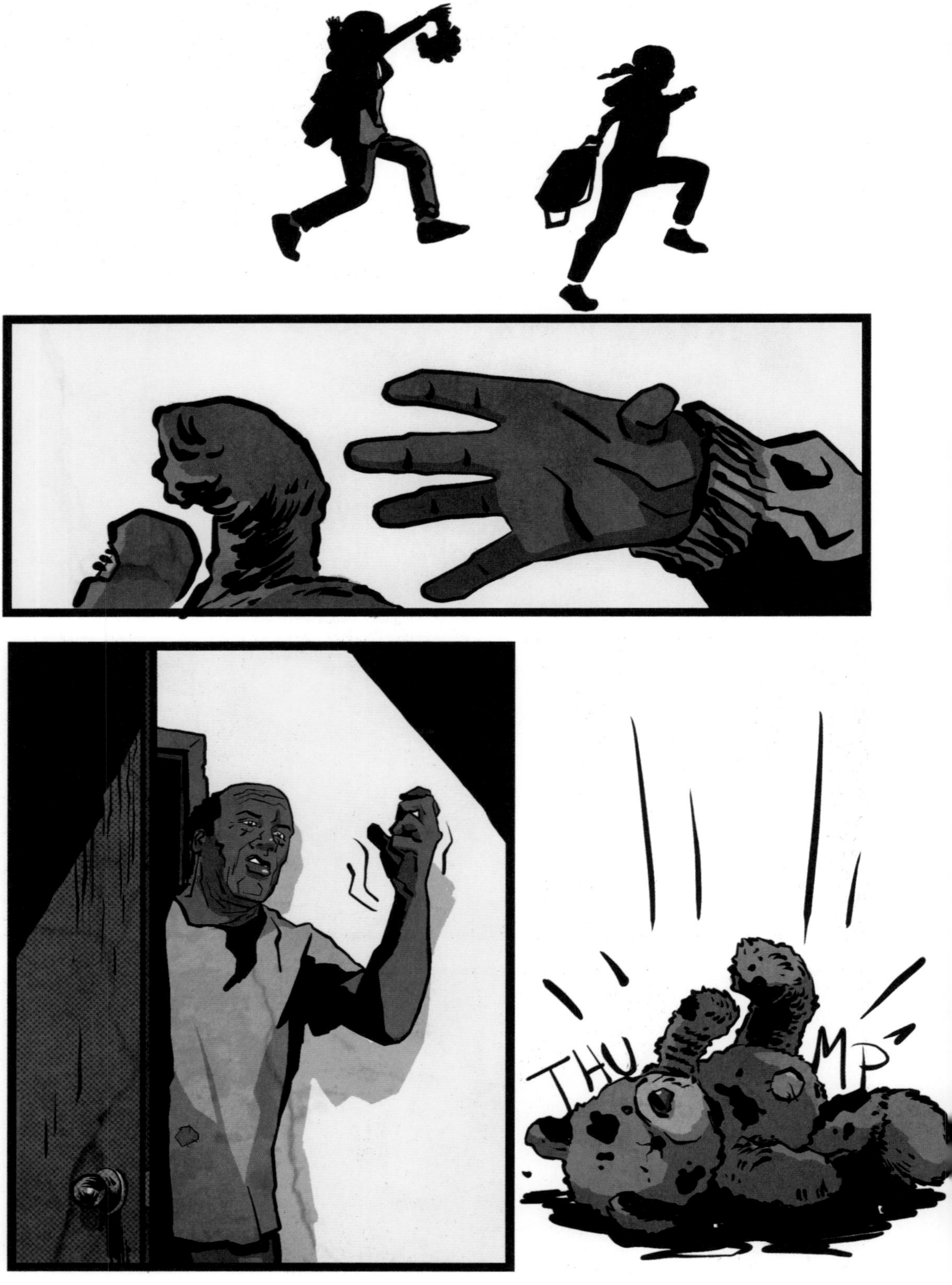
THUMP

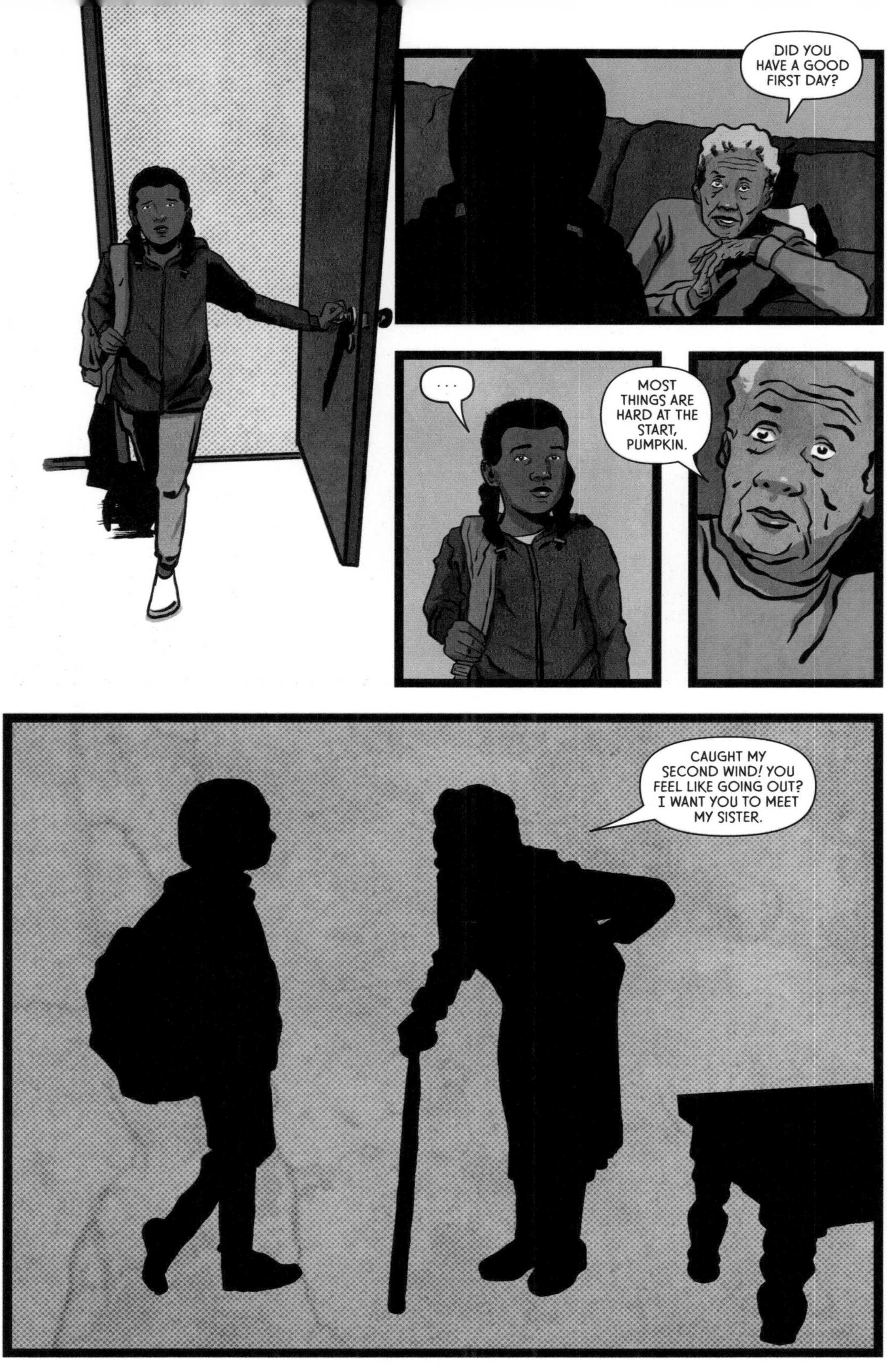
DID YOU HAVE A GOOD FIRST DAY?
. . .
MOST THINGS ARE HARD AT THE START, PUMPKIN.
CAUGHT MY SECOND WIND! YOU FEEL LIKE GOING OUT? I WANT YOU TO MEET MY SISTER.

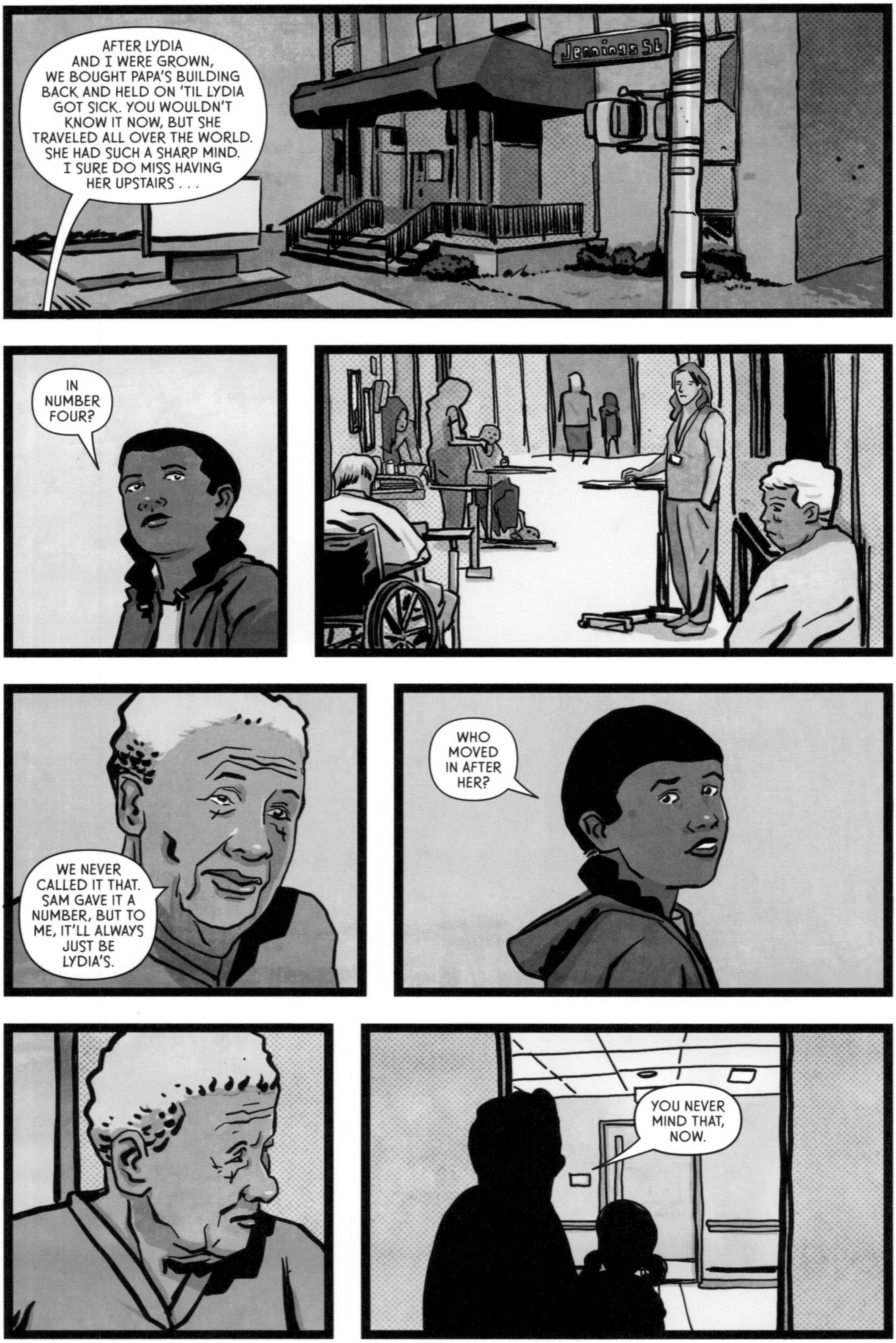
AFTER LYDIA AND I WERE GROWN, WE BOUGHT PAPA'S BUILDING BACK AND HELD ON 'TIL LYDIA GOT SICK. YOU WOULDN'T KNOW IT NOW, BUT SHE TRAVELED ALL OVER THE WORLD. SHE HAD SUCH A SHARP MIND. I SURE DO MISS HAVING HER UPSTAIRS . . .
Jennings St
IN NUMBER FOUR?
WE NEVER CALLED IT THAT. SAM GAVE IT A NUMBER, BUT TO ME, IT'LL ALWAYS JUST BE LYDIA'S.
WHO MOVED IN AFTER HER?
YOU NEVER MIND THAT, NOW.

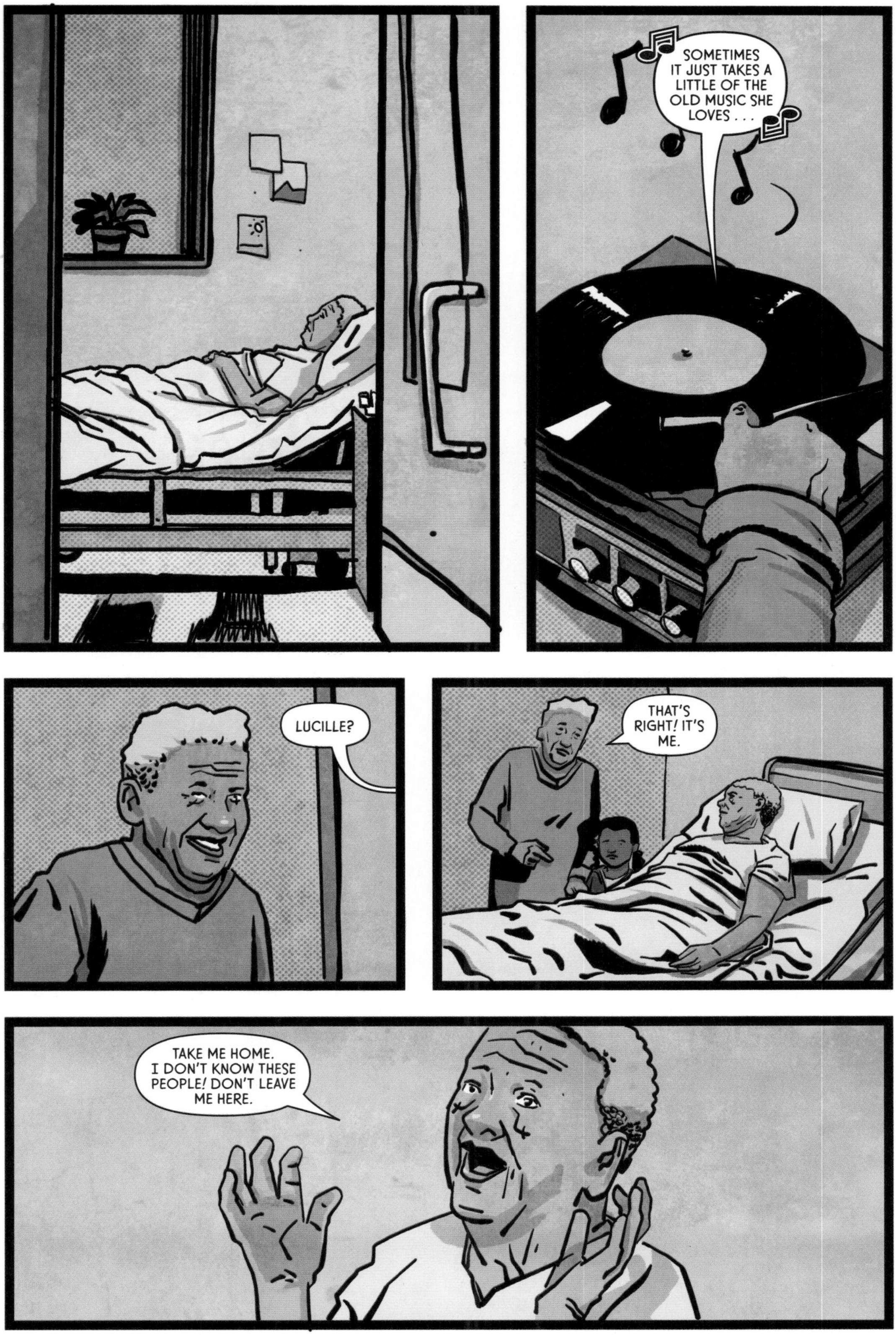
SOMETIMES IT JUST TAKES A LITTLE OF THE OLD MUSIC SHE LOVES . . .
LUCILLE?
THAT'S RIGHT! IT'S ME.
TAKE ME HOME. I DON'T KNOW THESE PEOPLE! DON'T LEAVE ME HERE.

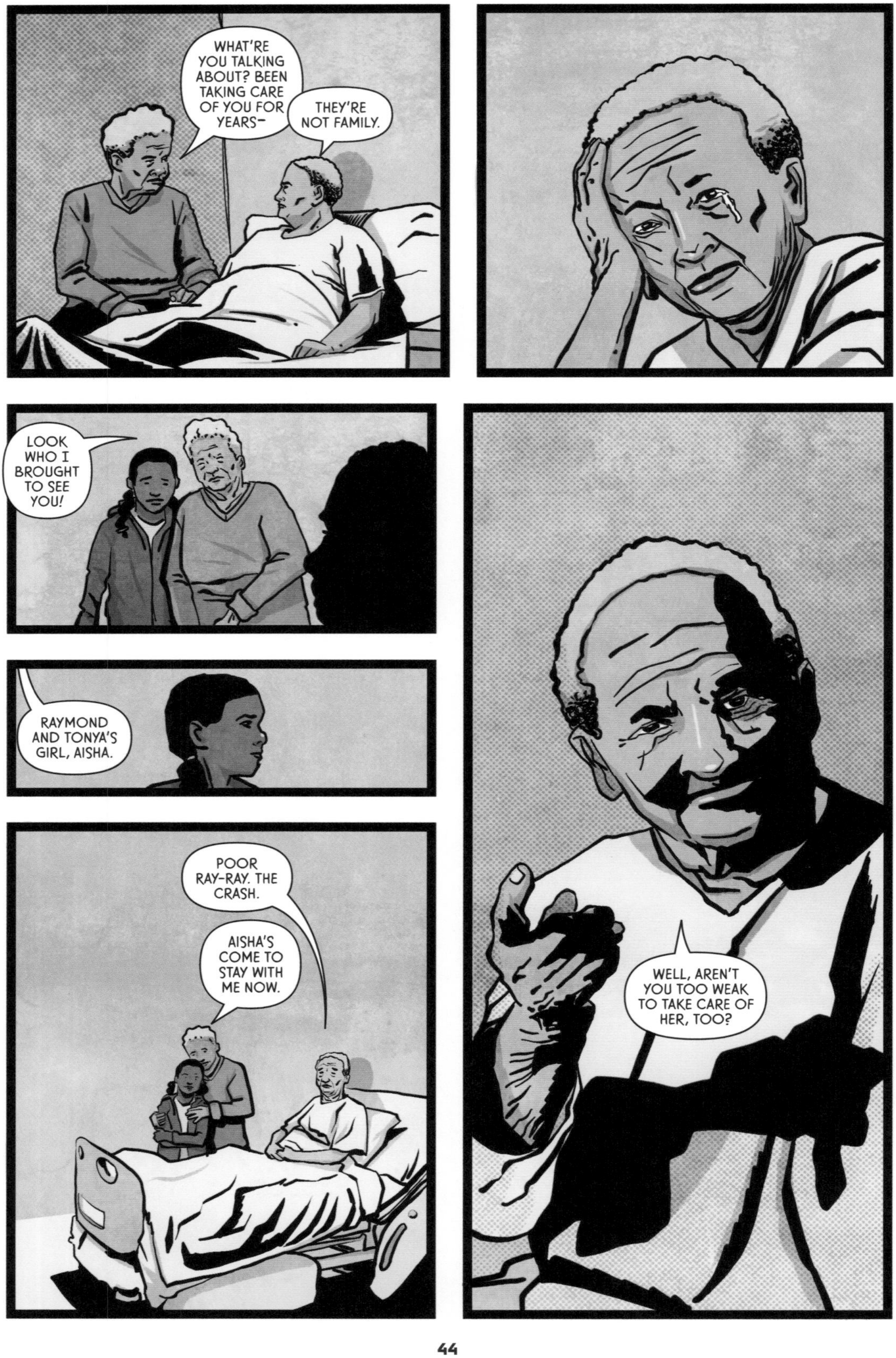
WHAT'RE YOU TALKING ABOUT? BEEN TAKING CARE OF YOU FOR YEARS—
THEY'RE NOT FAMILY.
LOOK WHO I BROUGHT TO SEE YOU!
RAYMOND AND TONYA'S GIRL, AISHA.
POOR RAY-RAY. THE CRASH.
AISHA'S COME TO STAY WITH ME NOW.
WELL, AREN'T YOU TOO WEAK TO TAKE CARE OF HER, TOO?

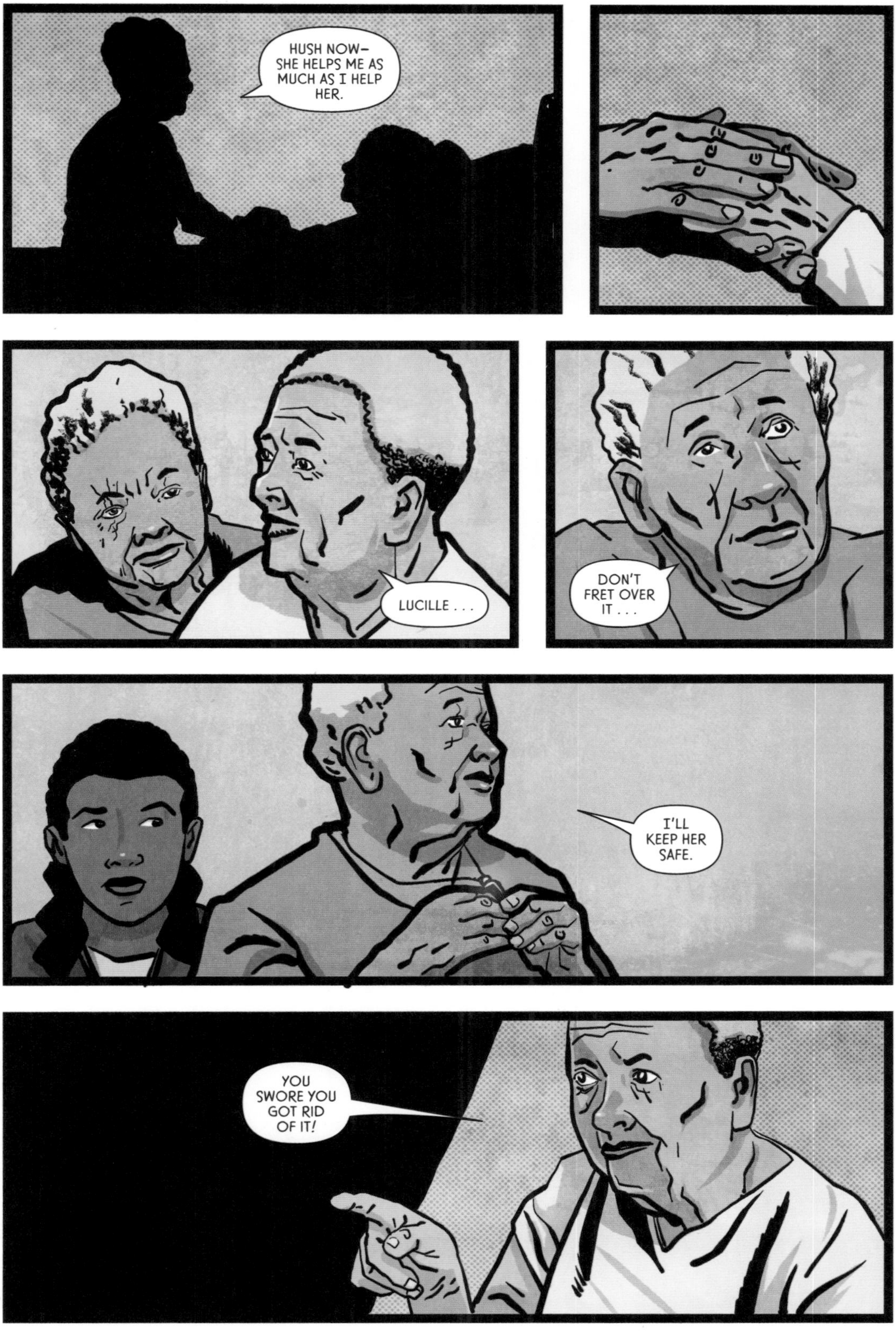

HUSH NOW—
SHE HELPS ME AS MUCH AS I HELP HER.
LUCILLE . . .
DON'T FRET OVER IT . . .
I'LL KEEP HER SAFE.
YOU SWORE YOU GOT RID OF IT!

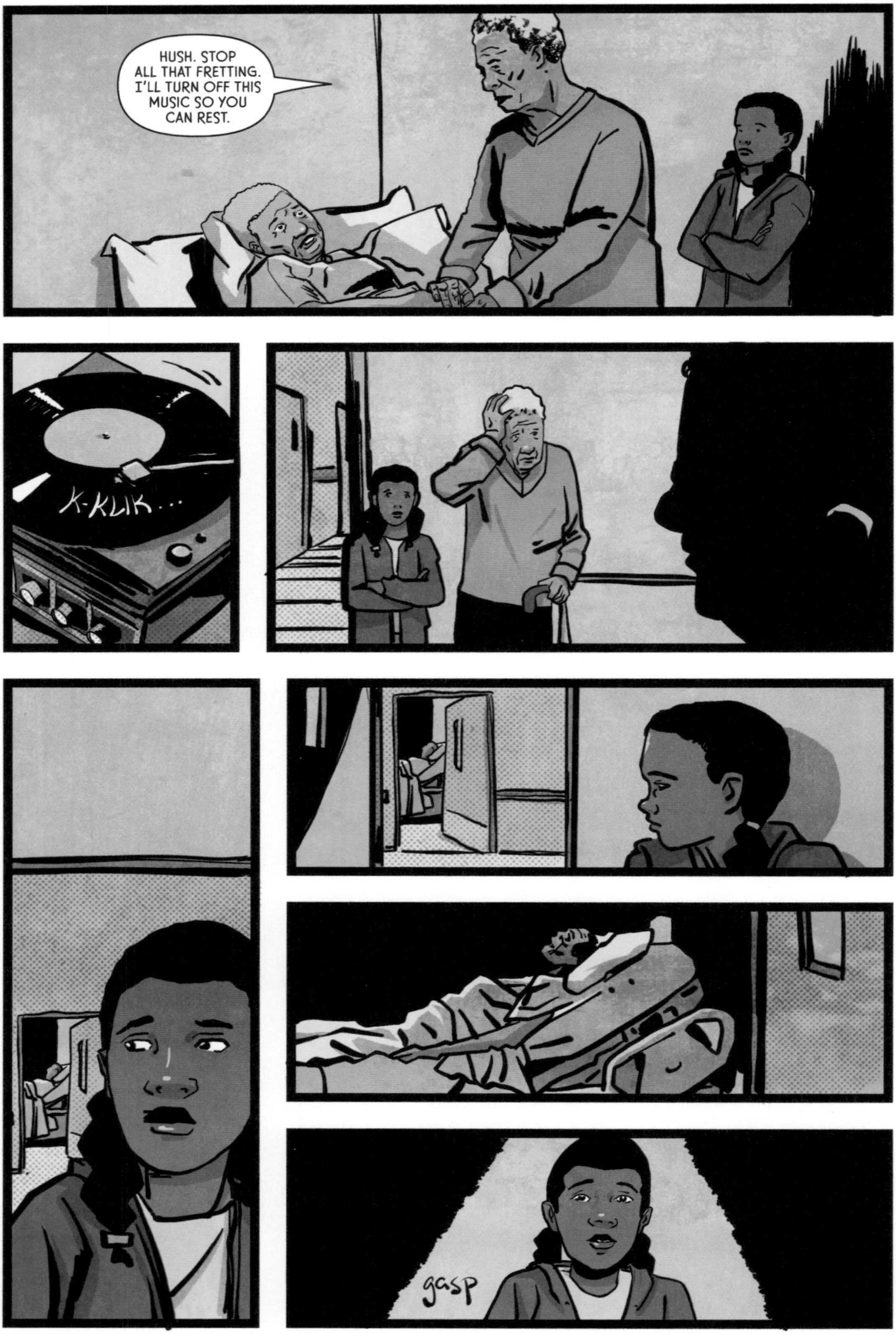
HUSH. STOP ALL THAT FRETTING. I'LL TURN OFF THIS MUSIC SO YOU CAN REST.
K-KLIK...
gasp

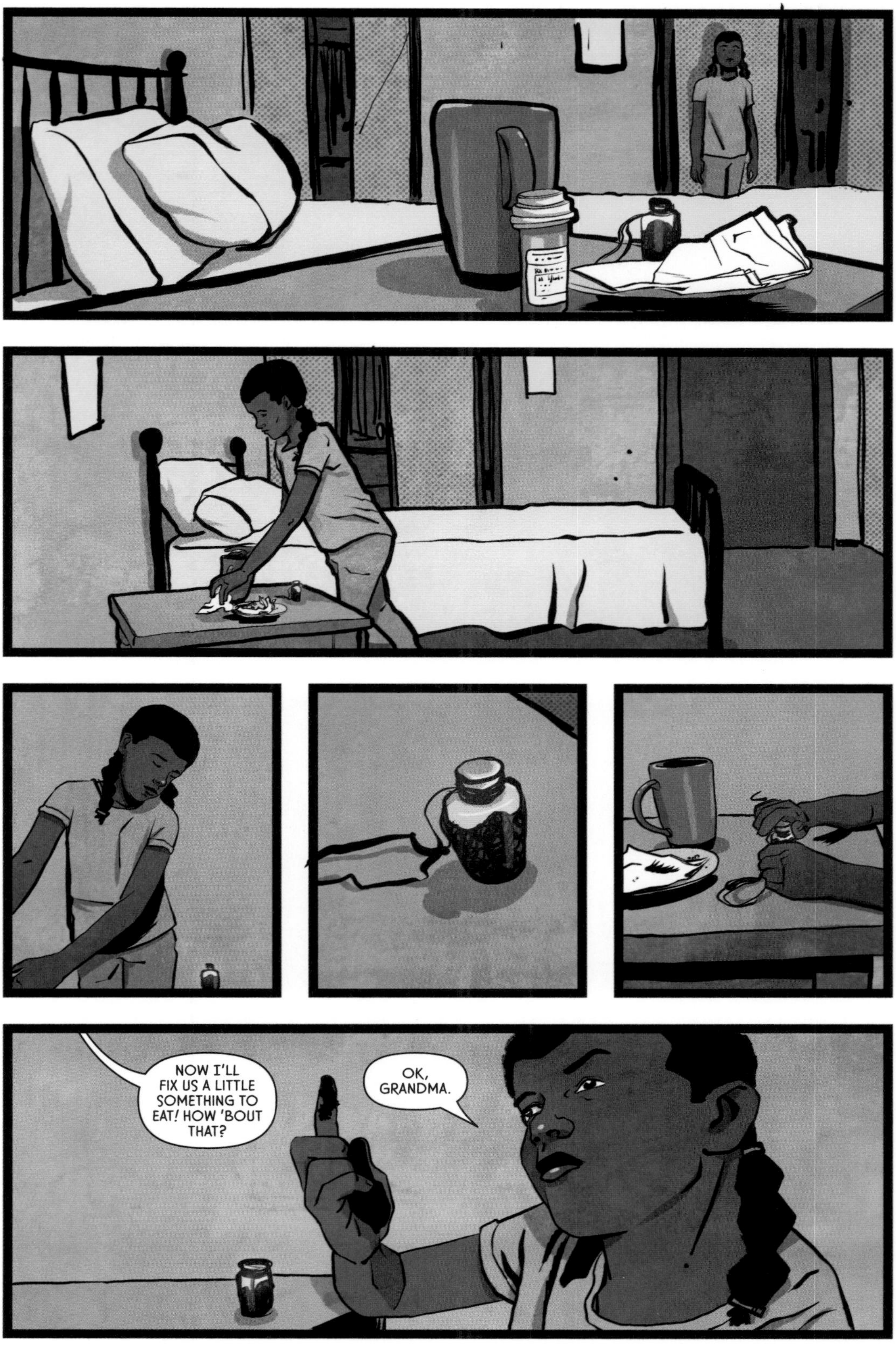
NOW I'LL FIX US A LITTLE SOMETHING TO EAT! HOW 'BOUT THAT?
OK, GRANDMA.

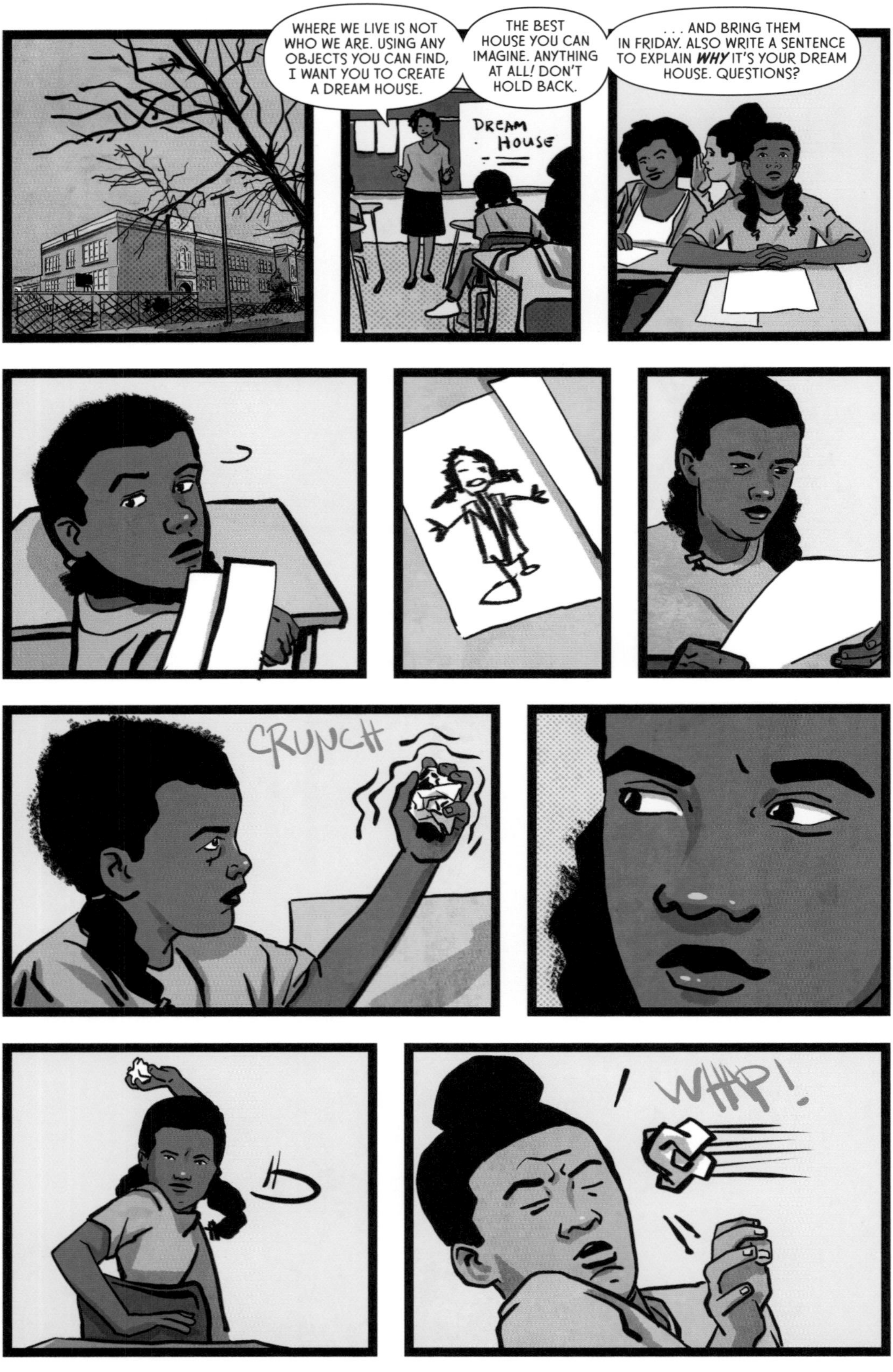
WHERE WE LIVE IS NOT WHO WE ARE. USING ANY OBJECTS YOU CAN FIND, I WANT YOU TO CREATE A DREAM HOUSE.
THE BEST HOUSE YOU CAN IMAGINE. ANYTHING AT ALL! DON'T HOLD BACK.
DREAM HOUSE
. . . AND BRING THEM IN FRIDAY. ALSO WRITE A SENTENCE TO EXPLAIN WHY IT'S YOUR DREAM HOUSE. QUESTIONS?
CRUNCH
WHAP!

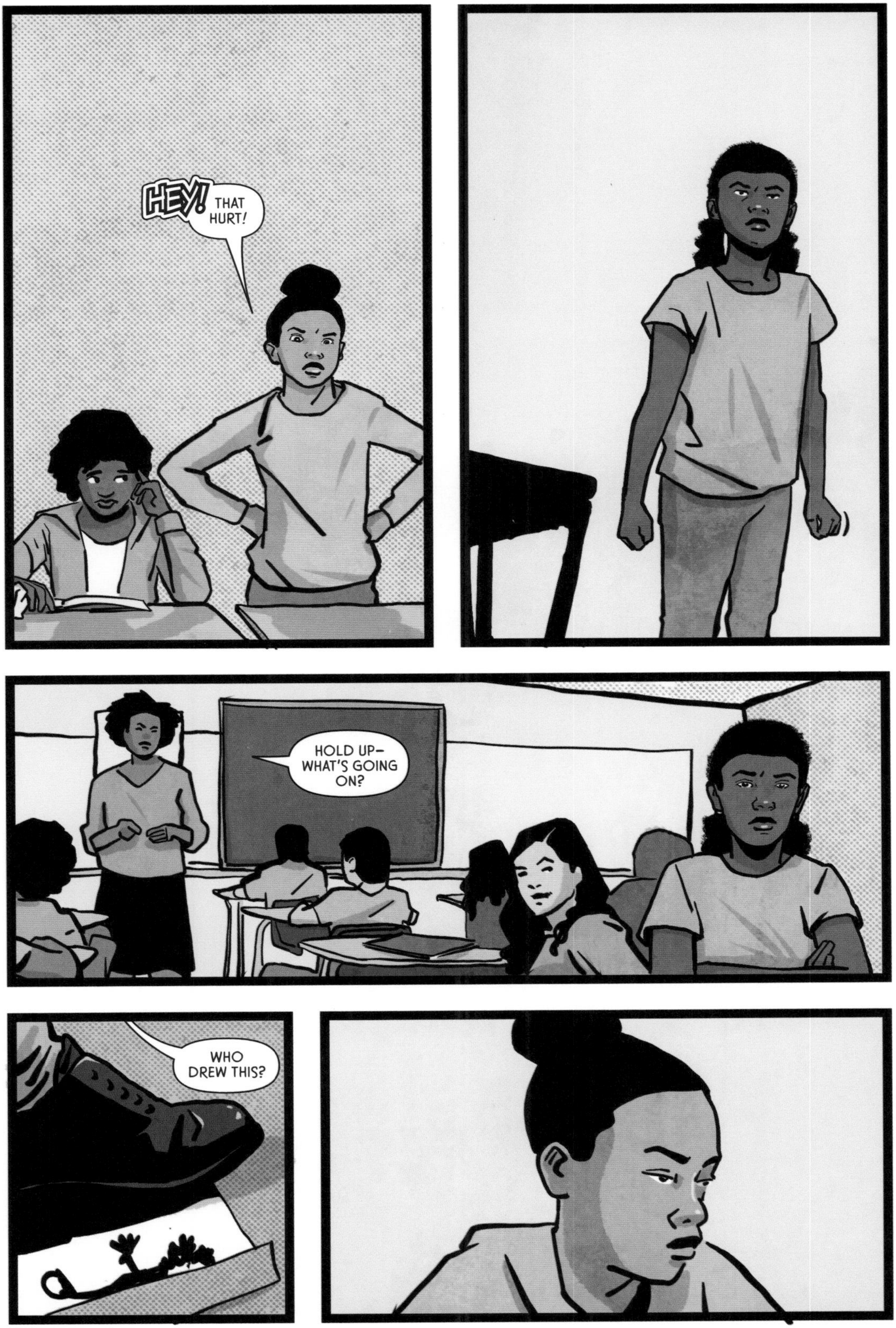
HEY! THAT HURT!
HOLD UP— WHAT'S GOING ON?
WHO DREW THIS?

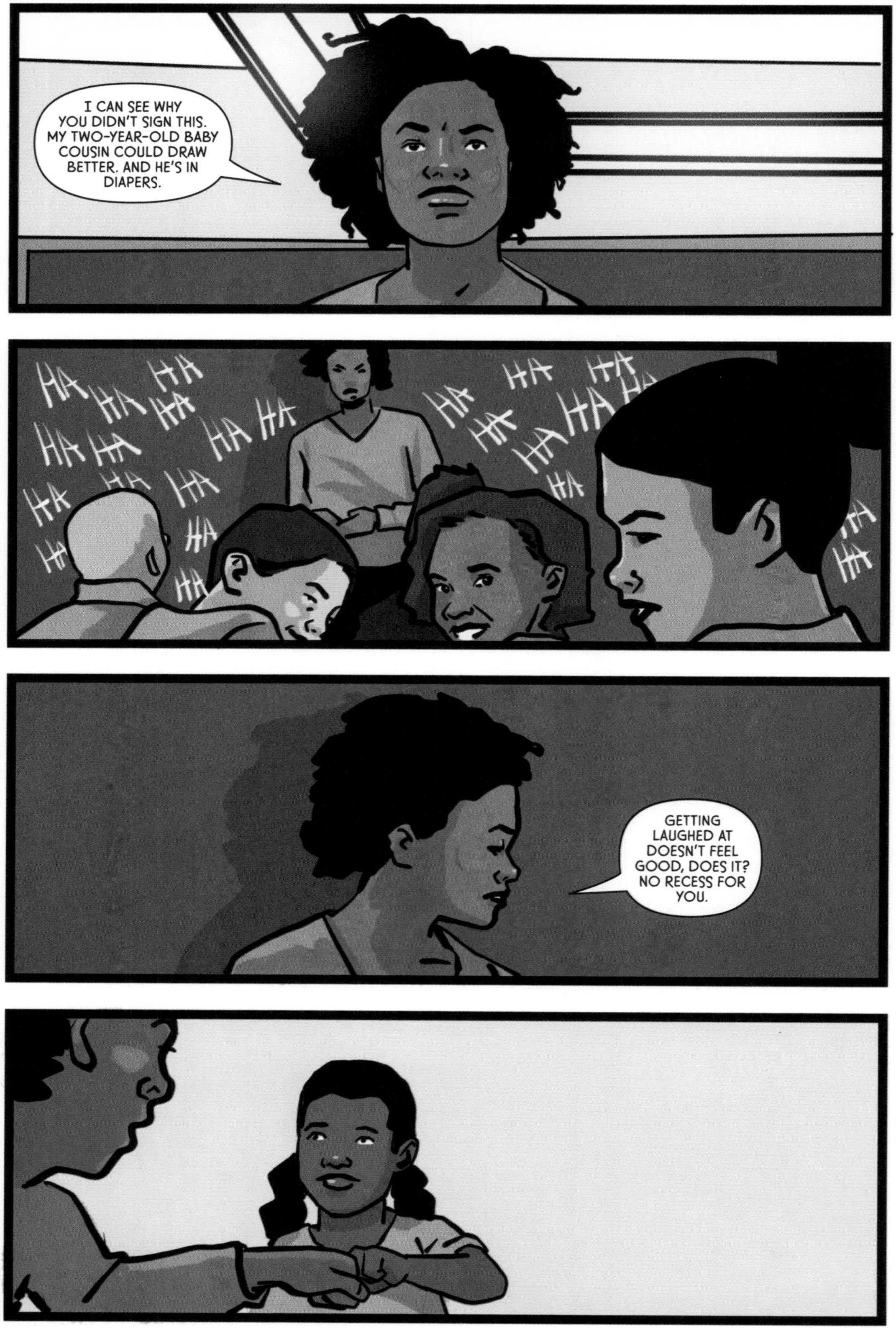
I CAN SEE WHY YOU DIDN'T SIGN THIS. MY TWO-YEAR-OLD BABY COUSIN COULD DRAW BETTER. AND HE'S IN DIAPERS.
HA HA HA HA HA HA HA HA HA HA HA HA HA HA HA HA HA HA HA HA HA HA
GETTING LAUGHED AT DOESN'T FEEL GOOD, DOES IT? NO RECESS FOR YOU.

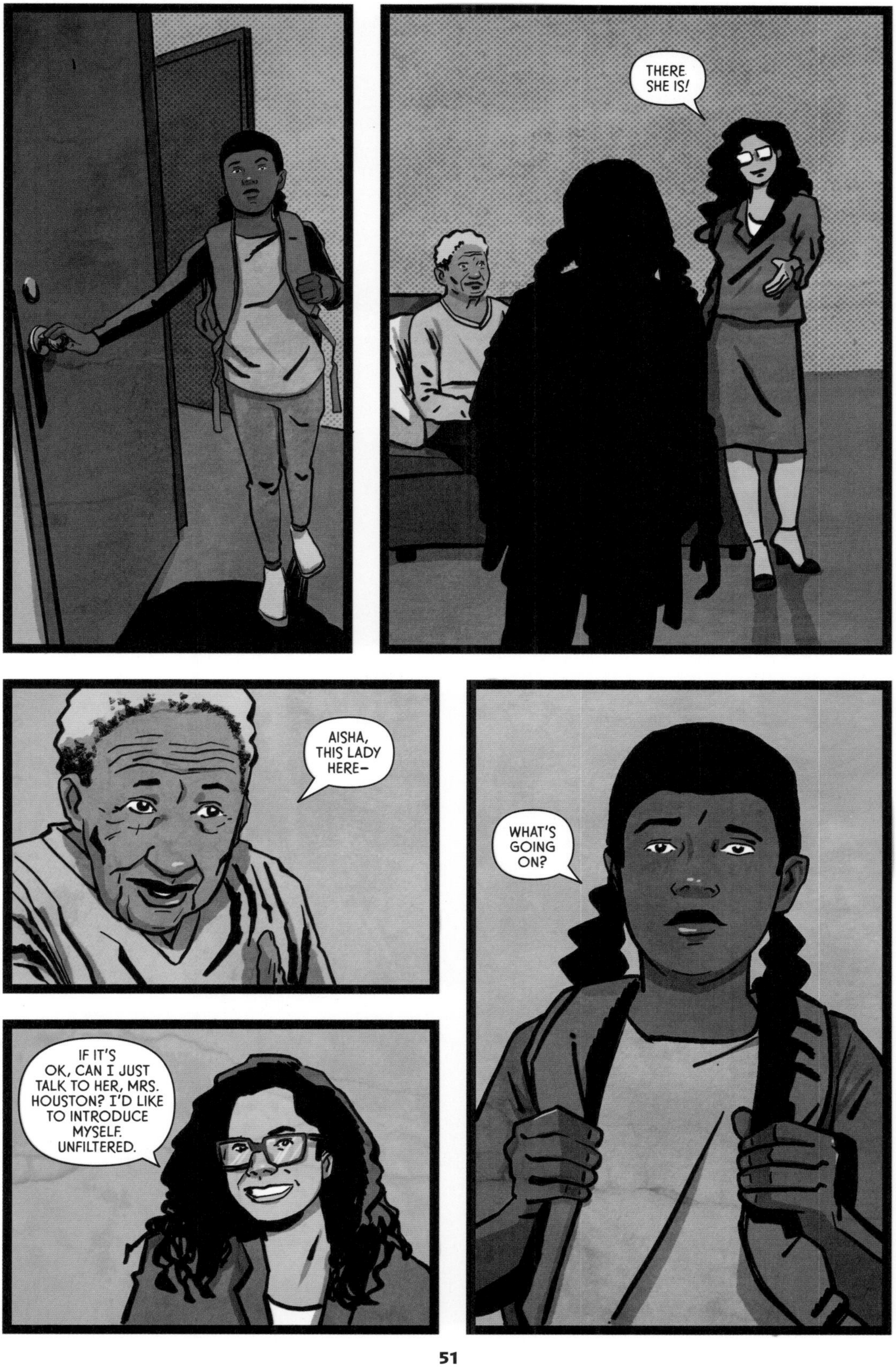
THERE SHE IS!
AISHA, THIS LADY HERE-
WHAT'S GOING ON?
IF IT'S OK, CAN I JUST TALK TO HER, MRS. HOUSTON? I'D LIKE TO INTRODUCE MYSELF. UNFILTERED.

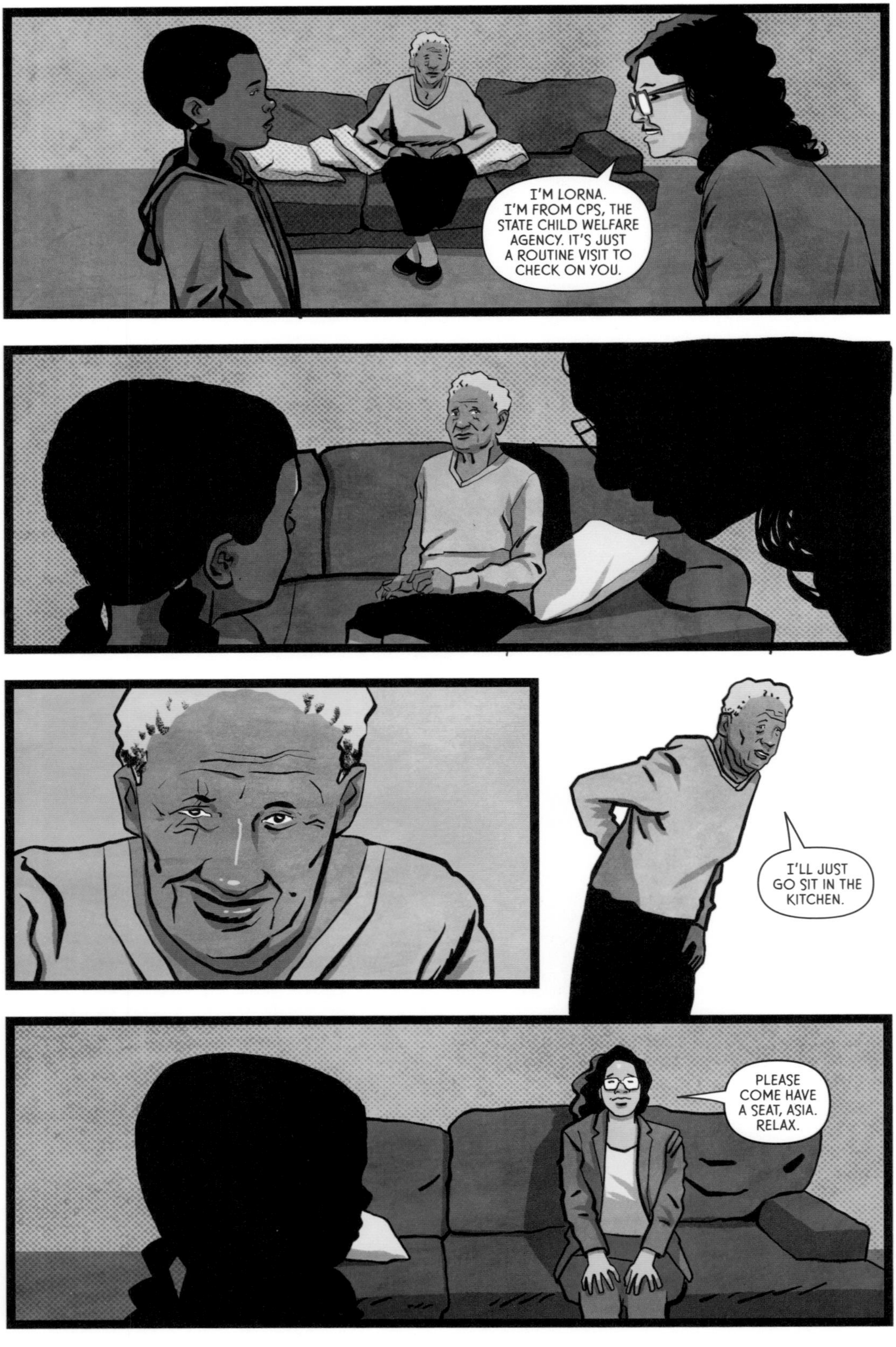
I'M LORNA. I'M FROM CPS, THE STATE CHILD WELFARE AGENCY. IT'S JUST A ROUTINE VISIT TO CHECK ON YOU.
I'LL JUST GO SIT IN THE KITCHEN.
PLEASE COME HAVE A SEAT, ASIA. RELAX.

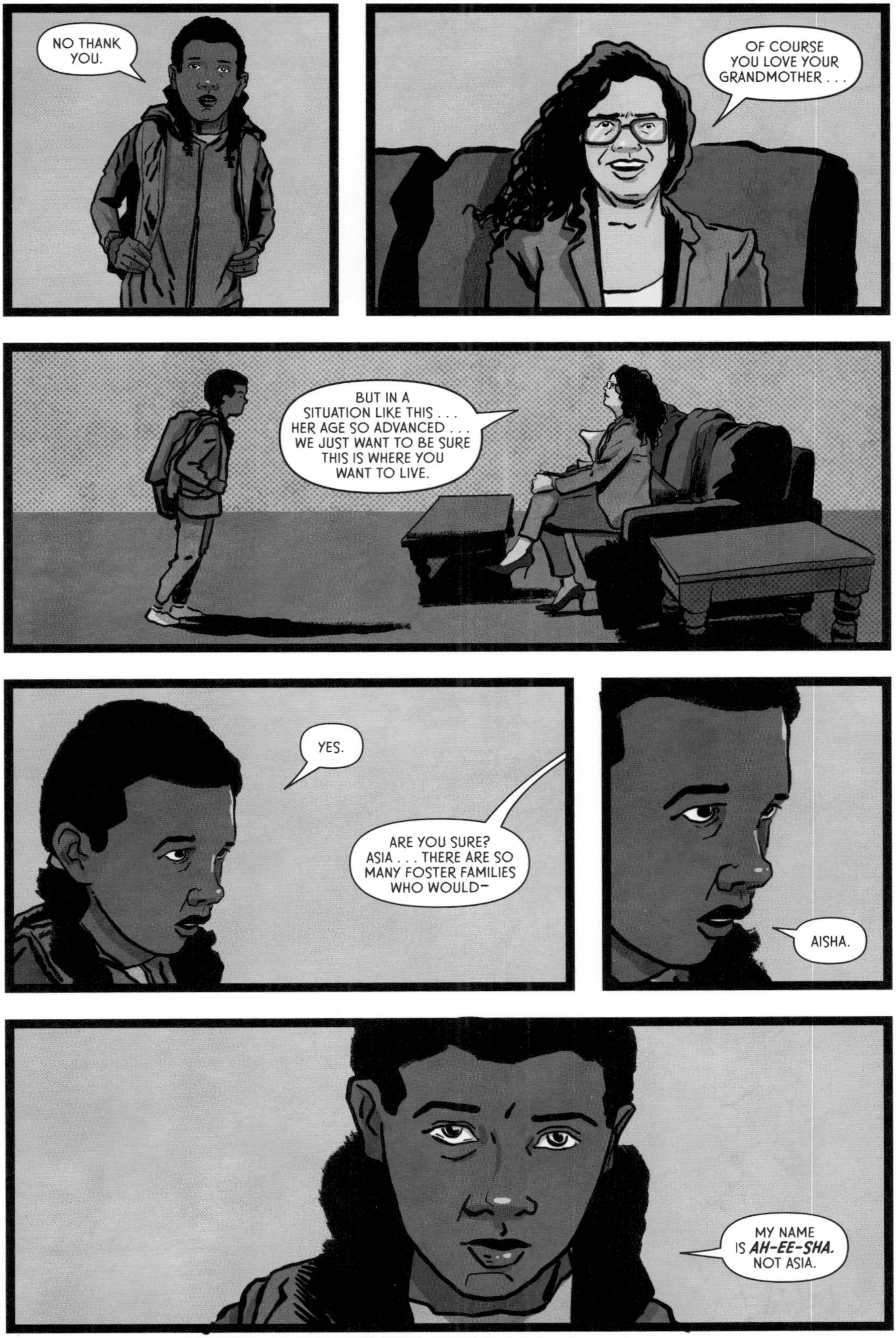
NO THANK YOU.
OF COURSE YOU LOVE YOUR GRANDMOTHER . . .
BUT IN A SITUATION LIKE THIS . . . HER AGE SO ADVANCED . . . WE JUST WANT TO BE SURE THIS IS WHERE YOU WANT TO LIVE.
YES.
ARE YOU SURE? ASIA . . . THERE ARE SO MANY FOSTER FAMILIES WHO WOULD—
AISHA.
MY NAME IS ***AH-EE-SHA.*** NOT ASIA.

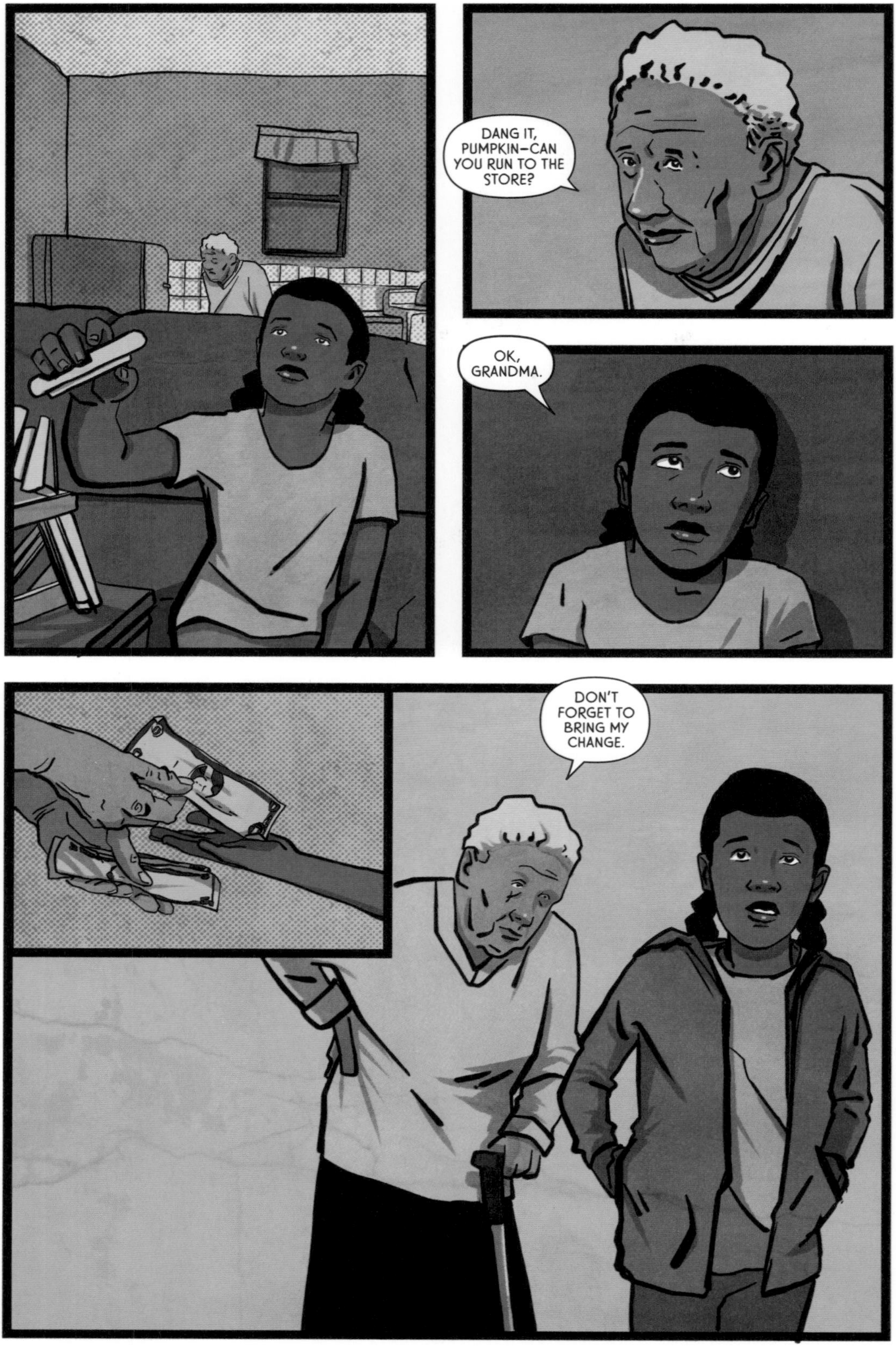
DANG IT, PUMPKIN—CAN YOU RUN TO THE STORE?
OK, GRANDMA.
DON'T FORGET TO BRING MY CHANGE.

JUST LIKE THE BARRETTES MOM GAVE ME.

HERE'S YOUR CHANGE.

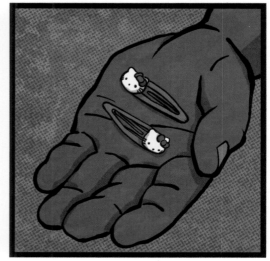

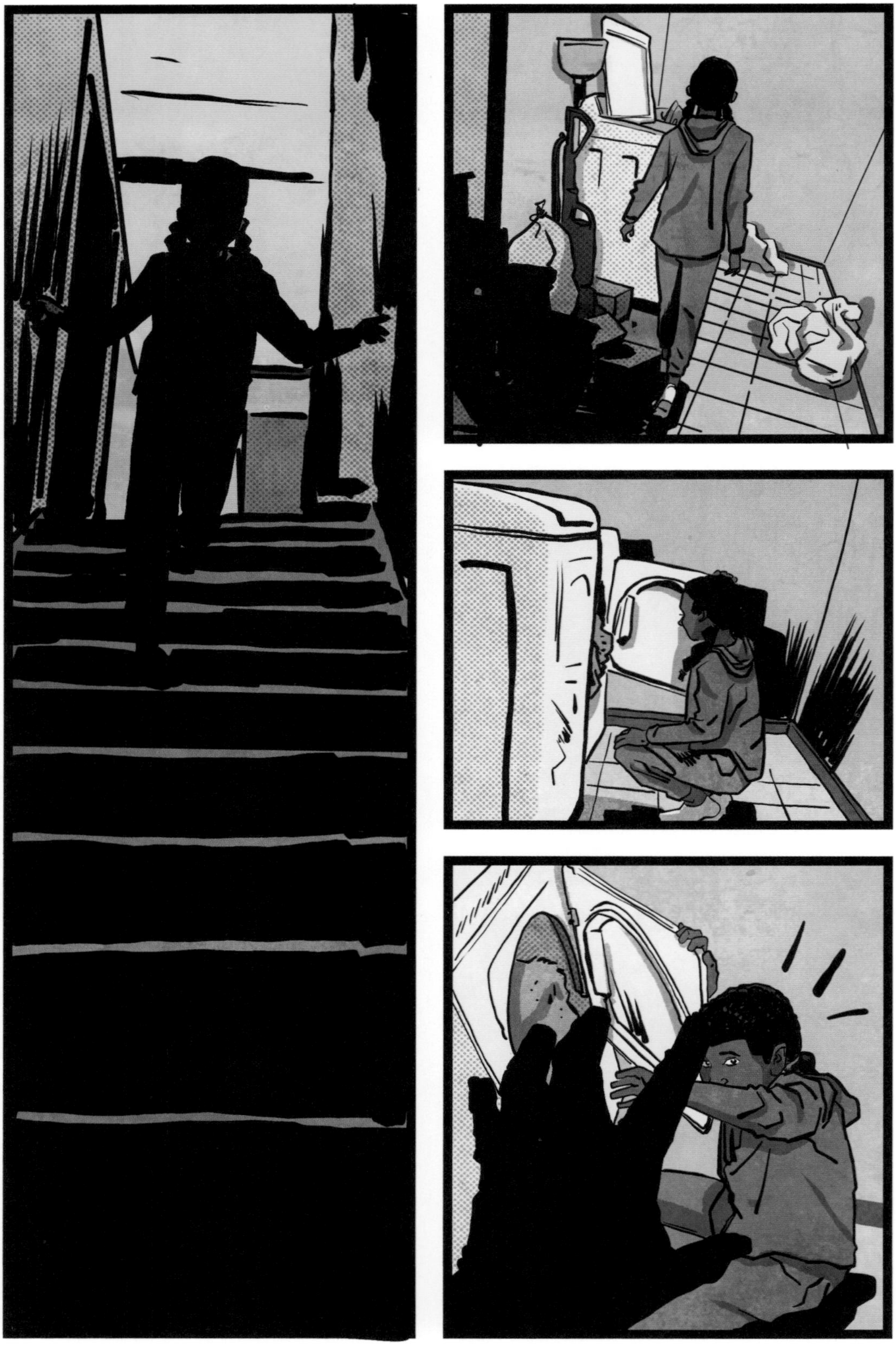

HELP ME UPSTAIRS.

I NEED TO CALL FOR HELP—

NO, PUMPKIN.

JUST NEED TO CATCH MY BREATH. DIDN'T WANT EVERYTHING ON YOU . . .

YOU DESERVE BETTER THAN THIS . . .

NOTHING'S BETTER THAN FAMILY.

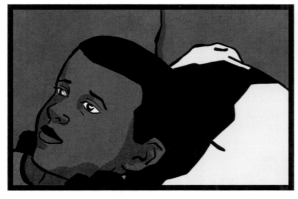

ARE YOU OK, GRANDMA?

SOME JUICE?

57

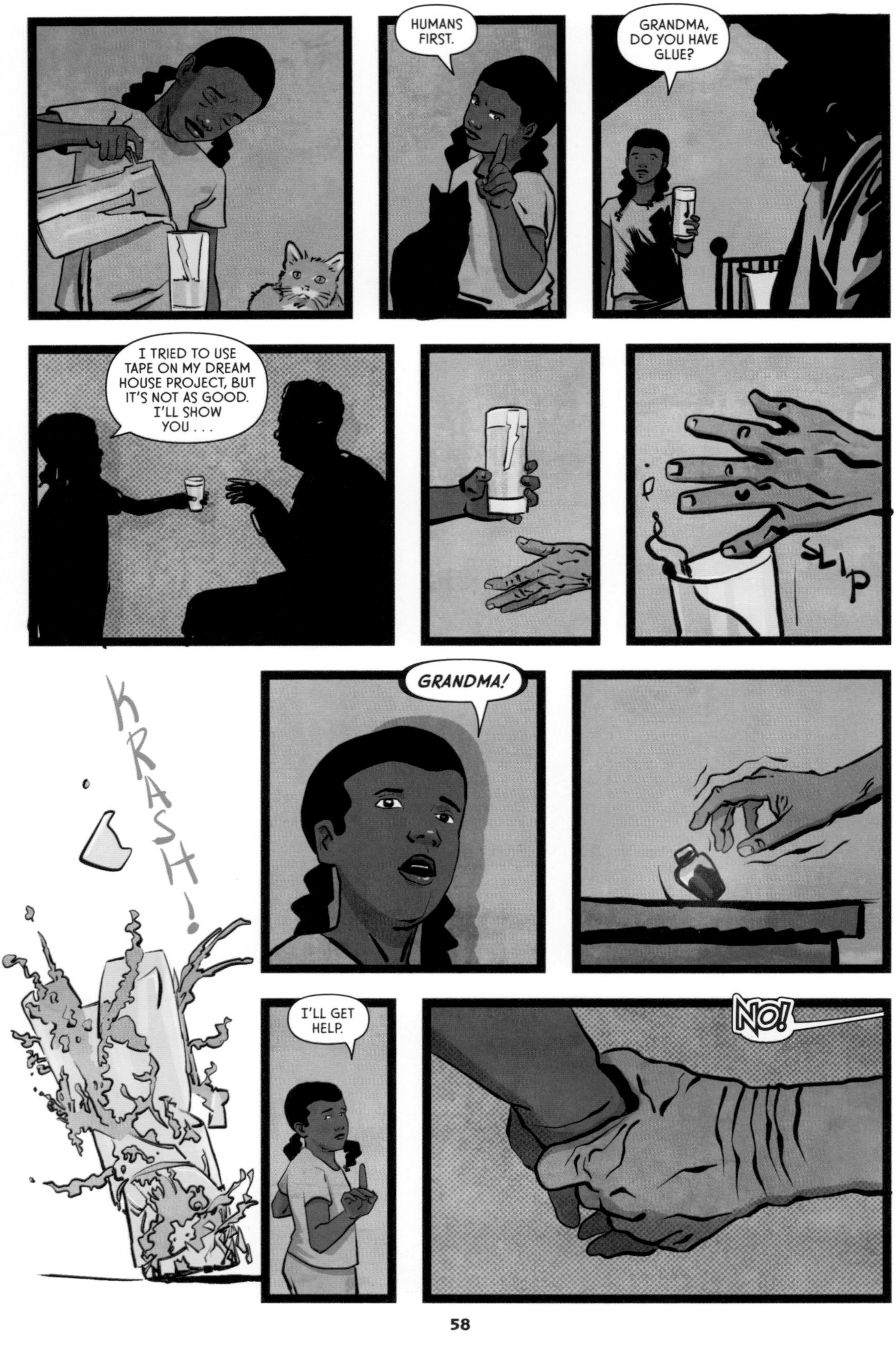
HUMANS FIRST.
GRANDMA, DO YOU HAVE GLUE?
I TRIED TO USE TAPE ON MY DREAM HOUSE PROJECT, BUT IT'S NOT AS GOOD. I'LL SHOW YOU . . .
SLIP
KRASH!
GRANDMA!
I'LL GET HELP.
NO!

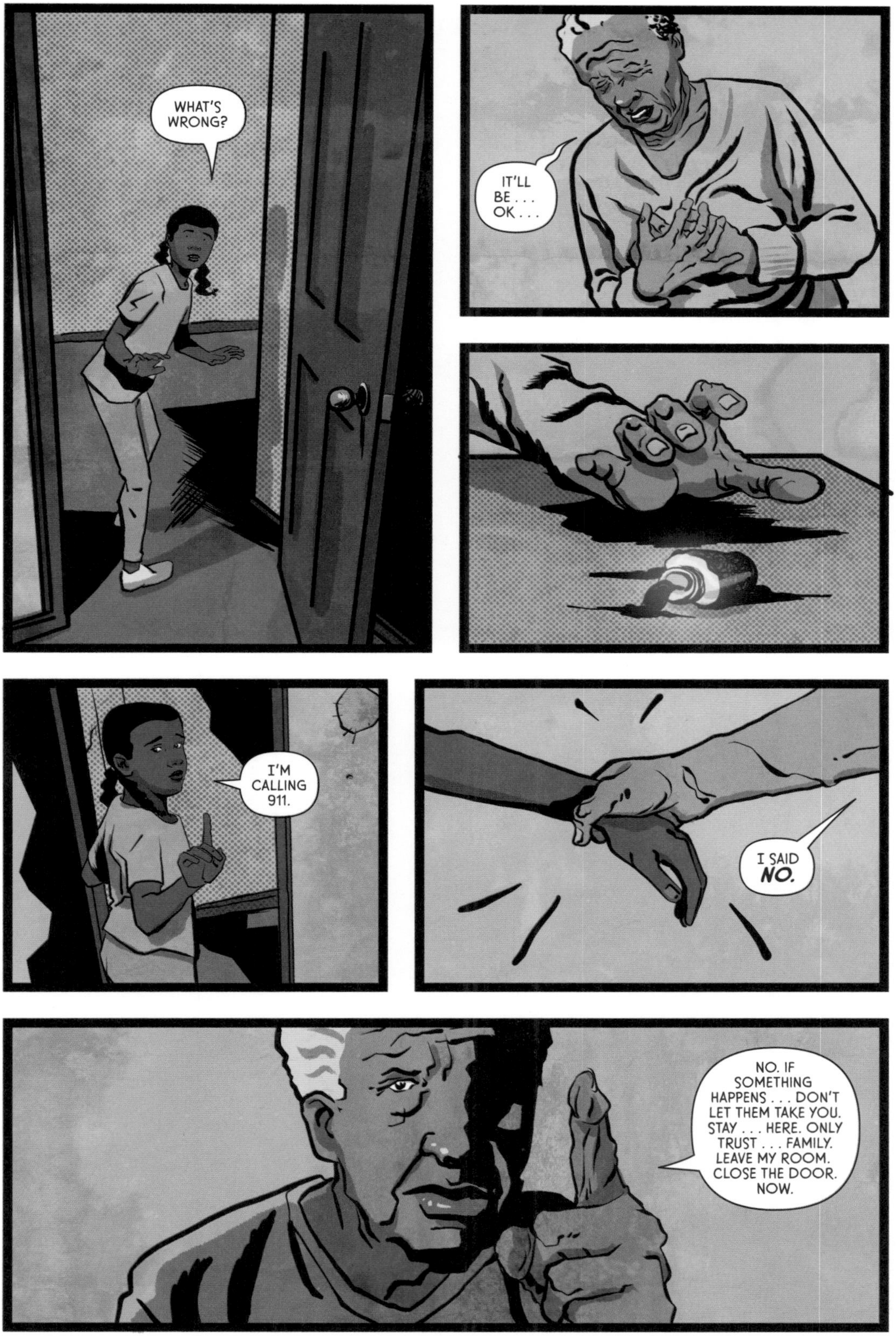
WHAT'S WRONG?
IT'LL BE . . . OK . . .
I'M CALLING 911.
I SAID *NO.*
NO. IF SOMETHING HAPPENS . . . DON'T LET THEM TAKE YOU. STAY . . . HERE. ONLY TRUST . . . FAMILY. LEAVE MY ROOM. CLOSE THE DOOR. NOW.

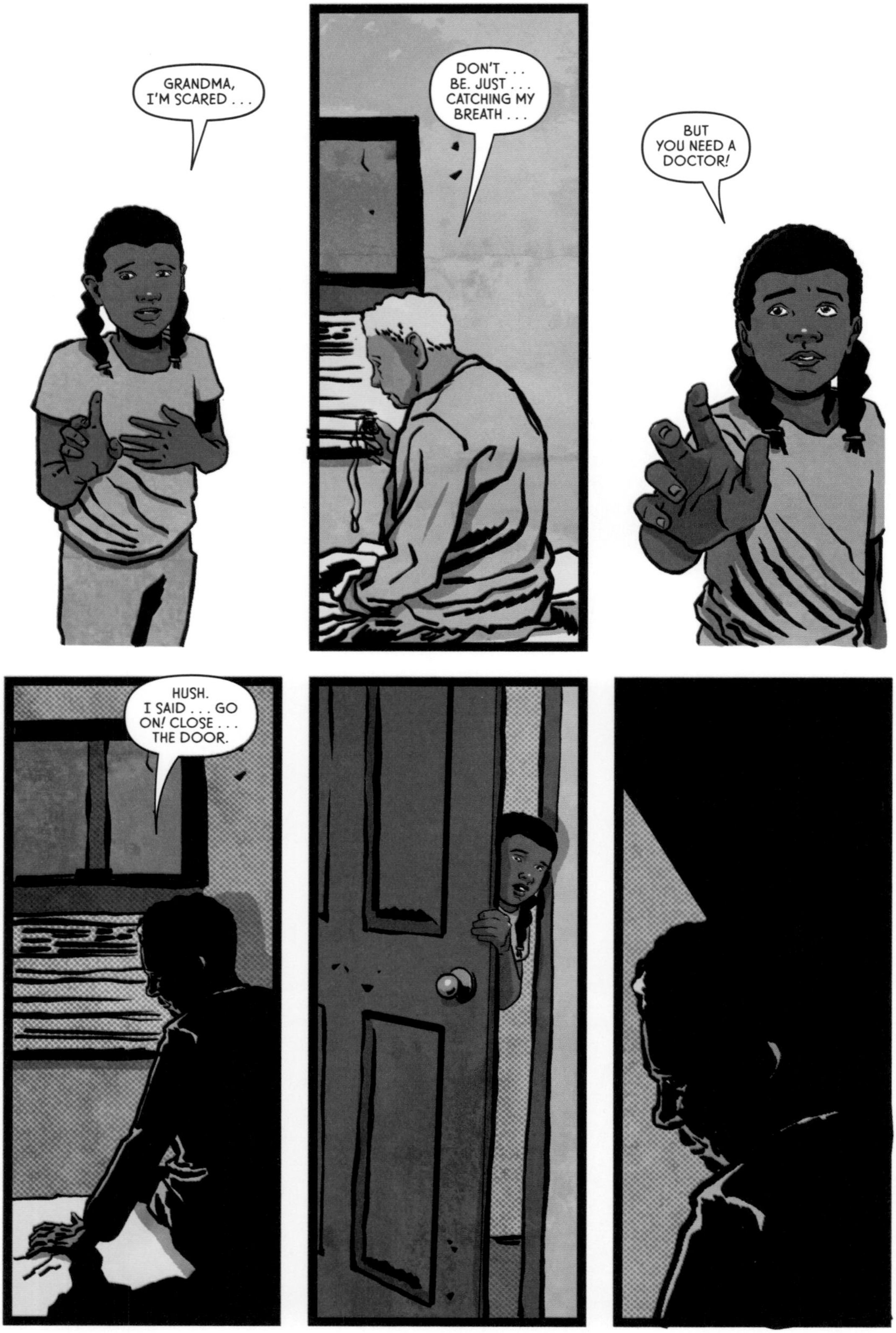
GRANDMA, I'M SCARED . . .
DON'T . . . BE. JUST . . . CATCHING MY BREATH . . .
BUT YOU NEED A DOCTOR!
HUSH. I SAID . . . GO ON! CLOSE . . . THE DOOR.

PROTECT MY GRANDBABY. TAKE CARE OF HER. I BEG YOU. KEEP HER . . . SAFE . . .

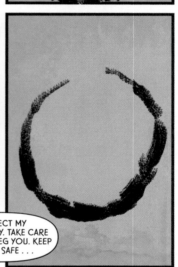

rrattle

KRAK!

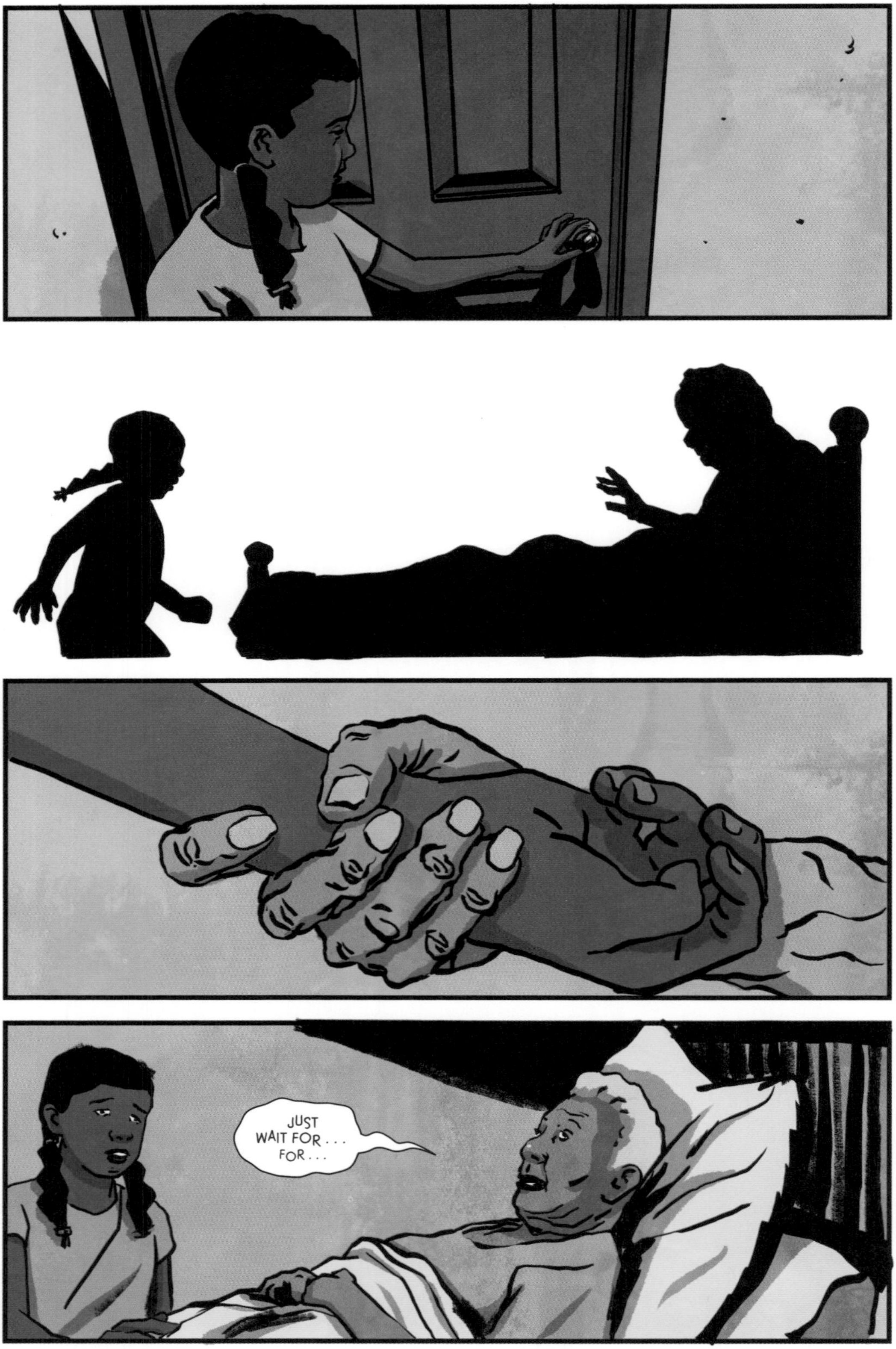
JUST WAIT FOR . . . FOR . . .

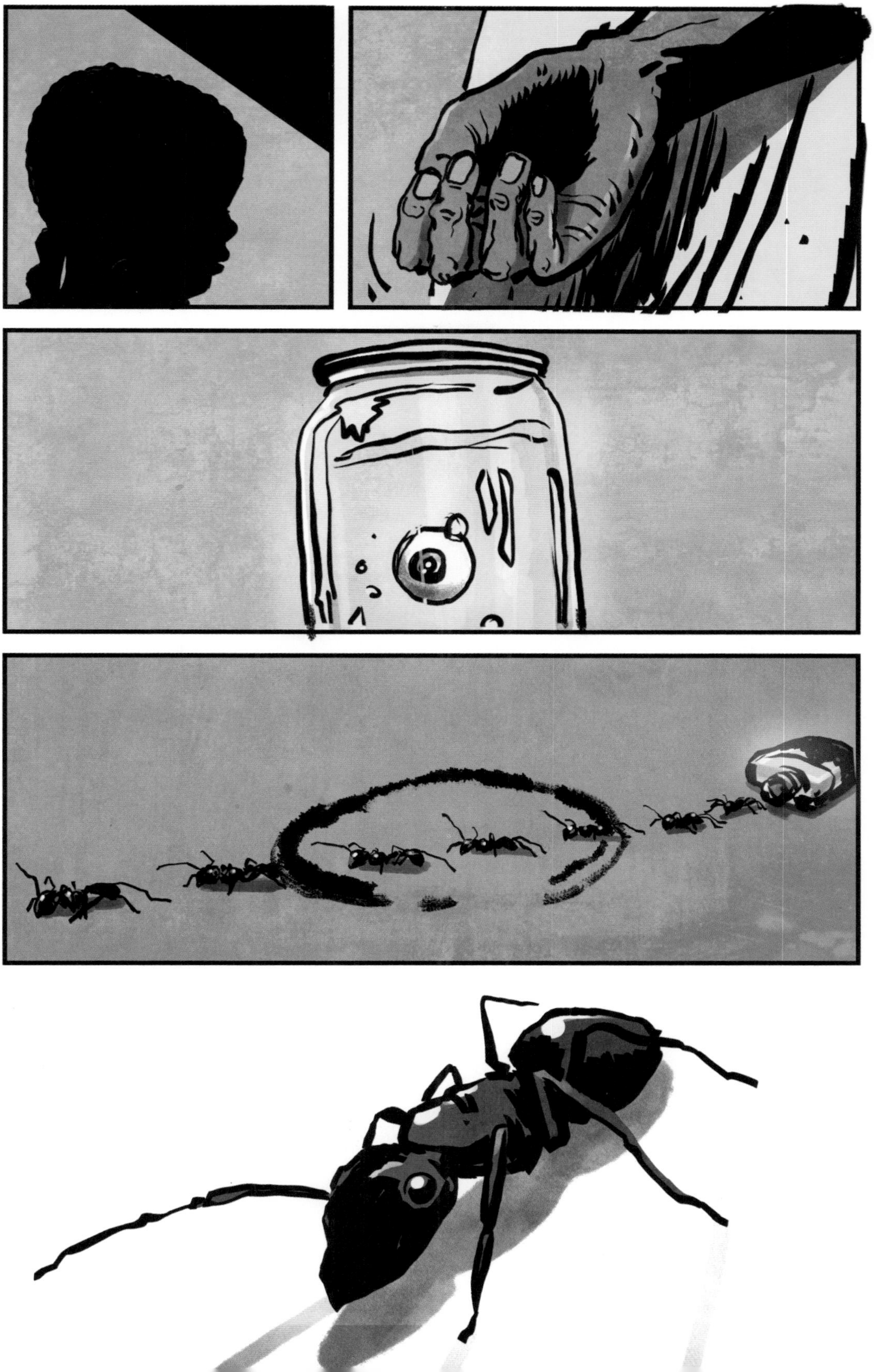

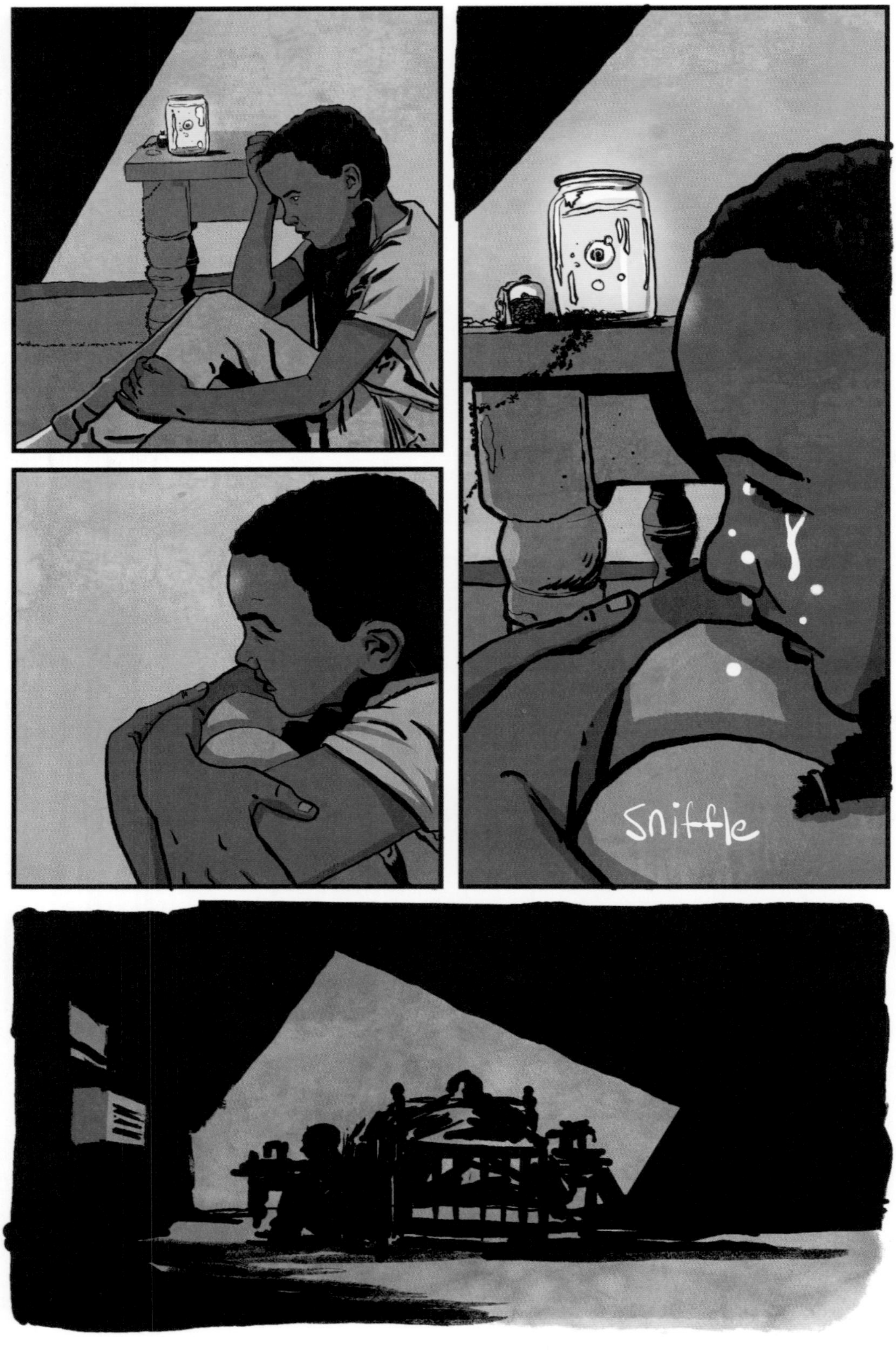
sniffle

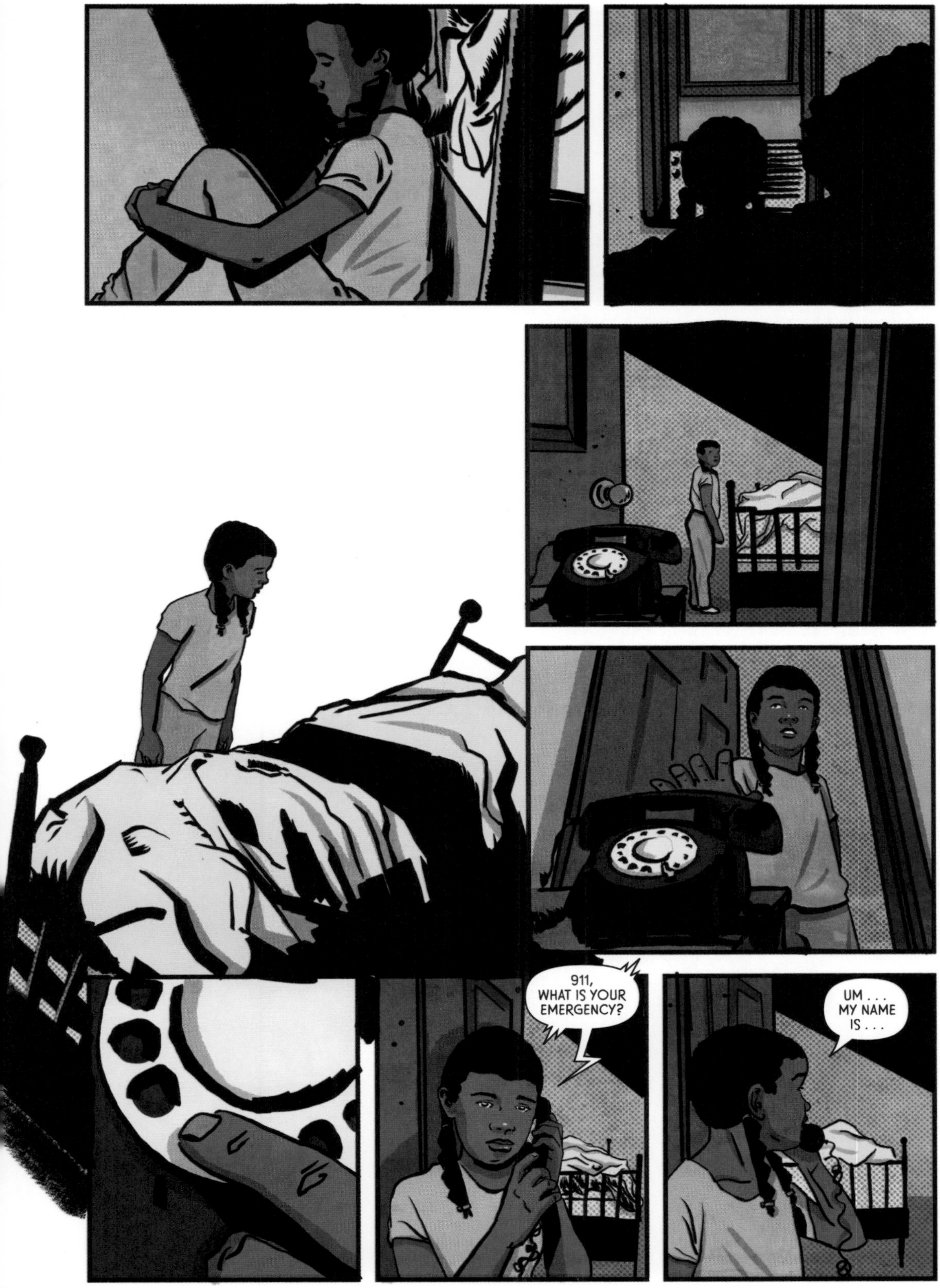
911,
WHAT IS YOUR
EMERGENCY?
UM . . .
MY NAME
IS . . .

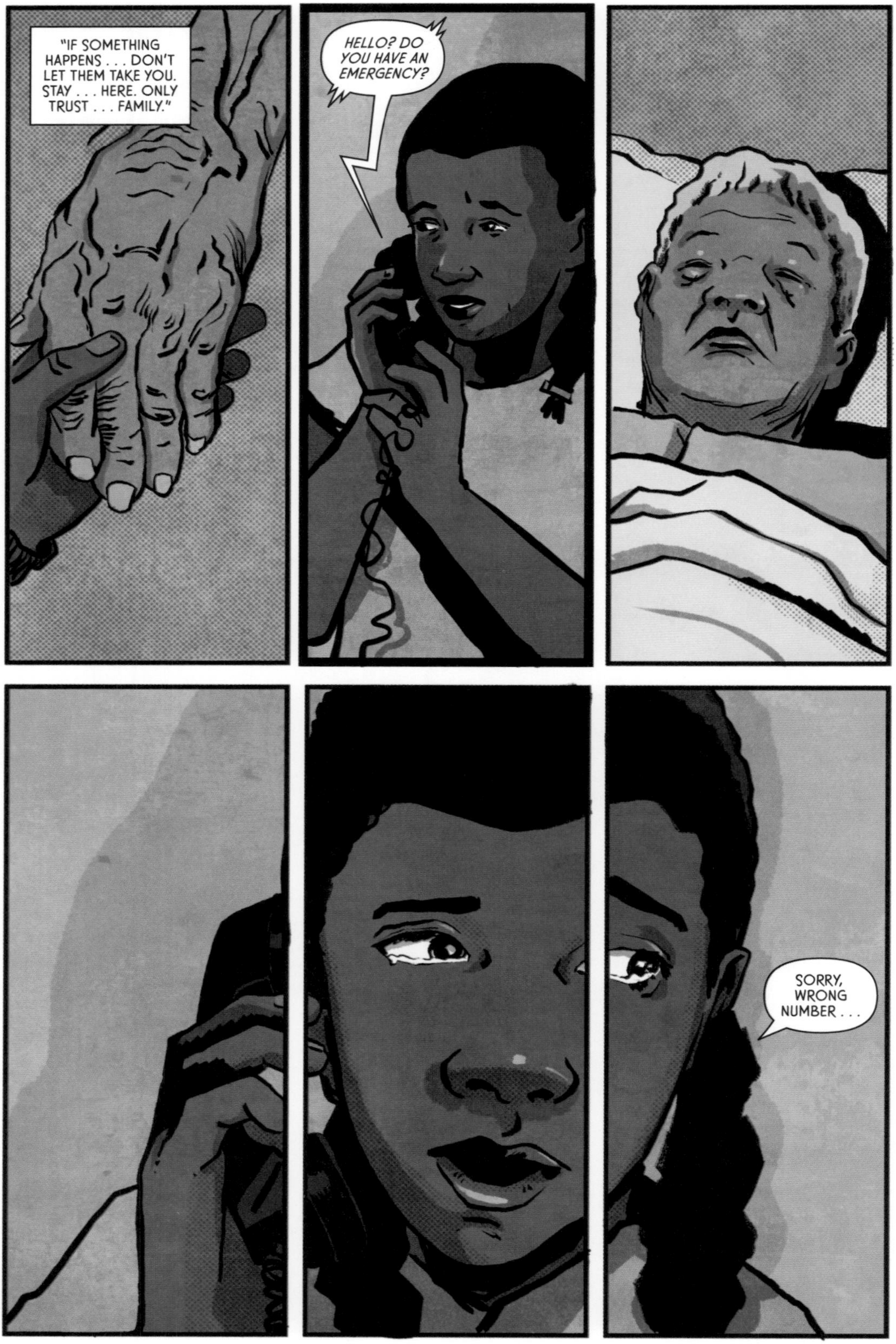
"IF SOMETHING HAPPENS . . . DON'T LET THEM TAKE YOU. STAY . . . HERE. ONLY TRUST . . . FAMILY."
HELLO? DO YOU HAVE AN EMERGENCY?
SORRY, WRONG NUMBER . . .

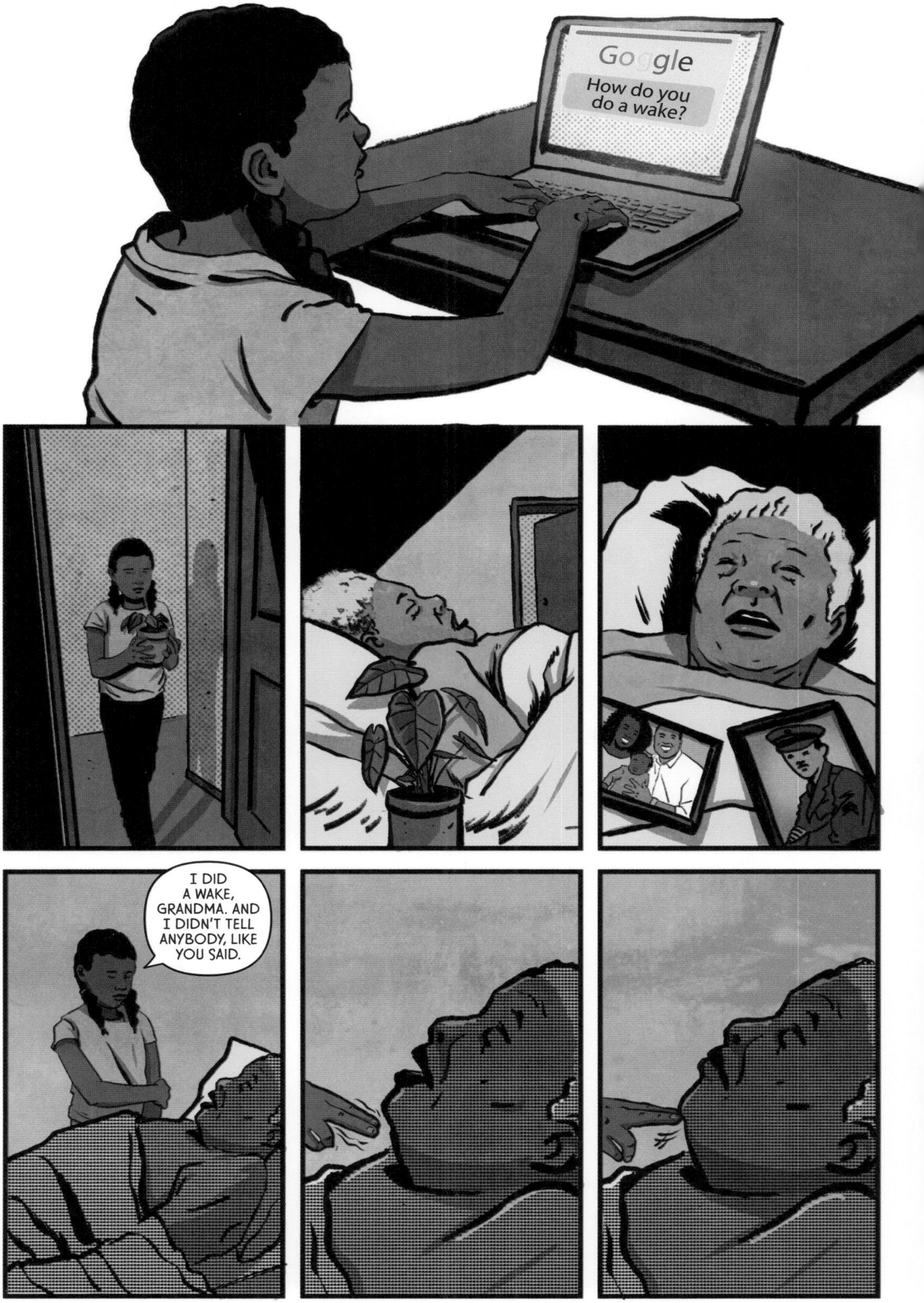
Goggle
How do you do a wake?
I DID A WAKE, GRANDMA. AND I DIDN'T TELL ANYBODY, LIKE YOU SAID.

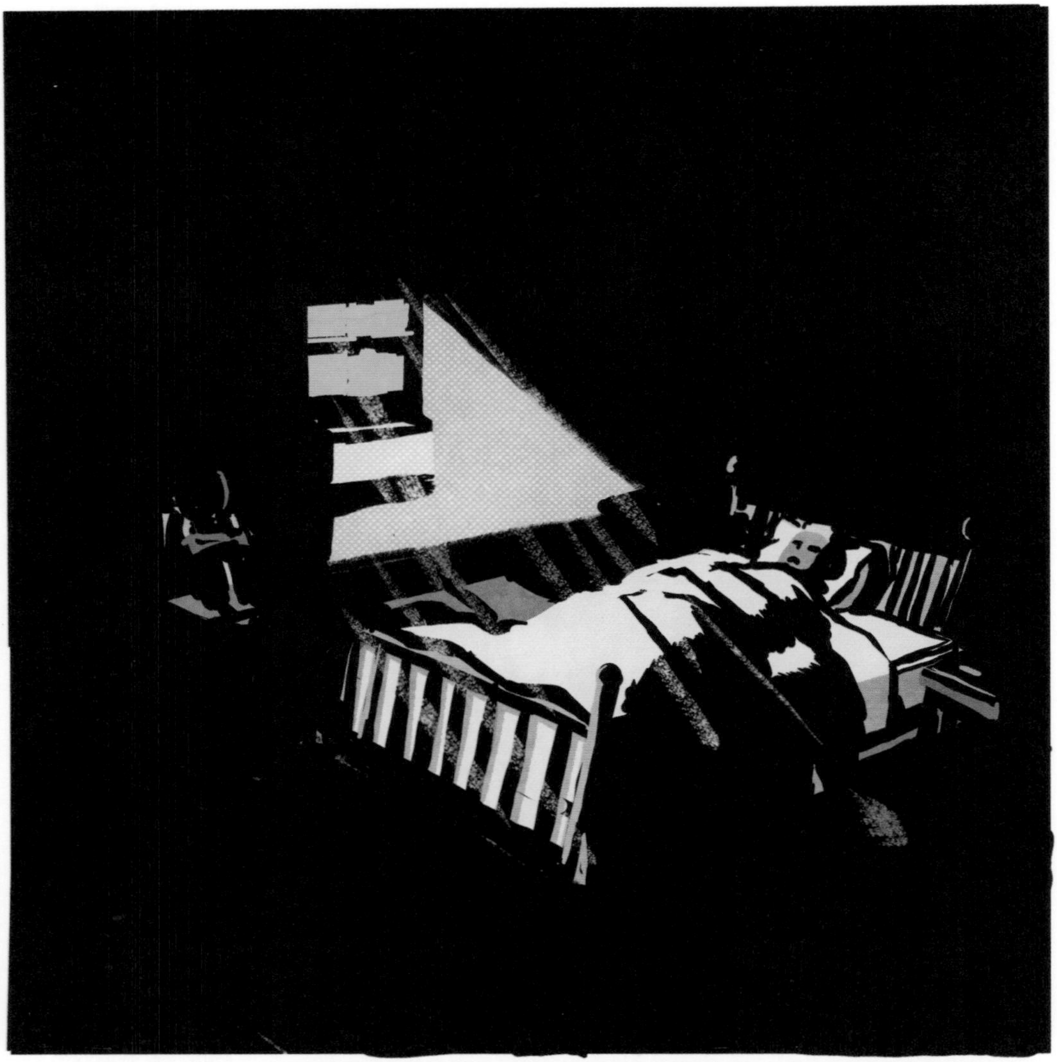

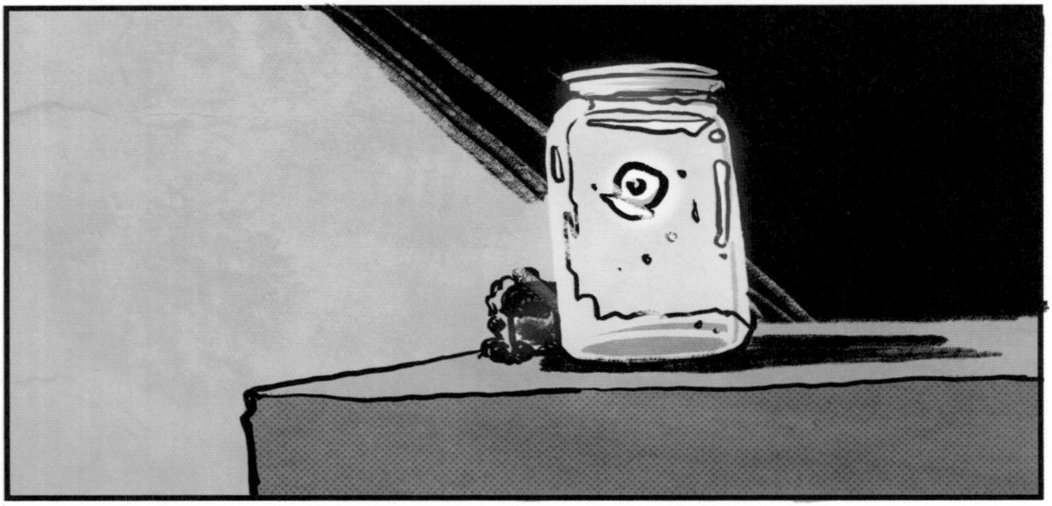

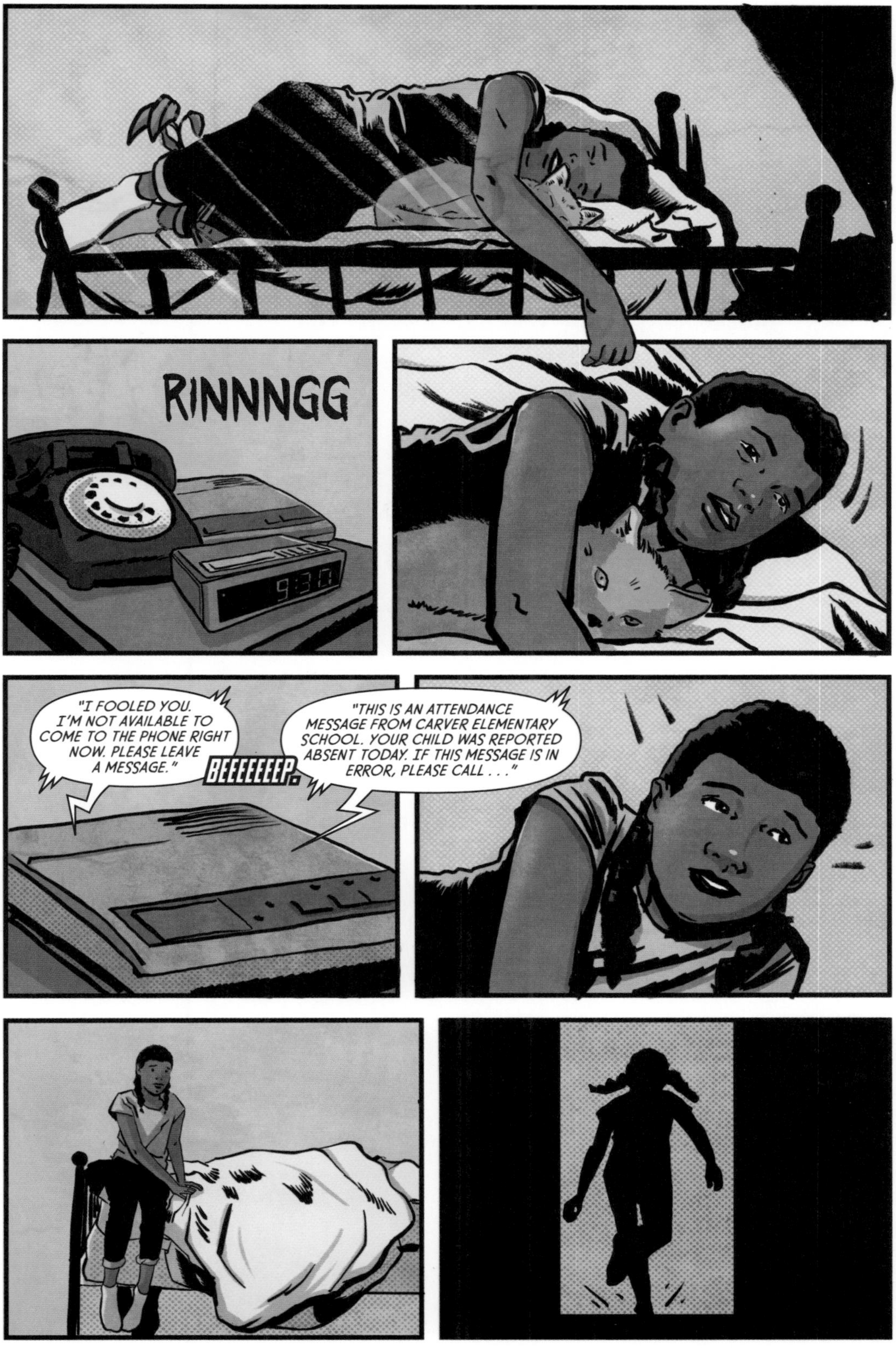
RINNNGG
"I FOOLED YOU. I'M NOT AVAILABLE TO COME TO THE PHONE RIGHT NOW. PLEASE LEAVE A MESSAGE."
BEEEEEEEP.
"THIS IS AN ATTENDANCE MESSAGE FROM CARVER ELEMENTARY SCHOOL. YOUR CHILD WAS REPORTED ABSENT TODAY. IF THIS MESSAGE IS IN ERROR, PLEASE CALL . . ."

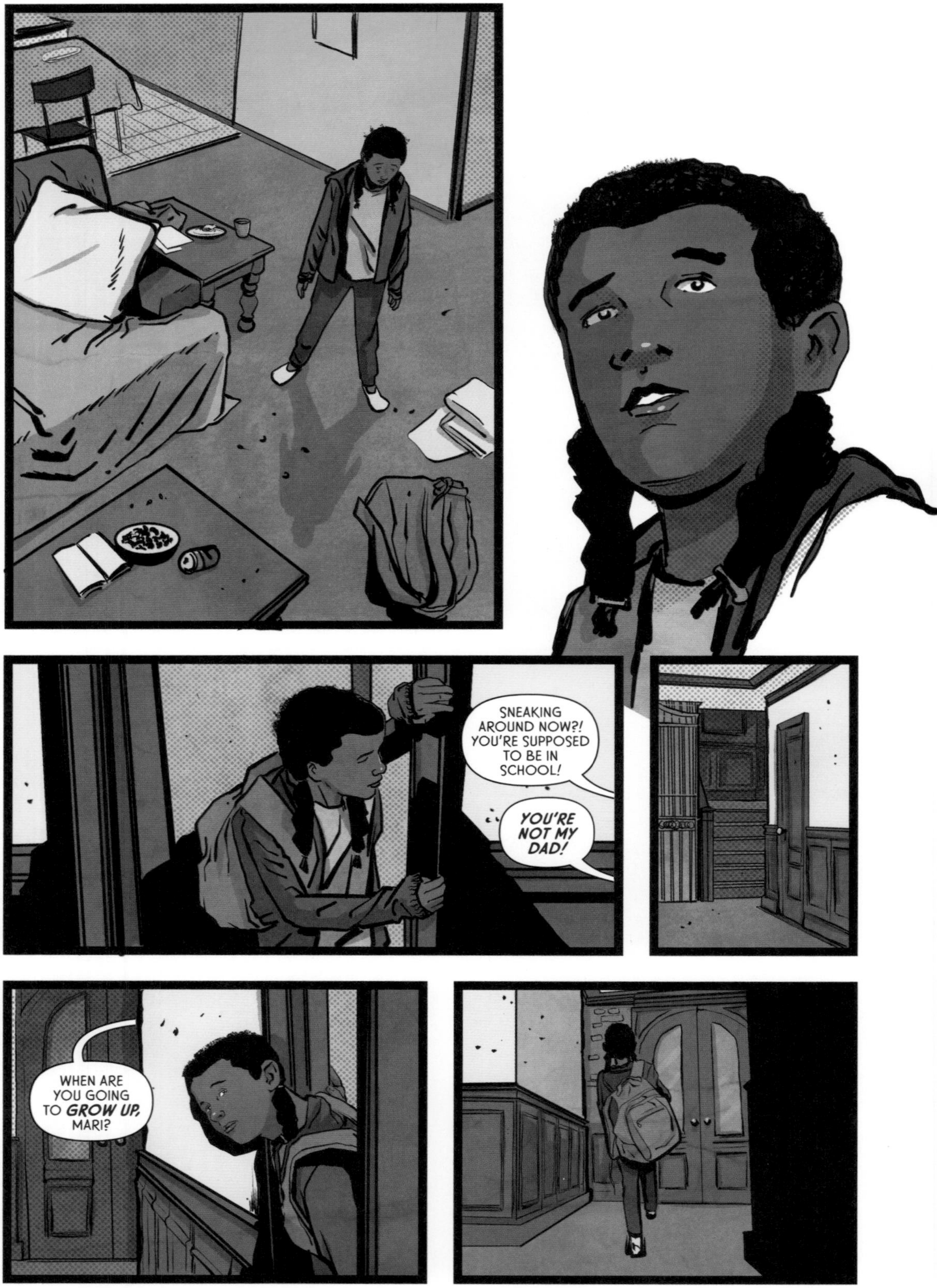
SNEAKING AROUND NOW?! YOU'RE SUPPOSED TO BE IN SCHOOL!
YOU'RE NOT MY DAD!
WHEN ARE YOU GOING TO GROW UP, MARI?

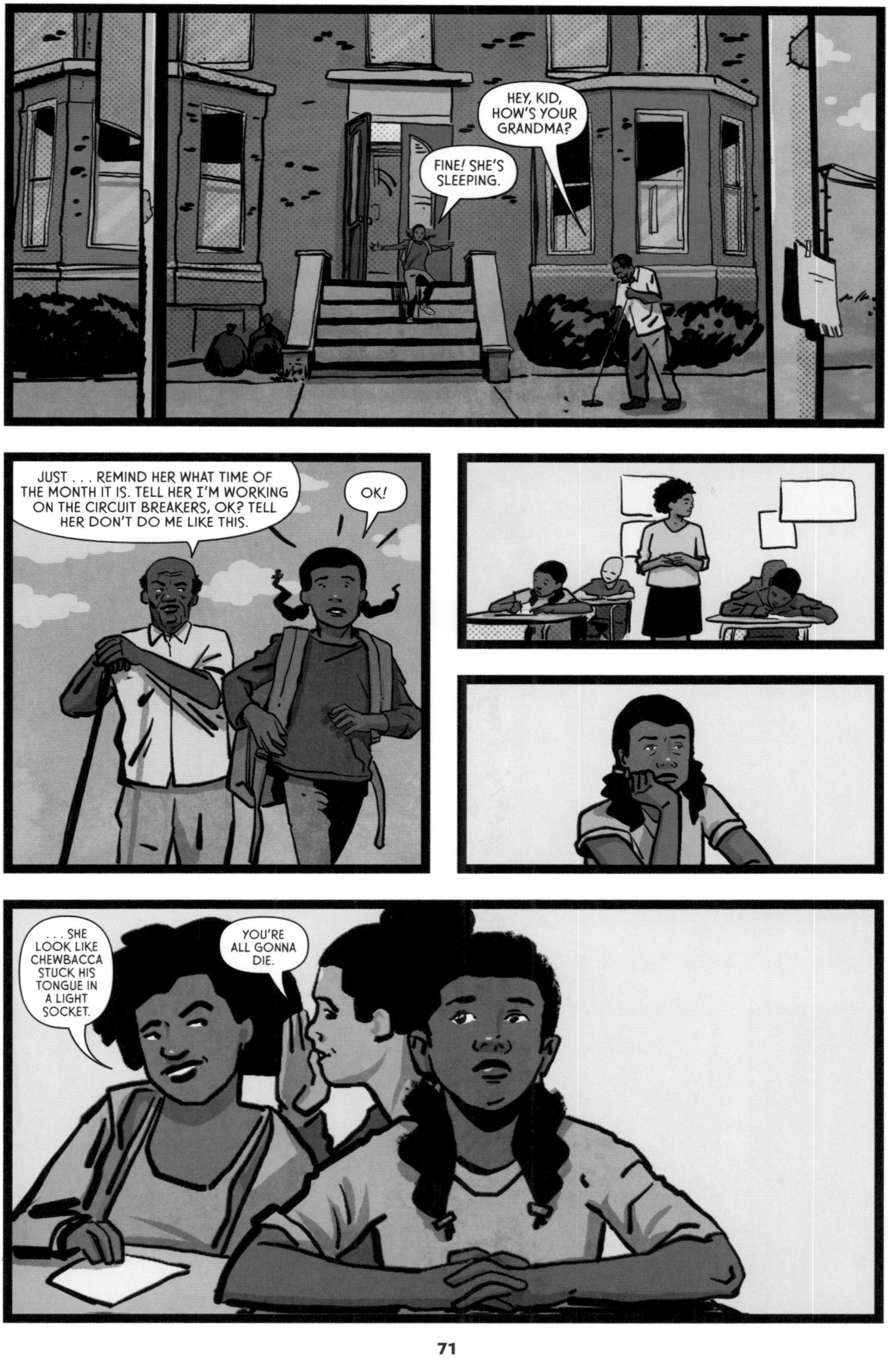
HEY, KID, HOW'S YOUR GRANDMA?
FINE! SHE'S SLEEPING.
JUST . . . REMIND HER WHAT TIME OF THE MONTH IT IS. TELL HER I'M WORKING ON THE CIRCUIT BREAKERS, OK? TELL HER DON'T DO ME LIKE THIS.
OK!
. . . SHE LOOK LIKE CHEWBACCA STUCK HIS TONGUE IN A LIGHT SOCKET.
YOU'RE ALL GONNA DIE.

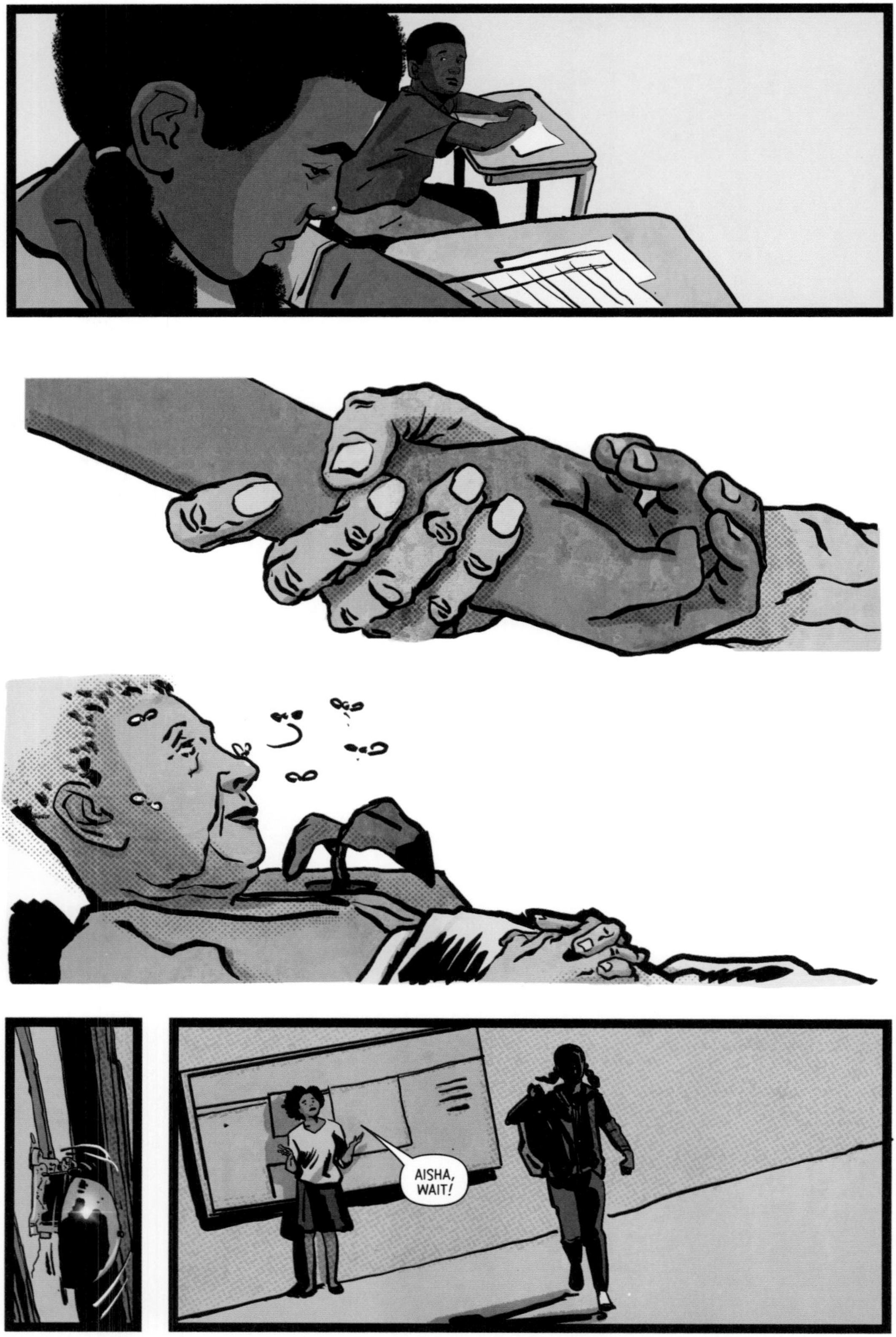
AISHA, WAIT!

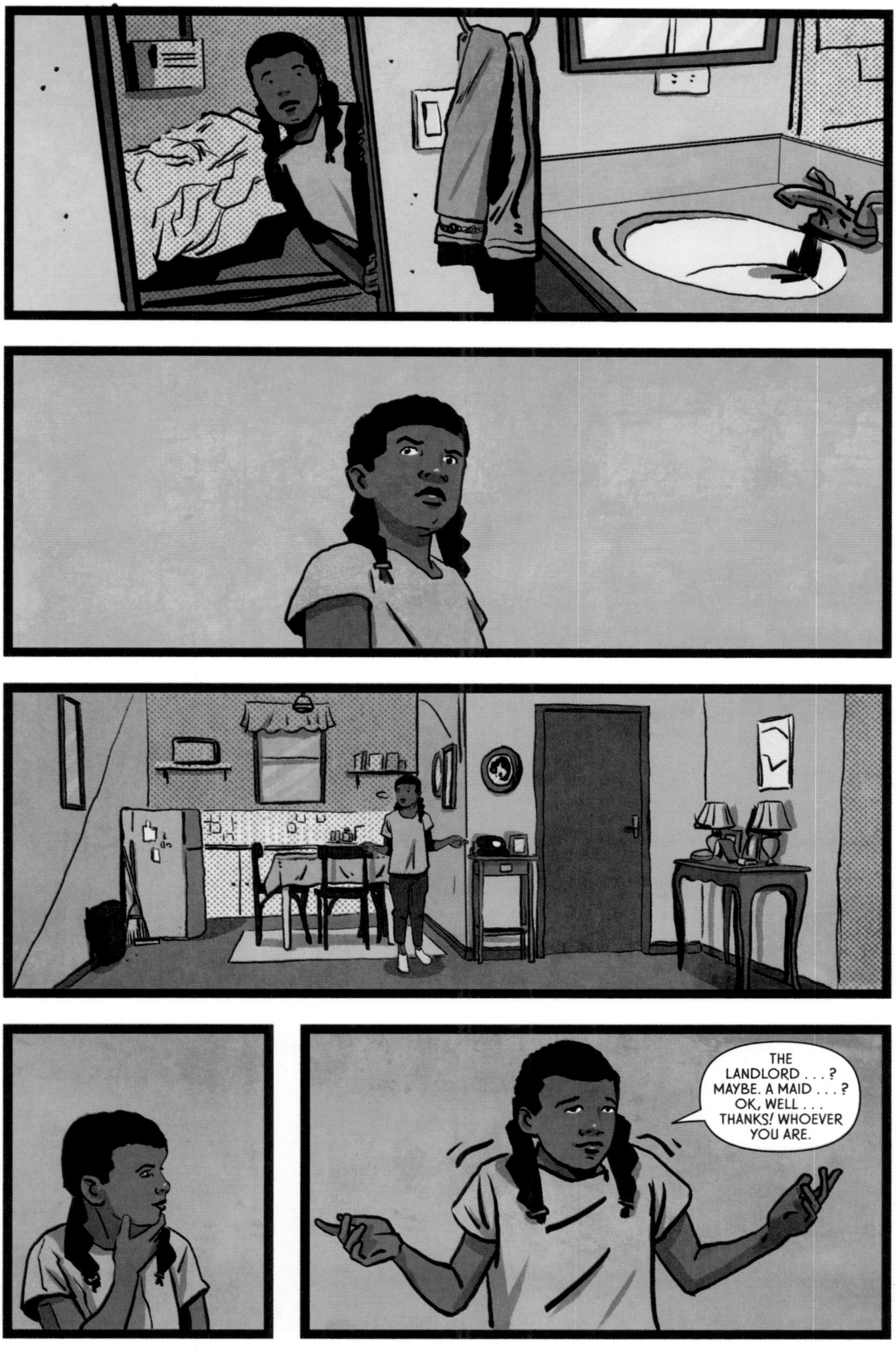
THE LANDLORD . . . ? MAYBE. A MAID . . . ? OK, WELL . . . THANKS! WHOEVER YOU ARE.

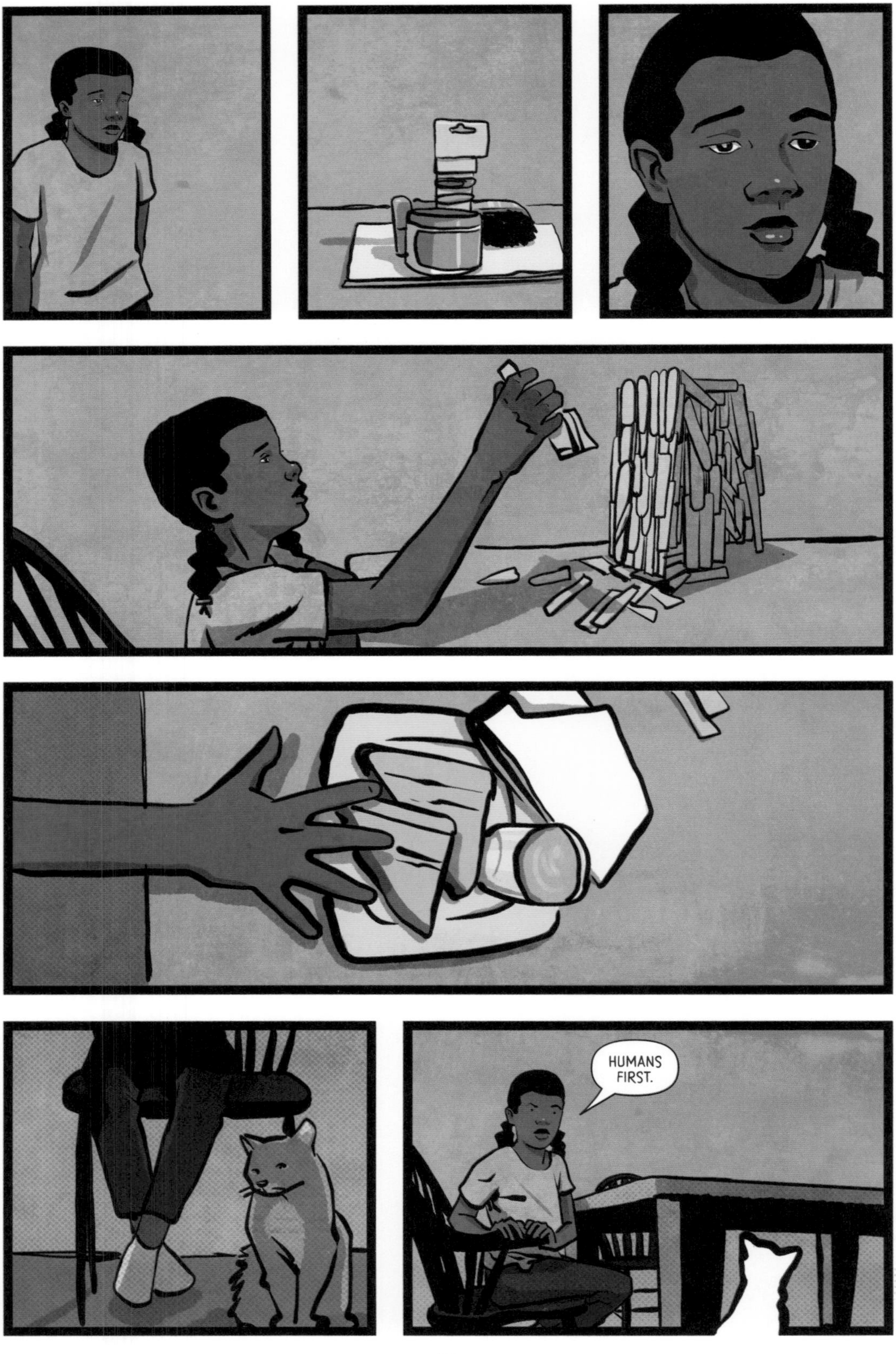
HUMANS
FIRST.

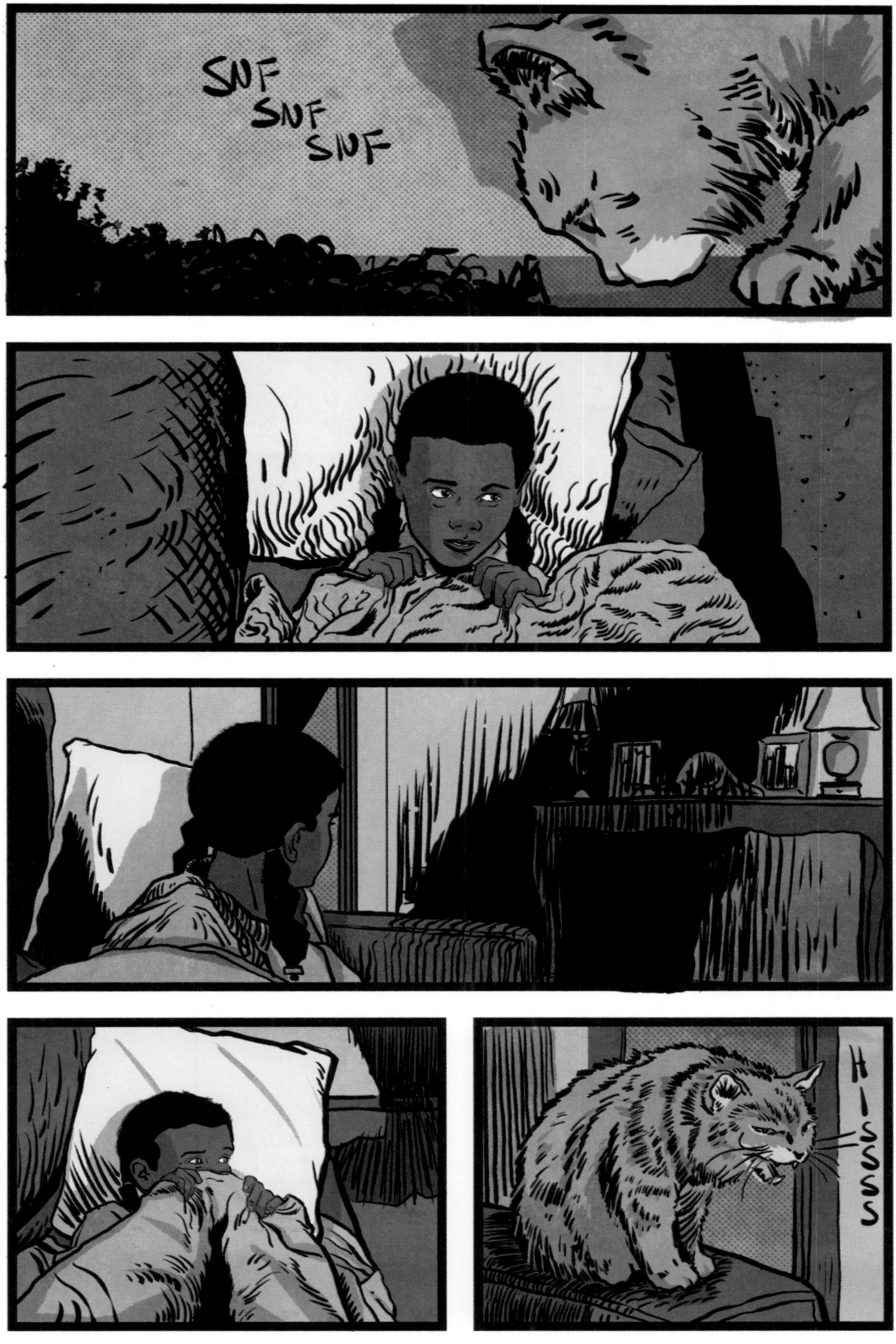
SNF
SNF
SNF
HISSSS

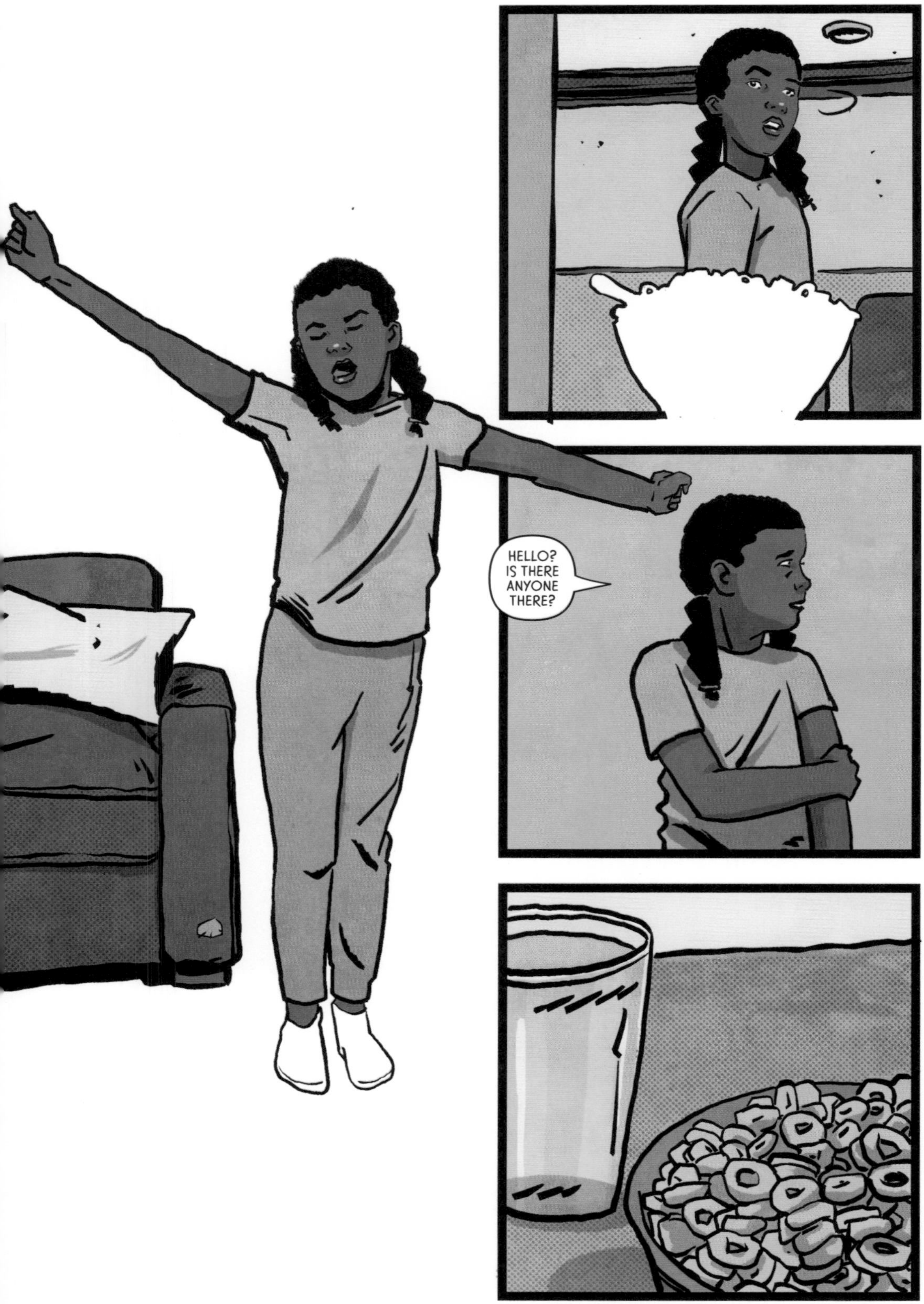
HELLO? IS THERE ANYONE THERE?

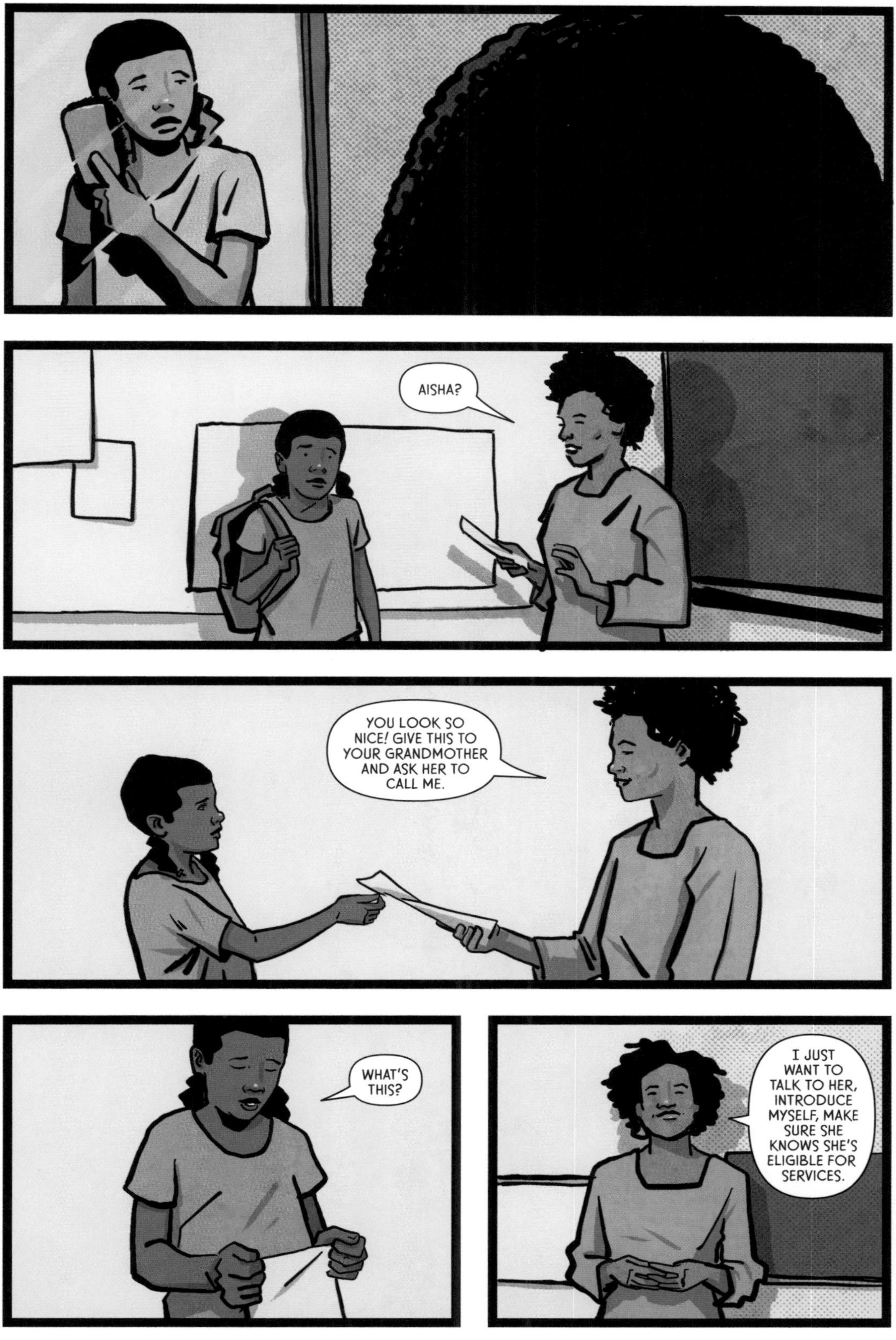
AISHA?
YOU LOOK SO NICE! GIVE THIS TO YOUR GRANDMOTHER AND ASK HER TO CALL ME.
WHAT'S THIS?
I JUST WANT TO TALK TO HER, INTRODUCE MYSELF, MAKE SURE SHE KNOWS SHE'S ELIGIBLE FOR SERVICES.

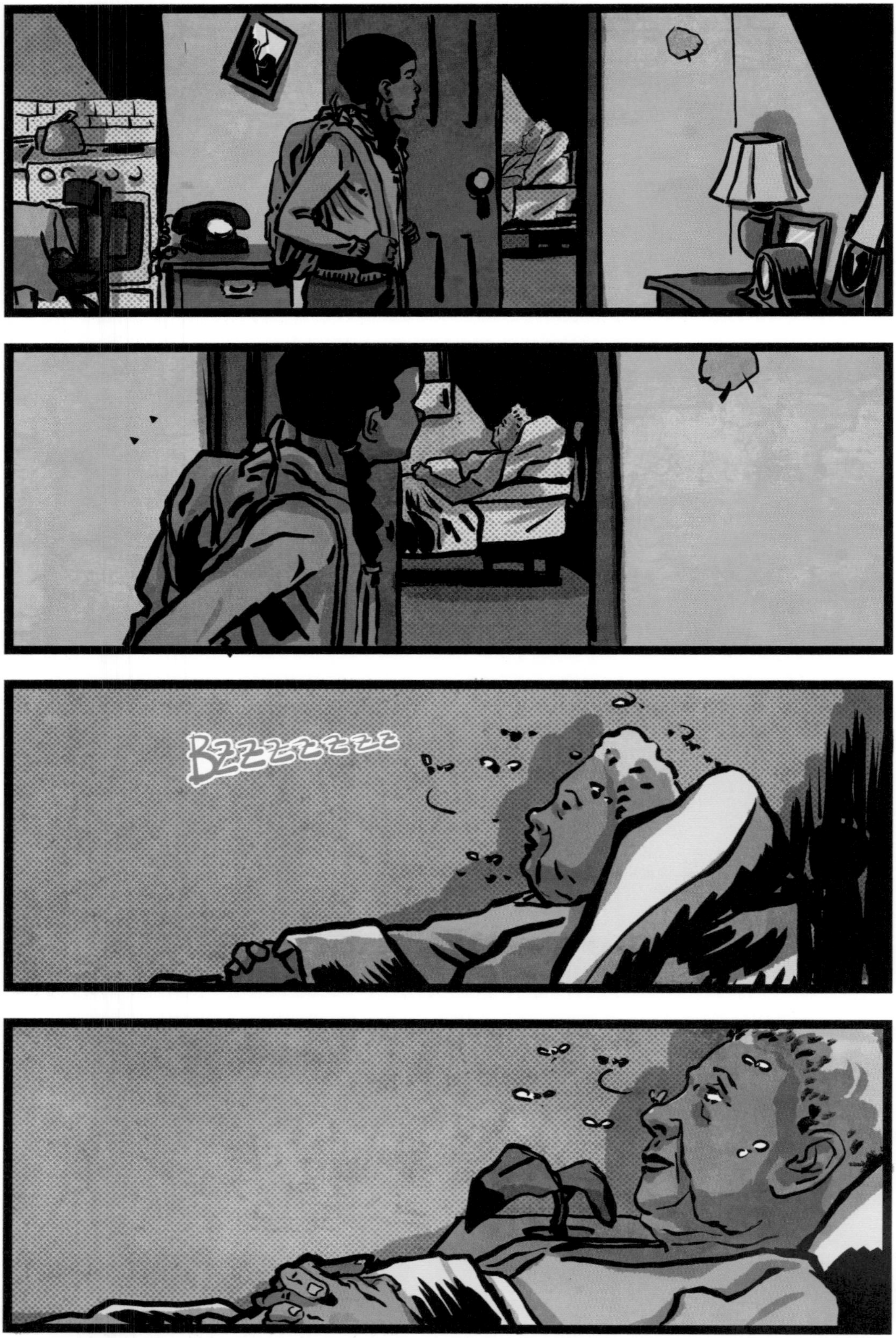
Bzzzzzzzz

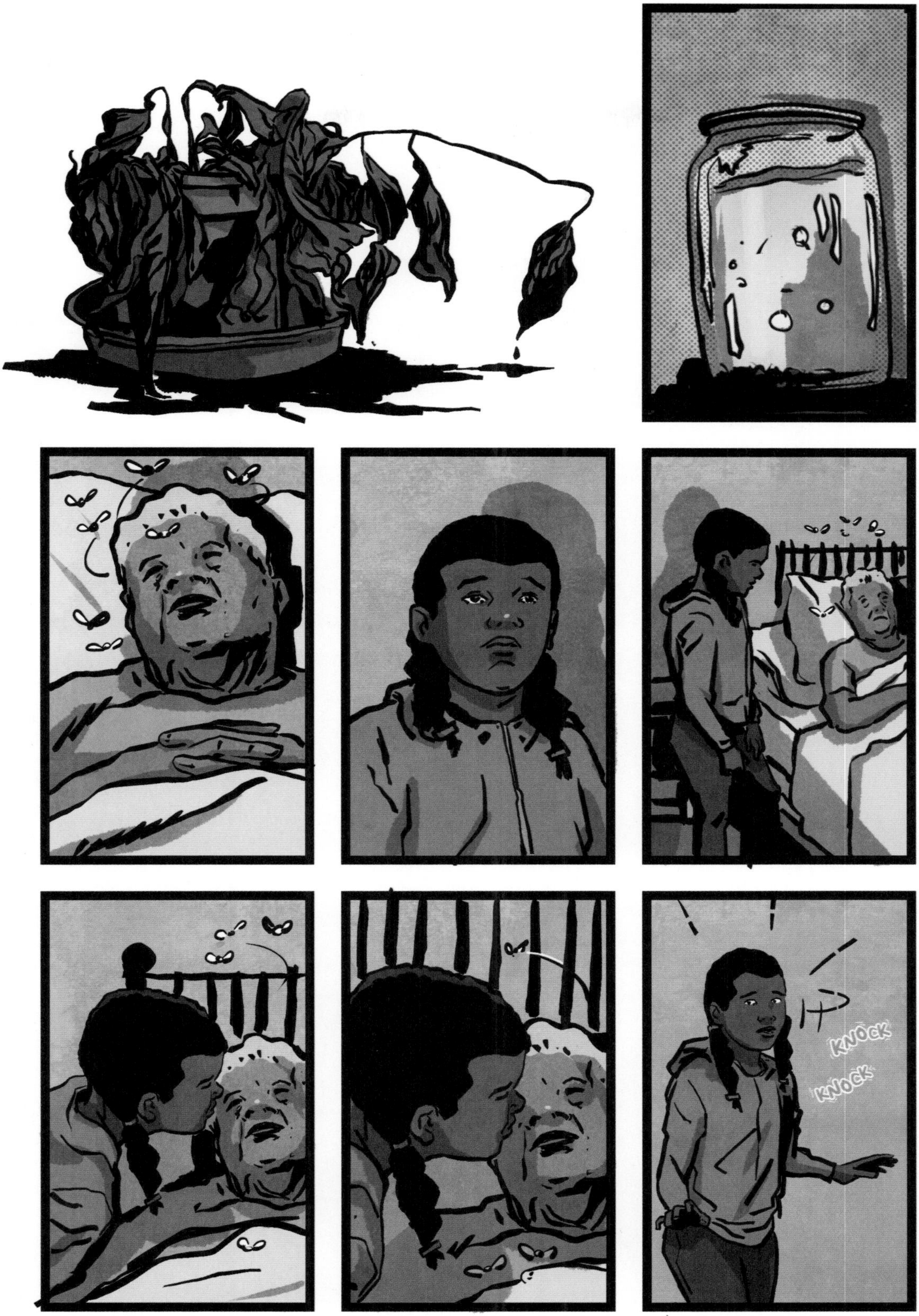
KNOCK
KNOCK

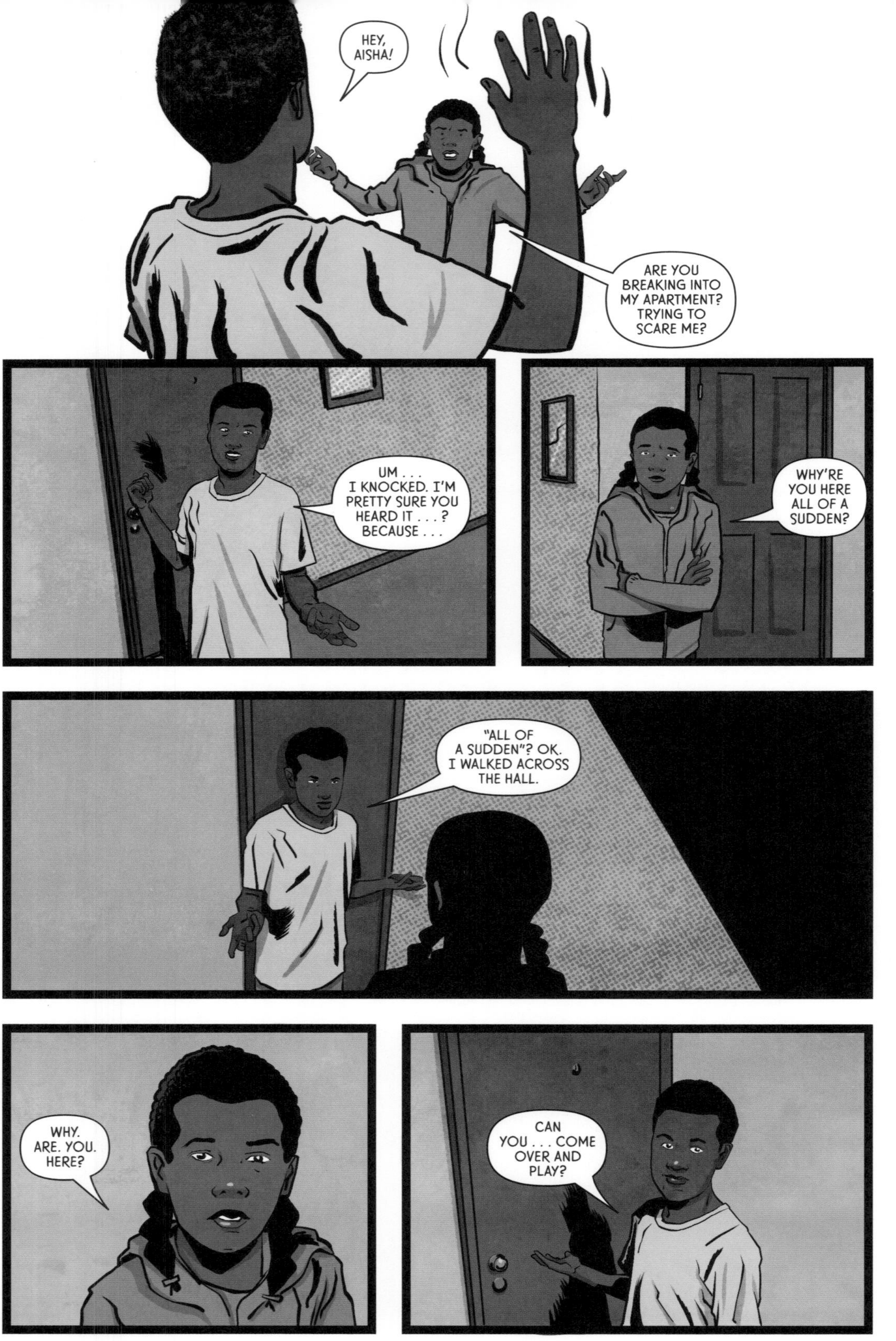
HEY, AISHA!
ARE YOU BREAKING INTO MY APARTMENT? TRYING TO SCARE ME?
UM . . . I KNOCKED. I'M PRETTY SURE YOU HEARD IT . . . ? BECAUSE . . .
WHY'RE YOU HERE ALL OF A SUDDEN?
"ALL OF A SUDDEN"? OK. I WALKED ACROSS THE HALL.
WHY. ARE. YOU. HERE?
CAN YOU . . . COME OVER AND PLAY?

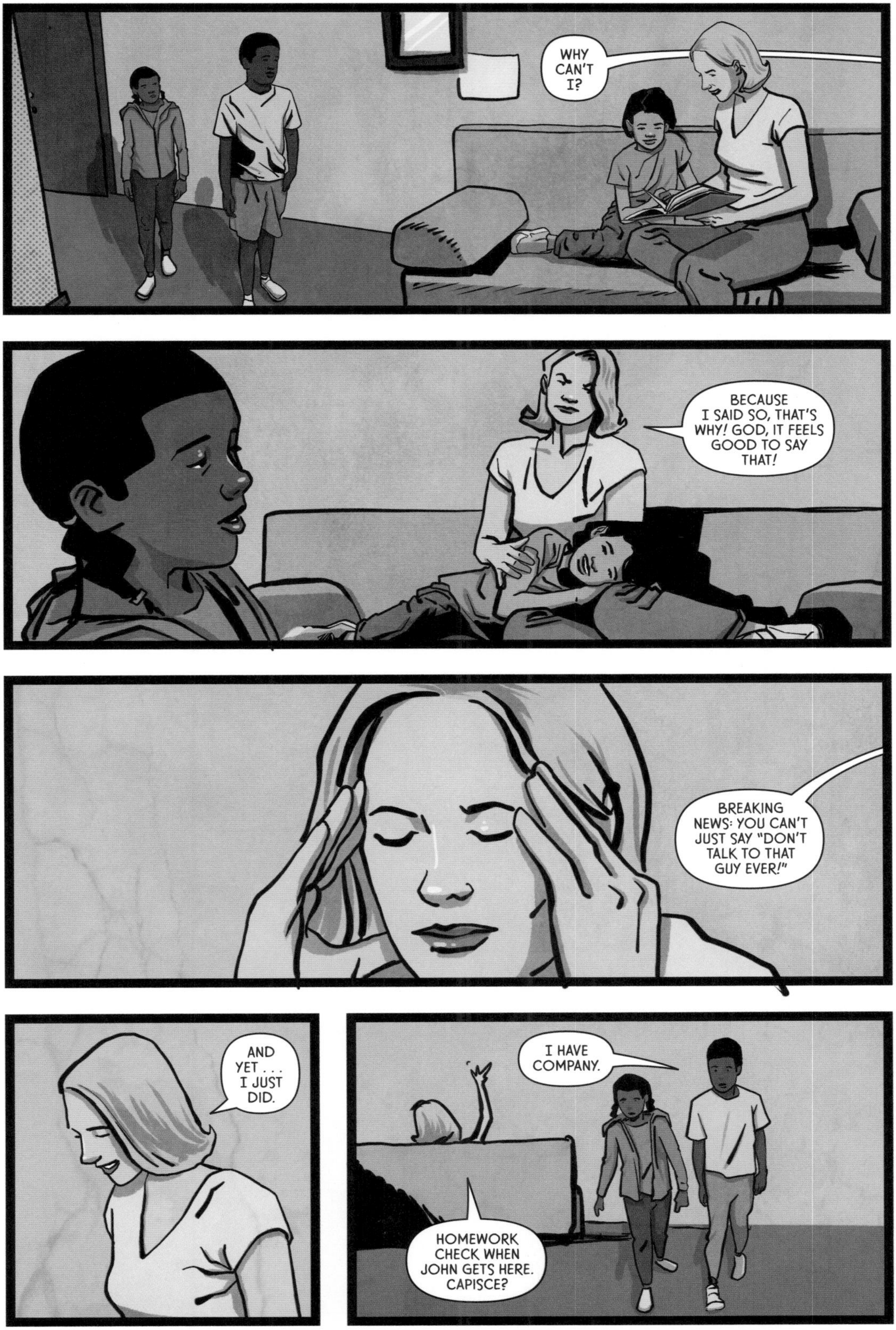
WHY CAN'T I?
BECAUSE I SAID SO, THAT'S WHY! GOD, IT FEELS GOOD TO SAY THAT!
BREAKING NEWS: YOU CAN'T JUST SAY "DON'T TALK TO THAT GUY EVER!"
AND YET . . . I JUST DID.
I HAVE COMPANY.
HOMEWORK CHECK WHEN JOHN GETS HERE. CAPISCE?

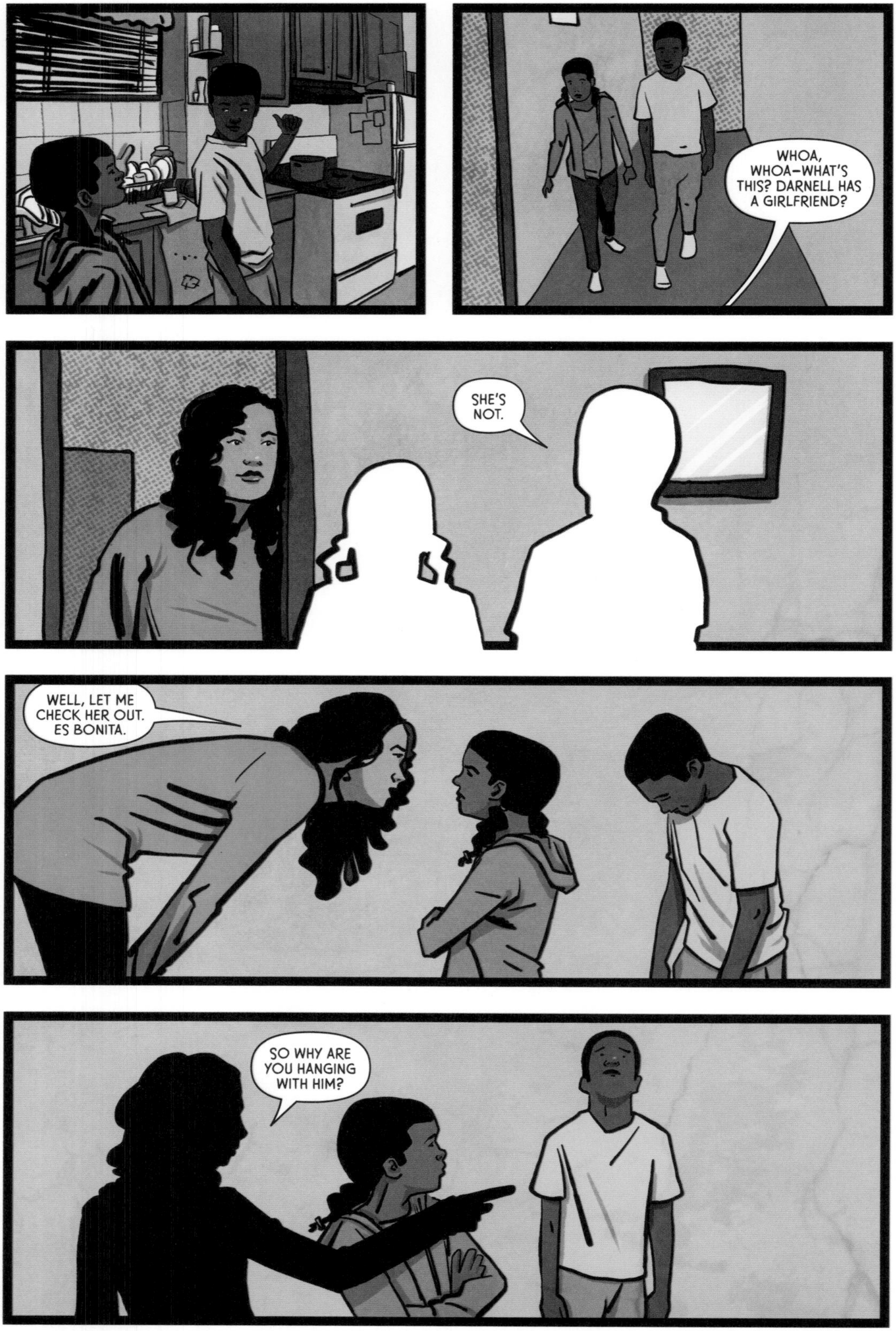
WHOA, WHOA—WHAT'S THIS? DARNELL HAS A GIRLFRIEND?
SHE'S NOT.
WELL, LET ME CHECK HER OUT. ES BONITA.
SO WHY ARE YOU HANGING WITH HIM?

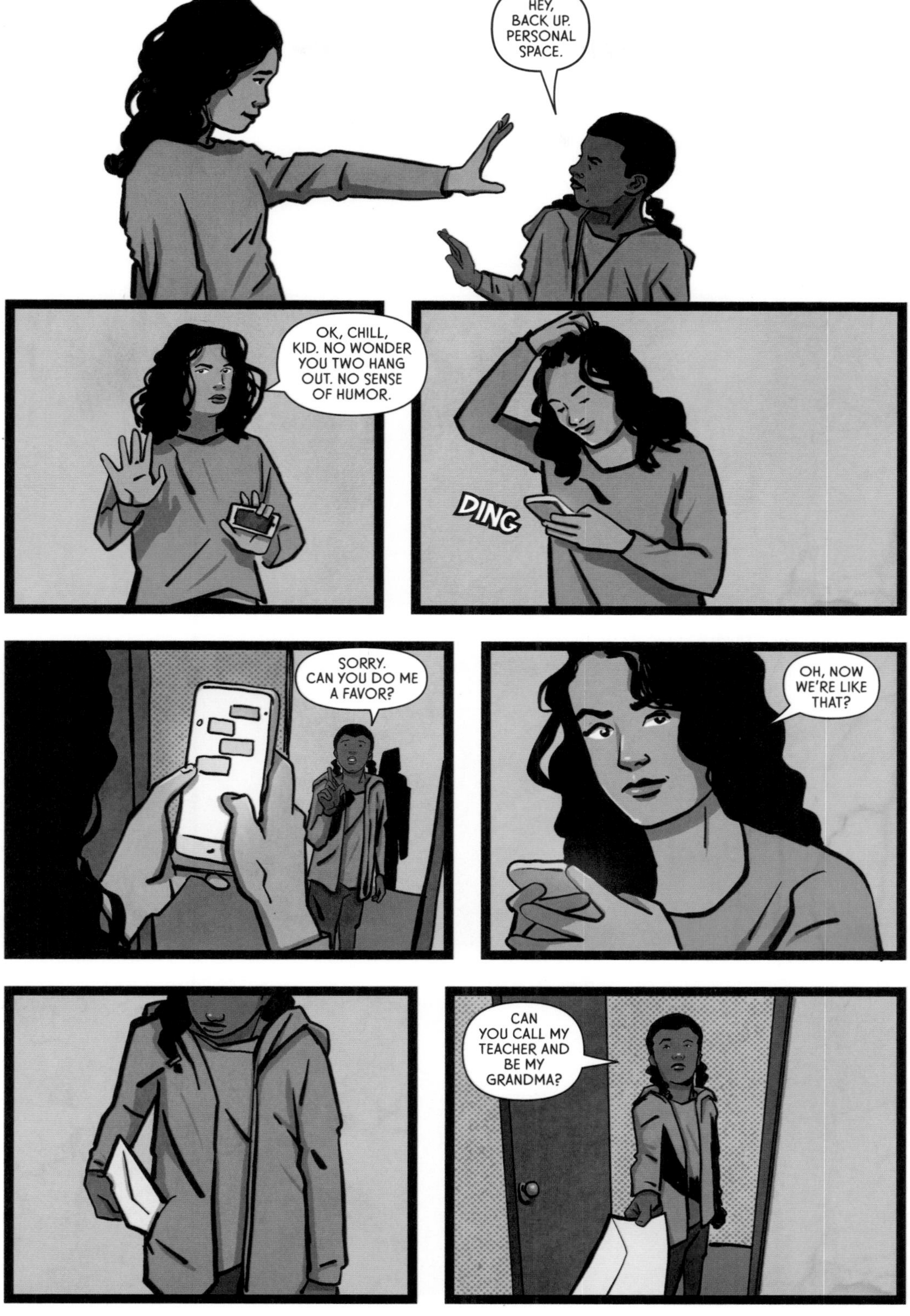
HEY, BACK UP. PERSONAL SPACE.
OK, CHILL, KID. NO WONDER YOU TWO HANG OUT. NO SENSE OF HUMOR.
DING
SORRY. CAN YOU DO ME A FAVOR?
OH, NOW WE'RE LIKE THAT?
CAN YOU CALL MY TEACHER AND BE MY GRANDMA?

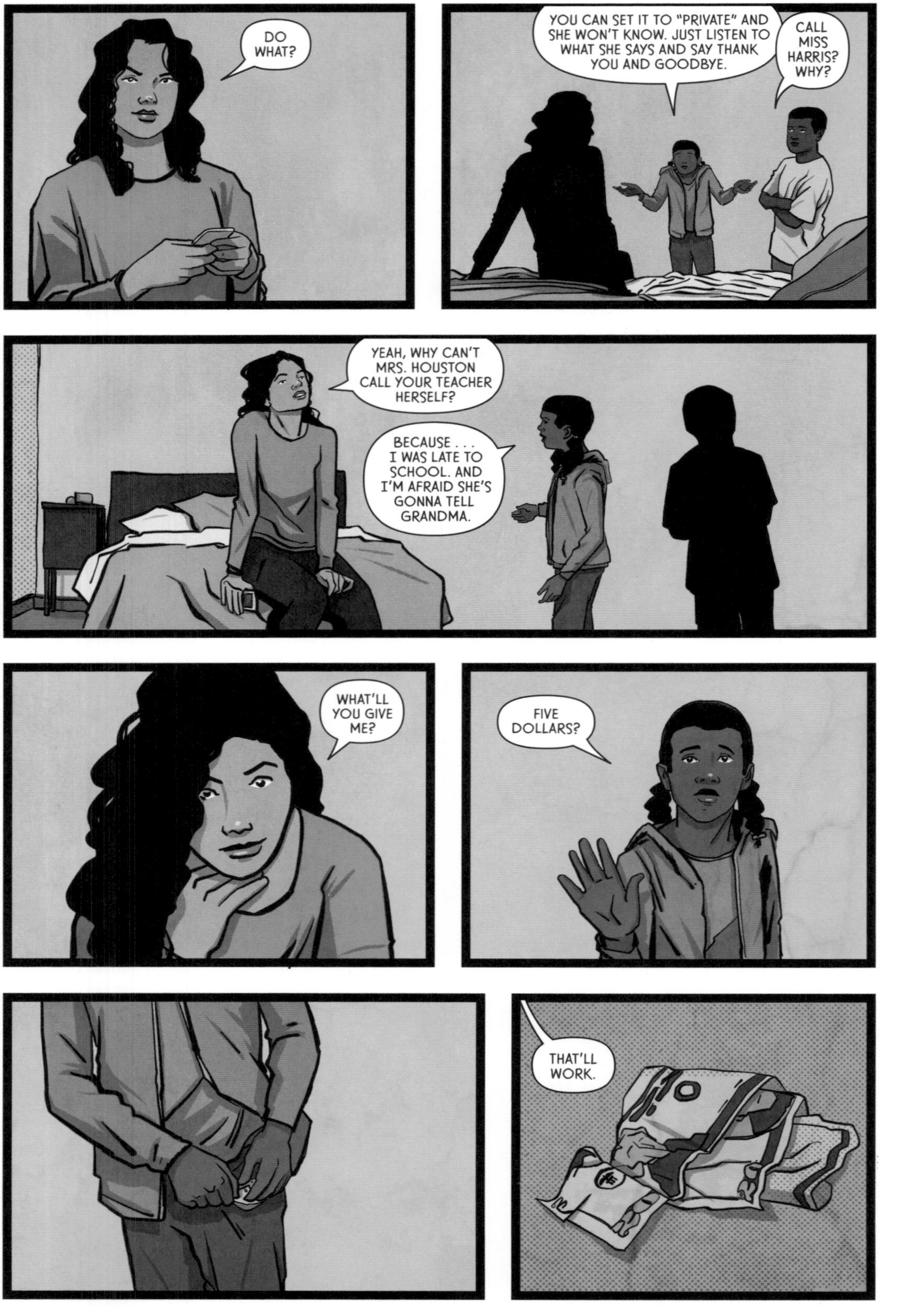
DO WHAT?
YOU CAN SET IT TO "PRIVATE" AND SHE WON'T KNOW. JUST LISTEN TO WHAT SHE SAYS AND SAY THANK YOU AND GOODBYE.
CALL MISS HARRIS? WHY?
YEAH, WHY CAN'T MRS. HOUSTON CALL YOUR TEACHER HERSELF?
BECAUSE . . . I WAS LATE TO SCHOOL. AND I'M AFRAID SHE'S GONNA TELL GRANDMA.
WHAT'LL YOU GIVE ME?
FIVE DOLLARS?
THAT'LL WORK.

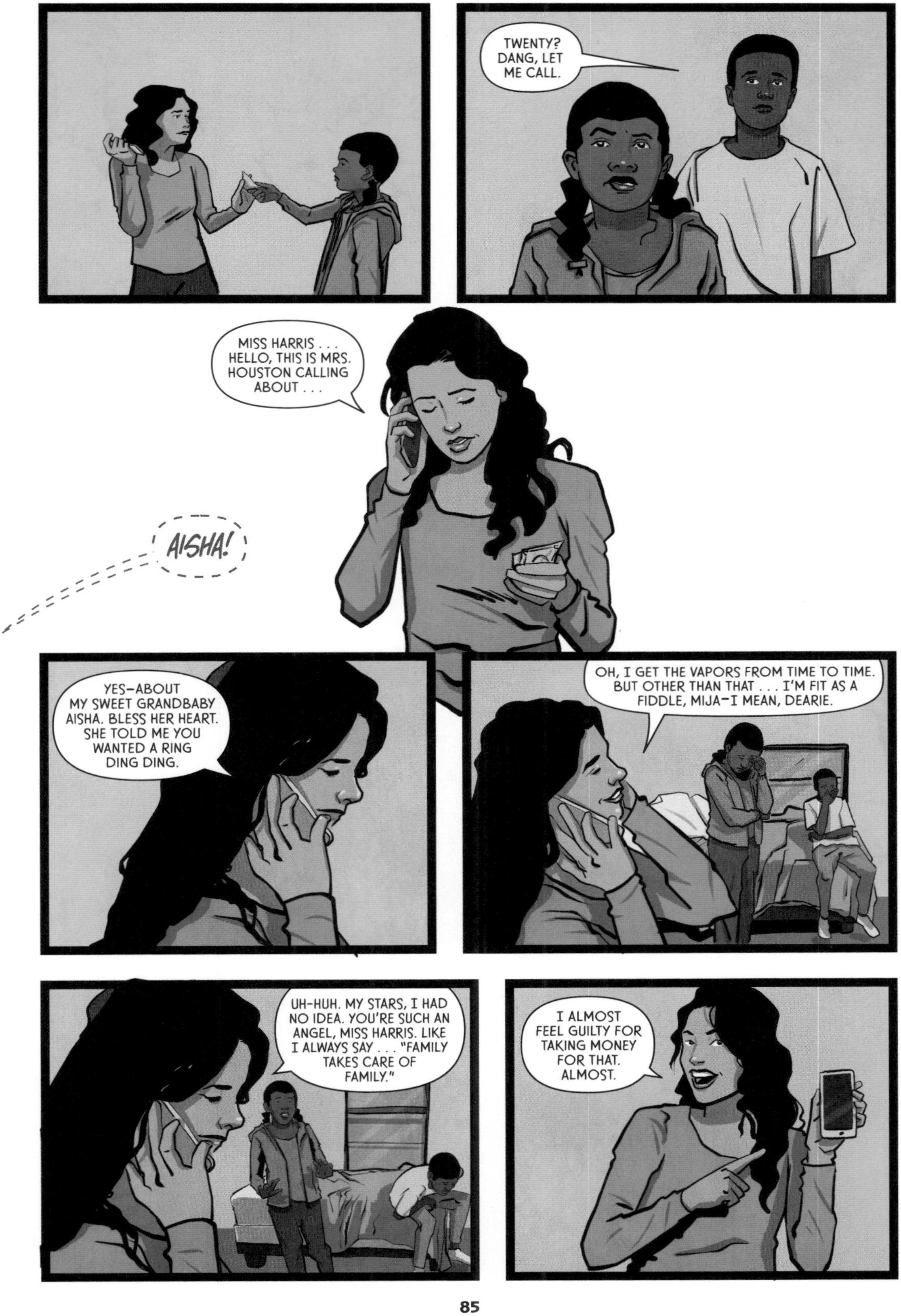
TWENTY? DANG, LET ME CALL.
MISS HARRIS . . . HELLO, THIS IS MRS. HOUSTON CALLING ABOUT . . .
AISHA!
YES—ABOUT MY SWEET GRANDBABY AISHA. BLESS HER HEART. SHE TOLD ME YOU WANTED A RING DING DING.
OH, I GET THE VAPORS FROM TIME TO TIME. BUT OTHER THAN THAT . . . I'M FIT AS A FIDDLE, MIJA—I MEAN, DEARIE.
UH-HUH. MY STARS, I HAD NO IDEA. YOU'RE SUCH AN ANGEL, MISS HARRIS. LIKE I ALWAYS SAY . . . "FAMILY TAKES CARE OF FAMILY."
I ALMOST FEEL GUILTY FOR TAKING MONEY FOR THAT. ALMOST.

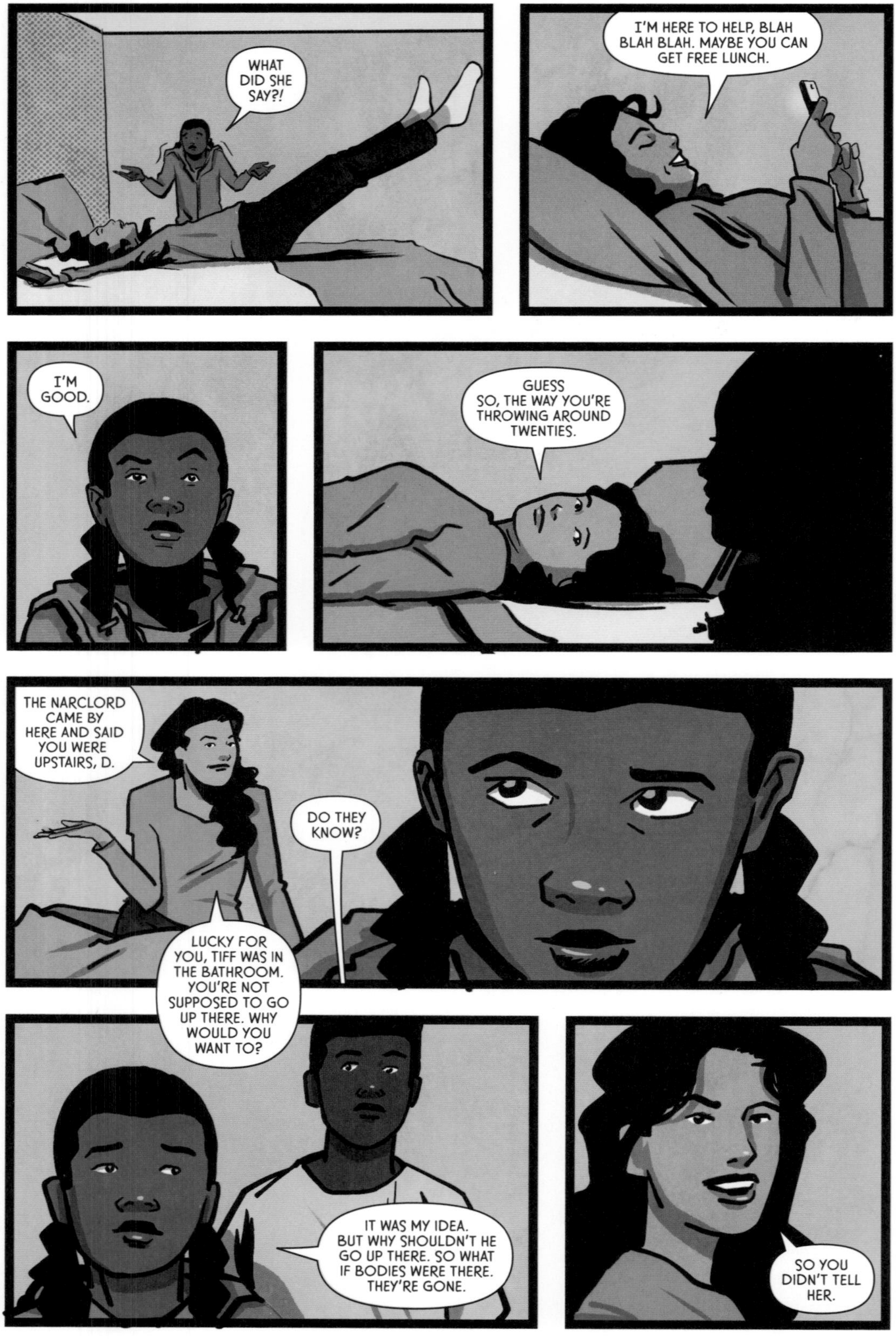
WHAT DID SHE SAY?!
I'M HERE TO HELP, BLAH BLAH BLAH. MAYBE YOU CAN GET FREE LUNCH.
I'M GOOD.
GUESS SO, THE WAY YOU'RE THROWING AROUND TWENTIES.
THE NARCLORD CAME BY HERE AND SAID YOU WERE UPSTAIRS, D.
DO THEY KNOW?
LUCKY FOR YOU, TIFF WAS IN THE BATHROOM. YOU'RE NOT SUPPOSED TO GO UP THERE. WHY WOULD YOU WANT TO?
IT WAS MY IDEA. BUT WHY SHOULDN'T HE GO UP THERE. SO WHAT IF BODIES WERE THERE. THEY'RE GONE.
SO YOU DIDN'T TELL HER.

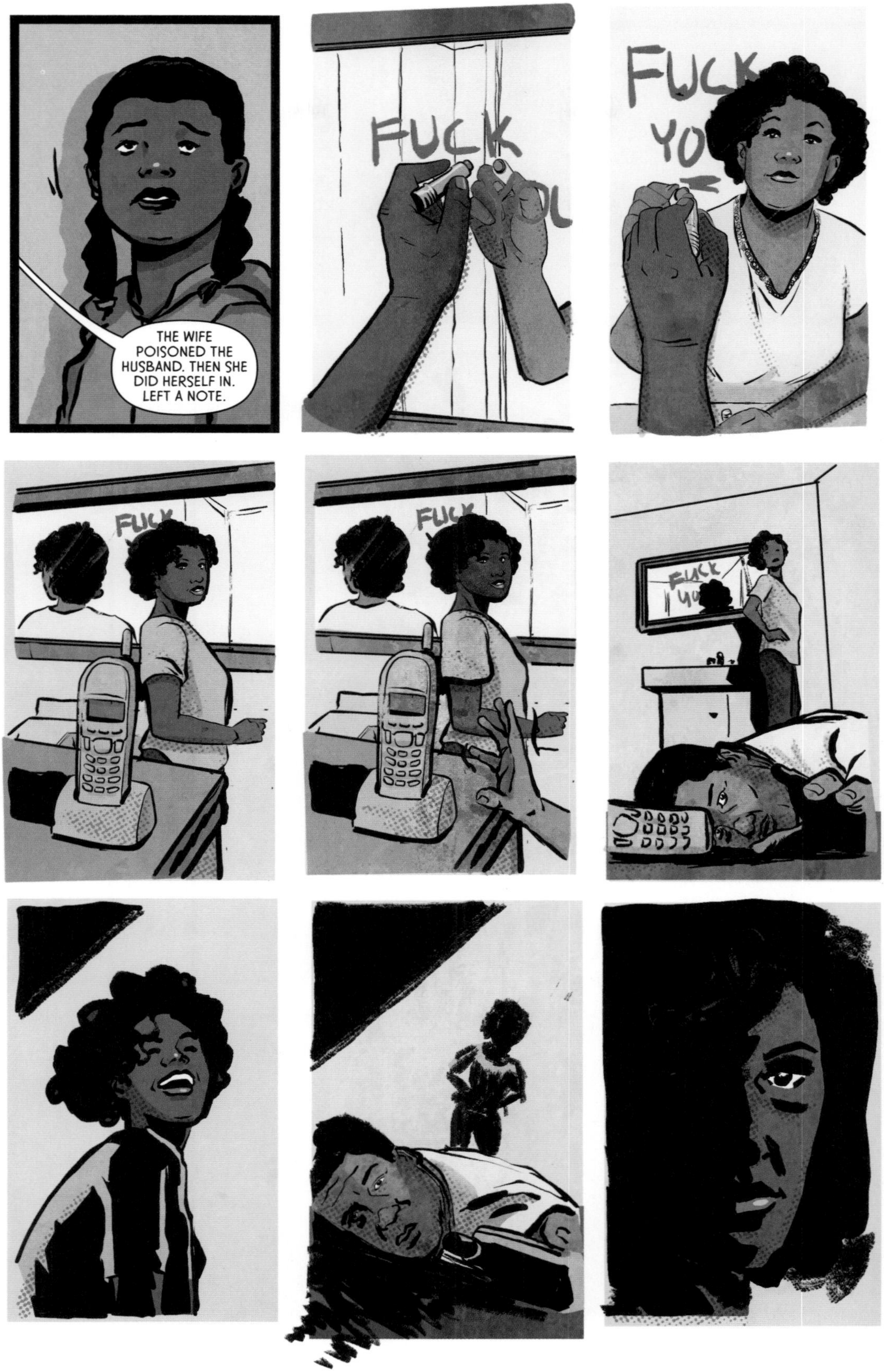
THE WIFE POISONED THE HUSBAND. THEN SHE DID HERSELF IN. LEFT A NOTE.
FUCK
FUCK
YO

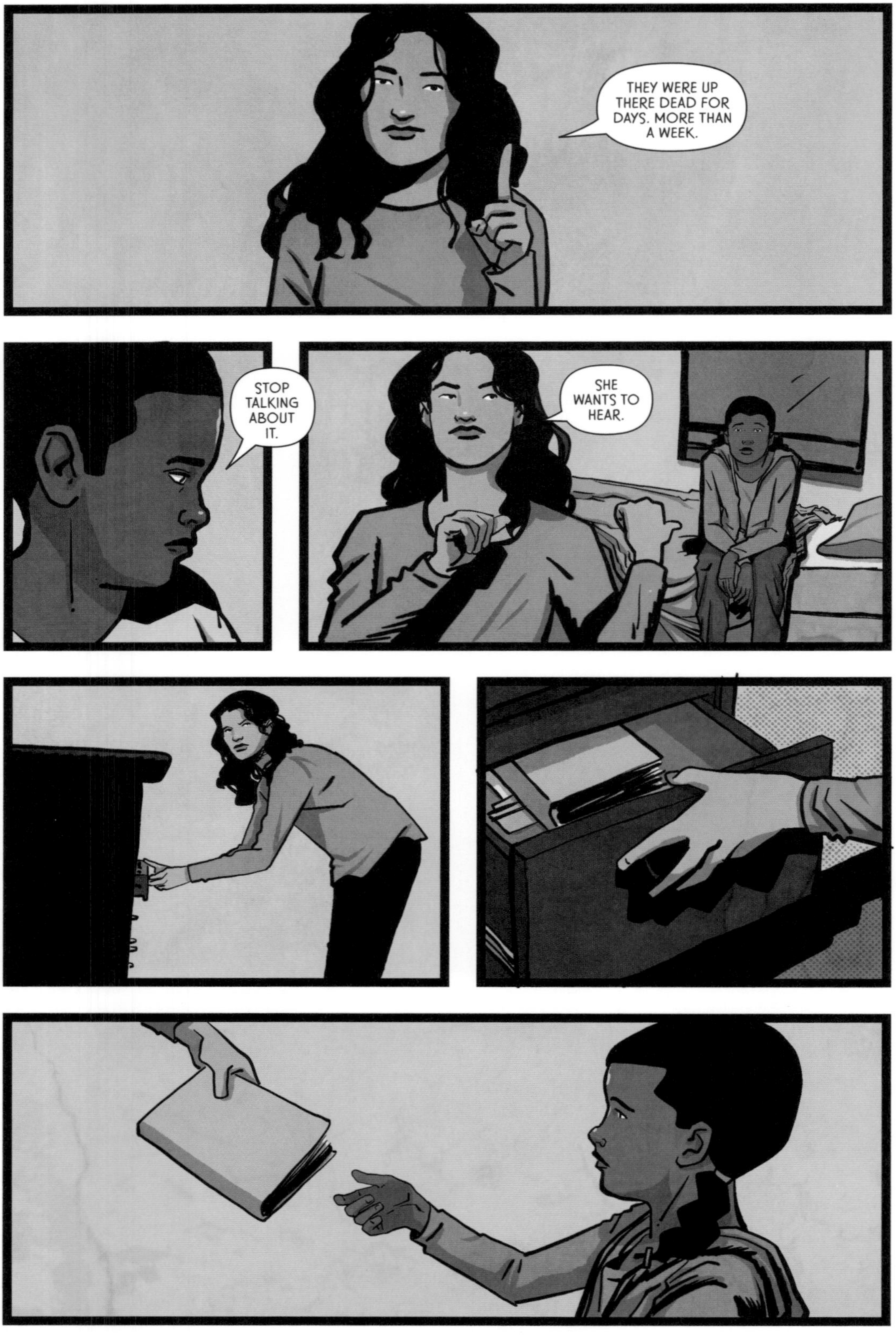
THEY WERE UP THERE DEAD FOR DAYS. MORE THAN A WEEK.
STOP TALKING ABOUT IT.
SHE WANTS TO HEAR.

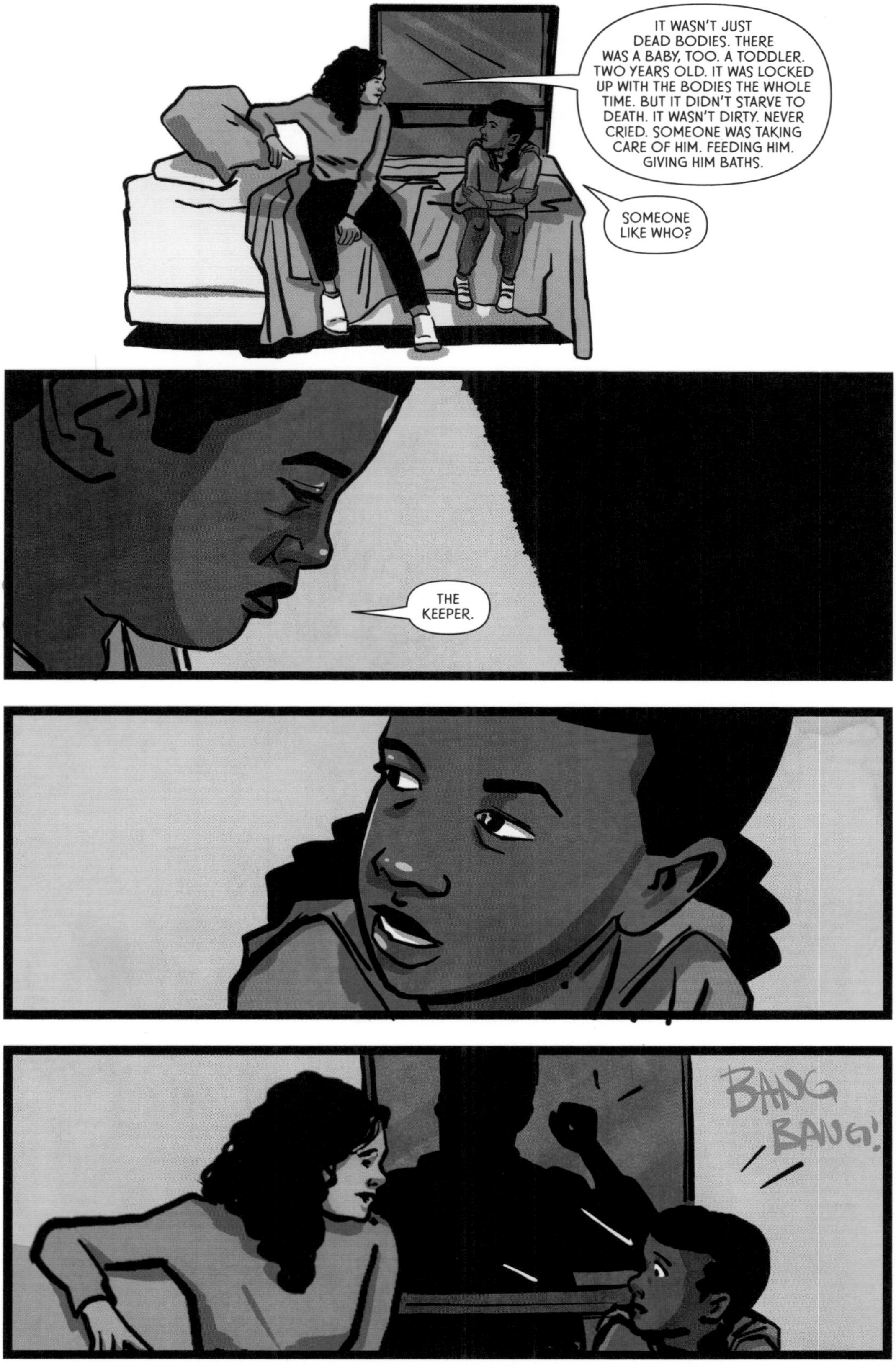
IT WASN'T JUST DEAD BODIES. THERE WAS A BABY, TOO. A TODDLER. TWO YEARS OLD. IT WAS LOCKED UP WITH THE BODIES THE WHOLE TIME. BUT IT DIDN'T STARVE TO DEATH. IT WASN'T DIRTY. NEVER CRIED. SOMEONE WAS TAKING CARE OF HIM. FEEDING HIM. GIVING HIM BATHS.
SOMEONE LIKE WHO?
THE KEEPER.
BANG BANG!

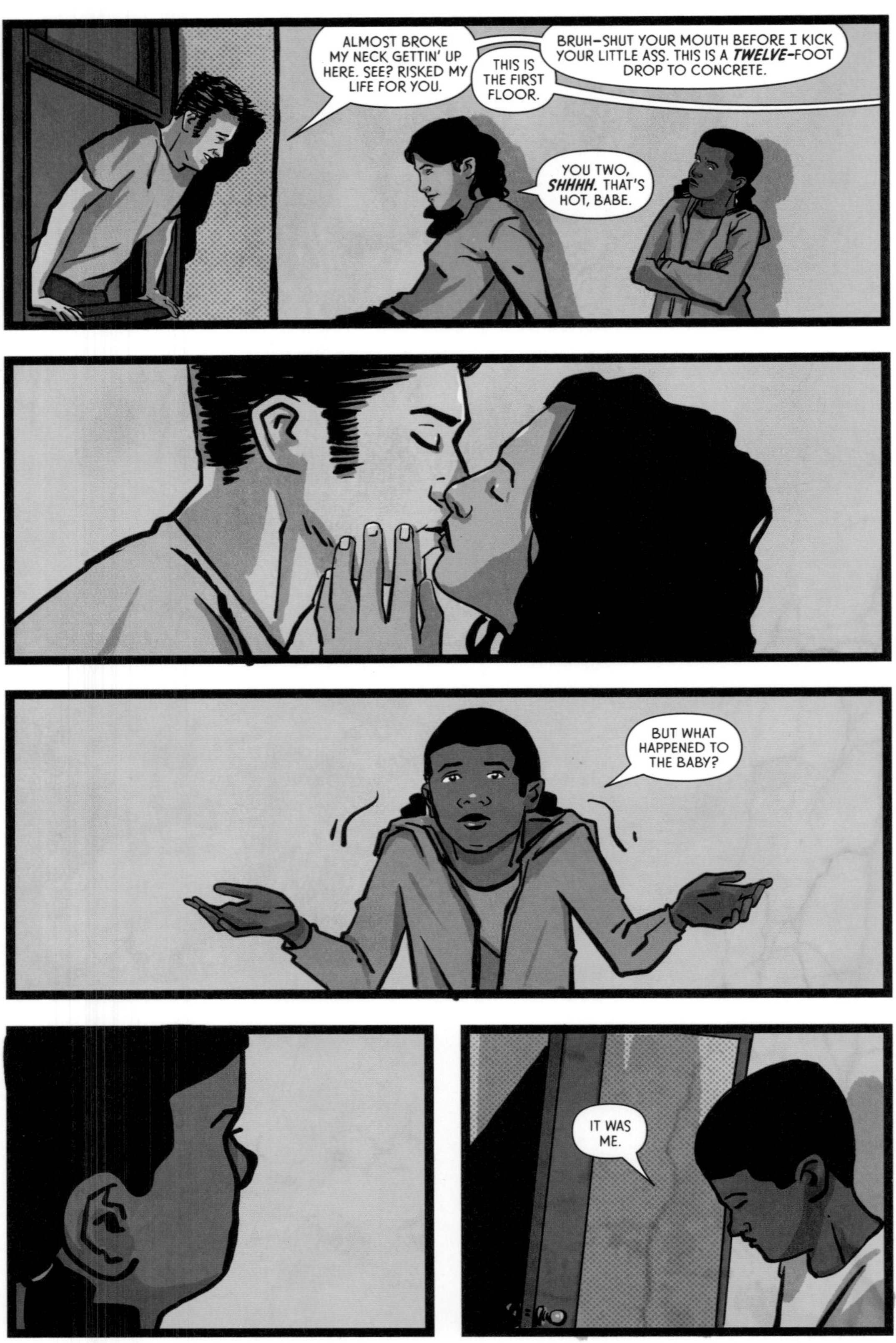
ALMOST BROKE MY NECK GETTIN' UP HERE. SEE? RISKED MY LIFE FOR YOU.
THIS IS THE FIRST FLOOR.
BRUH—SHUT YOUR MOUTH BEFORE I KICK YOUR LITTLE ASS. THIS IS A *TWELVE*-FOOT DROP TO CONCRETE.
YOU TWO, **SHHHH.** THAT'S HOT, BABE.
BUT WHAT HAPPENED TO THE BABY?
IT WAS ME.

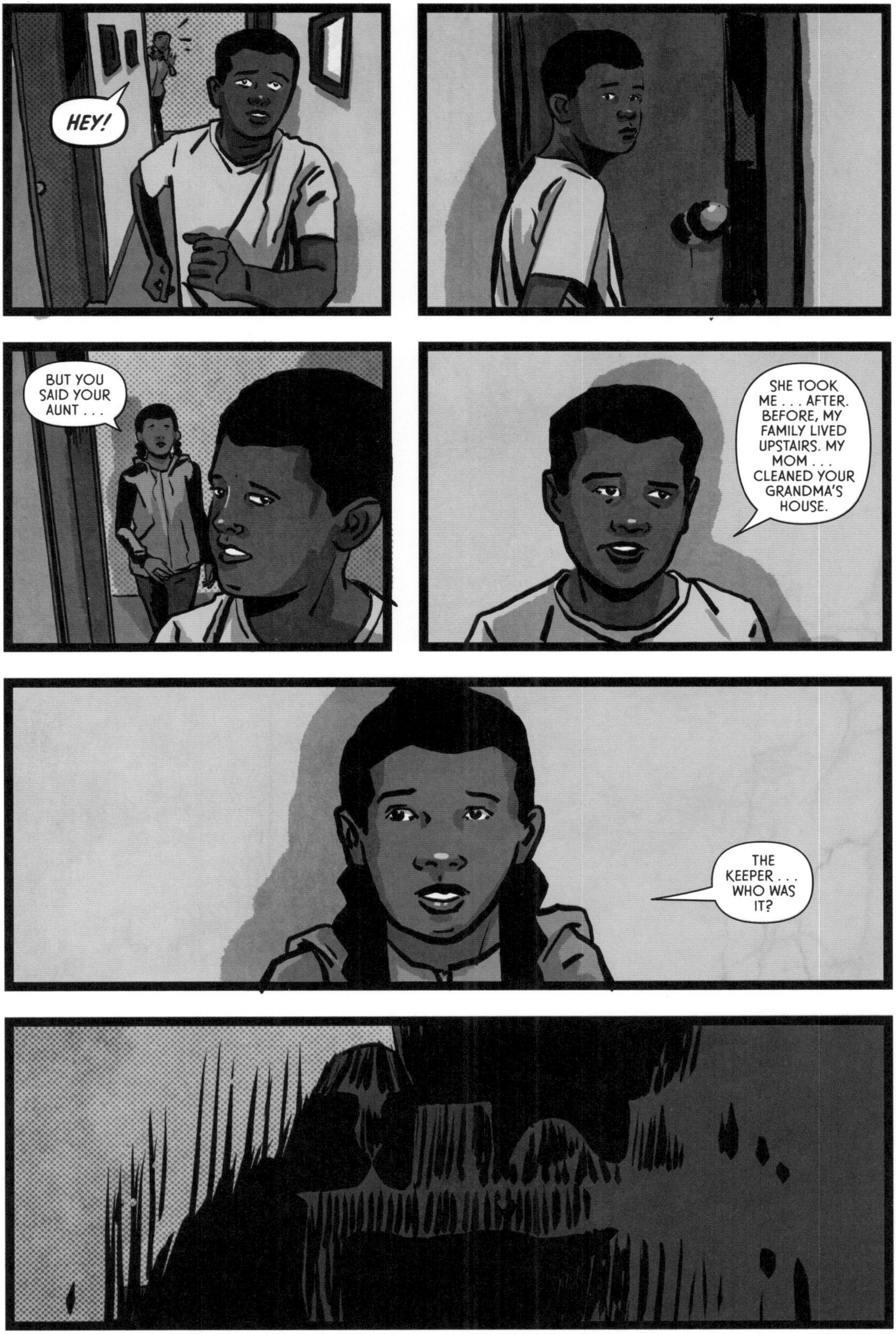
HEY!
BUT YOU SAID YOUR AUNT . . .
SHE TOOK ME . . . AFTER. BEFORE, MY FAMILY LIVED UPSTAIRS. MY MOM . . . CLEANED YOUR GRANDMA'S HOUSE.
THE KEEPER . . . WHO WAS IT?

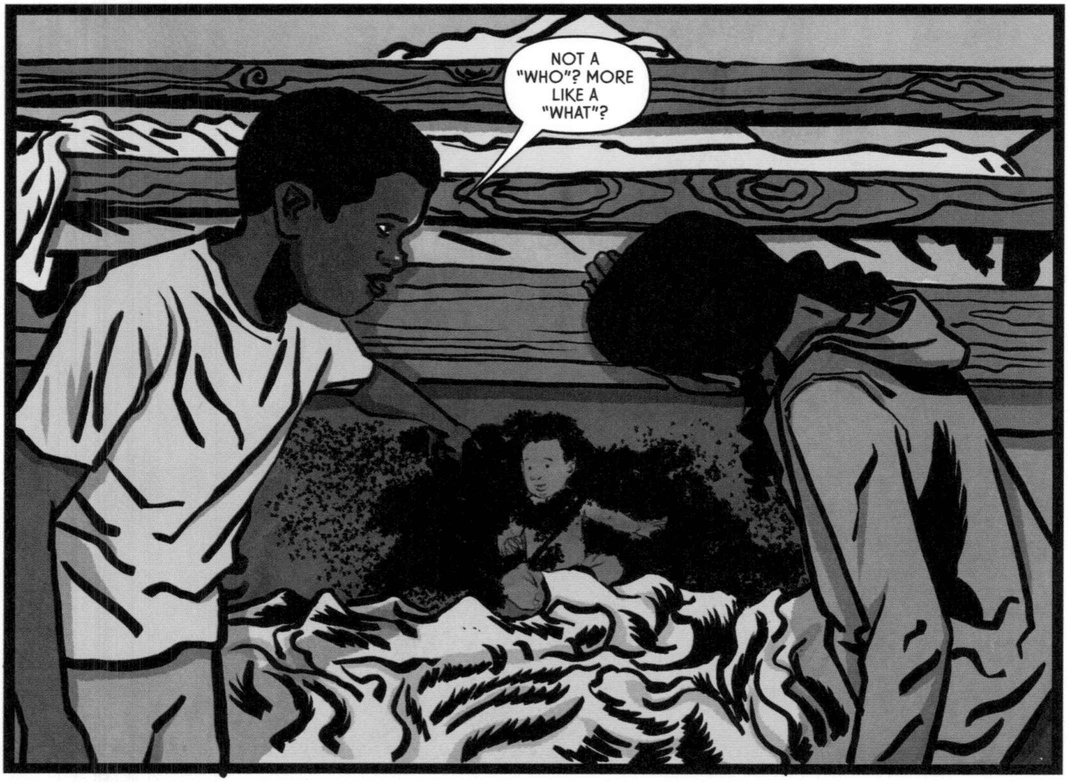
NOT A "WHO"? MORE LIKE A "WHAT"?

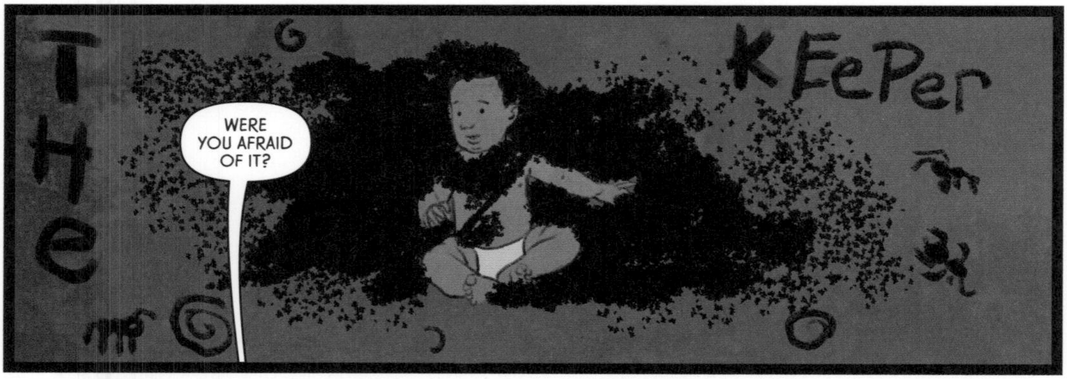
THE
KEEPER
WERE YOU AFRAID OF IT?

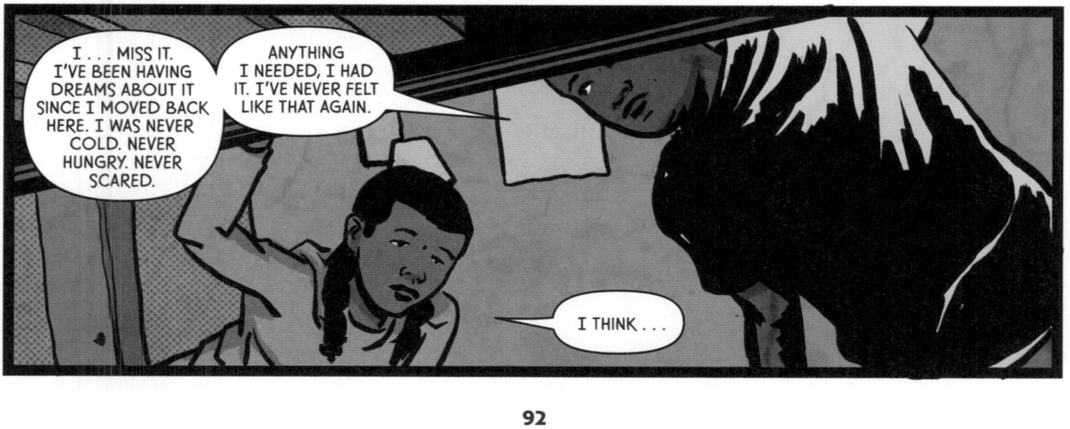
I . . . MISS IT. I'VE BEEN HAVING DREAMS ABOUT IT SINCE I MOVED BACK HERE. I WAS NEVER COLD. NEVER HUNGRY. NEVER SCARED.
ANYTHING I NEEDED, I HAD IT. I'VE NEVER FELT LIKE THAT AGAIN.
I THINK . . .

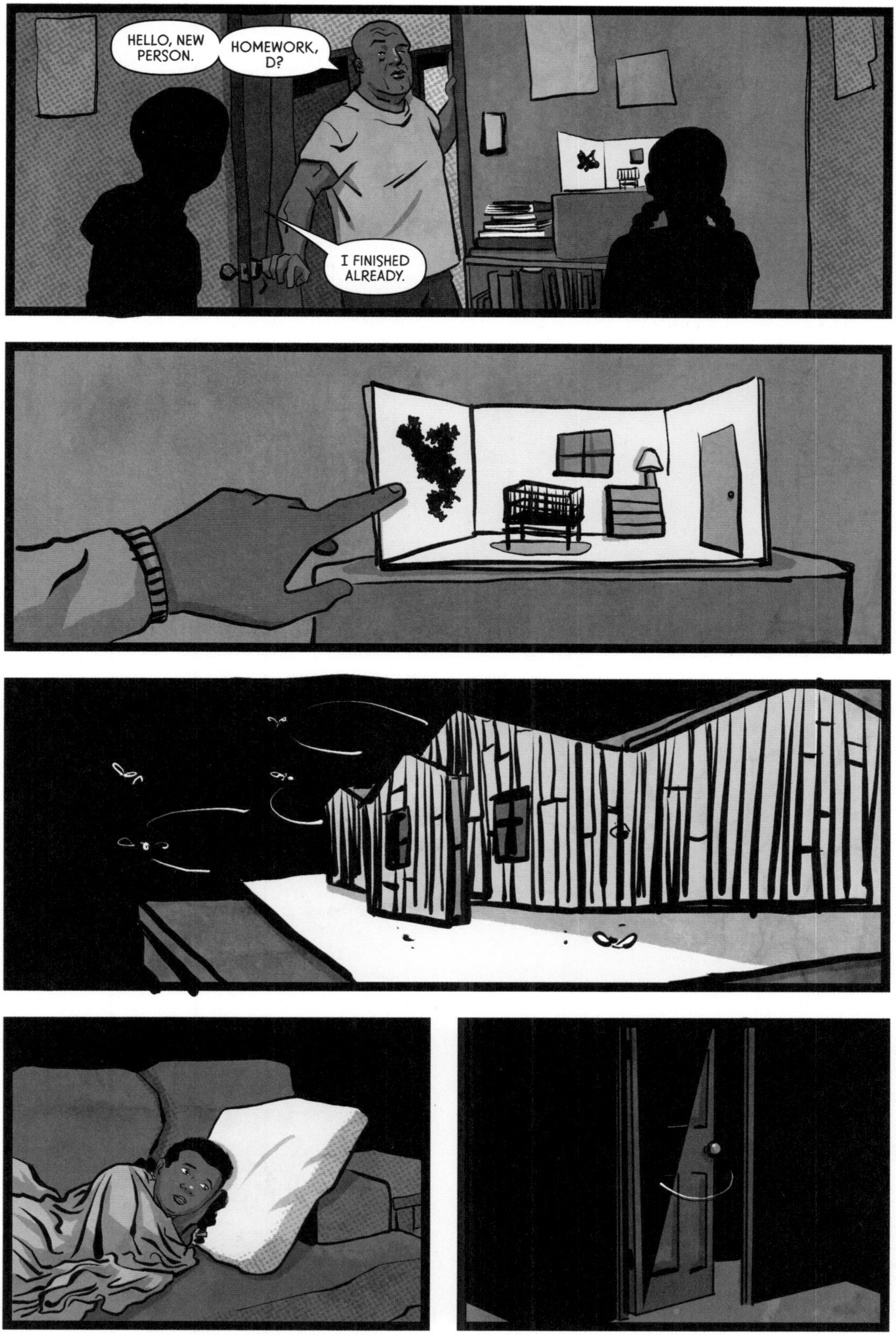
HELLO, NEW PERSON.
HOMEWORK, D?
I FINISHED ALREADY.

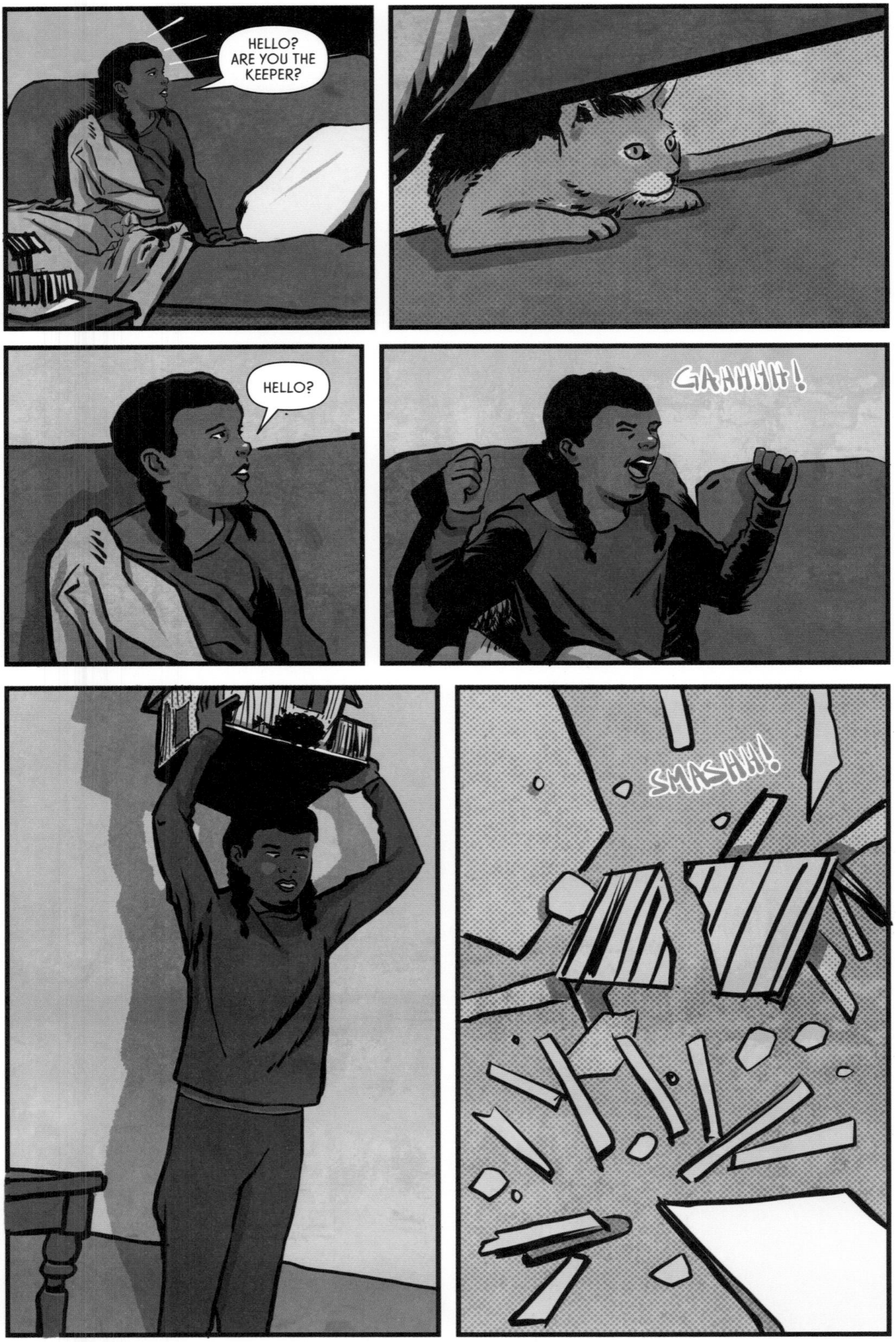
HELLO? ARE YOU THE KEEPER?
HELLO?
GAHHHH!
SMASHH!

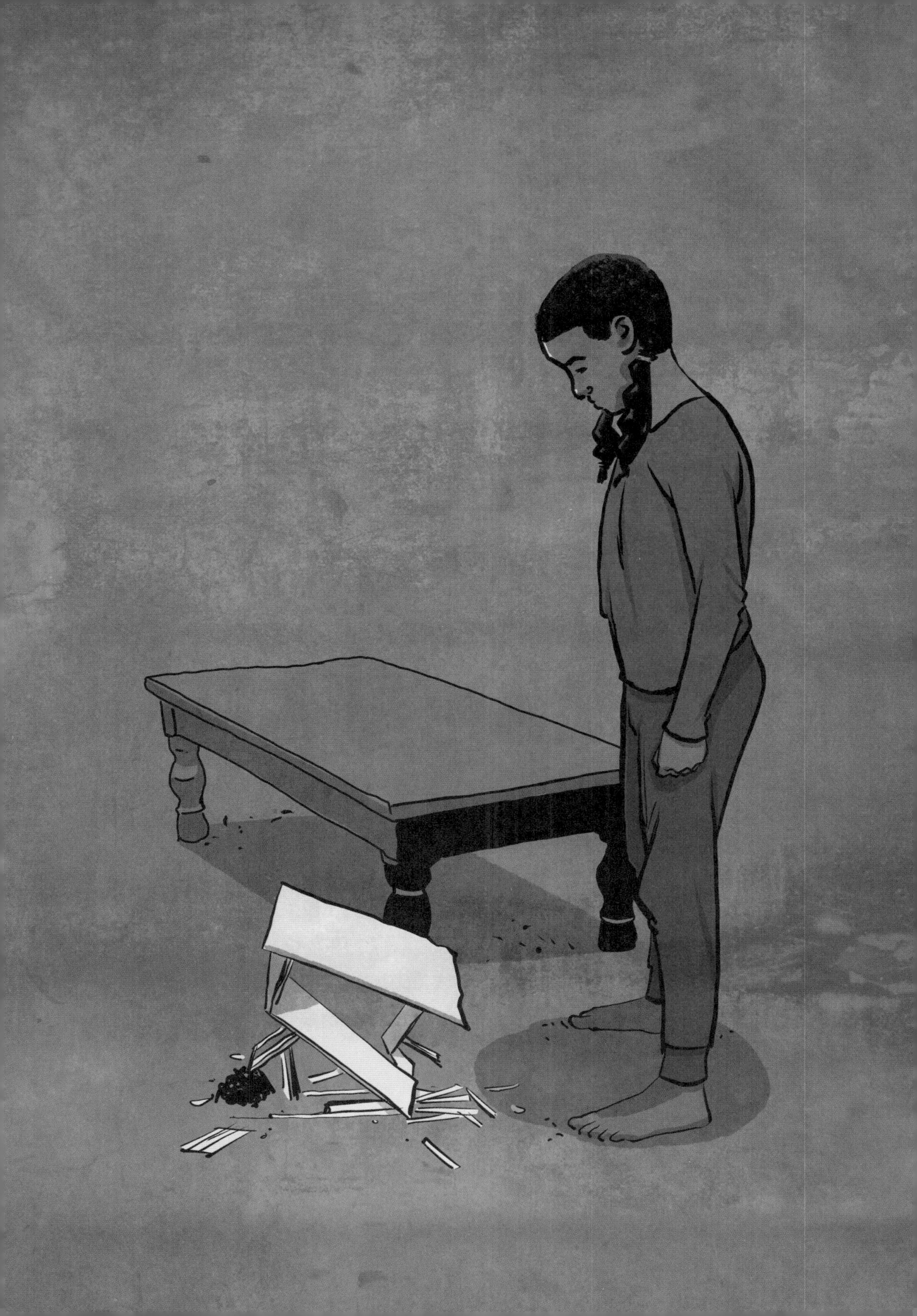

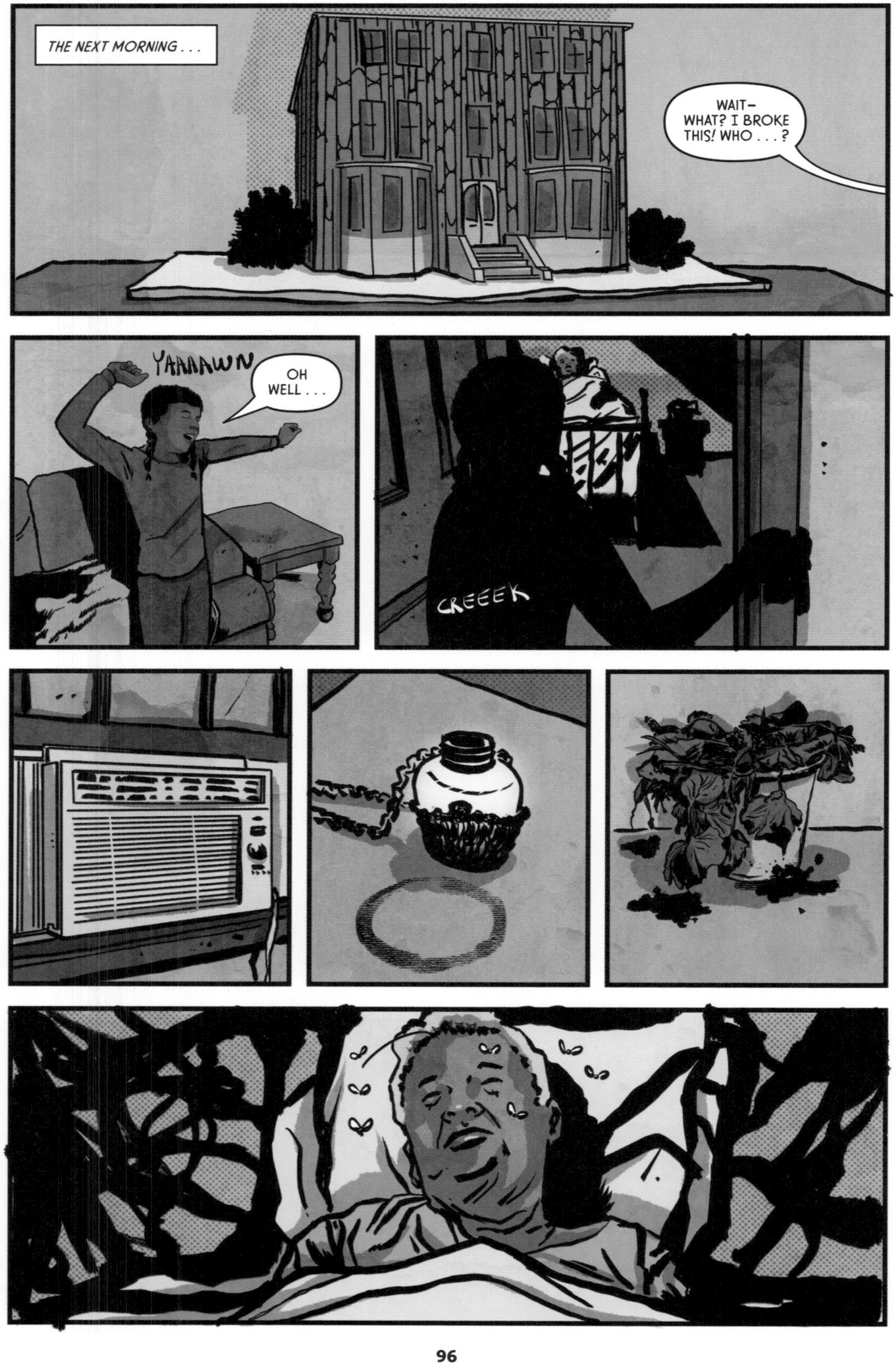
THE NEXT MORNING . . .
WAIT— WHAT? I BROKE THIS! WHO . . . ?
YAAAAWN
OH WELL . . .
CREEEK

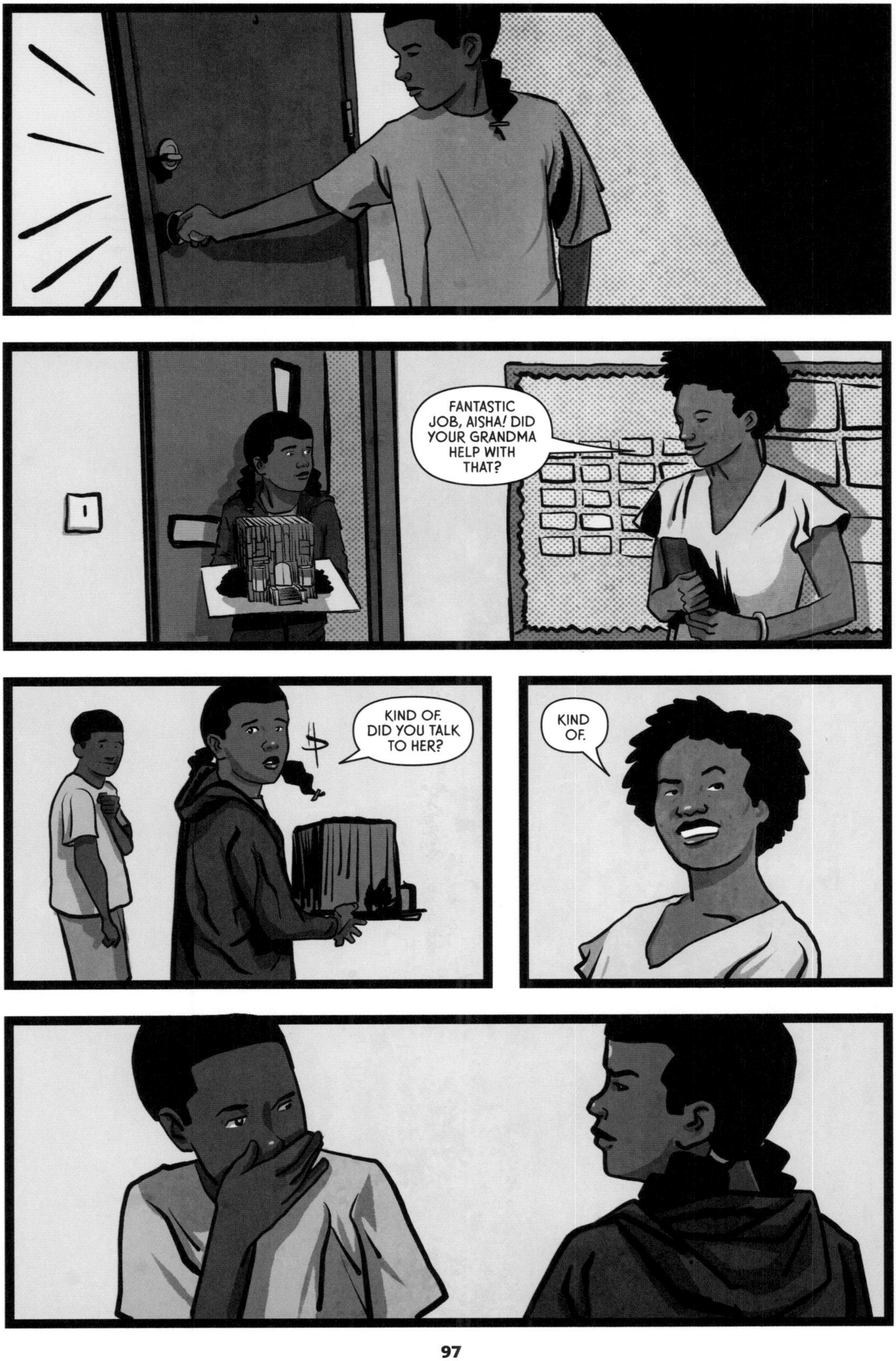
FANTASTIC JOB, AISHA! DID YOUR GRANDMA HELP WITH THAT?
KIND OF. DID YOU TALK TO HER?
KIND OF.

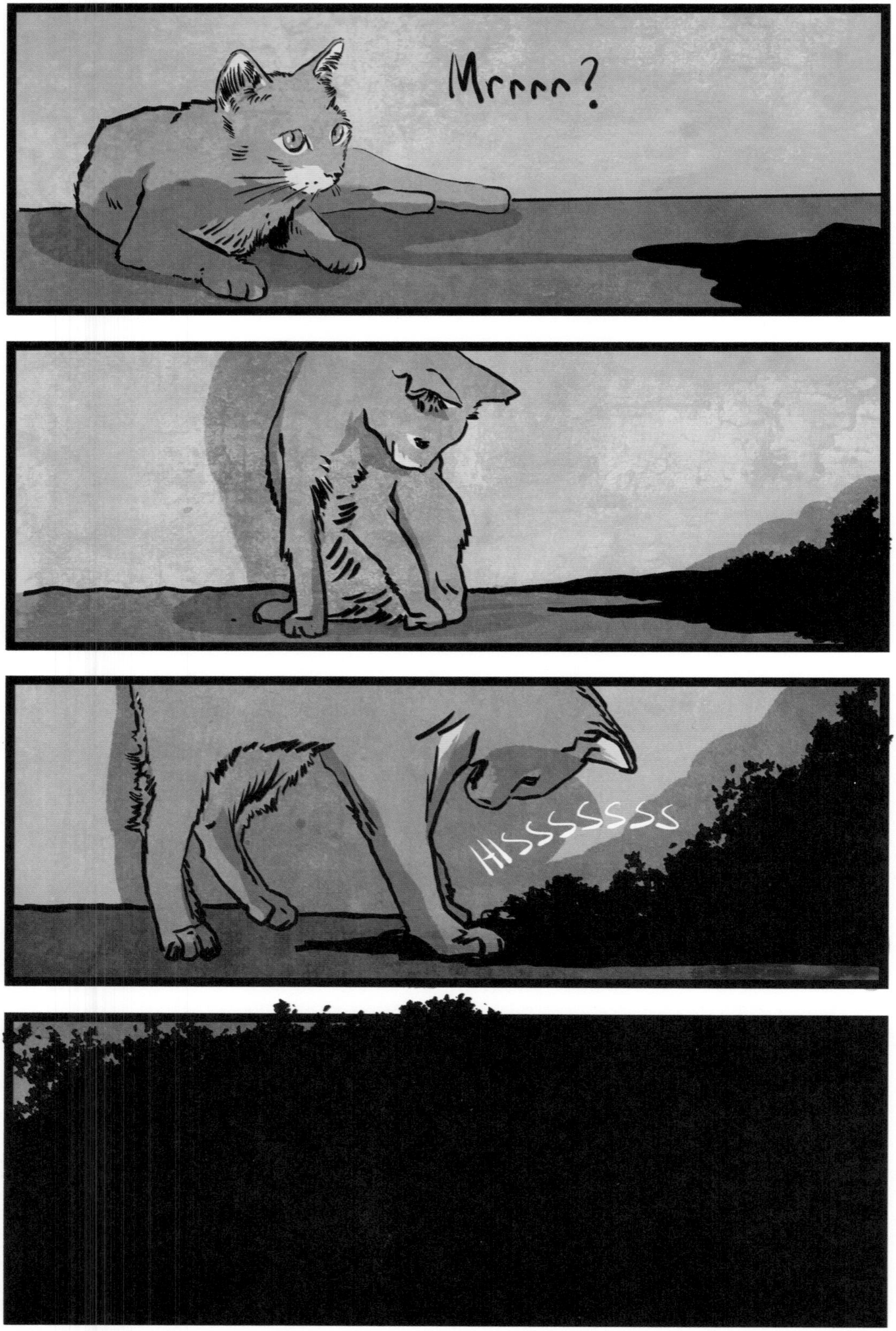
Mrrrr?
HISSSSSSS

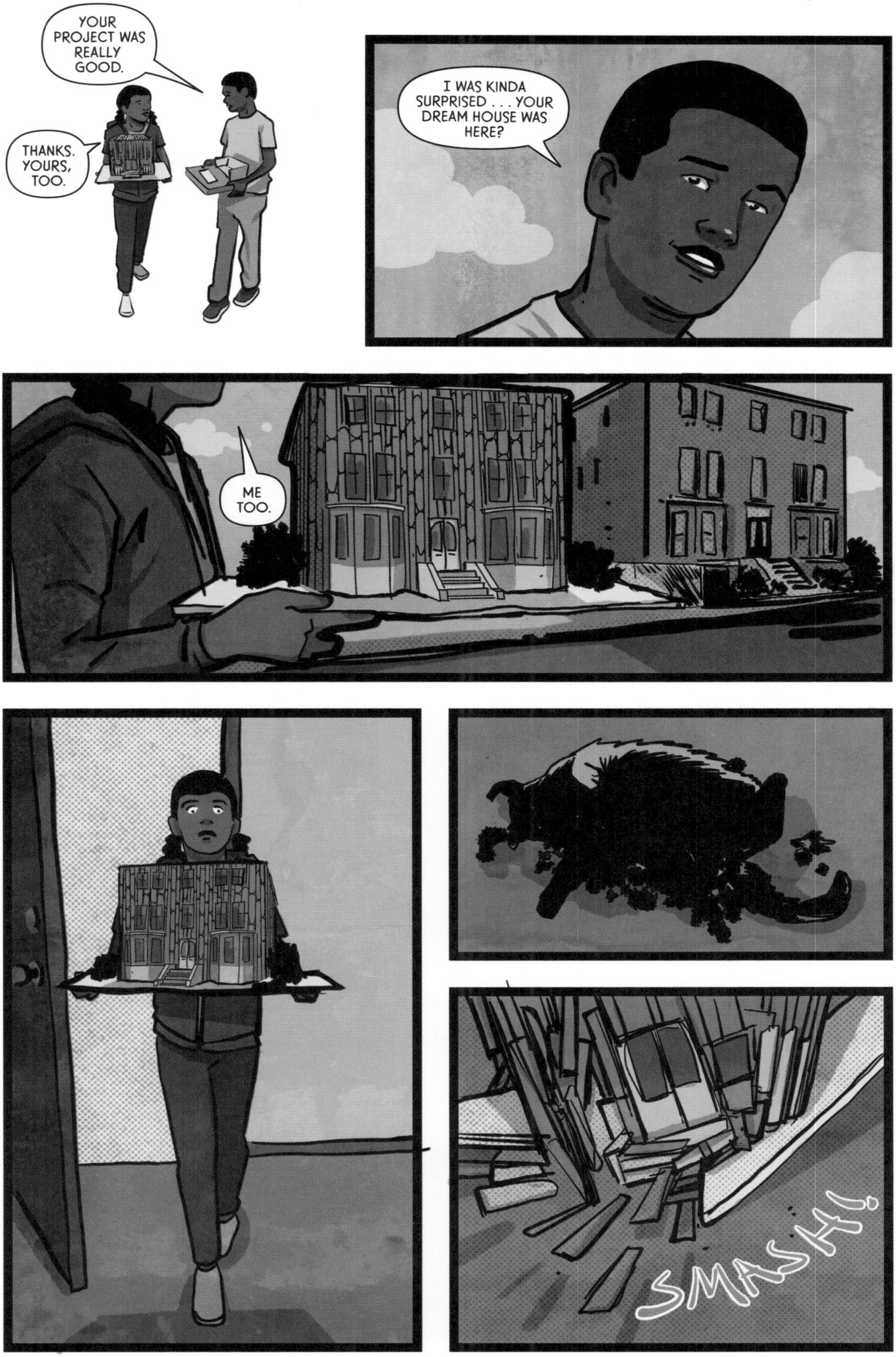
YOUR PROJECT WAS REALLY GOOD.
THANKS. YOURS, TOO.
I WAS KINDA SURPRISED . . . YOUR DREAM HOUSE WAS HERE?
ME TOO.
SMASH!

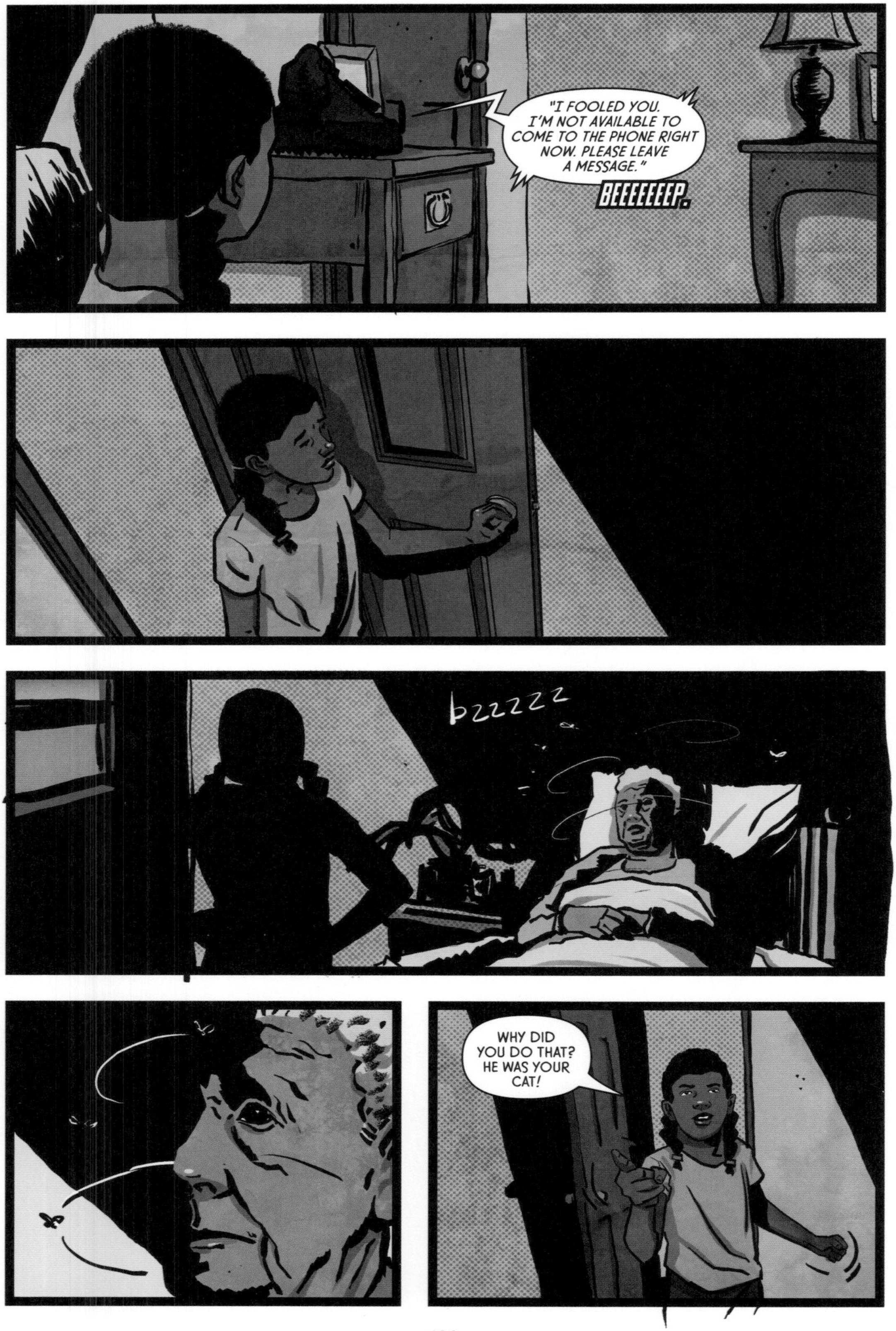
"I FOOLED YOU. I'M NOT AVAILABLE TO COME TO THE PHONE RIGHT NOW. PLEASE LEAVE A MESSAGE."
BEEEEEEEP.
bzzzzz
WHY DID YOU DO THAT? HE WAS YOUR CAT!

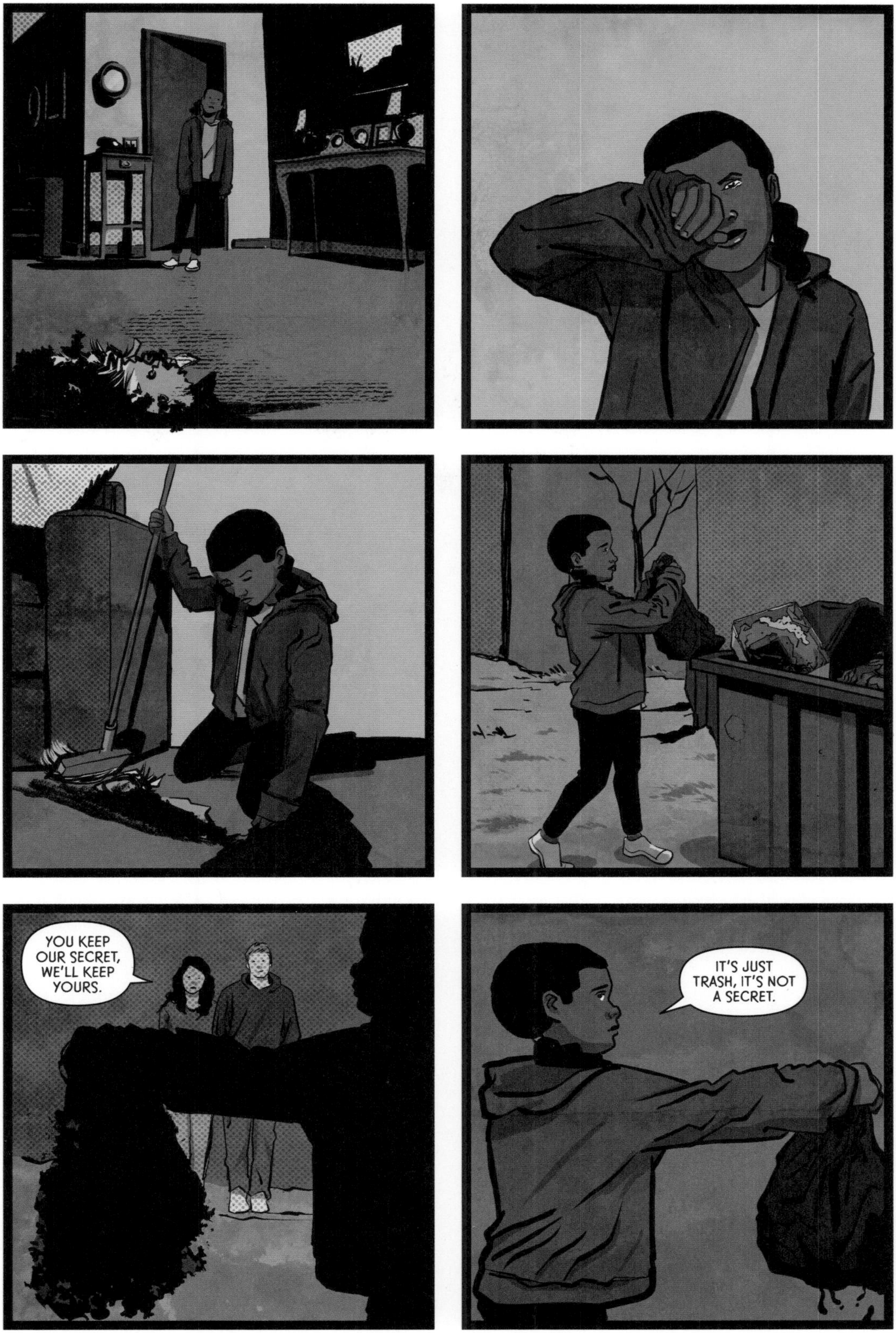
YOU KEEP OUR SECRET, WE'LL KEEP YOURS.
IT'S JUST TRASH, IT'S NOT A SECRET.

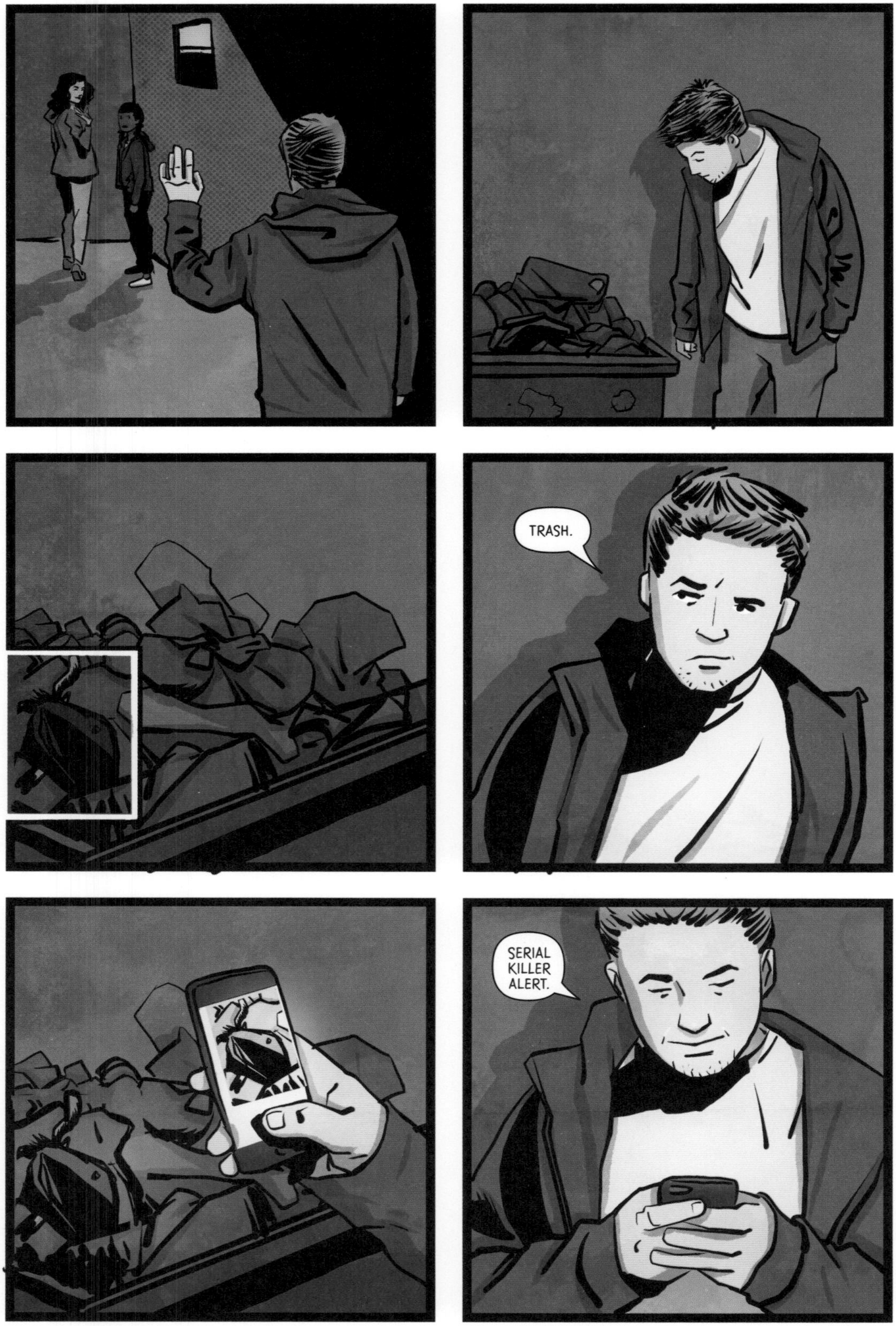
TRASH.
SERIAL KILLER ALERT.

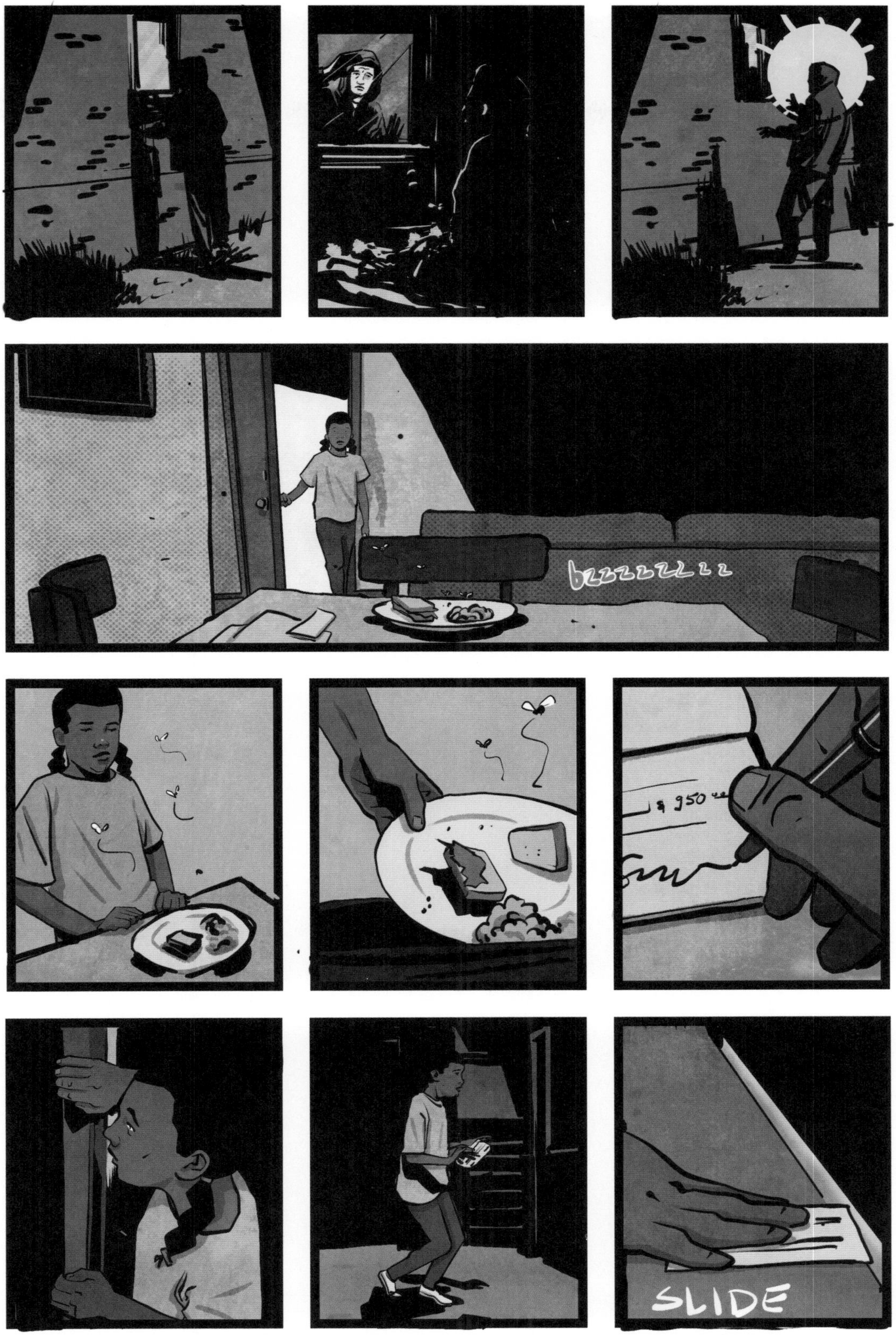
bzzzzzzzz
$950
SLIDE

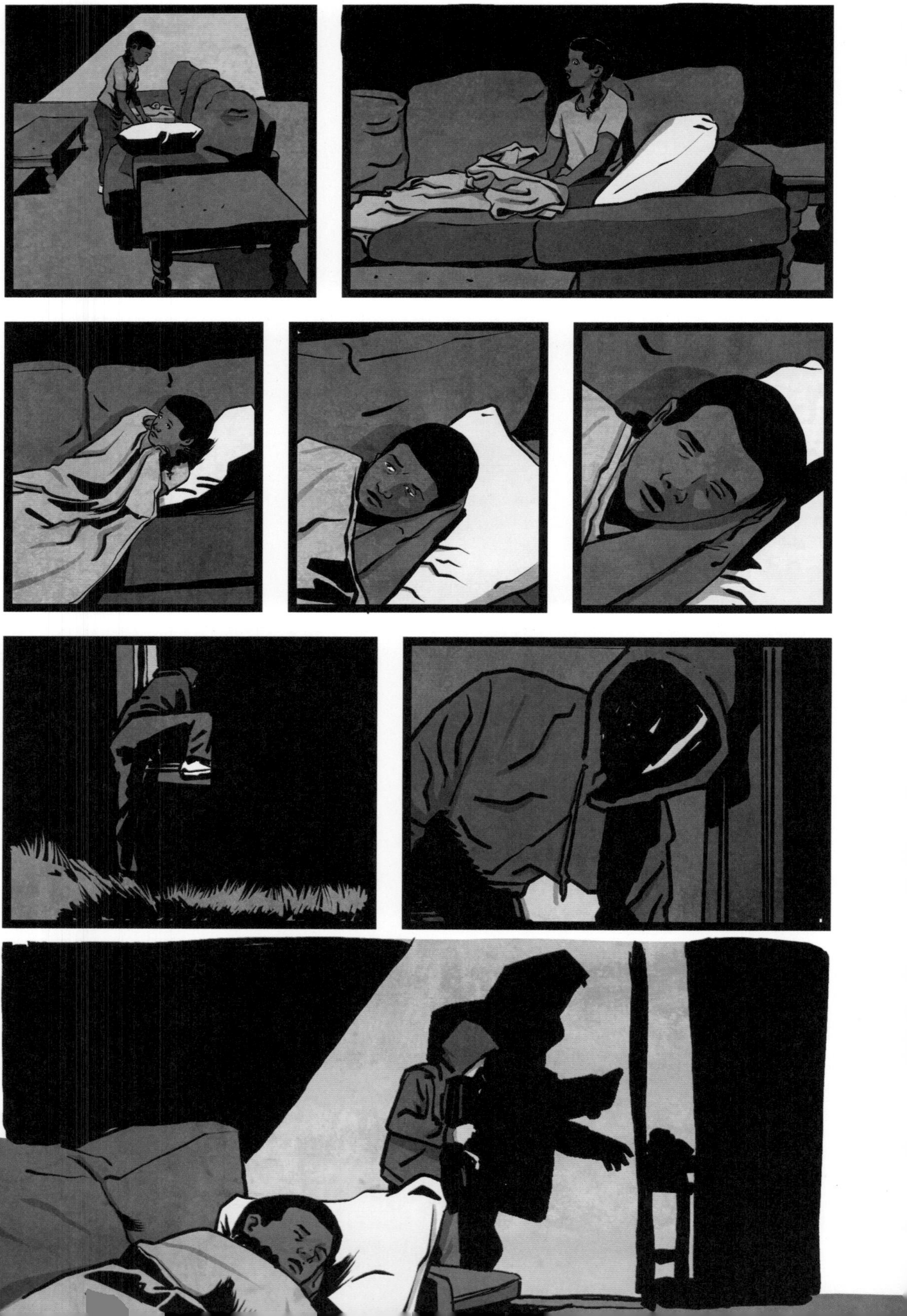

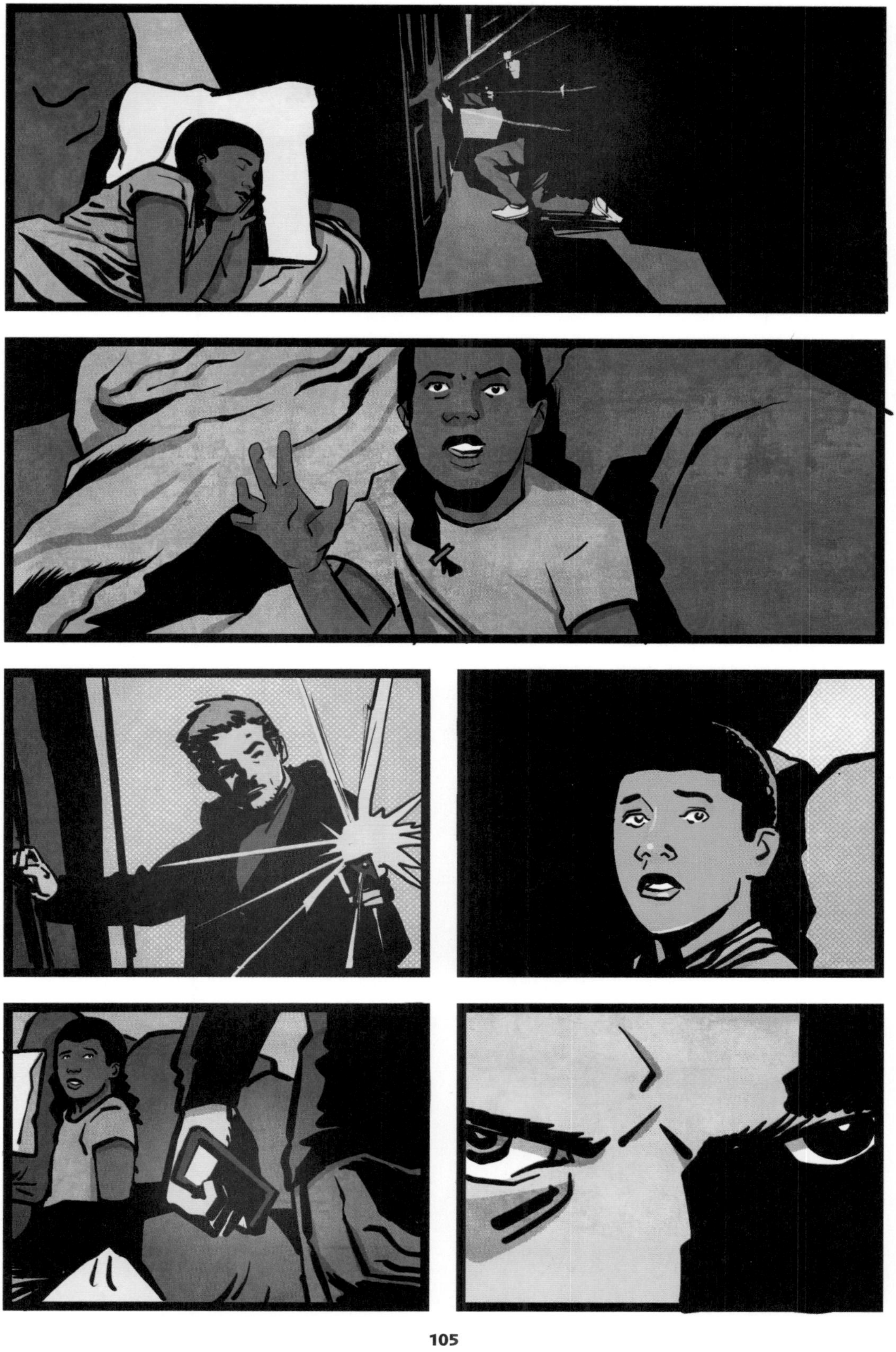

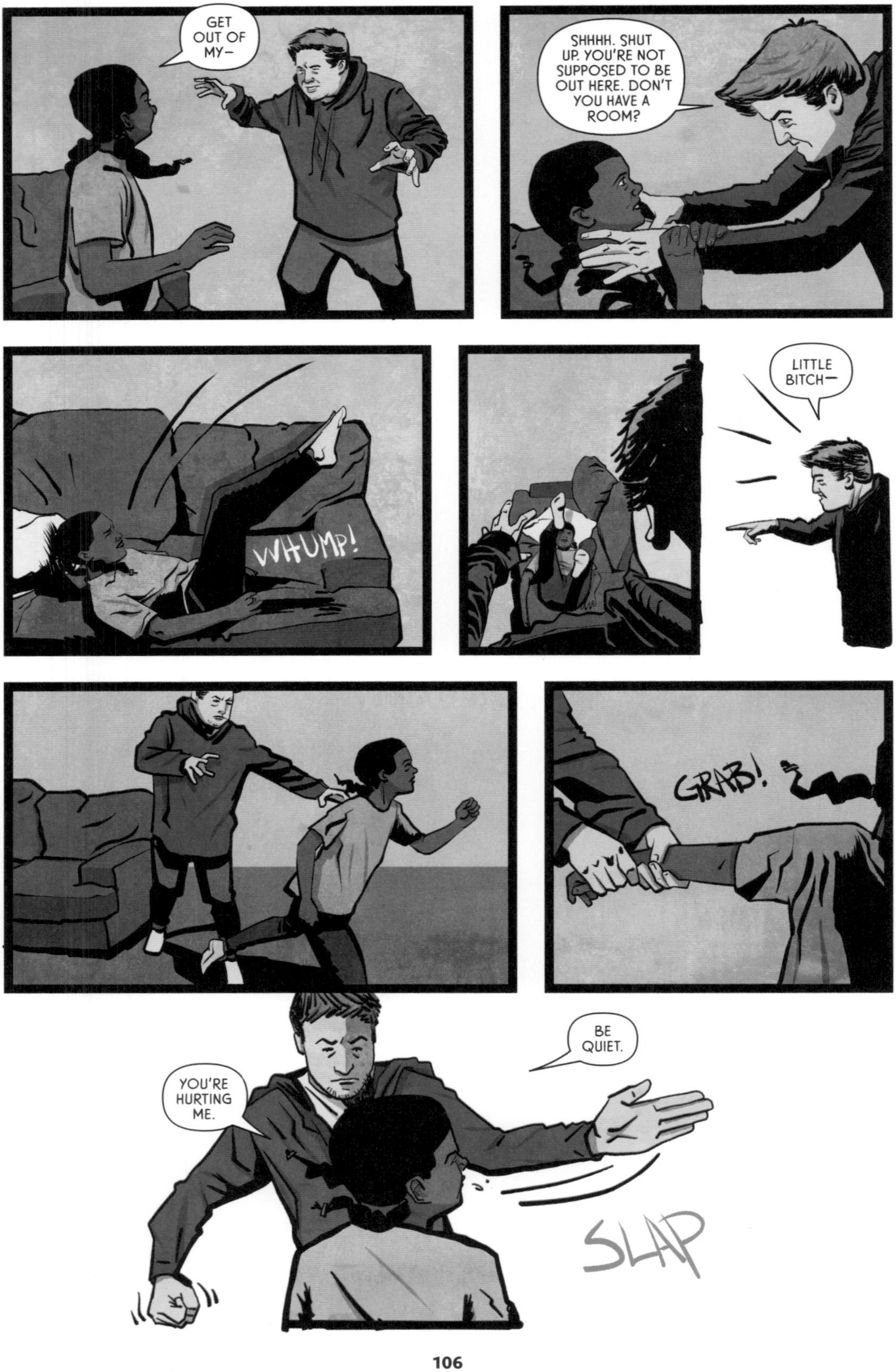
GET OUT OF MY—
SHHHH. SHUT UP. YOU'RE NOT SUPPOSED TO BE OUT HERE. DON'T YOU HAVE A ROOM?
WHUMP!
LITTLE BITCH—
GRAB!
YOU'RE HURTING ME.
BE QUIET.
SLAP

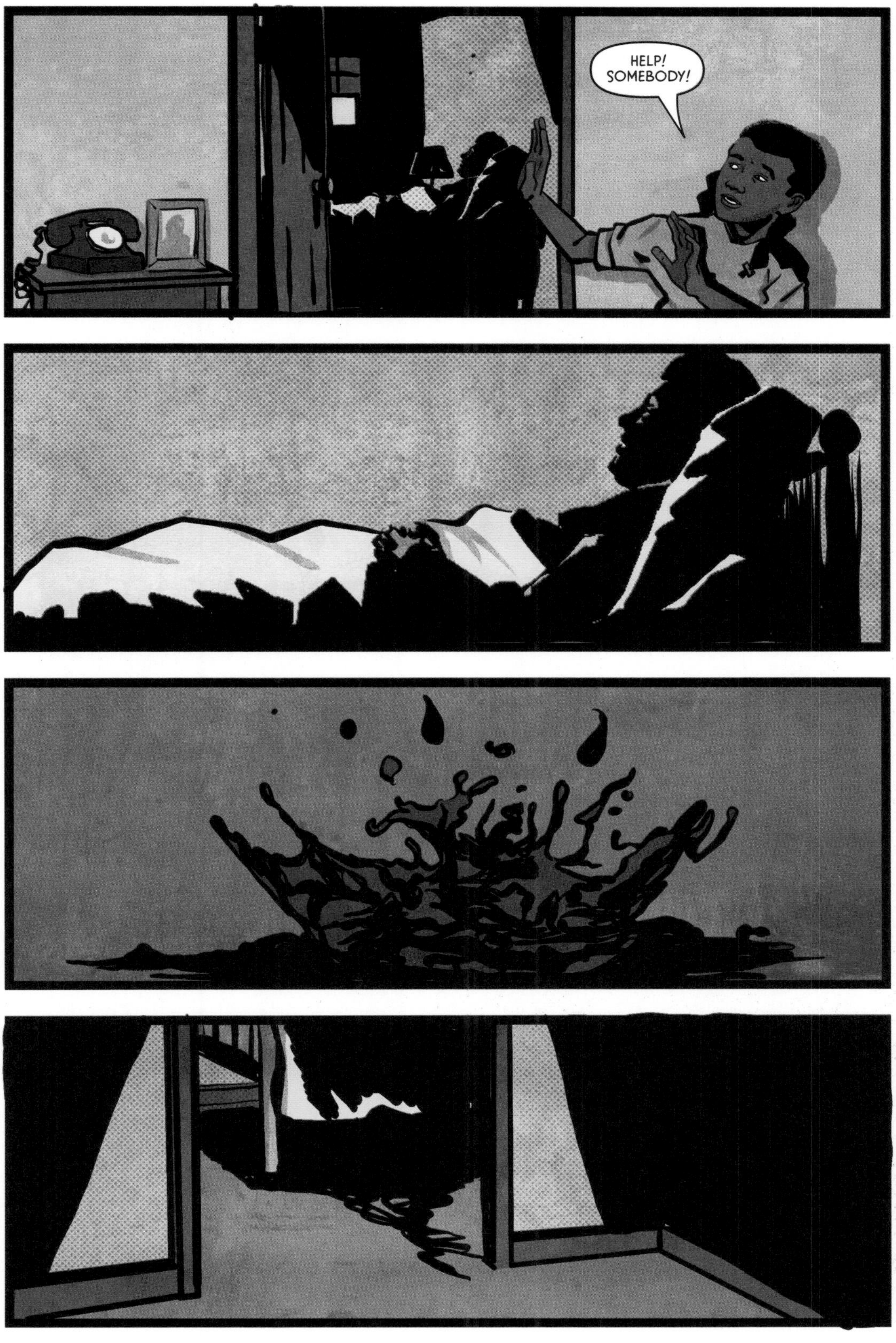
HELP! SOMEBODY!

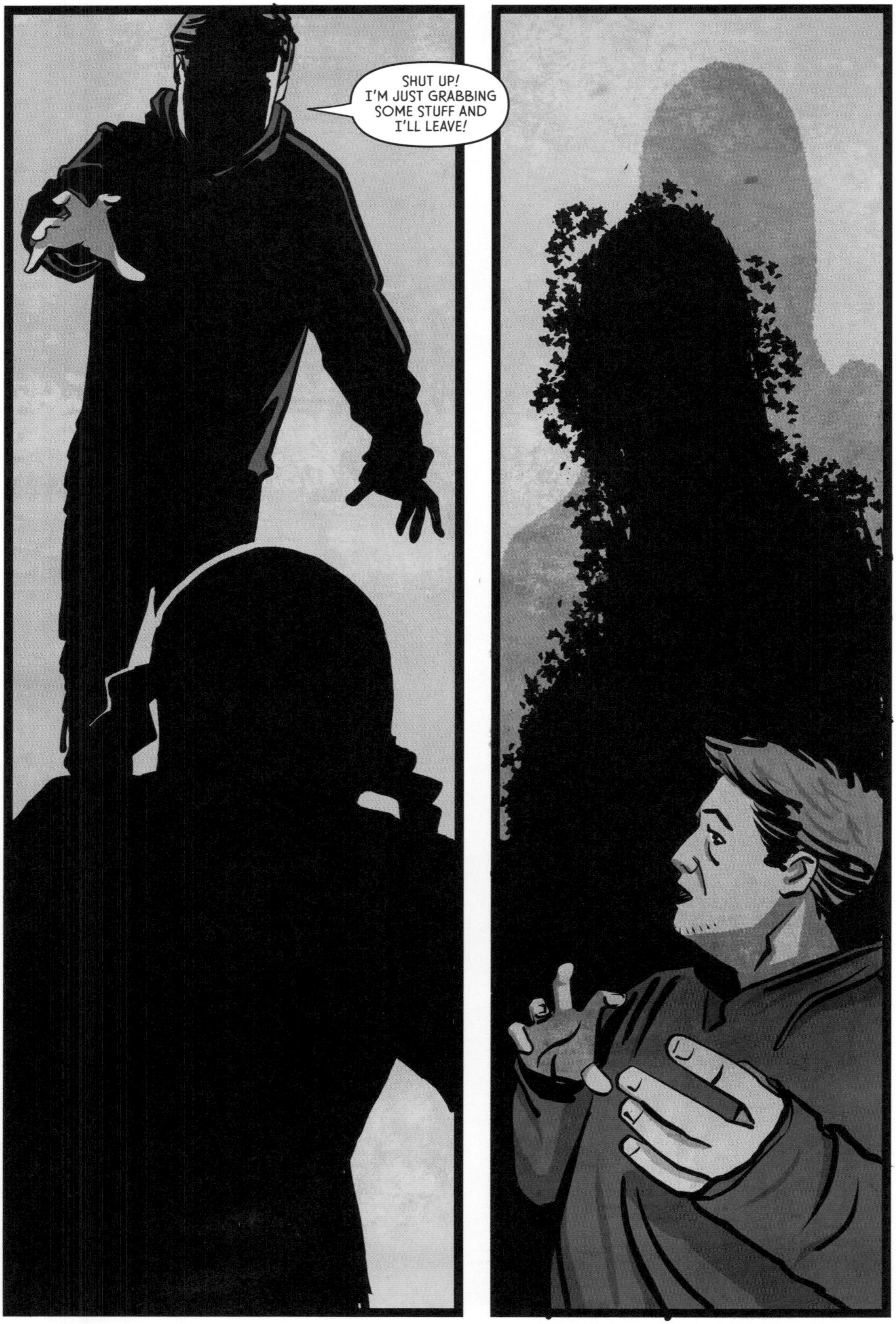
SHUT UP! I'M JUST GRABBING SOME STUFF AND I'LL LEAVE!

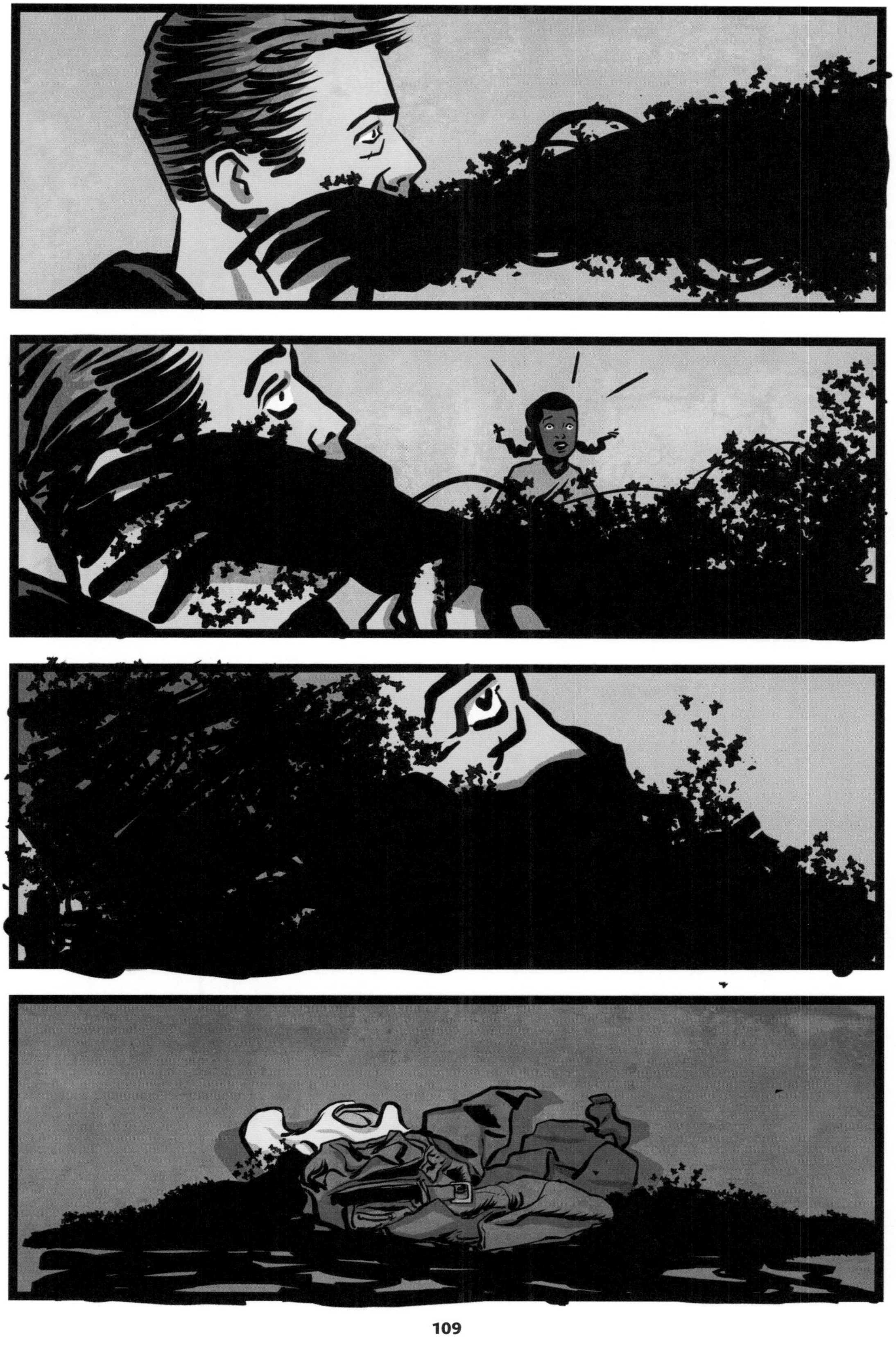

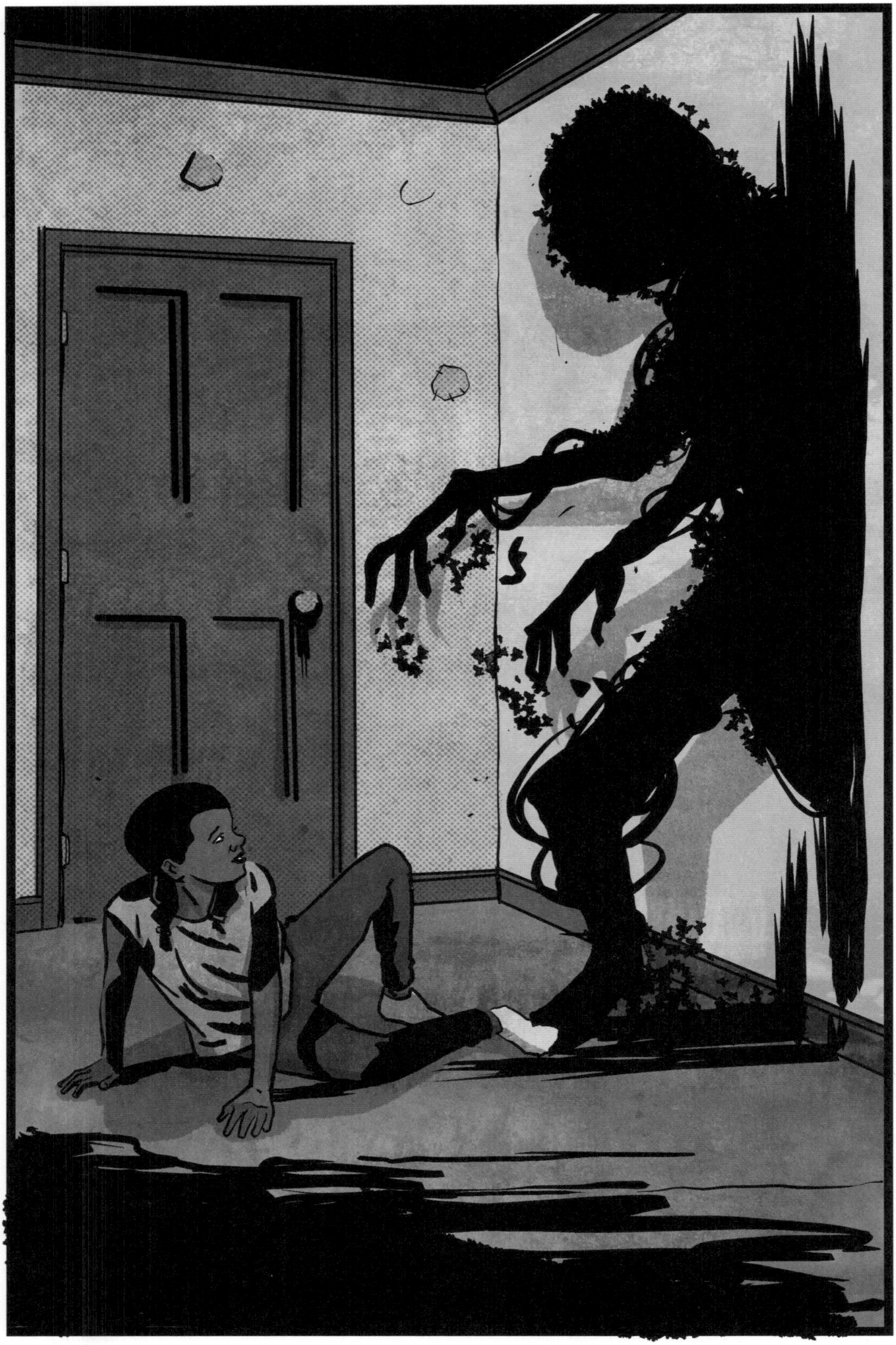

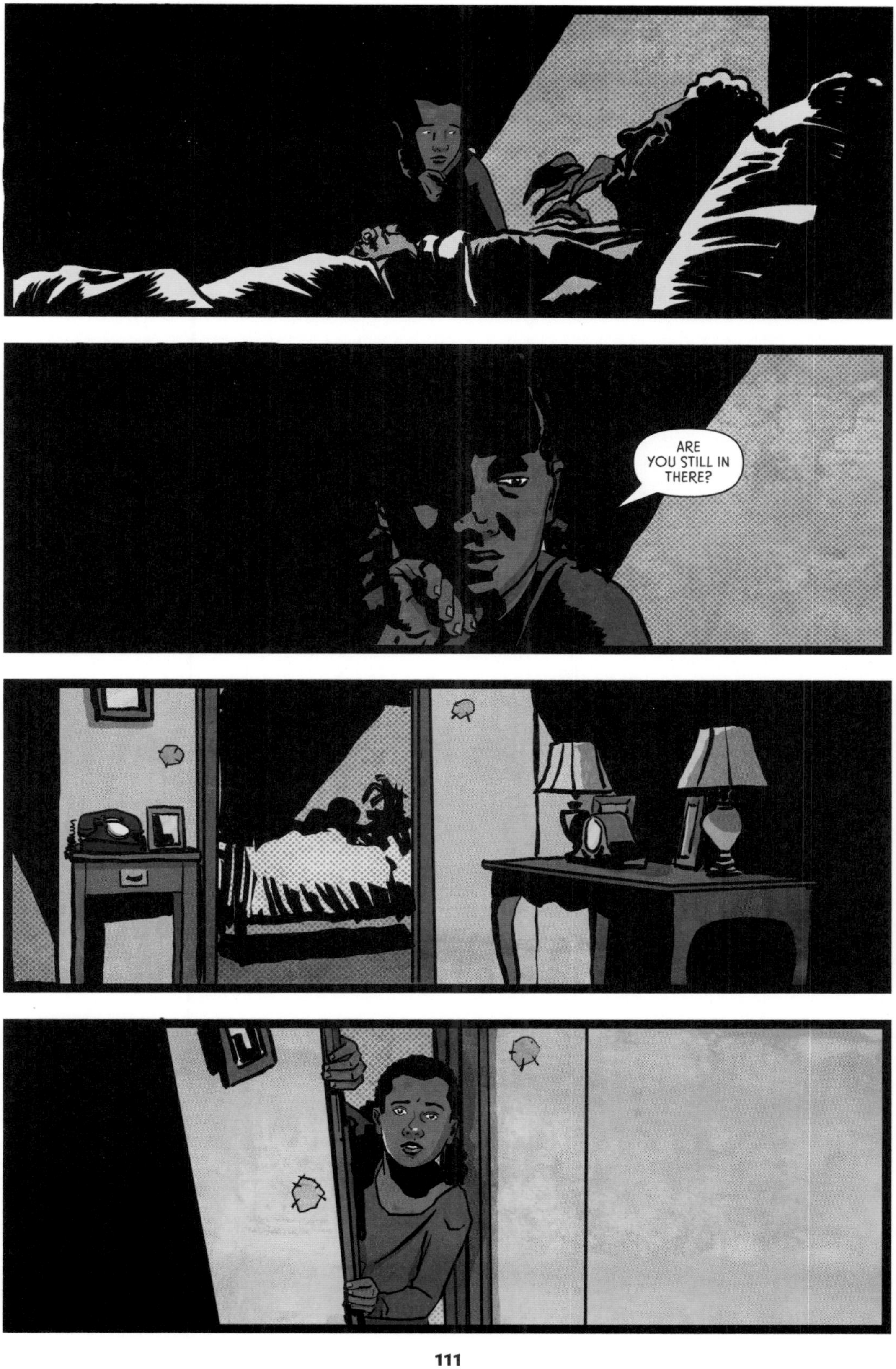
ARE YOU STILL IN THERE?

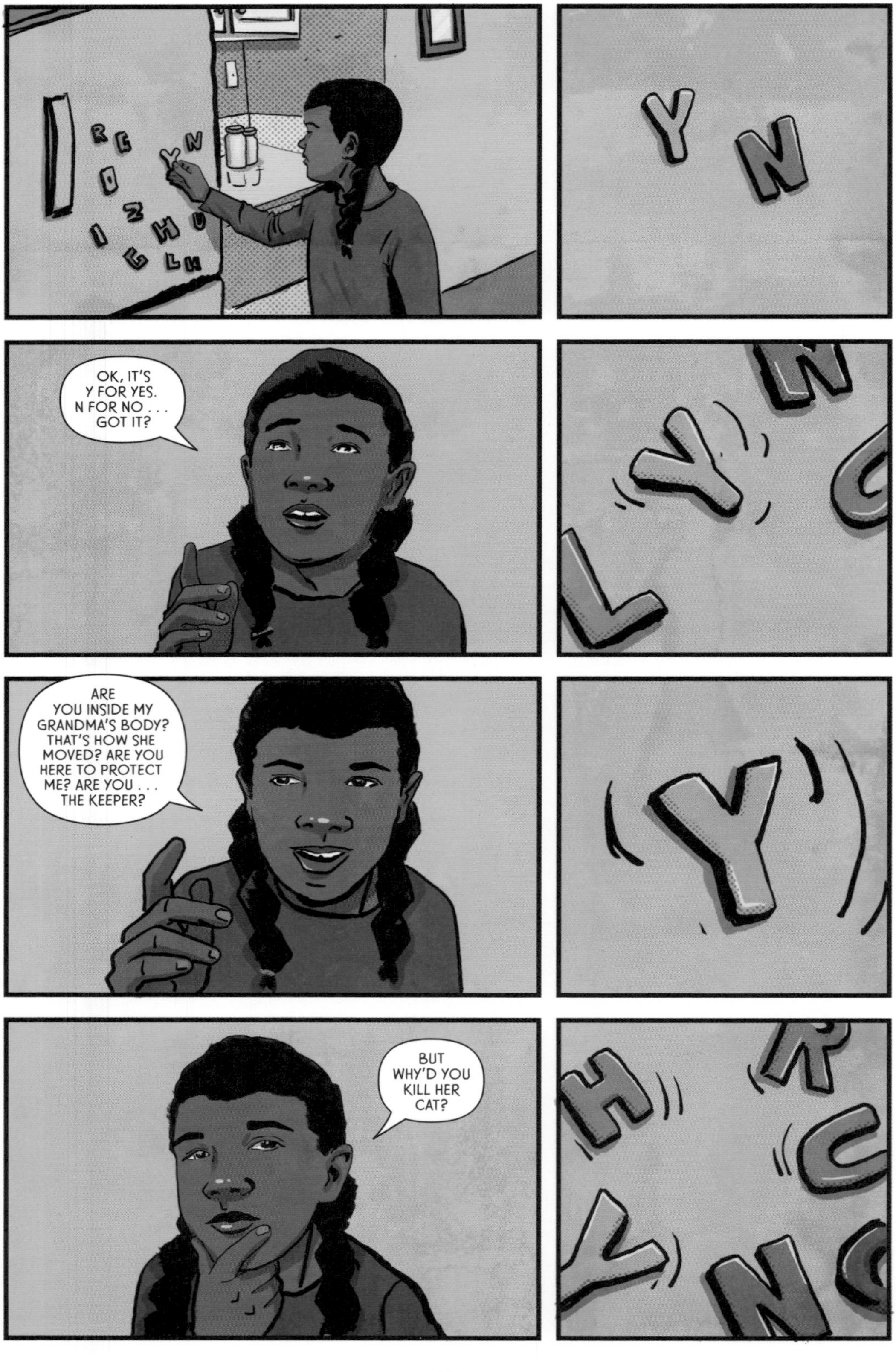
OK, IT'S Y FOR YES. N FOR NO . . . GOT IT?
ARE YOU INSIDE MY GRANDMA'S BODY? THAT'S HOW SHE MOVED? ARE YOU HERE TO PROTECT ME? ARE YOU . . . THE KEEPER?
BUT WHY'D YOU KILL HER CAT?

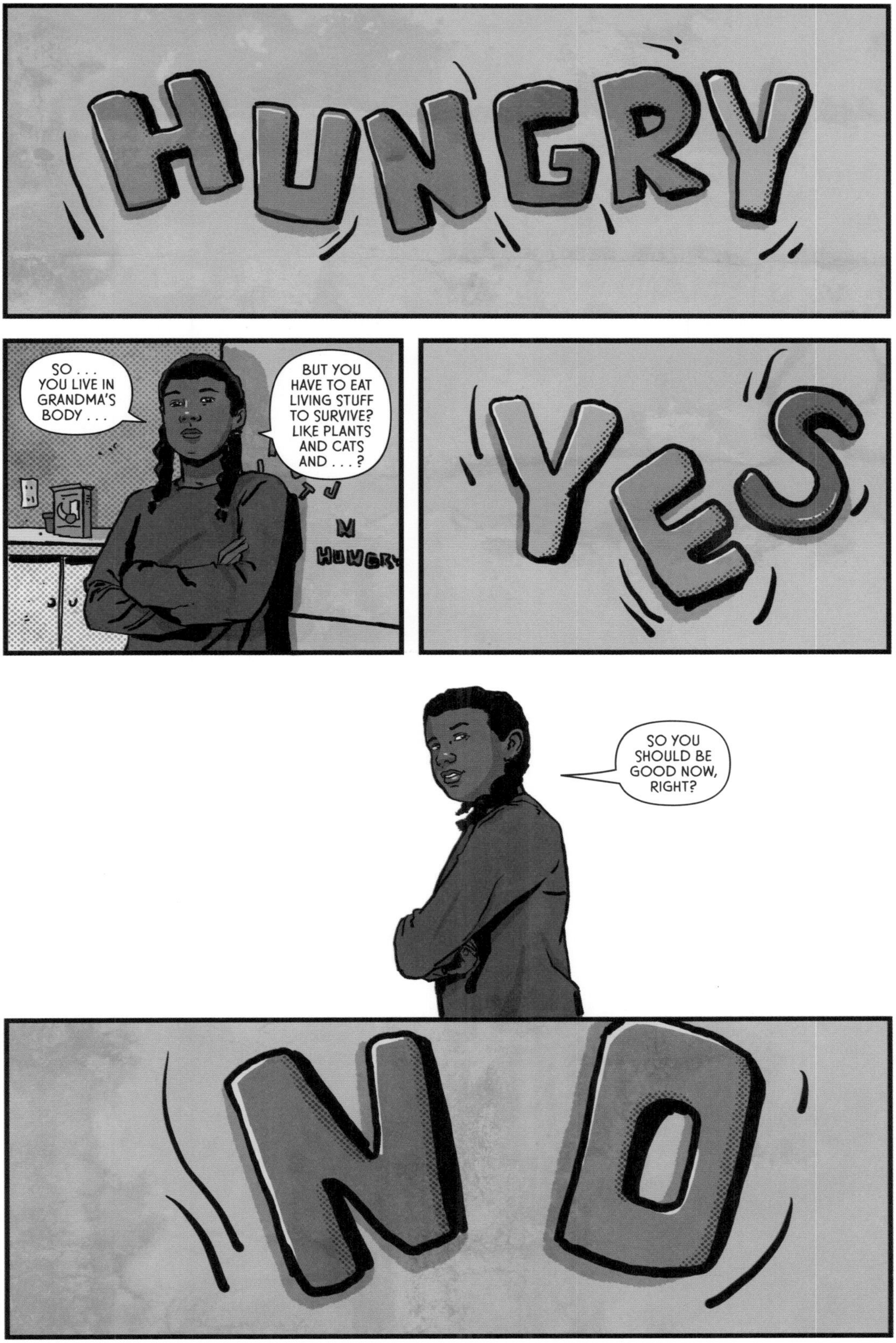
HUNGRY
SO . . . YOU LIVE IN GRANDMA'S BODY . . .
BUT YOU HAVE TO EAT LIVING STUFF TO SURVIVE? LIKE PLANTS AND CATS AND . . . ?
HUNGRY
YES
SO YOU SHOULD BE GOOD NOW, RIGHT?
NO

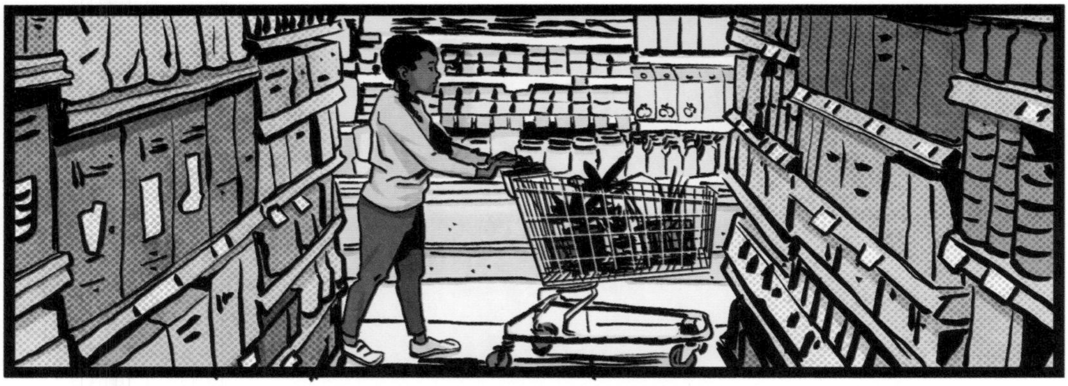

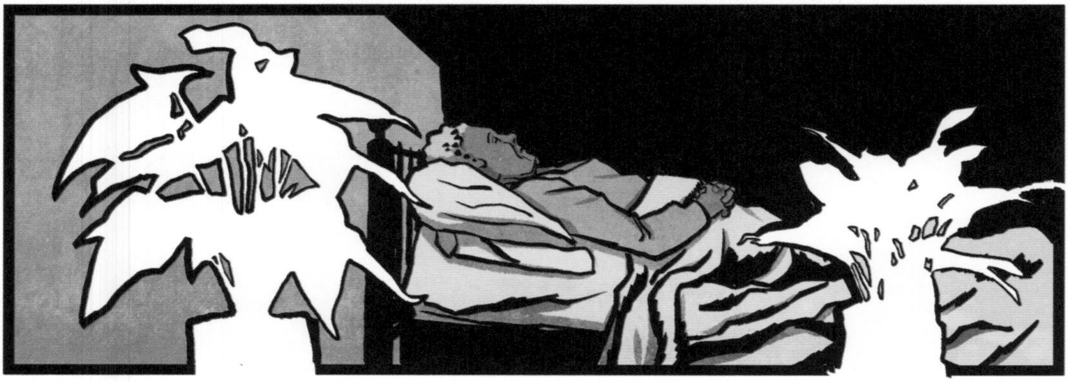

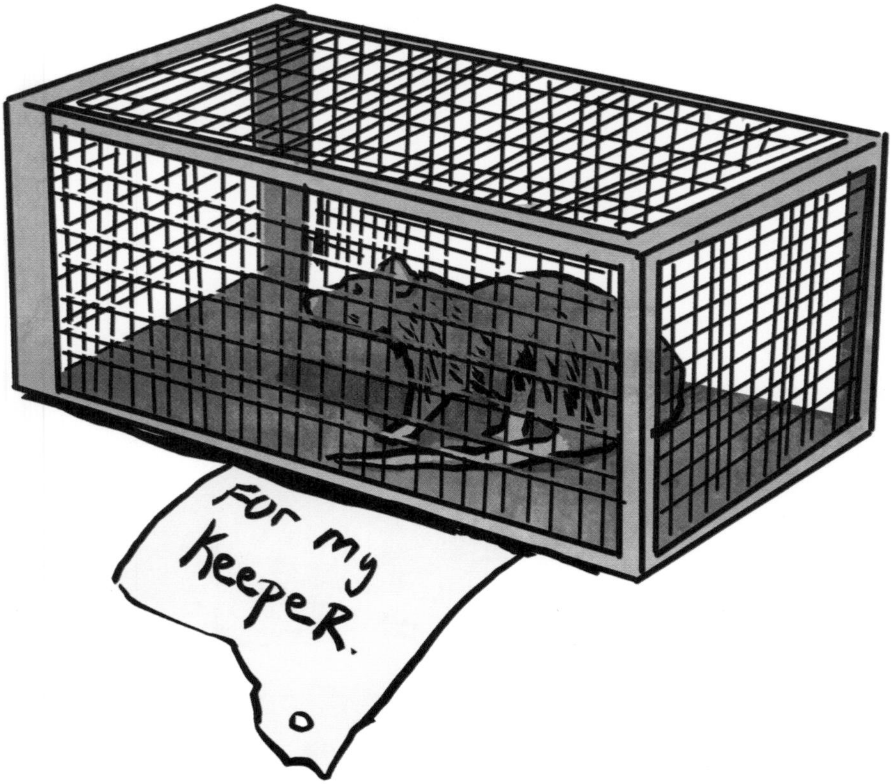
For my Keeper.

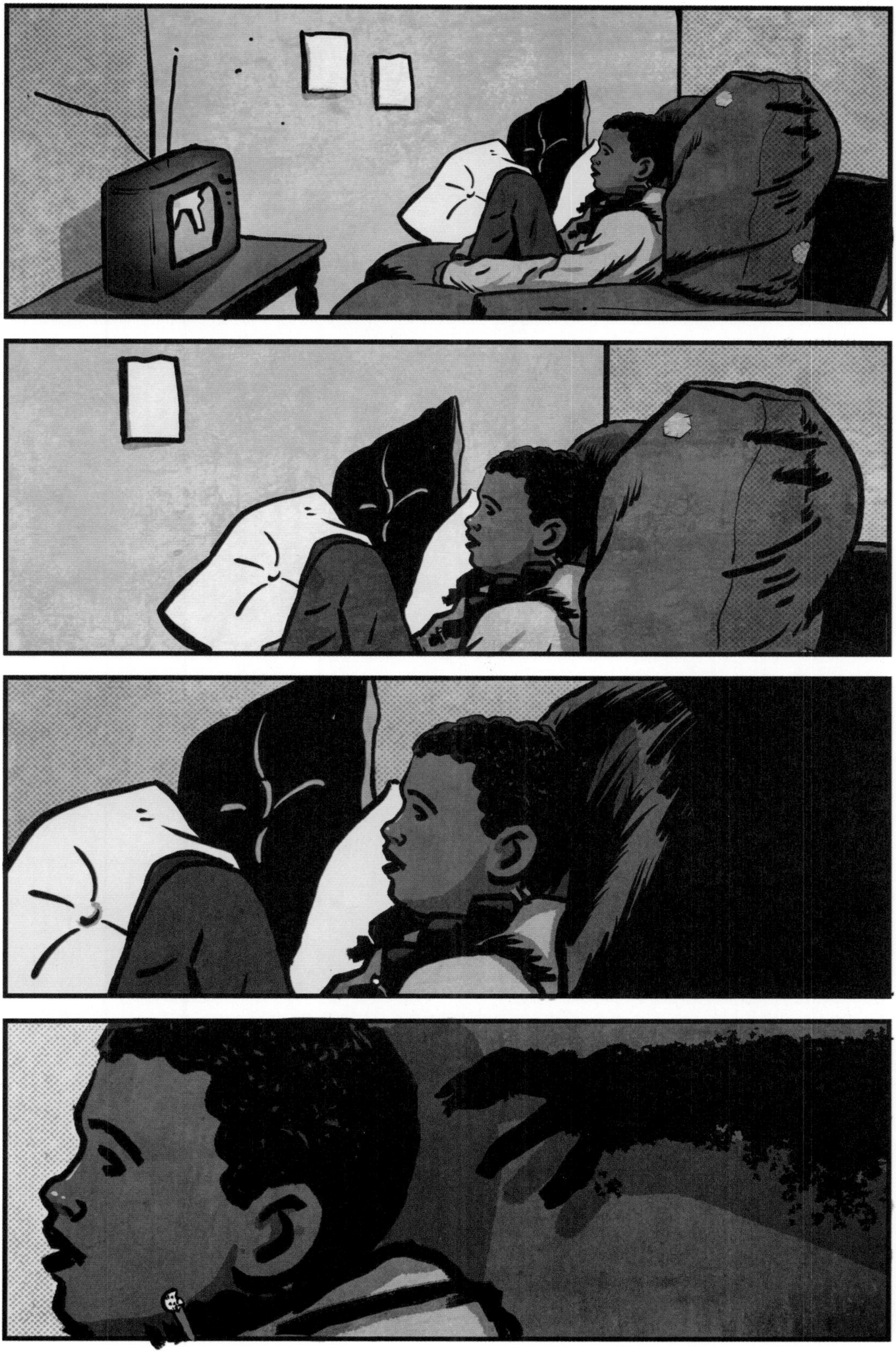

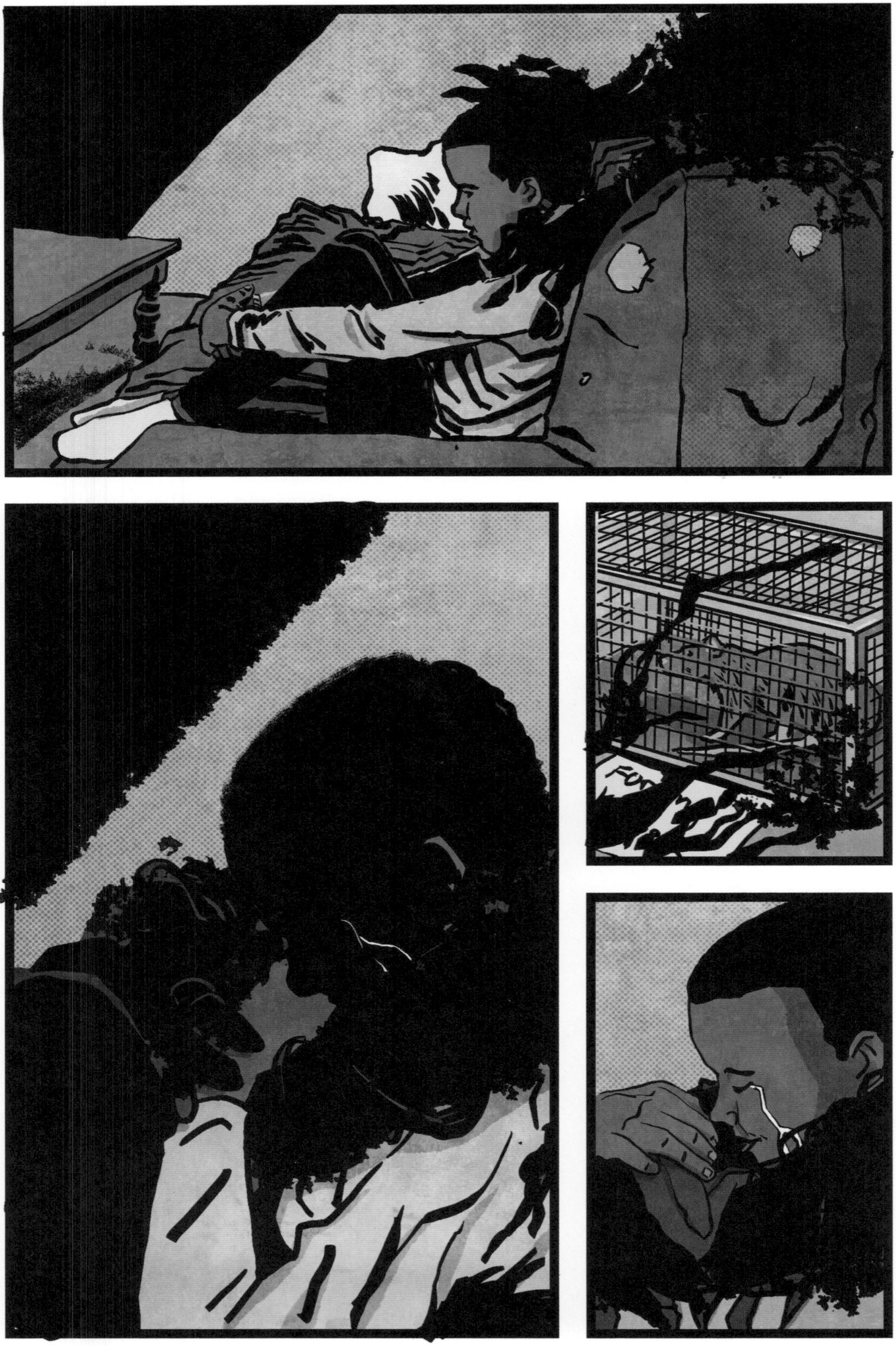

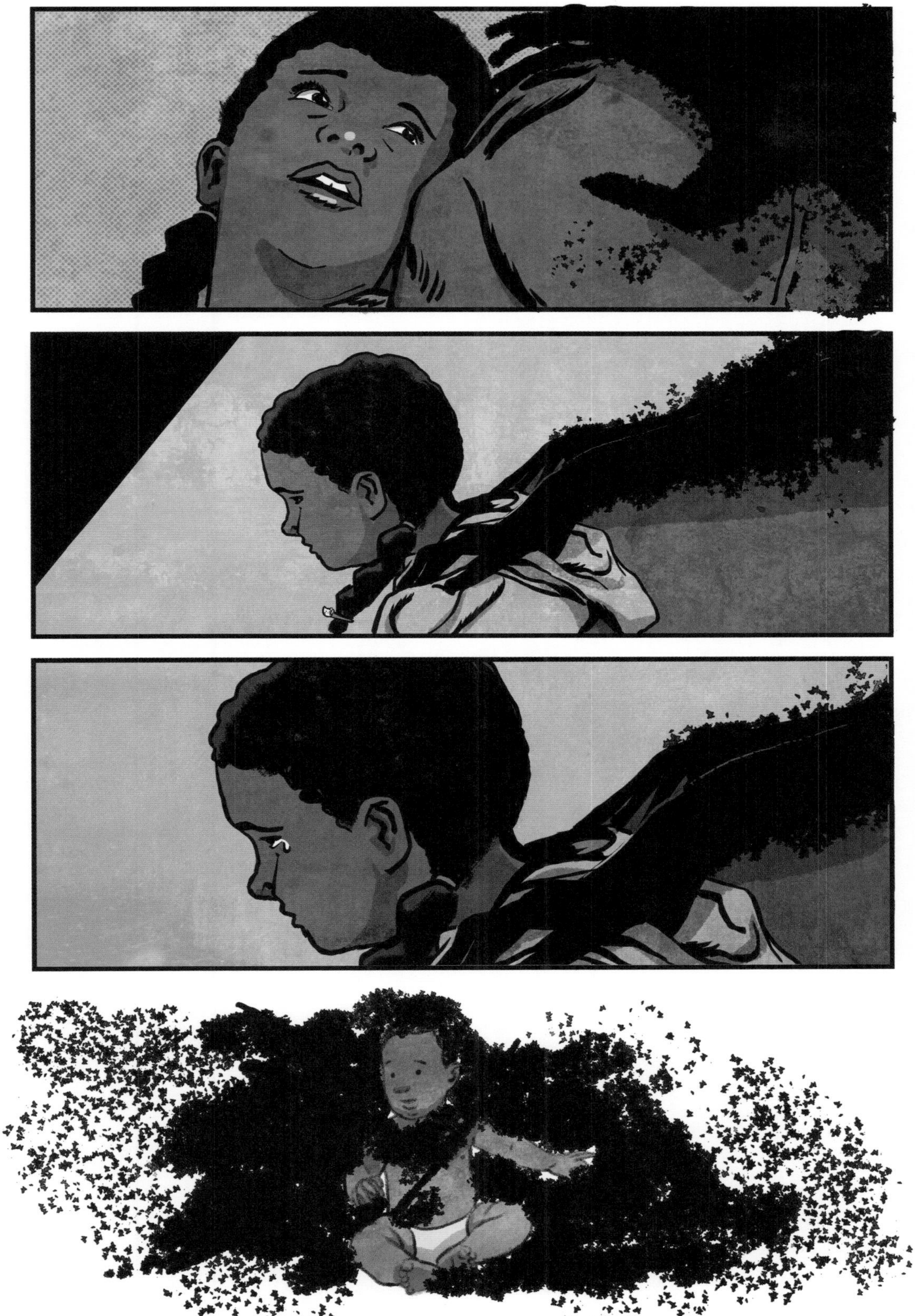

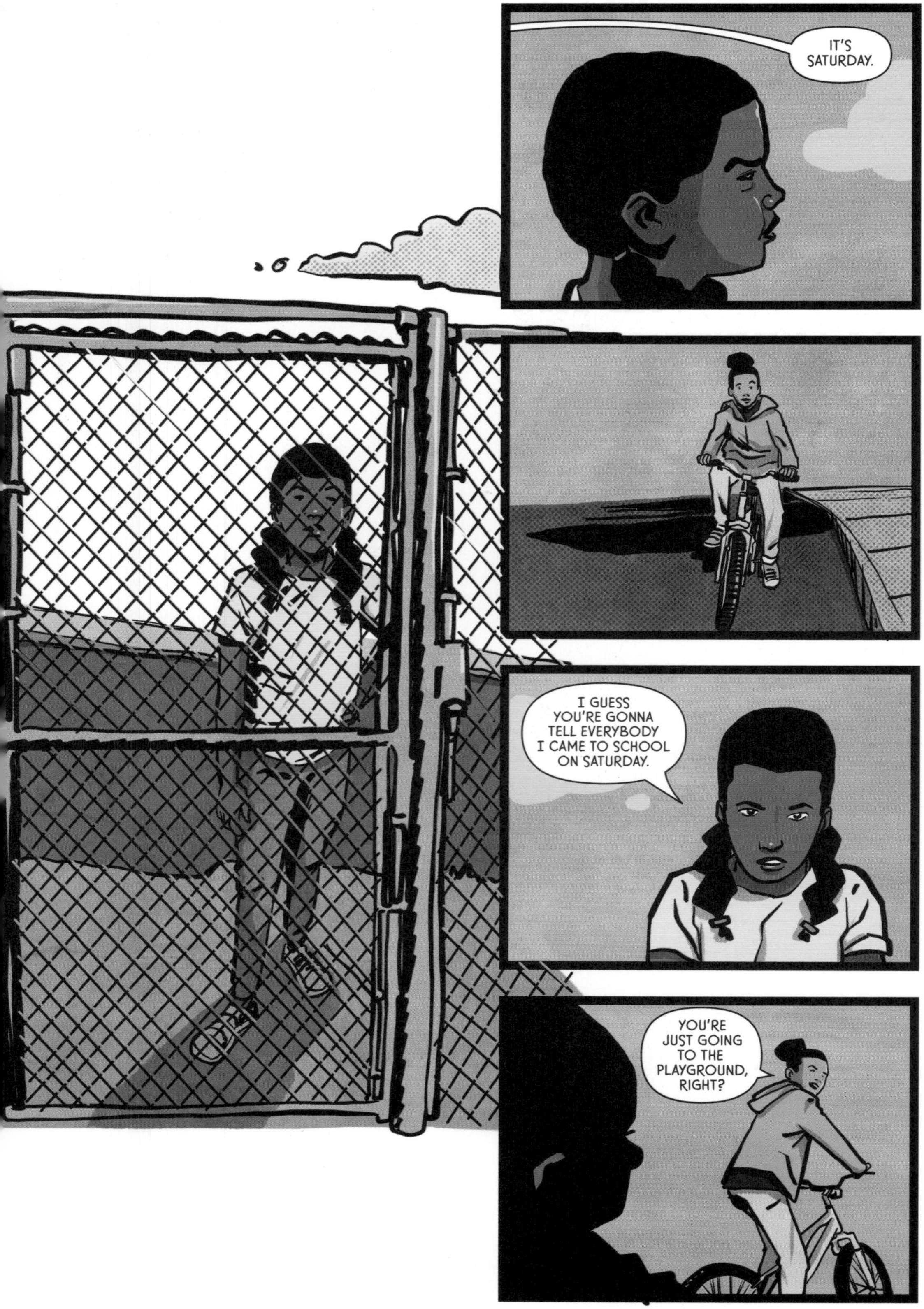
IT'S SATURDAY.
I GUESS YOU'RE GONNA TELL EVERYBODY I CAME TO SCHOOL ON SATURDAY.
YOU'RE JUST GOING TO THE PLAYGROUND, RIGHT?

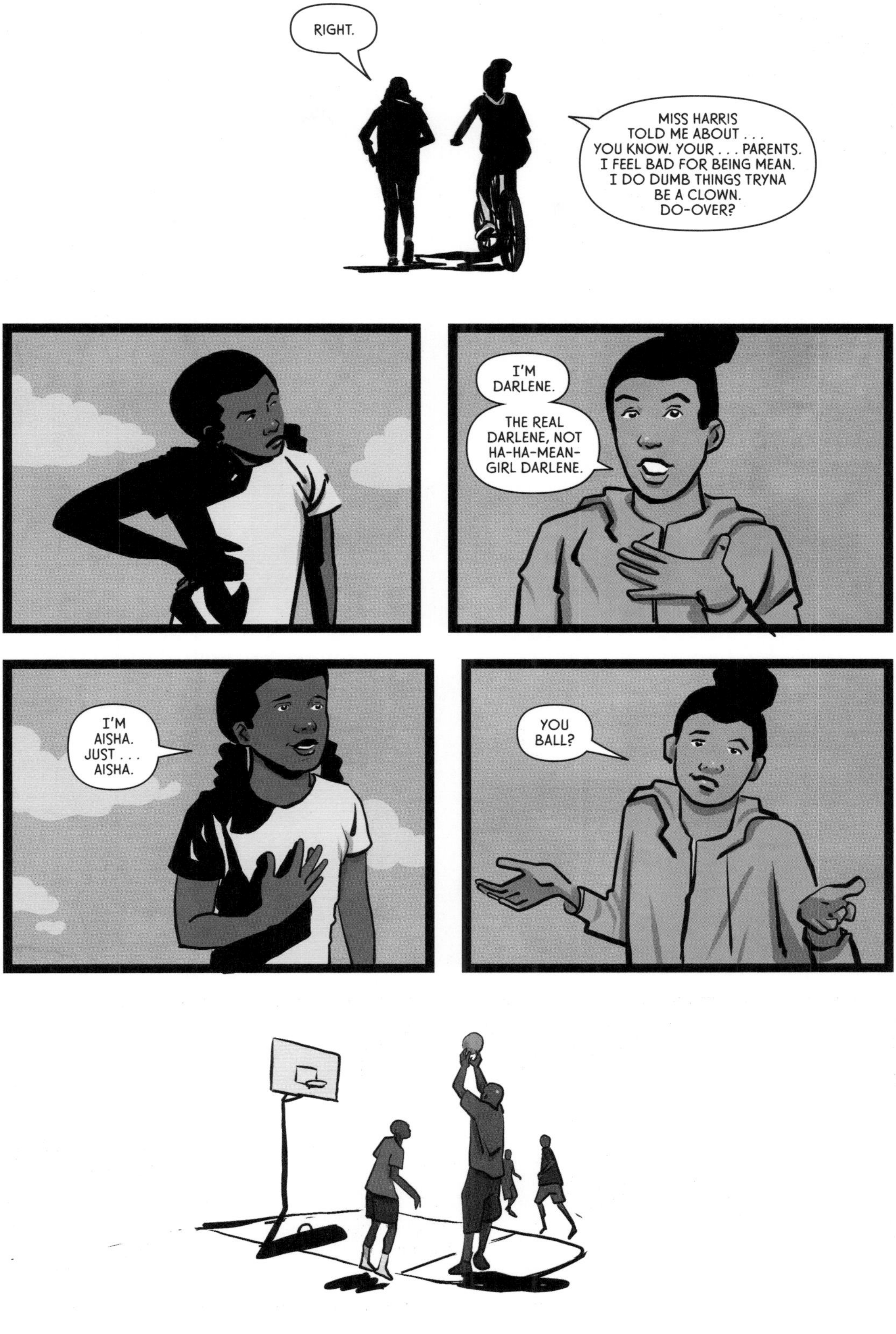
RIGHT.
MISS HARRIS TOLD ME ABOUT . . . YOU KNOW. YOUR . . . PARENTS. I FEEL BAD FOR BEING MEAN. I DO DUMB THINGS TRYNA BE A CLOWN. DO-OVER?
I'M DARLENE.
THE REAL DARLENE, NOT HA-HA-MEAN-GIRL DARLENE.
I'M AISHA. JUST . . . AISHA.
YOU BALL?

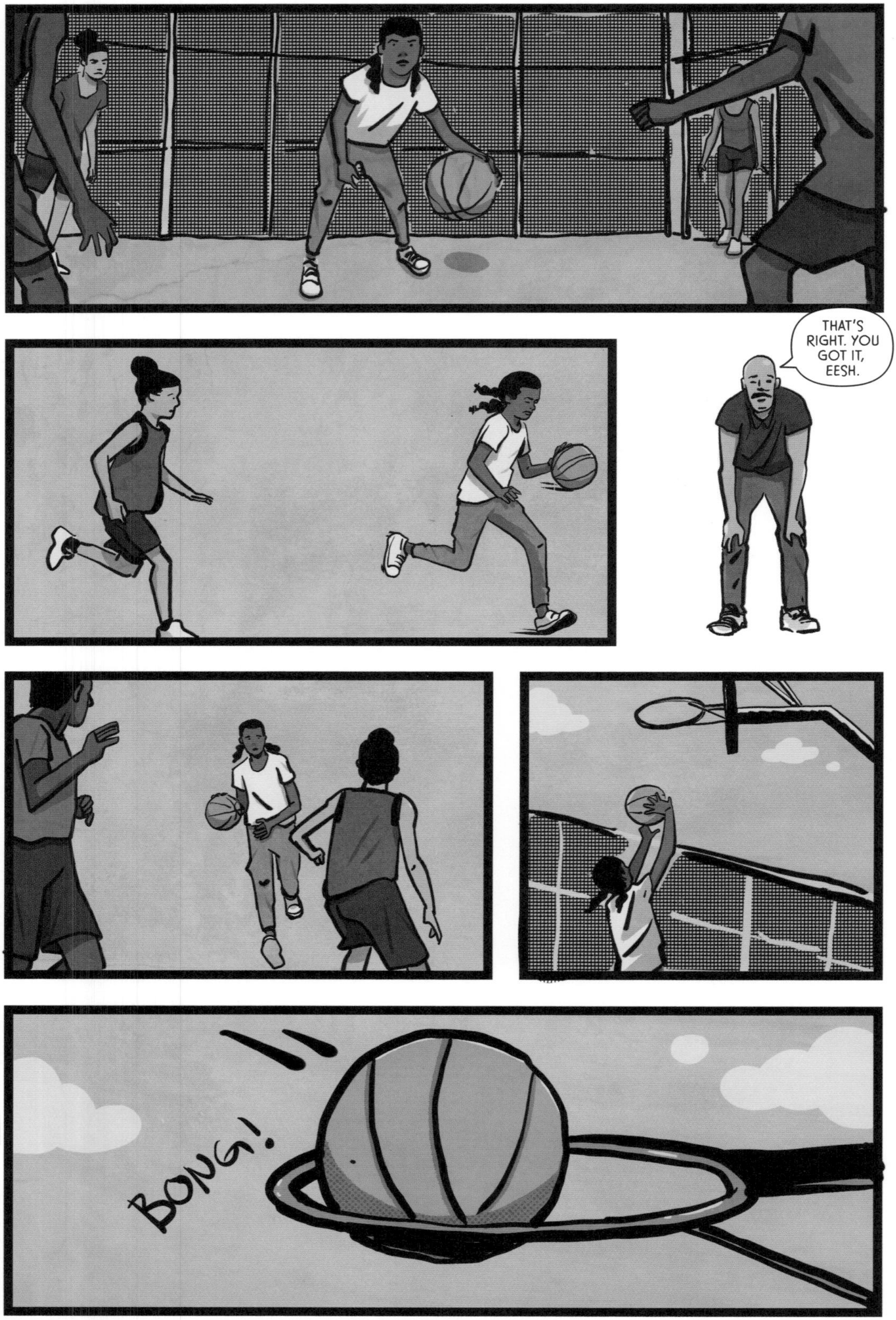
THAT'S RIGHT. YOU GOT IT, EESH.
BONG!

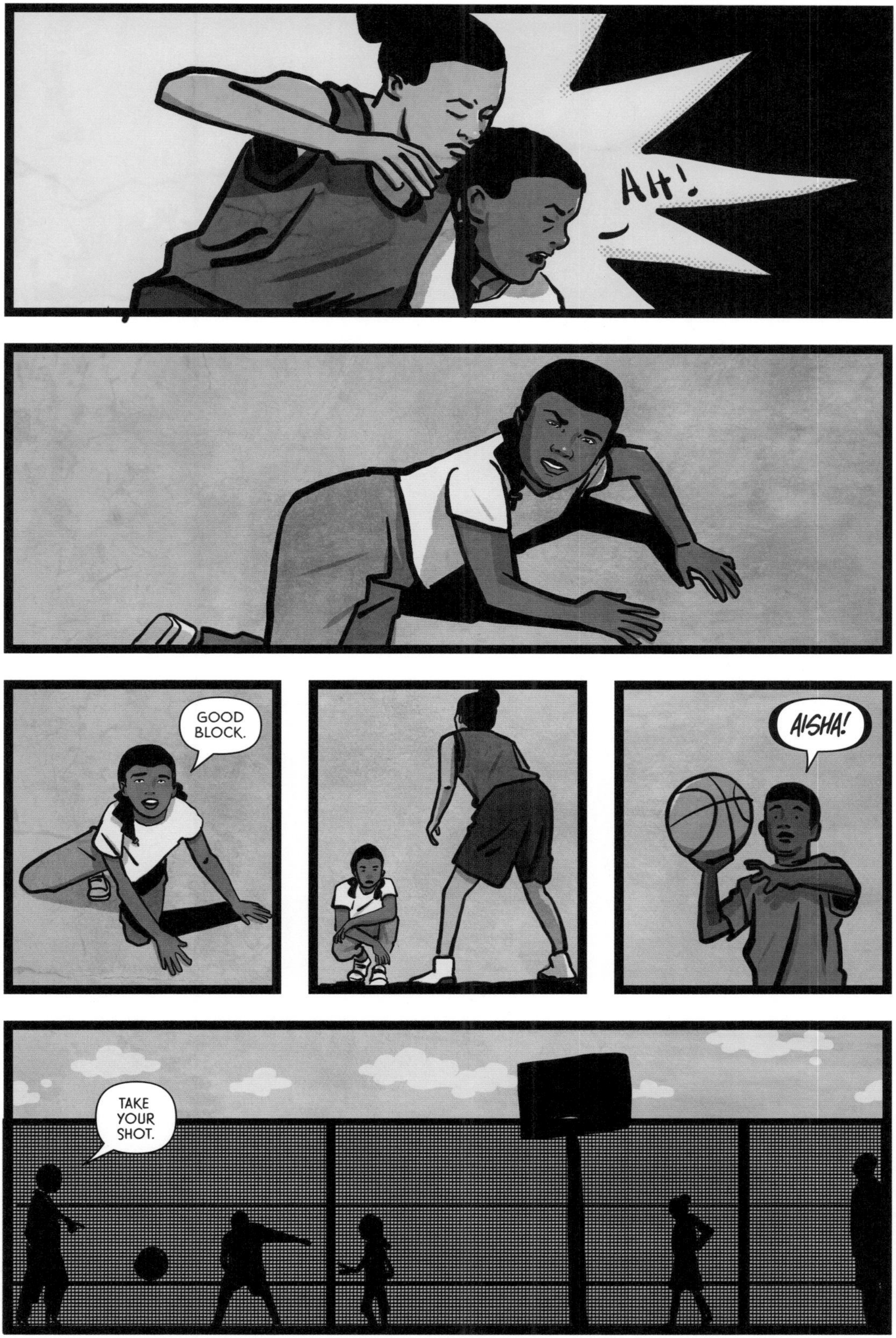
AH!
GOOD BLOCK.
AISHA!
TAKE YOUR SHOT.

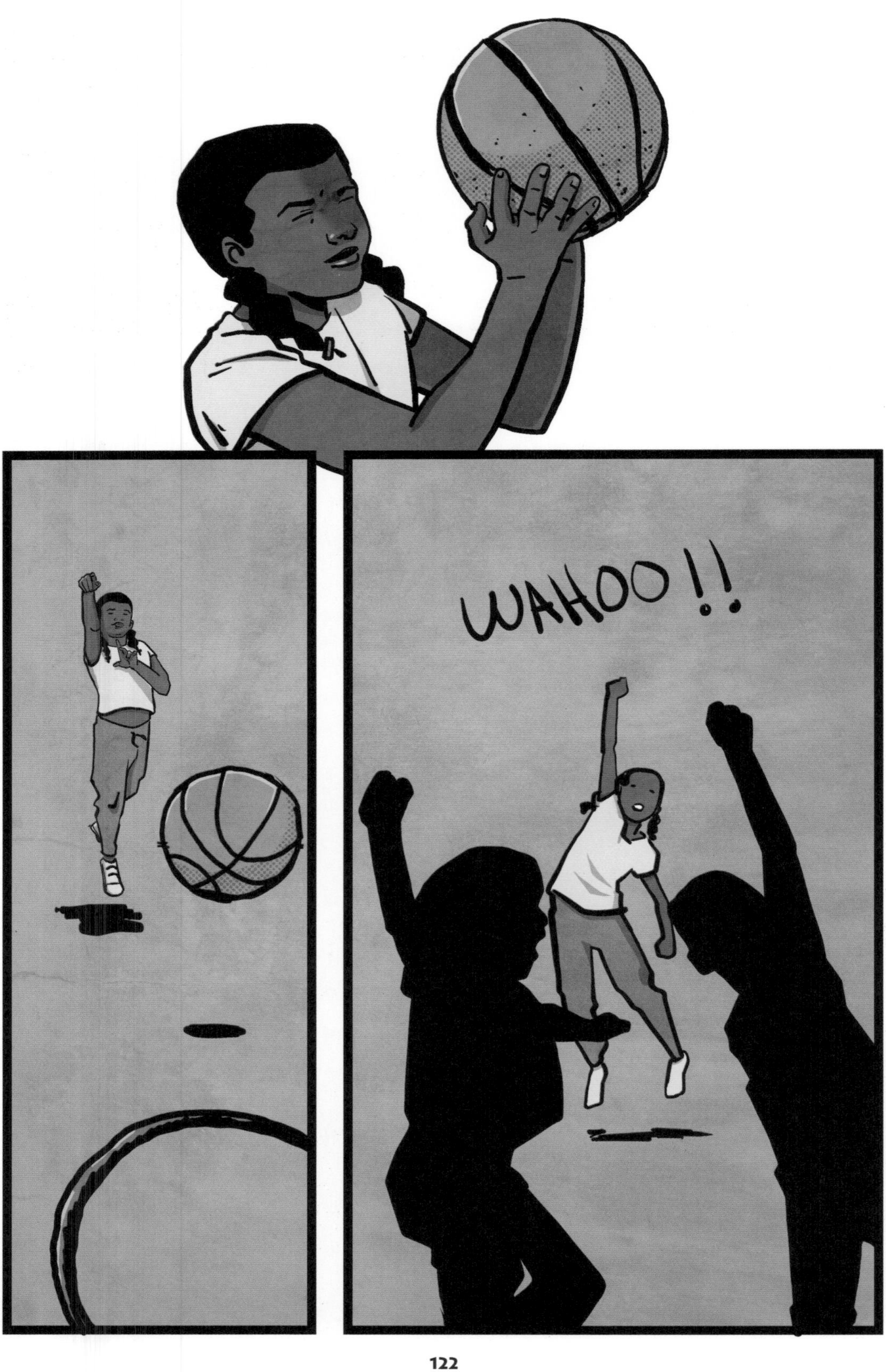
WAHOO!!

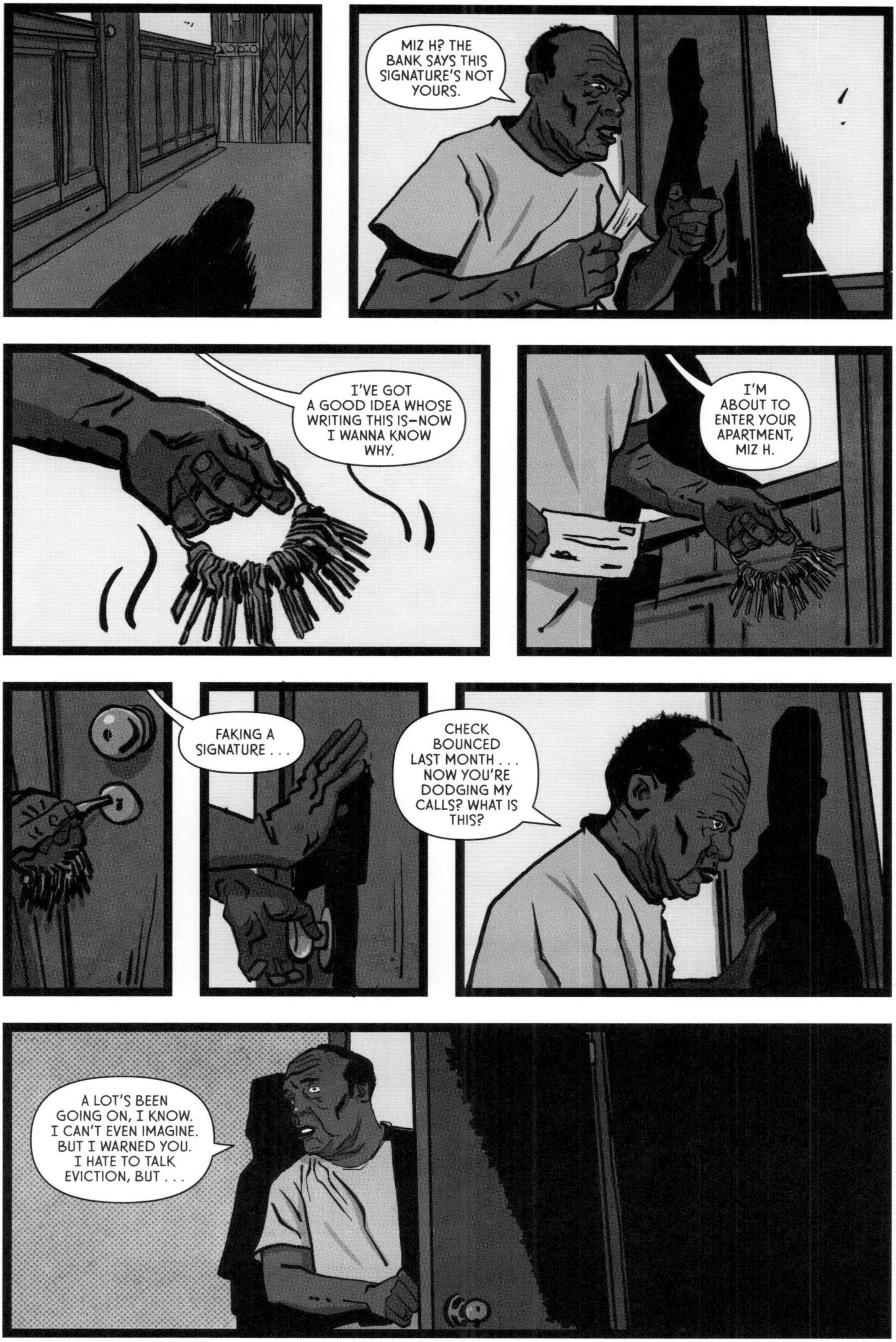
MIZ H? THE BANK SAYS THIS SIGNATURE'S NOT YOURS.
I'VE GOT A GOOD IDEA WHOSE WRITING THIS IS—NOW I WANNA KNOW WHY.
I'M ABOUT TO ENTER YOUR APARTMENT, MIZ H.
FAKING A SIGNATURE . . .
CHECK BOUNCED LAST MONTH . . . NOW YOU'RE DODGING MY CALLS? WHAT IS THIS?
A LOT'S BEEN GOING ON, I KNOW. I CAN'T EVEN IMAGINE. BUT I WARNED YOU. I HATE TO TALK EVICTION, BUT . . .

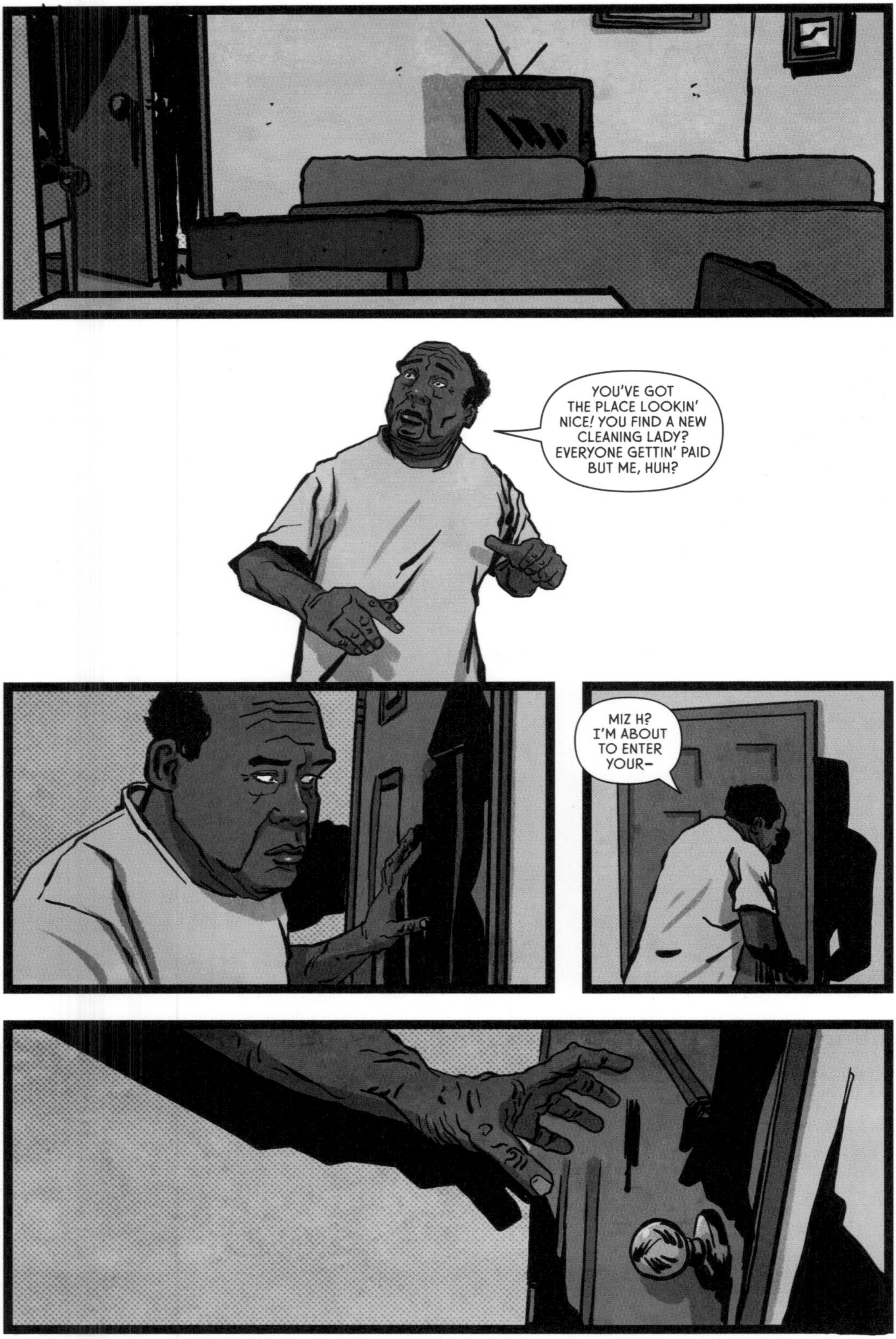
YOU'VE GOT THE PLACE LOOKIN' NICE! YOU FIND A NEW CLEANING LADY? EVERYONE GETTIN' PAID BUT ME, HUH?
MIZ H? I'M ABOUT TO ENTER YOUR–

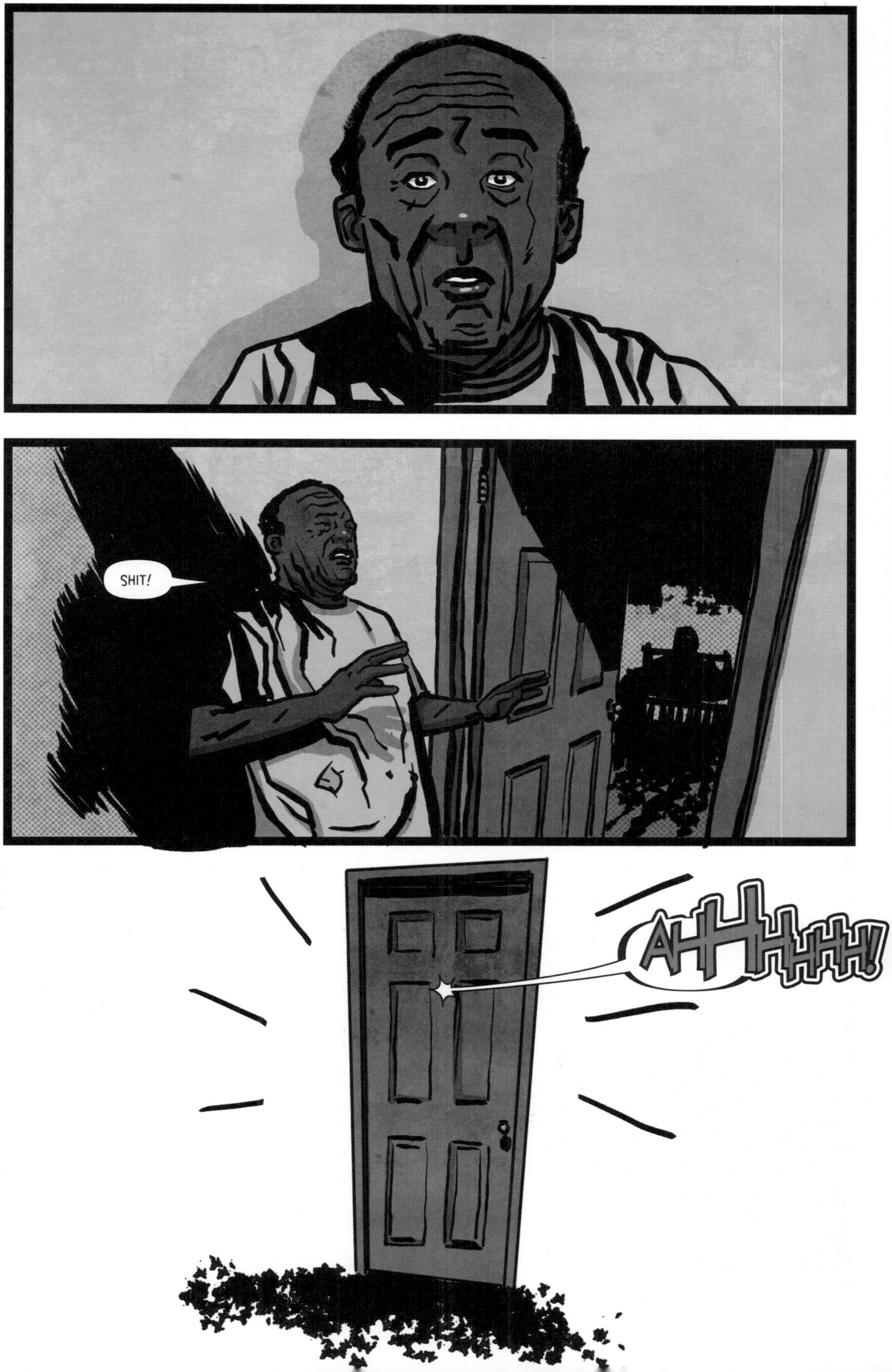
SHIT!
AHHHHHH!

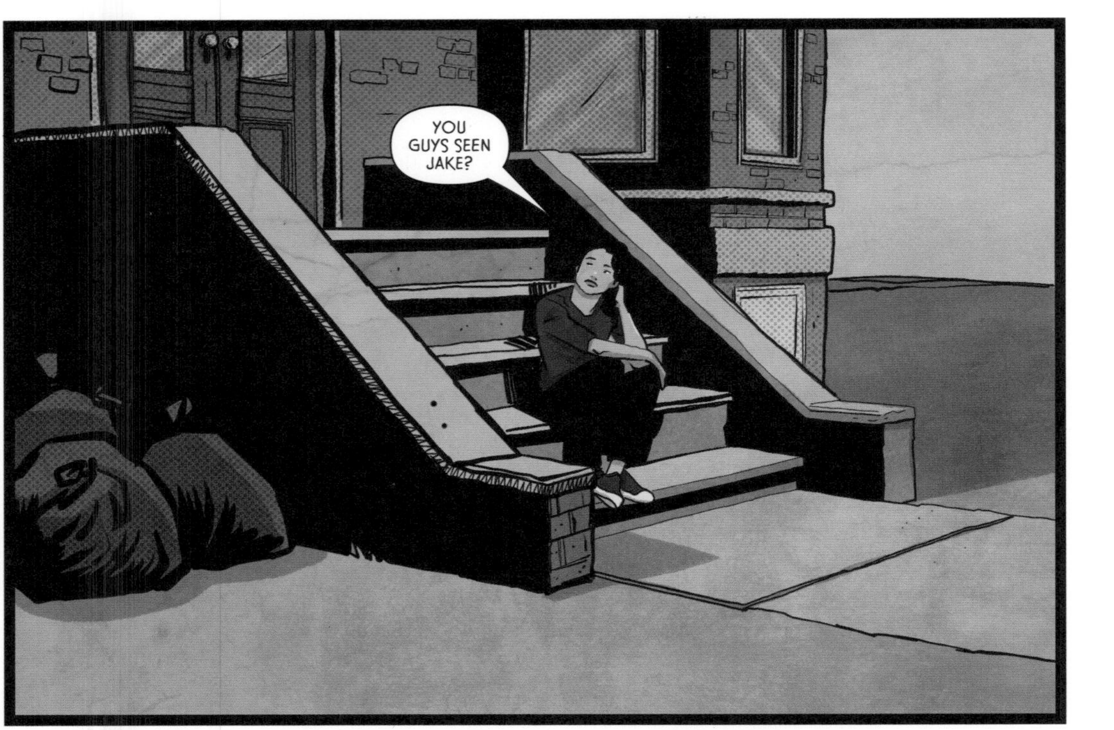
YOU GUYS SEEN JAKE?

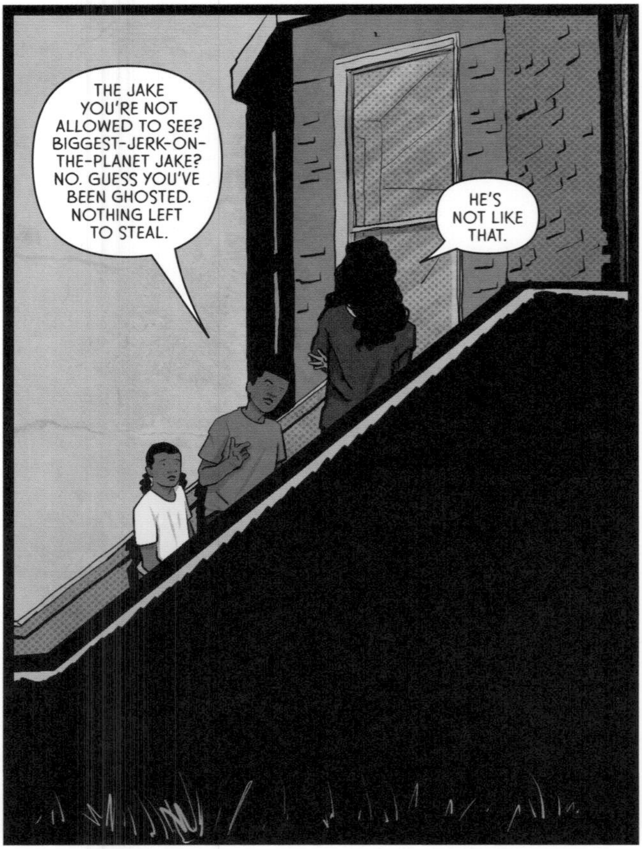
THE JAKE YOU'RE NOT ALLOWED TO SEE? BIGGEST-JERK-ON-THE-PLANET JAKE? NO. GUESS YOU'VE BEEN GHOSTED. NOTHING LEFT TO STEAL.
HE'S NOT LIKE THAT.

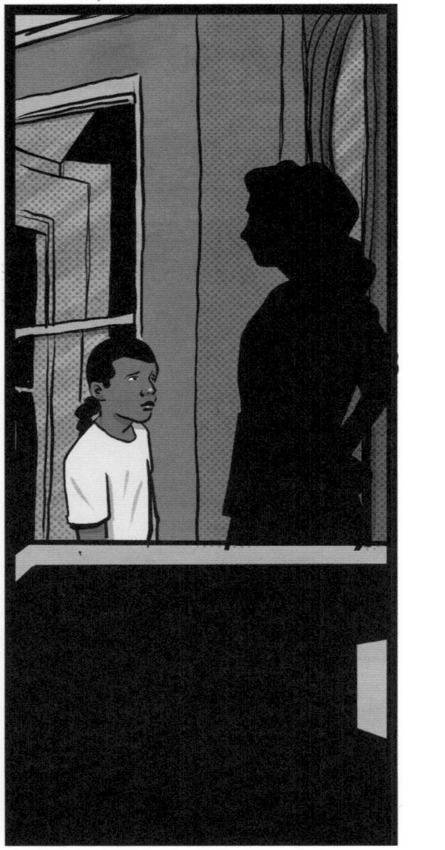

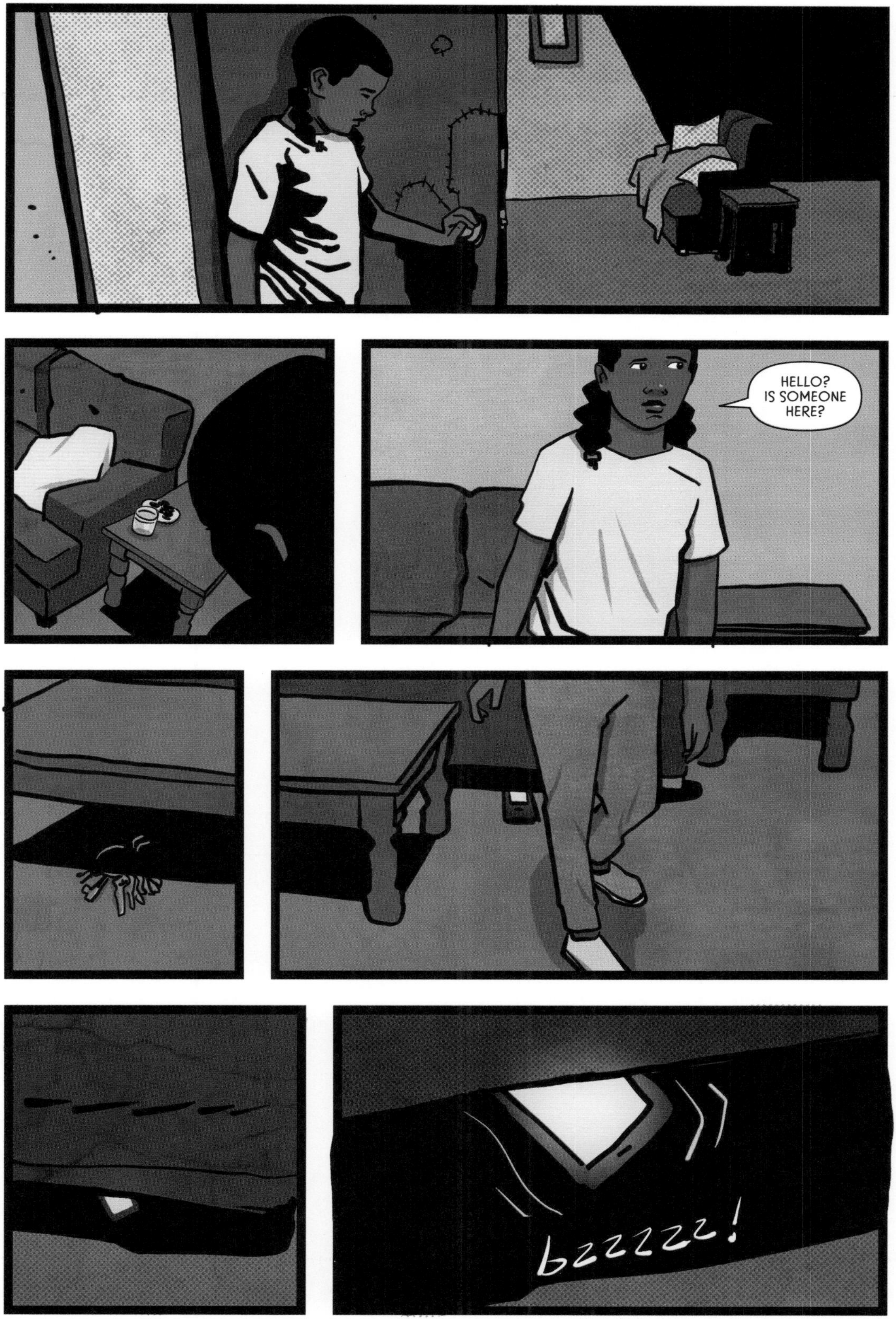
HELLO? IS SOMEONE HERE?
bzzzzz!

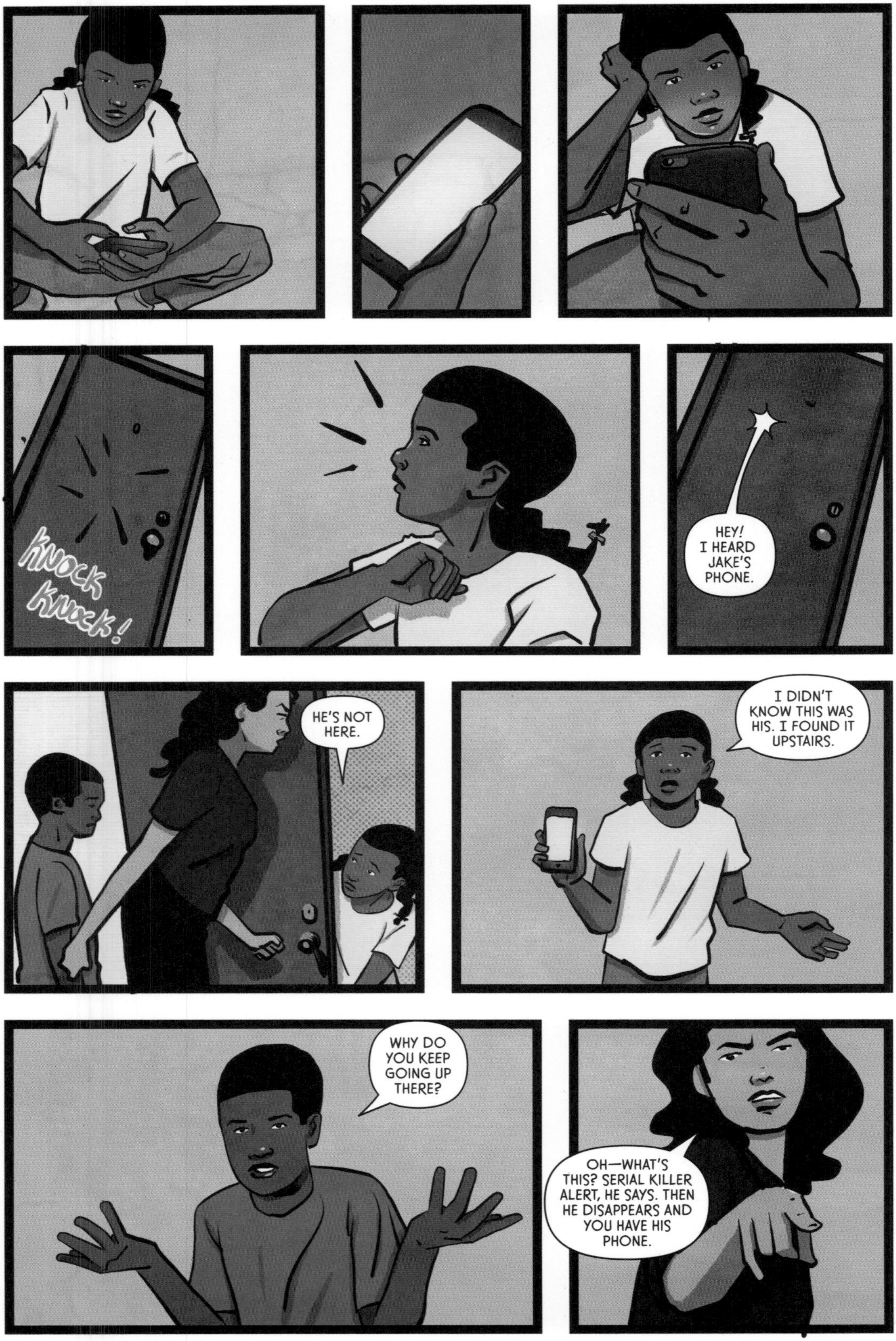
KNOCK KNOCK!
HEY! I HEARD JAKE'S PHONE.
HE'S NOT HERE.
I DIDN'T KNOW THIS WAS HIS. I FOUND IT UPSTAIRS.
WHY DO YOU KEEP GOING UP THERE?
OH—WHAT'S THIS? SERIAL KILLER ALERT, HE SAYS. THEN HE DISAPPEARS AND YOU HAVE HIS PHONE.

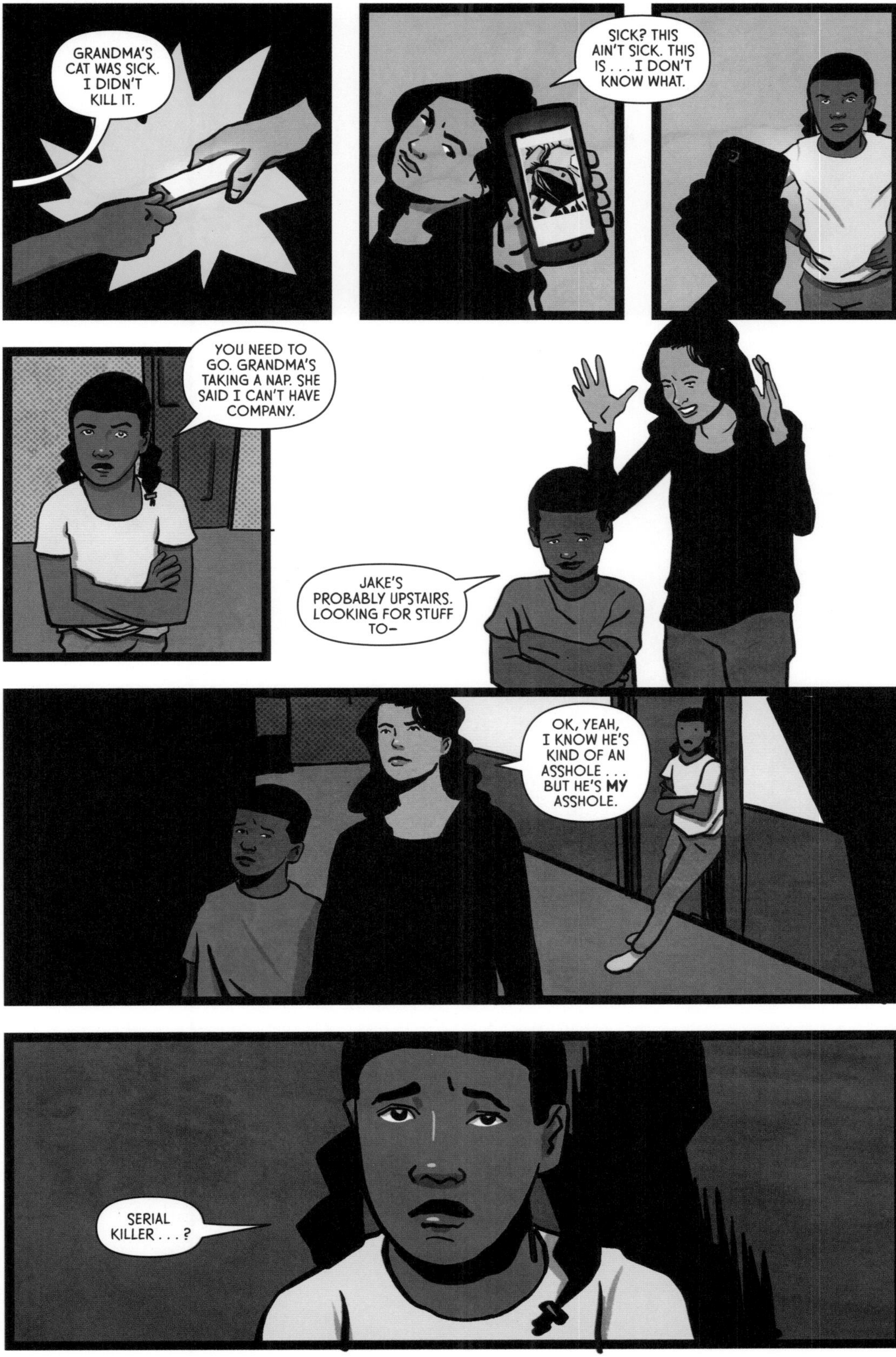
GRANDMA'S CAT WAS SICK. I DIDN'T KILL IT.
SICK? THIS AIN'T SICK. THIS IS . . . I DON'T KNOW WHAT.
YOU NEED TO GO. GRANDMA'S TAKING A NAP. SHE SAID I CAN'T HAVE COMPANY.
JAKE'S PROBABLY UPSTAIRS. LOOKING FOR STUFF TO–
OK, YEAH, I KNOW HE'S KIND OF AN ASSHOLE . . . BUT HE'S **MY** ASSHOLE.
SERIAL KILLER . . . ?

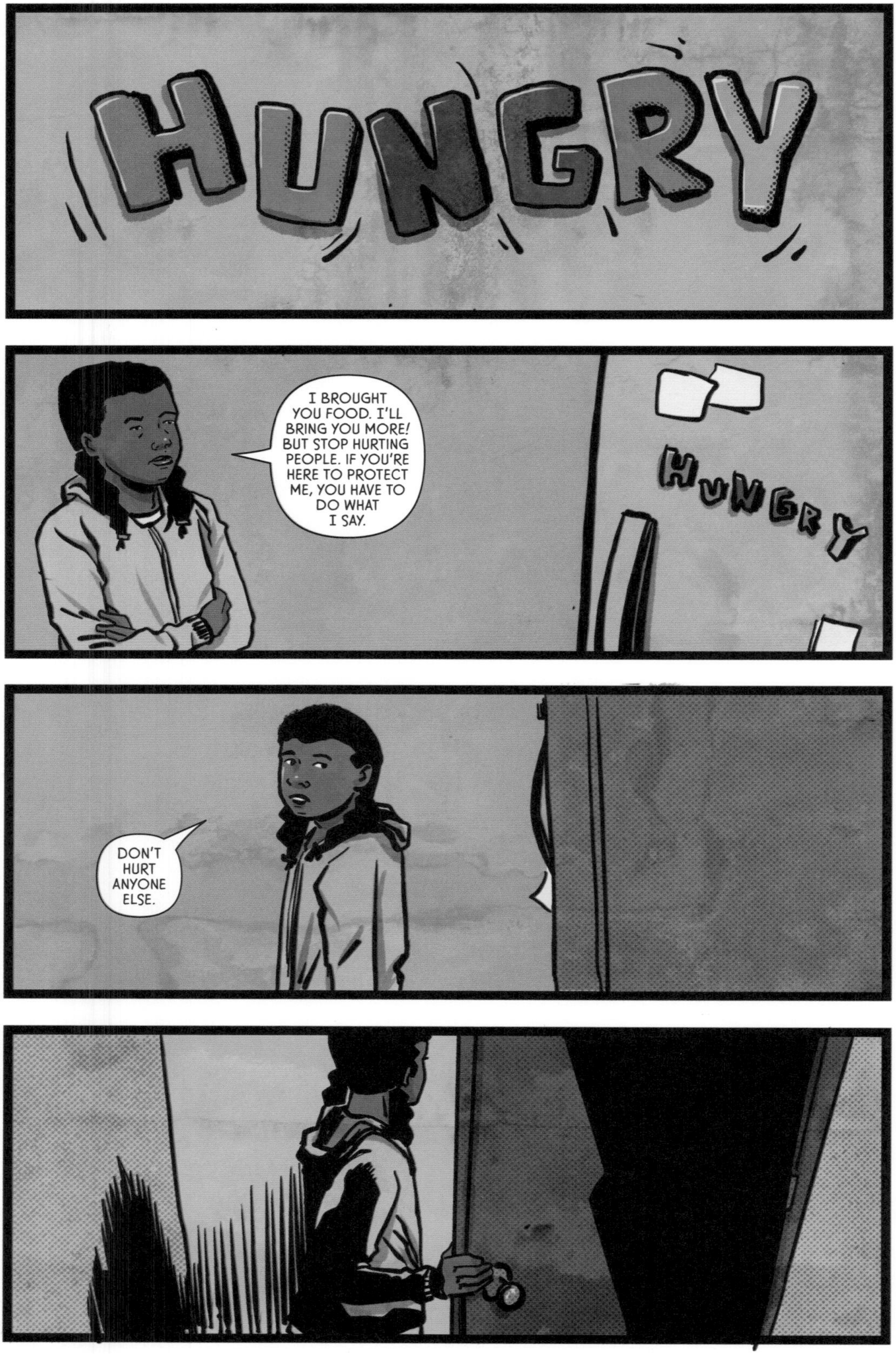
HUNGRY
I BROUGHT YOU FOOD. I'LL BRING YOU MORE! BUT STOP HURTING PEOPLE. IF YOU'RE HERE TO PROTECT ME, YOU HAVE TO DO WHAT I SAY.
HUNGRY
DON'T HURT ANYONE ELSE.

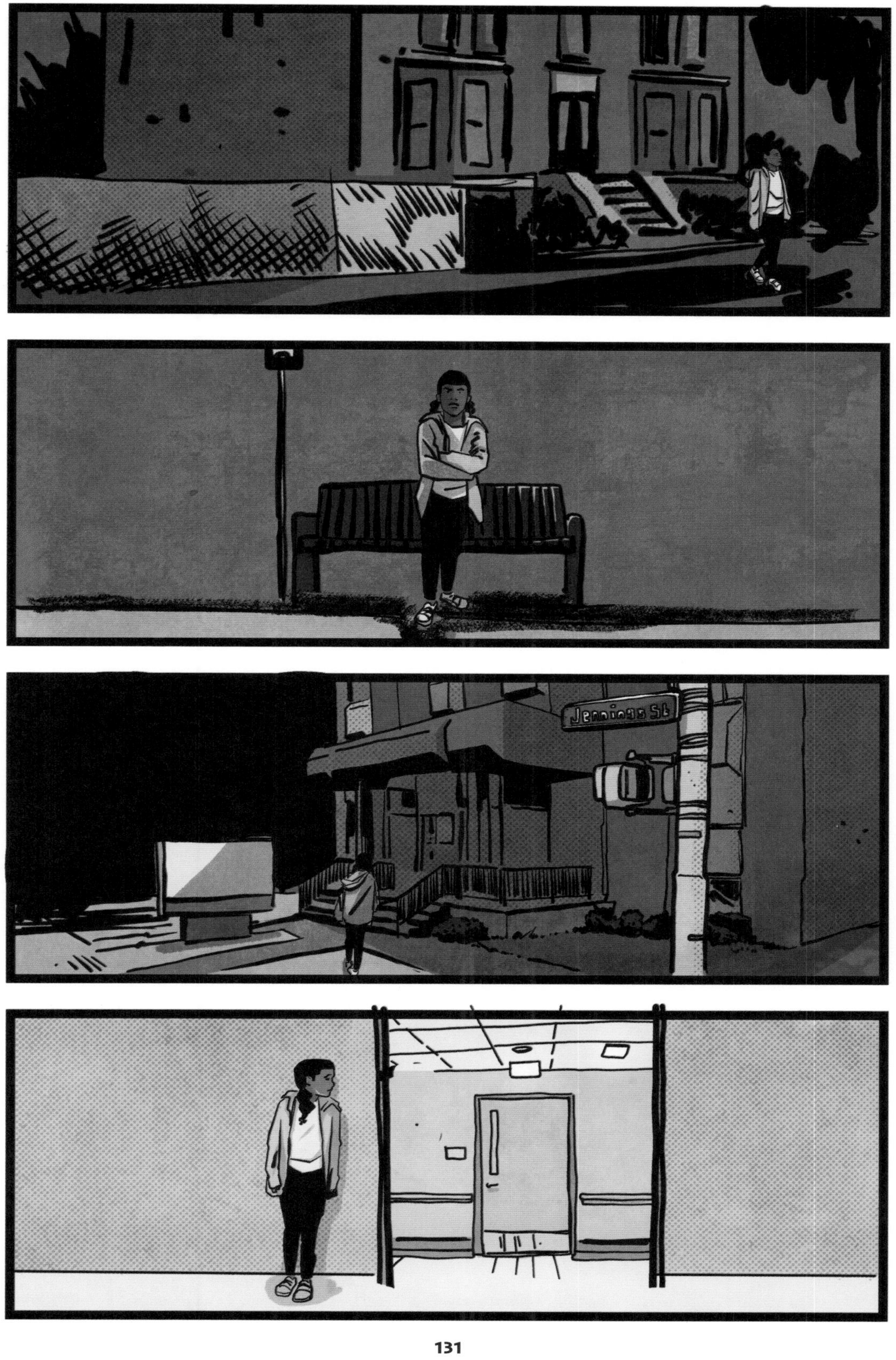
Jennings St

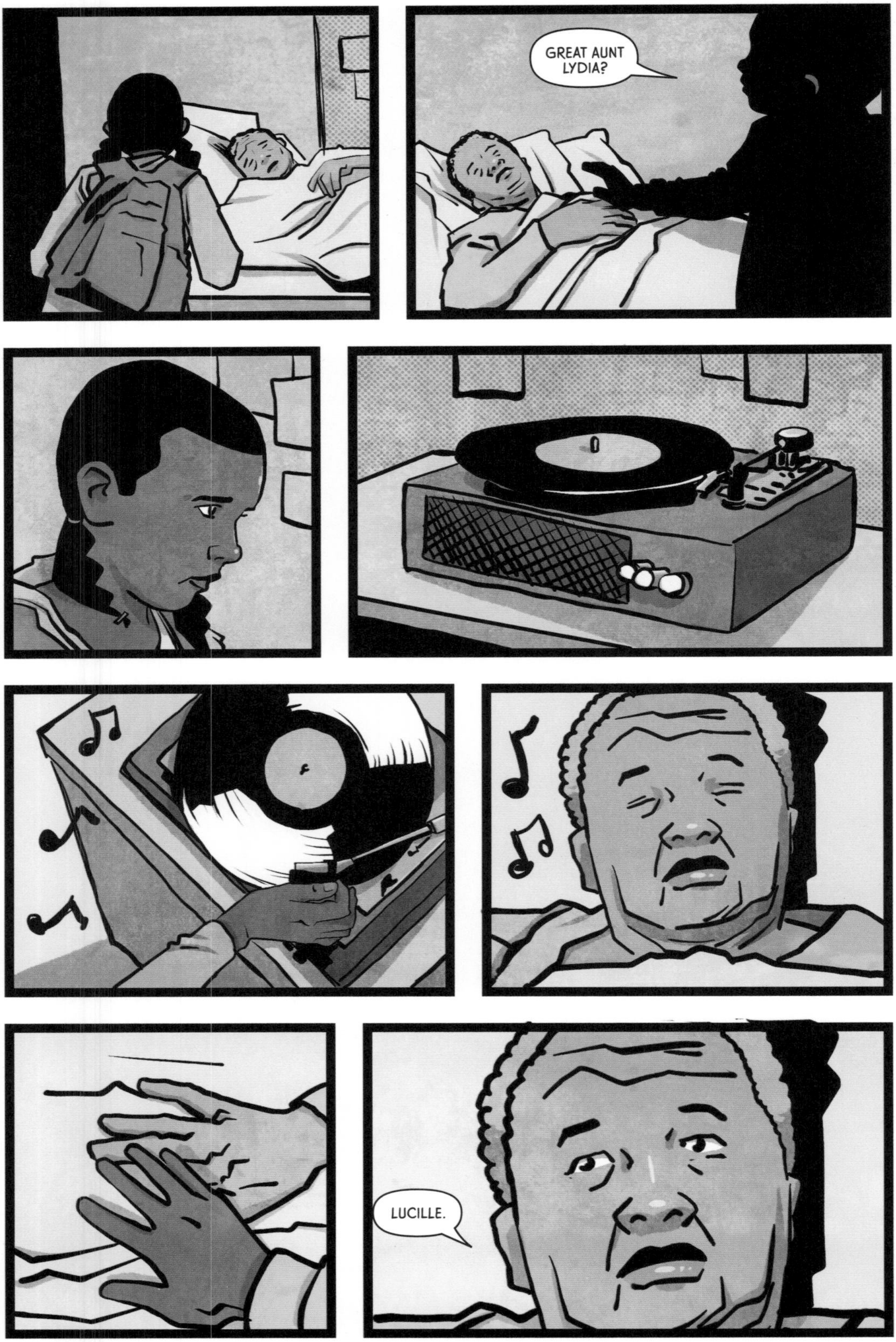
GREAT AUNT LYDIA?
LUCILLE.

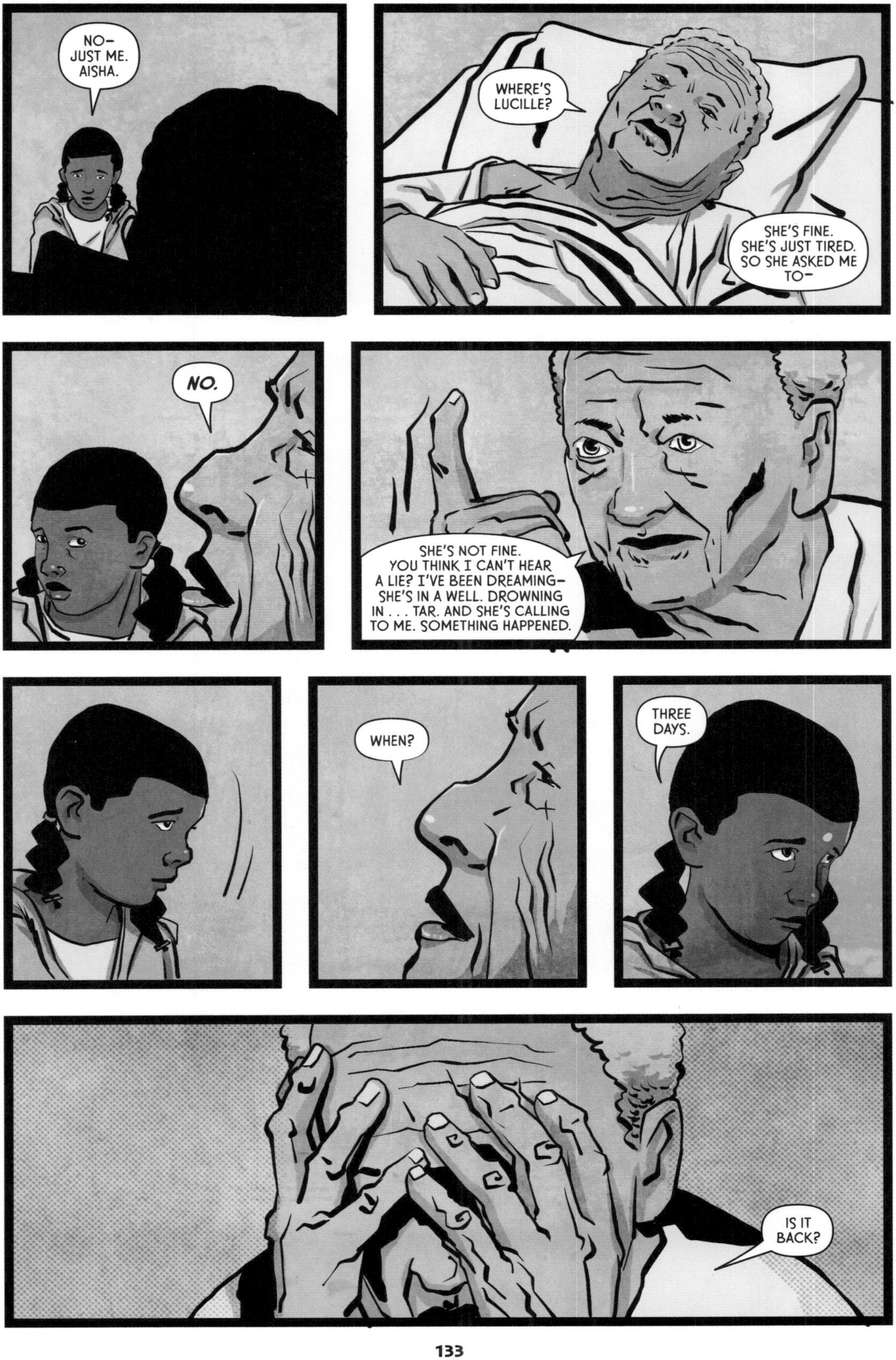
NO— JUST ME. AISHA.
WHERE'S LUCILLE?
SHE'S FINE. SHE'S JUST TIRED. SO SHE ASKED ME TO—
NO.
SHE'S NOT FINE. YOU THINK I CAN'T HEAR A LIE? I'VE BEEN DREAMING— SHE'S IN A WELL. DROWNING IN . . . TAR. AND SHE'S CALLING TO ME. SOMETHING HAPPENED.
WHEN?
THREE DAYS.
IS IT BACK?

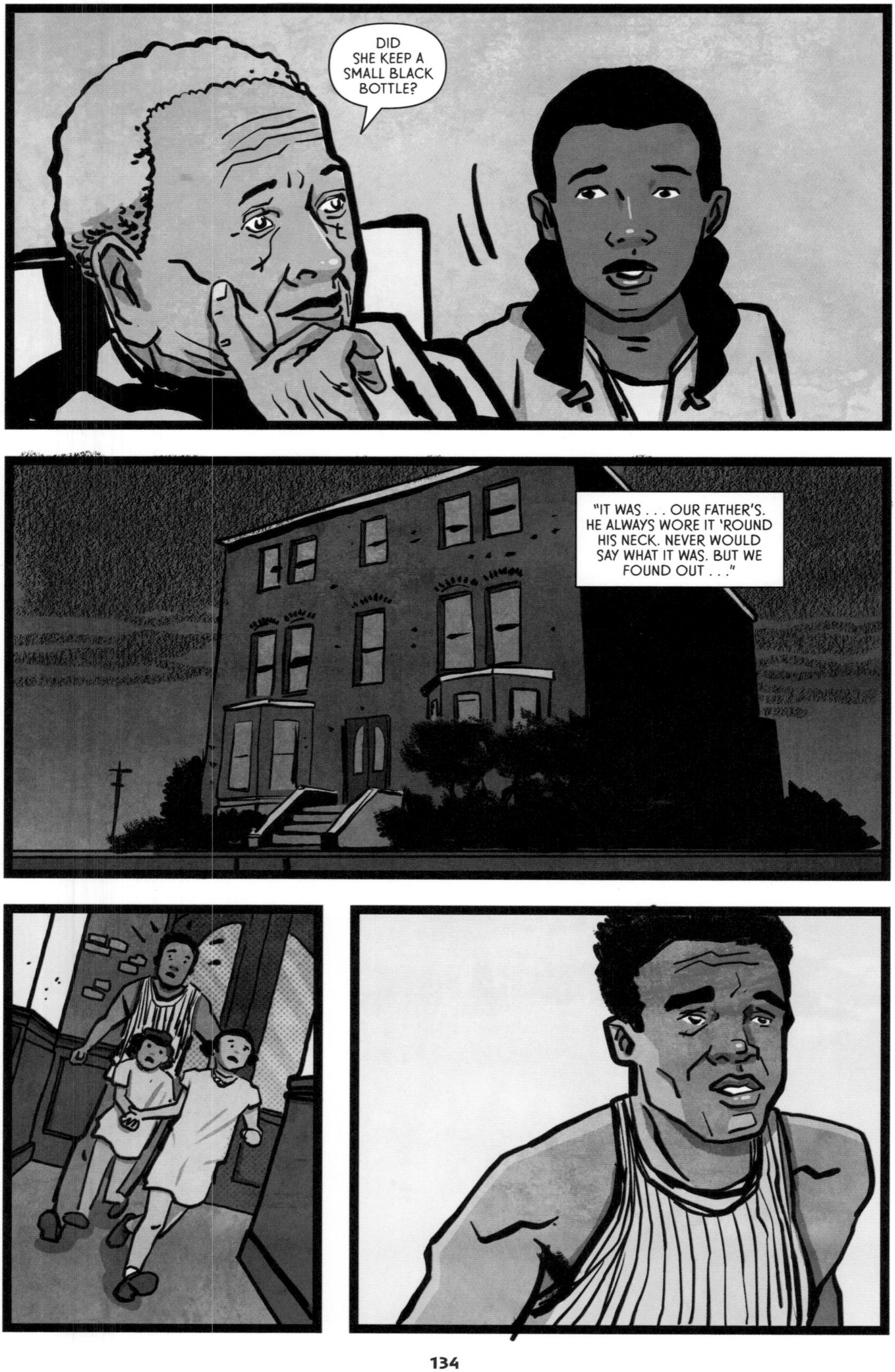
DID SHE KEEP A SMALL BLACK BOTTLE?
"IT WAS . . . OUR FATHER'S. HE ALWAYS WORE IT 'ROUND HIS NECK. NEVER WOULD SAY WHAT IT WAS. BUT WE FOUND OUT . . ."

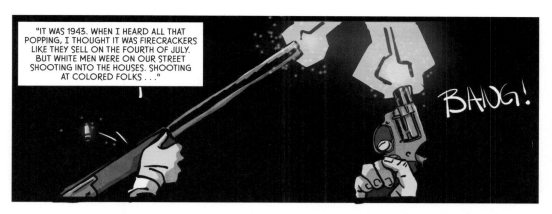

"IT WAS 1943. WHEN I HEARD ALL THAT POPPING, I THOUGHT IT WAS FIRECRACKERS LIKE THEY SELL ON THE FOURTH OF JULY. BUT WHITE MEN WERE ON OUR STREET SHOOTING INTO THE HOUSES. SHOOTING AT COLORED FOLKS . . ."

BANG!

KRASH!

HUSH, GIRLS. IT'LL BE ALL RIGHT—PROMISE. I'M GONNA HIDE YOU, BUT DON'T MAKE A SOUND.

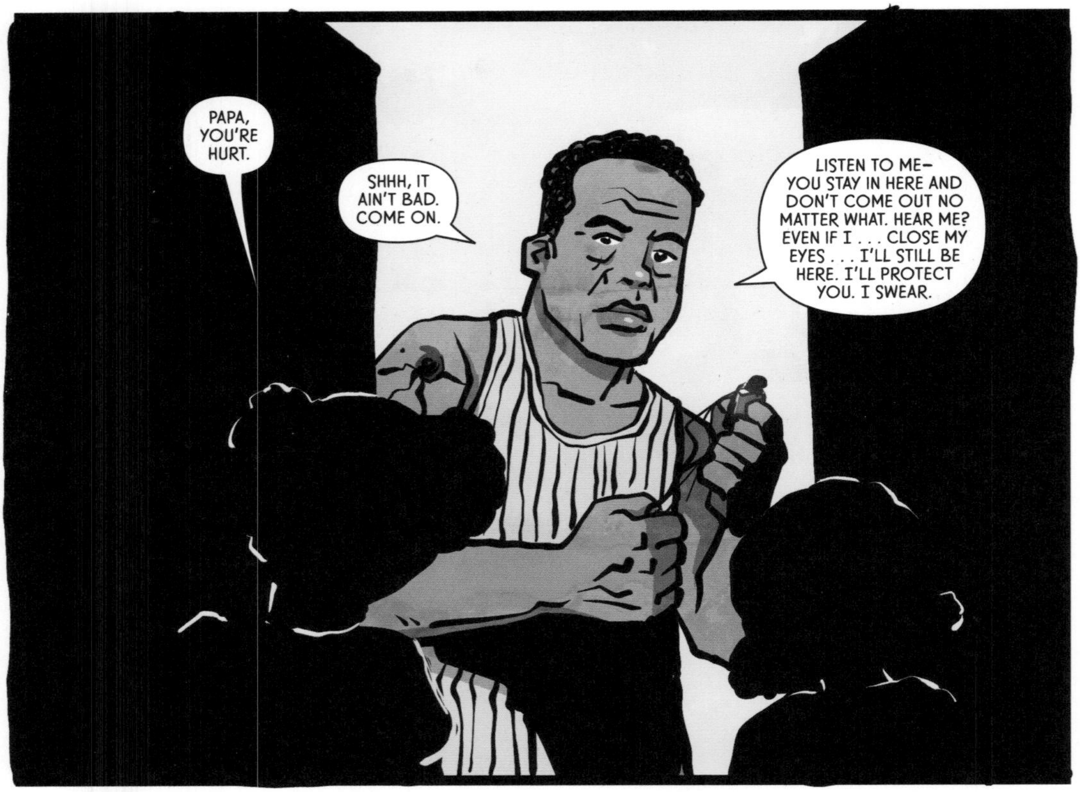
PAPA, YOU'RE HURT.
SHHH, IT AIN'T BAD. COME ON.
LISTEN TO ME— YOU STAY IN HERE AND DON'T COME OUT NO MATTER WHAT. HEAR ME? EVEN IF I . . . CLOSE MY EYES . . . I'LL STILL BE HERE. I'LL PROTECT YOU. I SWEAR.

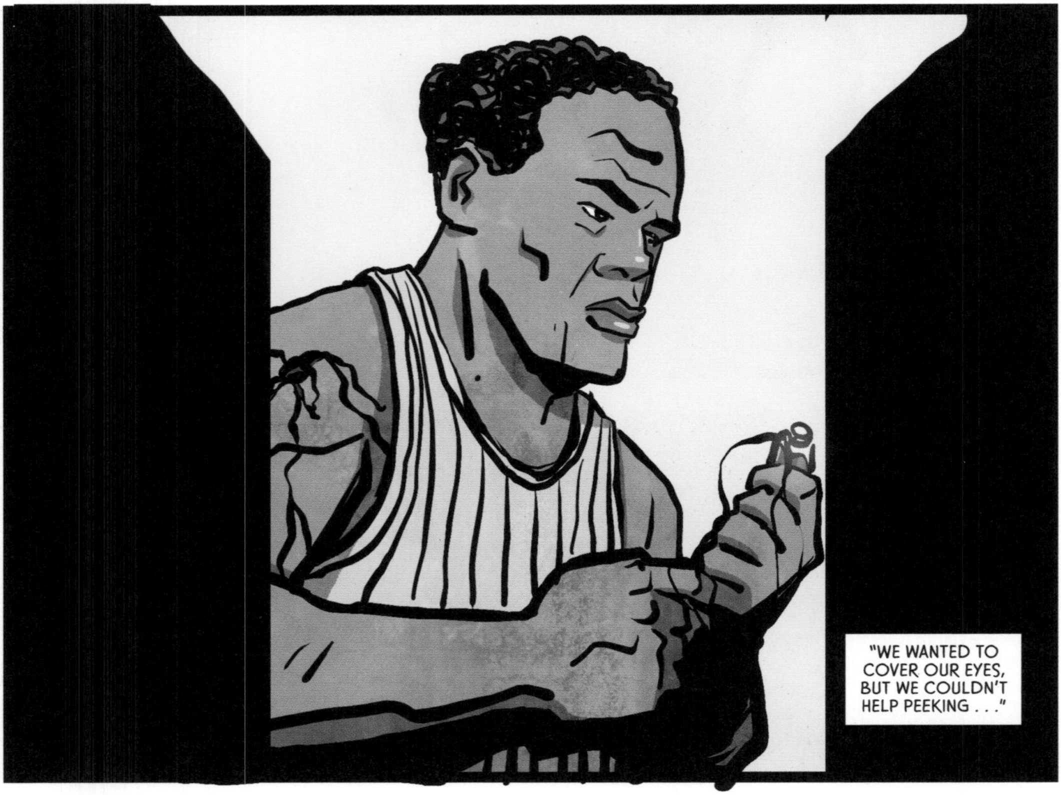
"WE WANTED TO COVER OUR EYES, BUT WE COULDN'T HELP PEEKING . . ."

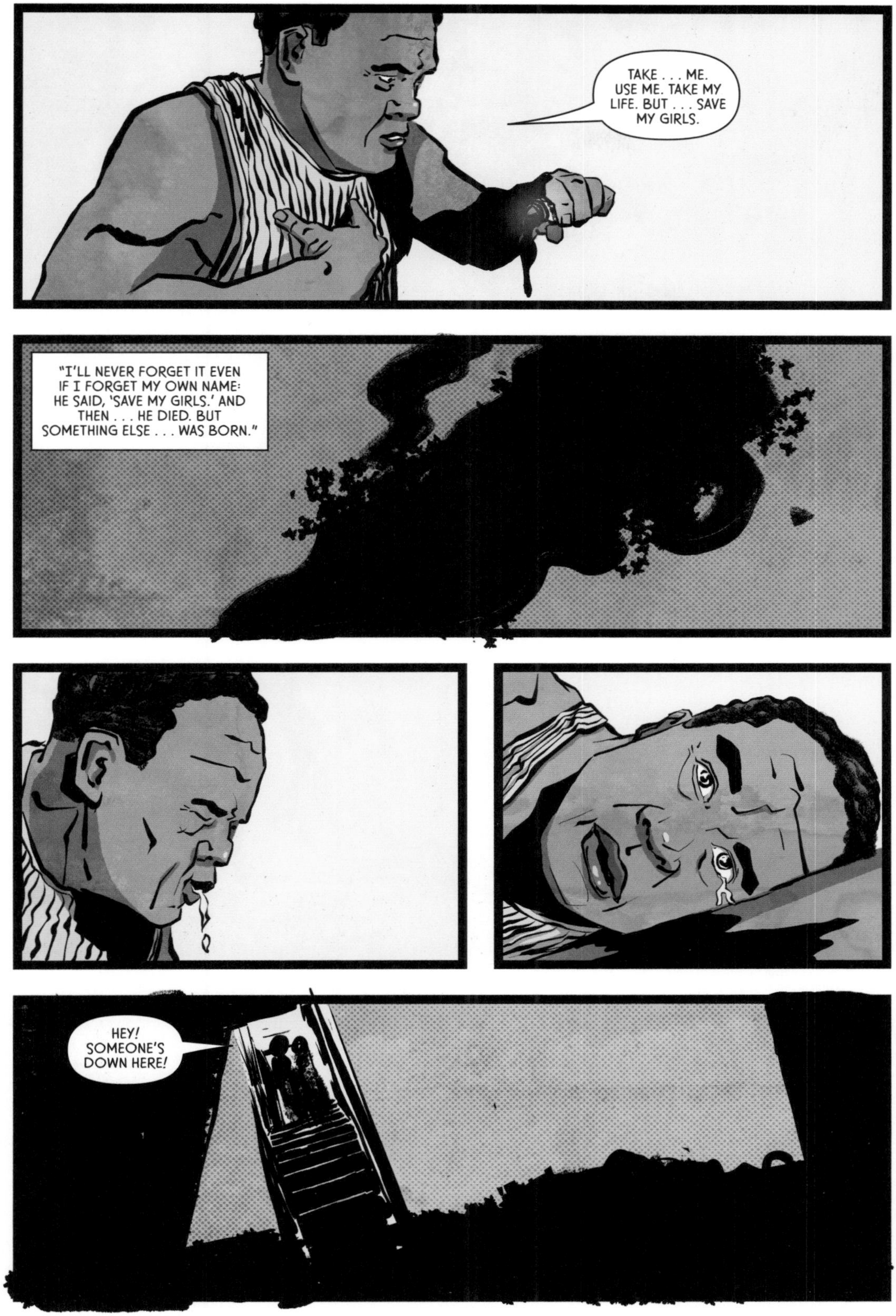
TAKE . . . ME. USE ME. TAKE MY LIFE. BUT . . . SAVE MY GIRLS.
"I'LL NEVER FORGET IT EVEN IF I FORGET MY OWN NAME: HE SAID, 'SAVE MY GIRLS.' AND THEN . . . HE DIED. BUT SOMETHING ELSE . . . WAS BORN."
HEY! SOMEONE'S DOWN HERE!

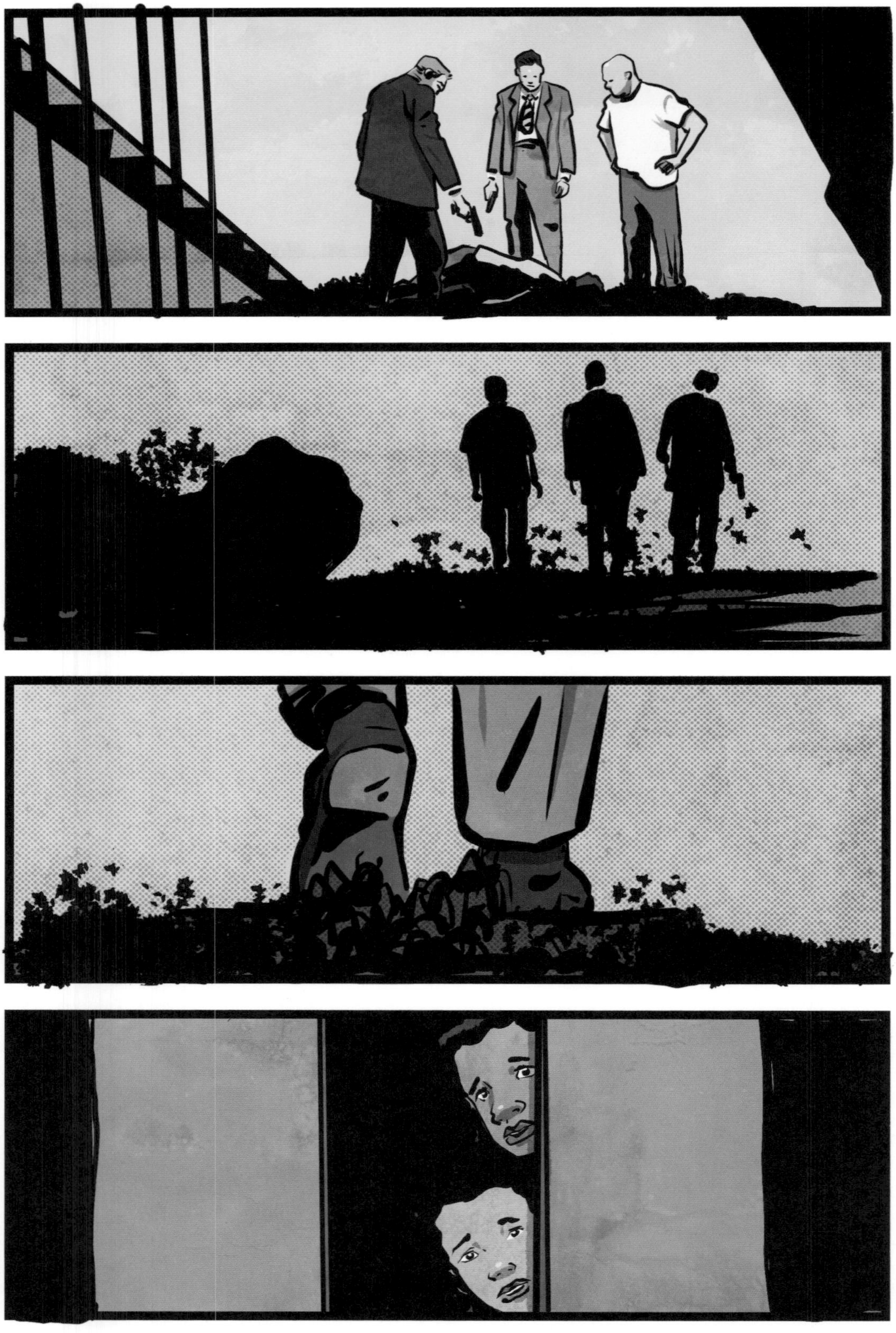

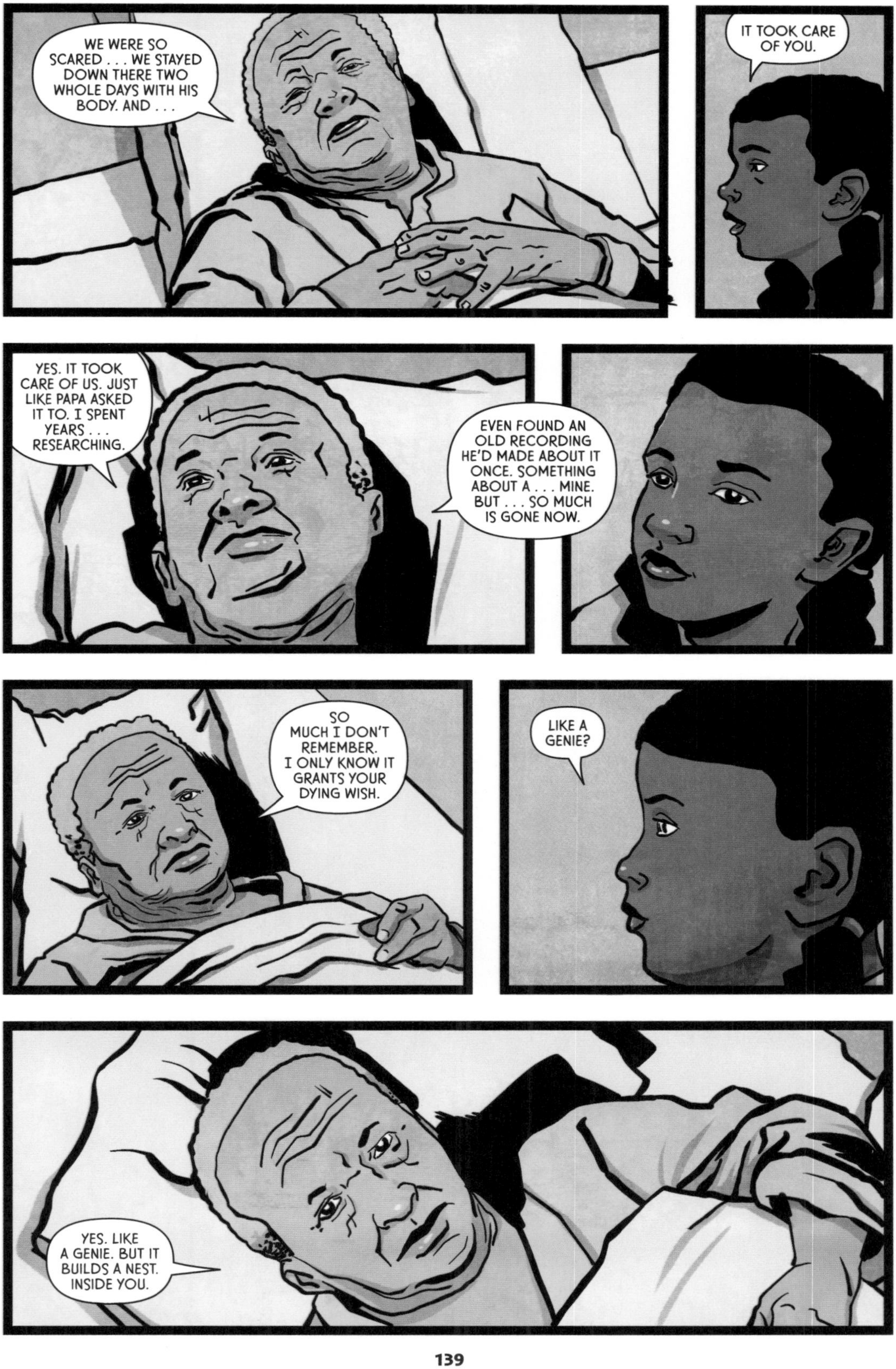

WE WERE SO SCARED . . . WE STAYED DOWN THERE TWO WHOLE DAYS WITH HIS BODY. AND . . .
IT TOOK CARE OF YOU.
YES. IT TOOK CARE OF US. JUST LIKE PAPA ASKED IT TO. I SPENT YEARS . . . RESEARCHING.
EVEN FOUND AN OLD RECORDING HE'D MADE ABOUT IT ONCE. SOMETHING ABOUT A . . . MINE. BUT . . . SO MUCH IS GONE NOW.
SO MUCH I DON'T REMEMBER. I ONLY KNOW IT GRANTS YOUR DYING WISH.
LIKE A GENIE?
YES. LIKE A GENIE. BUT IT BUILDS A NEST. INSIDE YOU.

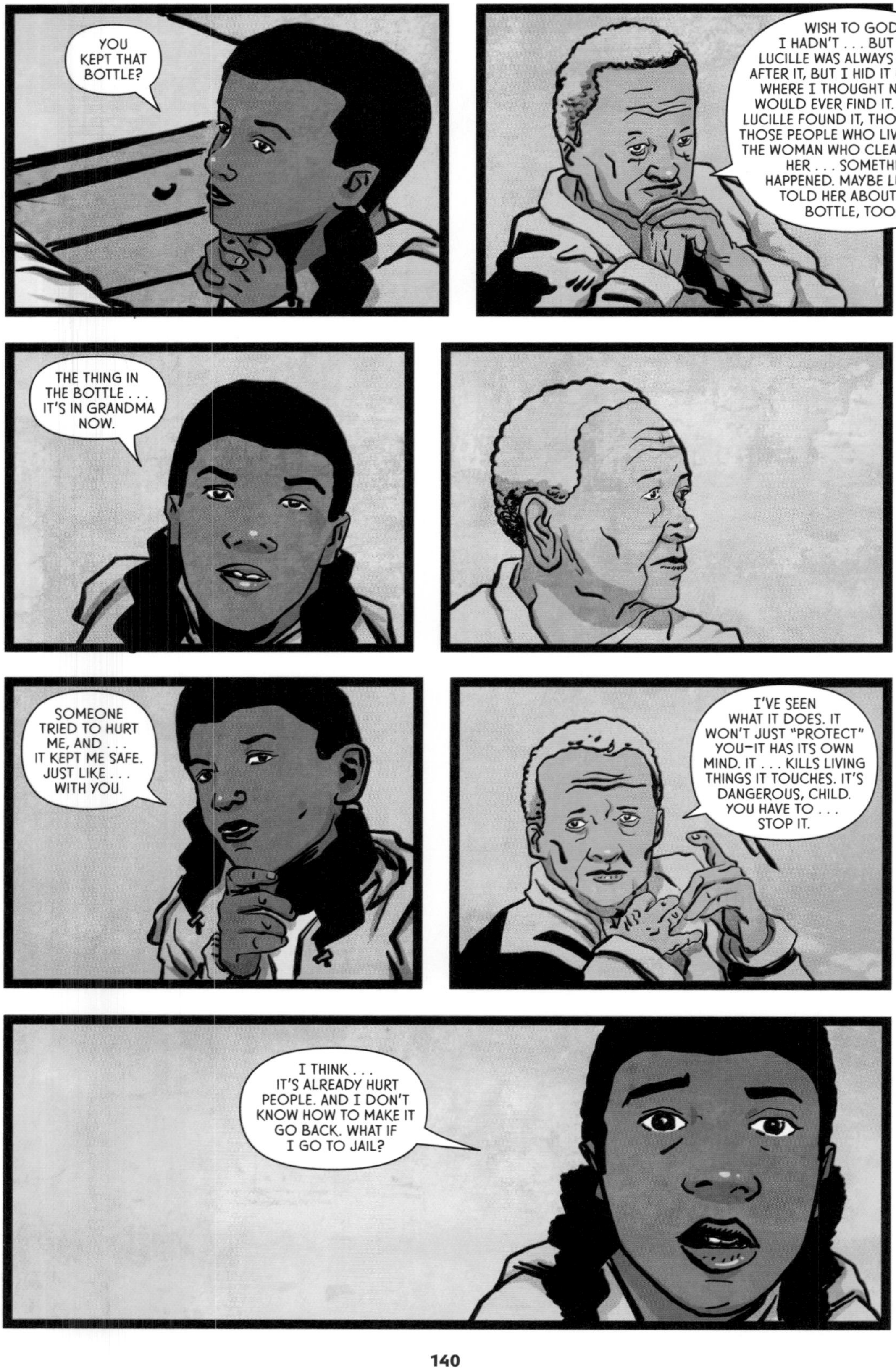
YOU KEPT THAT BOTTLE?
WISH TO GOD I HADN'T . . . BUT YES. LUCILLE WAS ALWAYS ASKING AFTER IT, BUT I HID IT UPSTAIRS WHERE I THOUGHT NO ONE WOULD EVER FIND IT. I THINK LUCILLE FOUND IT, THOUGH. AND THOSE PEOPLE WHO LIVED THERE, THE WOMAN WHO CLEANED FOR HER . . . SOMETHING HAPPENED. MAYBE LUCILLE TOLD HER ABOUT THE BOTTLE, TOO.
THE THING IN THE BOTTLE . . . IT'S IN GRANDMA NOW.
SOMEONE TRIED TO HURT ME, AND . . . IT KEPT ME SAFE. JUST LIKE . . . WITH YOU.
I'VE SEEN WHAT IT DOES. IT WON'T JUST "PROTECT" YOU—IT HAS ITS OWN MIND. IT . . . KILLS LIVING THINGS IT TOUCHES. IT'S DANGEROUS, CHILD. YOU HAVE TO . . . STOP IT.
I THINK . . . IT'S ALREADY HURT PEOPLE. AND I DON'T KNOW HOW TO MAKE IT GO BACK. WHAT IF I GO TO JAIL?

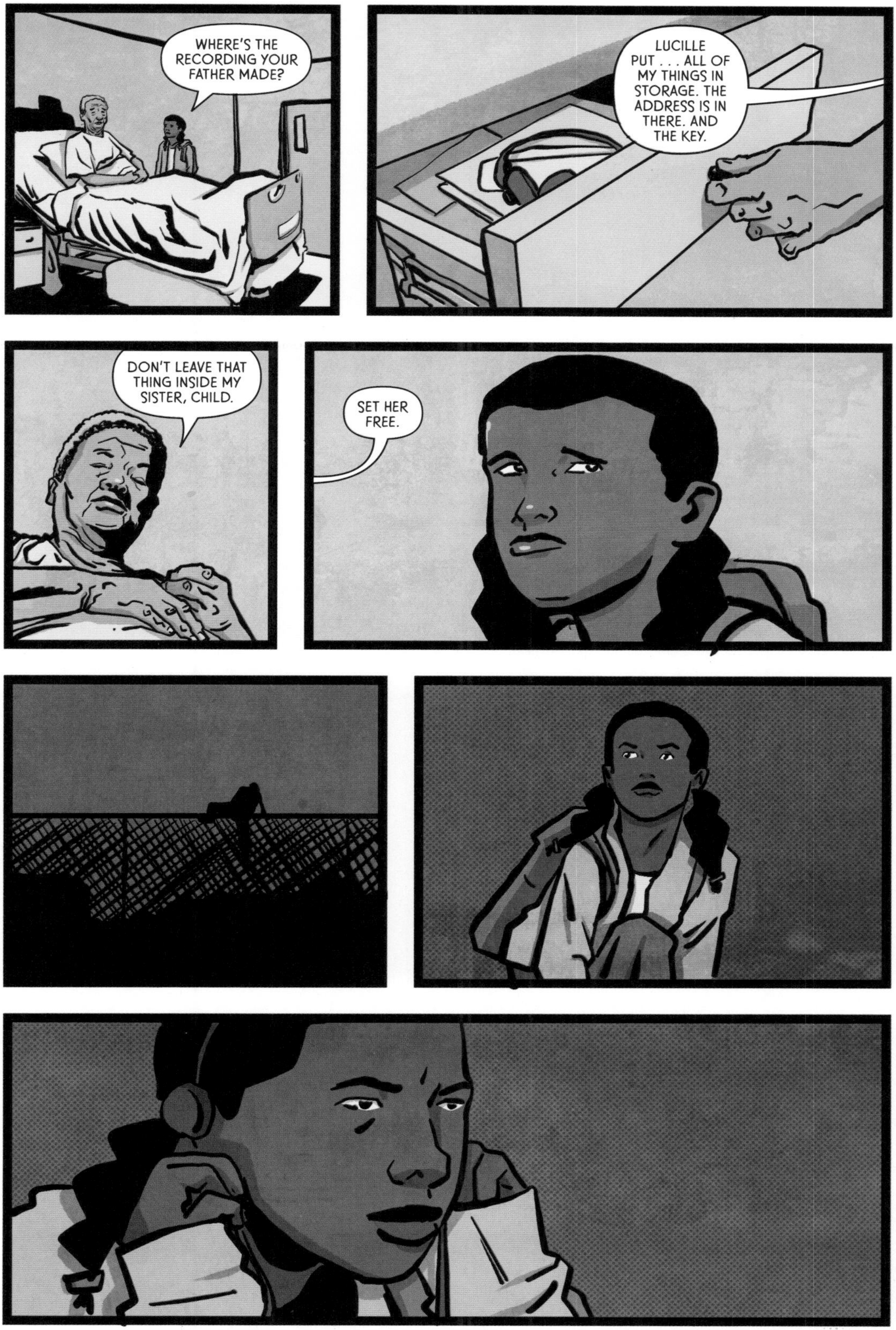
WHERE'S THE RECORDING YOUR FATHER MADE?
LUCILLE PUT . . . ALL OF MY THINGS IN STORAGE. THE ADDRESS IS IN THERE. AND THE KEY.
DON'T LEAVE THAT THING INSIDE MY SISTER, CHILD.
SET HER FREE.

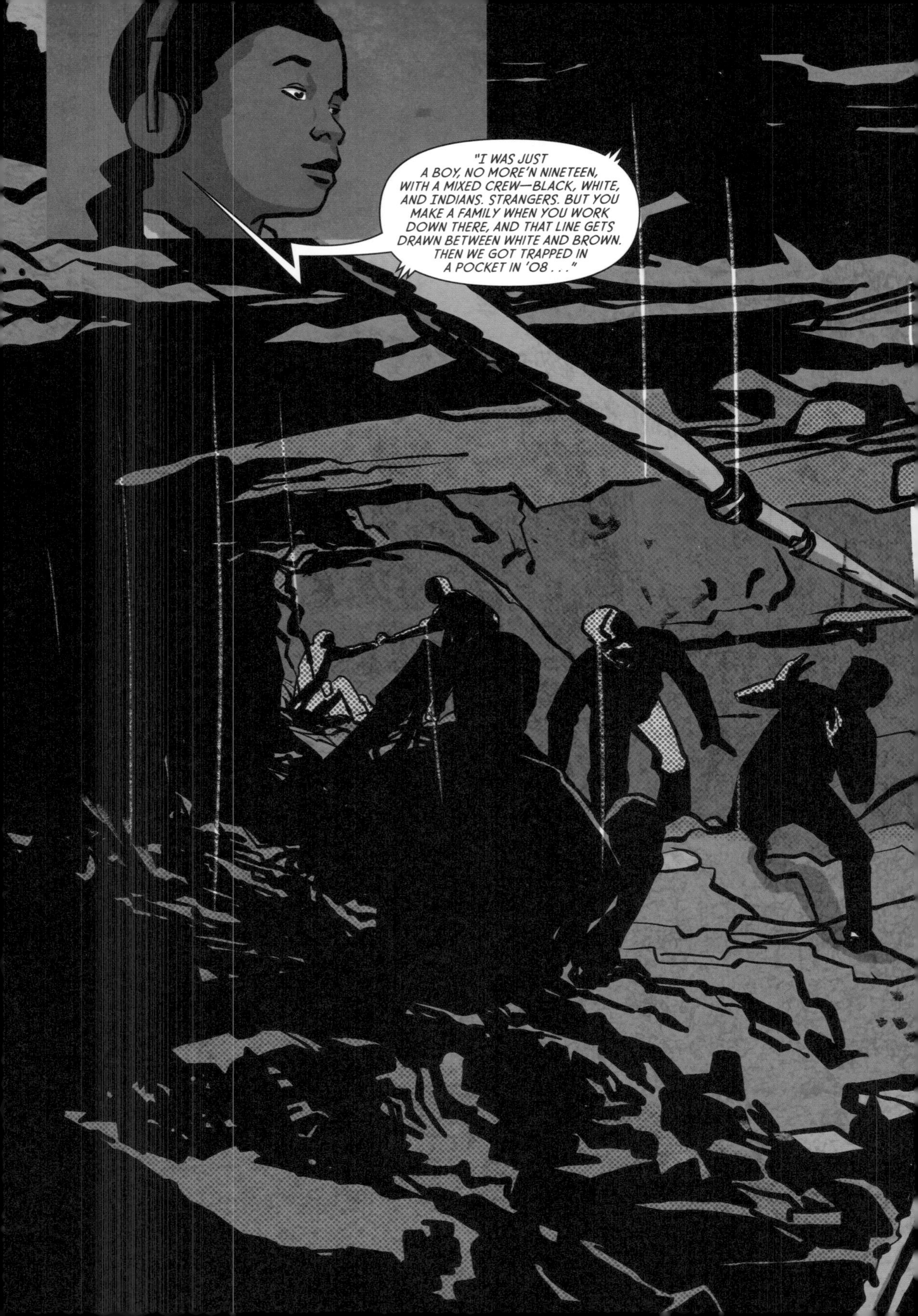
"I WAS JUST A BOY, NO MORE'N NINETEEN, WITH A MIXED CREW—BLACK, WHITE, AND INDIANS. STRANGERS. BUT YOU MAKE A FAMILY WHEN YOU WORK DOWN THERE, AND THAT LINE GETS DRAWN BETWEEN WHITE AND BROWN. THEN WE GOT TRAPPED IN A POCKET IN '08 . . ."

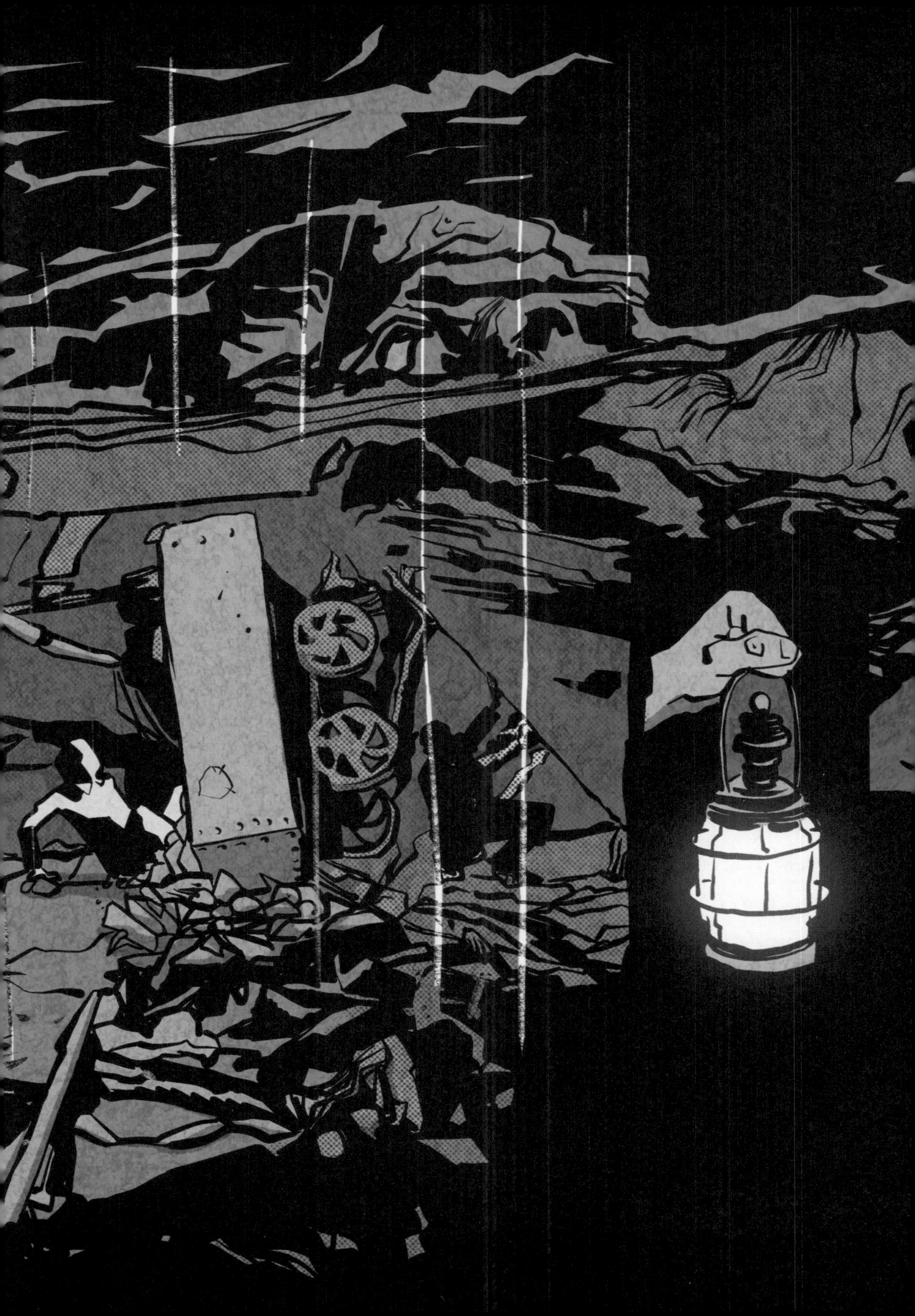

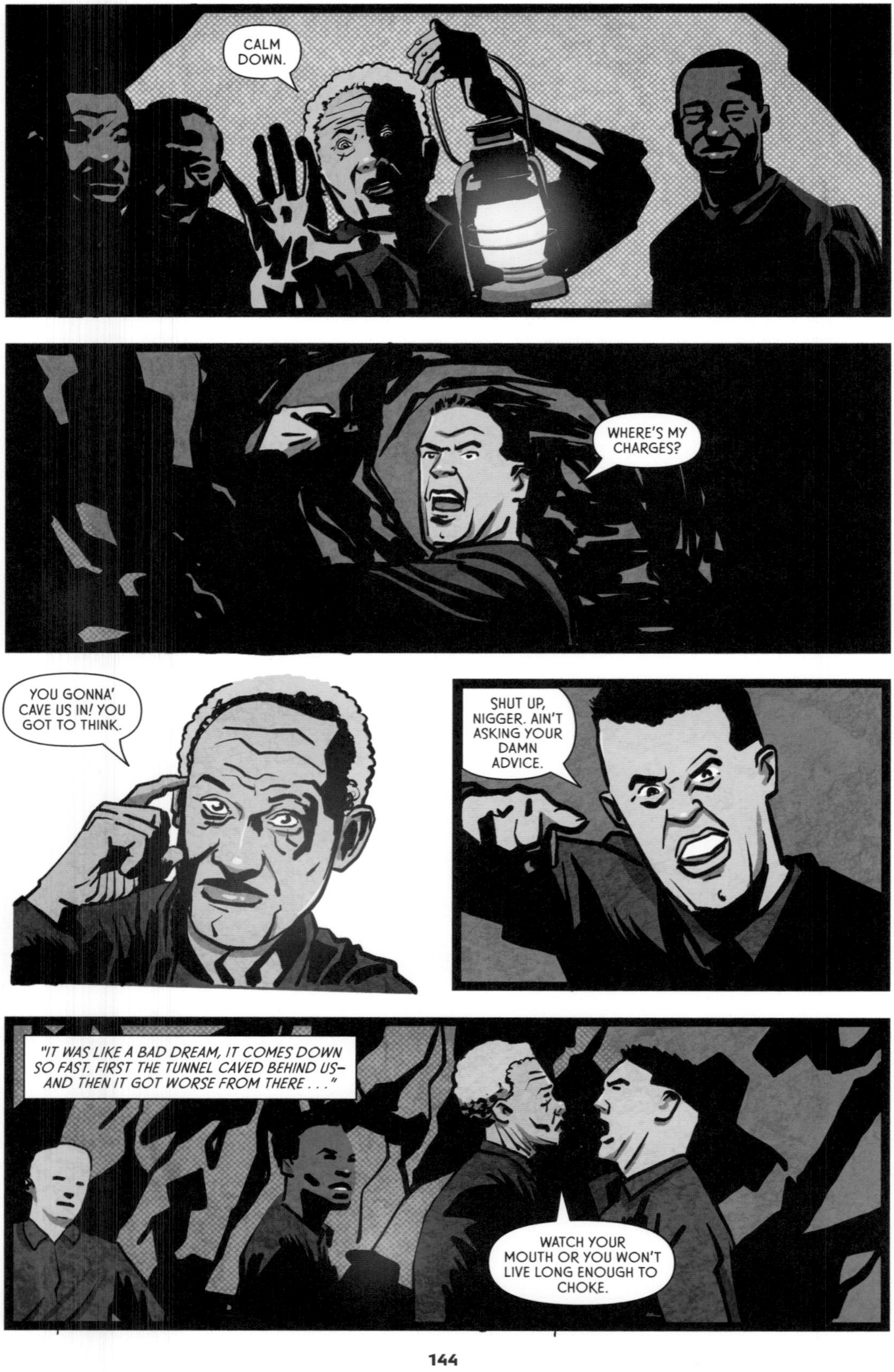
CALM DOWN.
WHERE'S MY CHARGES?
YOU GONNA' CAVE US IN! YOU GOT TO THINK.
SHUT UP, NIGGER. AIN'T ASKING YOUR DAMN ADVICE.
"IT WAS LIKE A BAD DREAM, IT COMES DOWN SO FAST. FIRST THE TUNNEL CAVED BEHIND US— AND THEN IT GOT WORSE FROM THERE . . ."
WATCH YOUR MOUTH OR YOU WON'T LIVE LONG ENOUGH TO CHOKE.

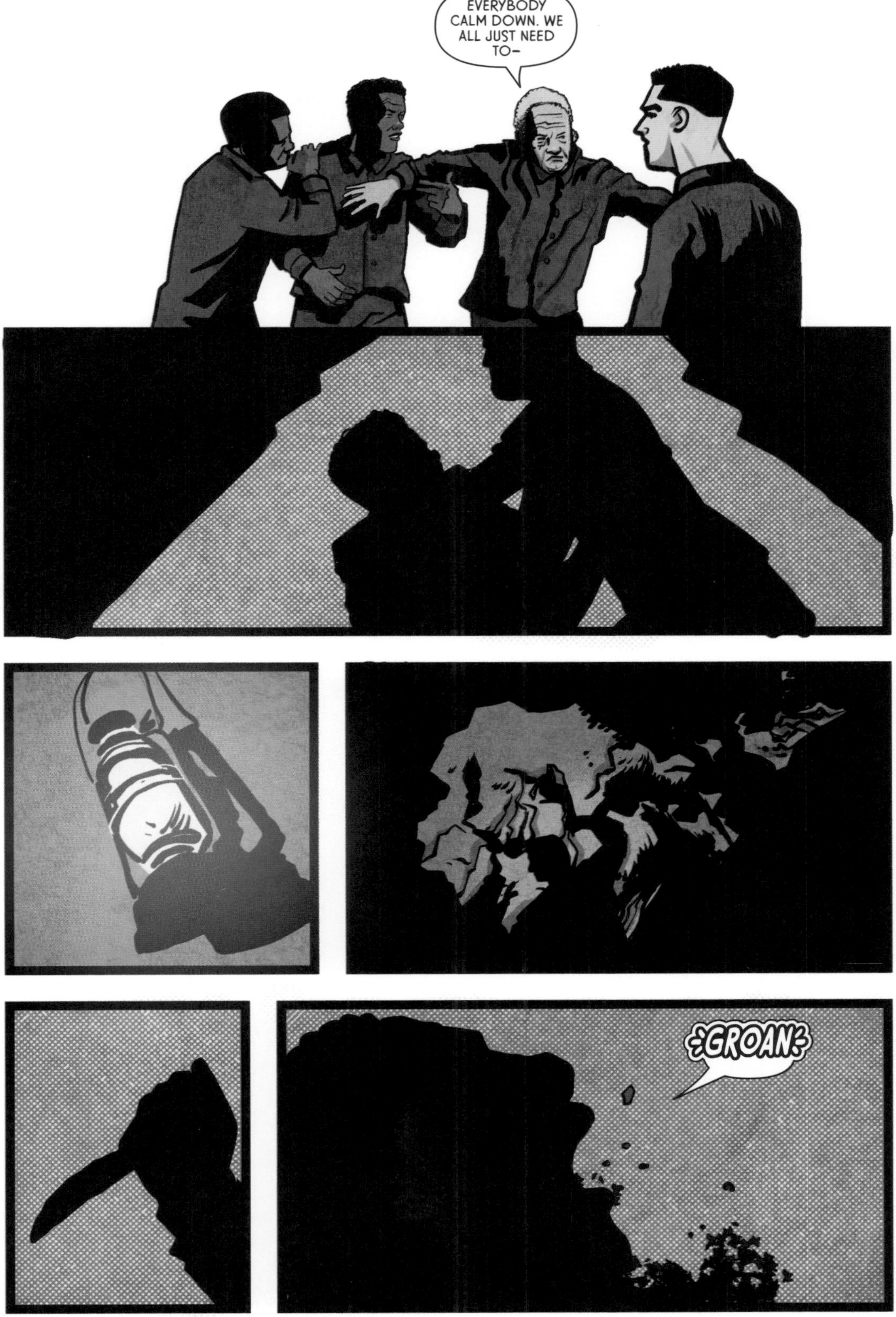
EVERYBODY CALM DOWN. WE ALL JUST NEED TO–
GROAN

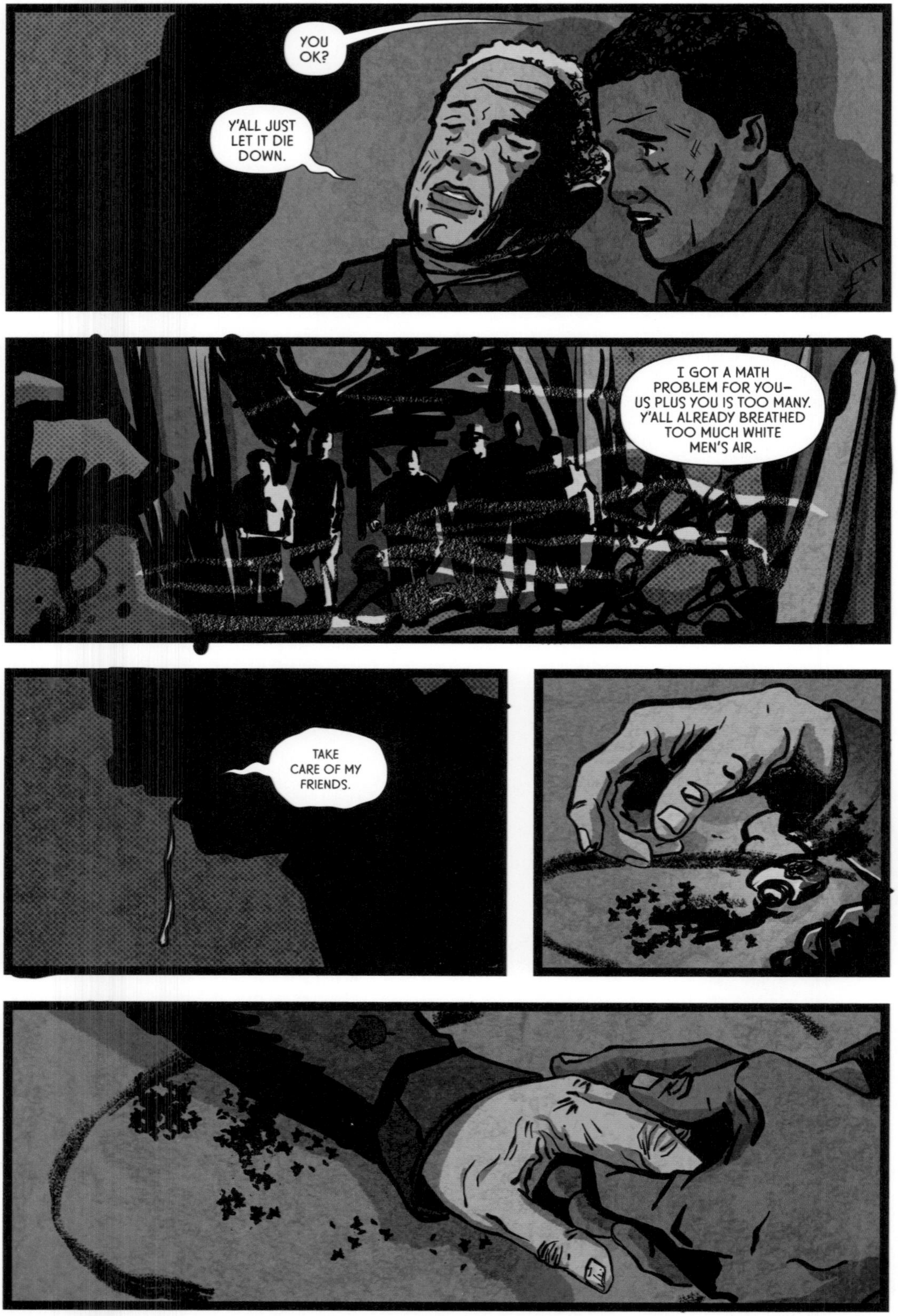
YOU OK?
Y'ALL JUST LET IT DIE DOWN.
I GOT A MATH PROBLEM FOR YOU— US PLUS YOU IS TOO MANY. Y'ALL ALREADY BREATHED TOO MUCH WHITE MEN'S AIR.
TAKE CARE OF MY FRIENDS.

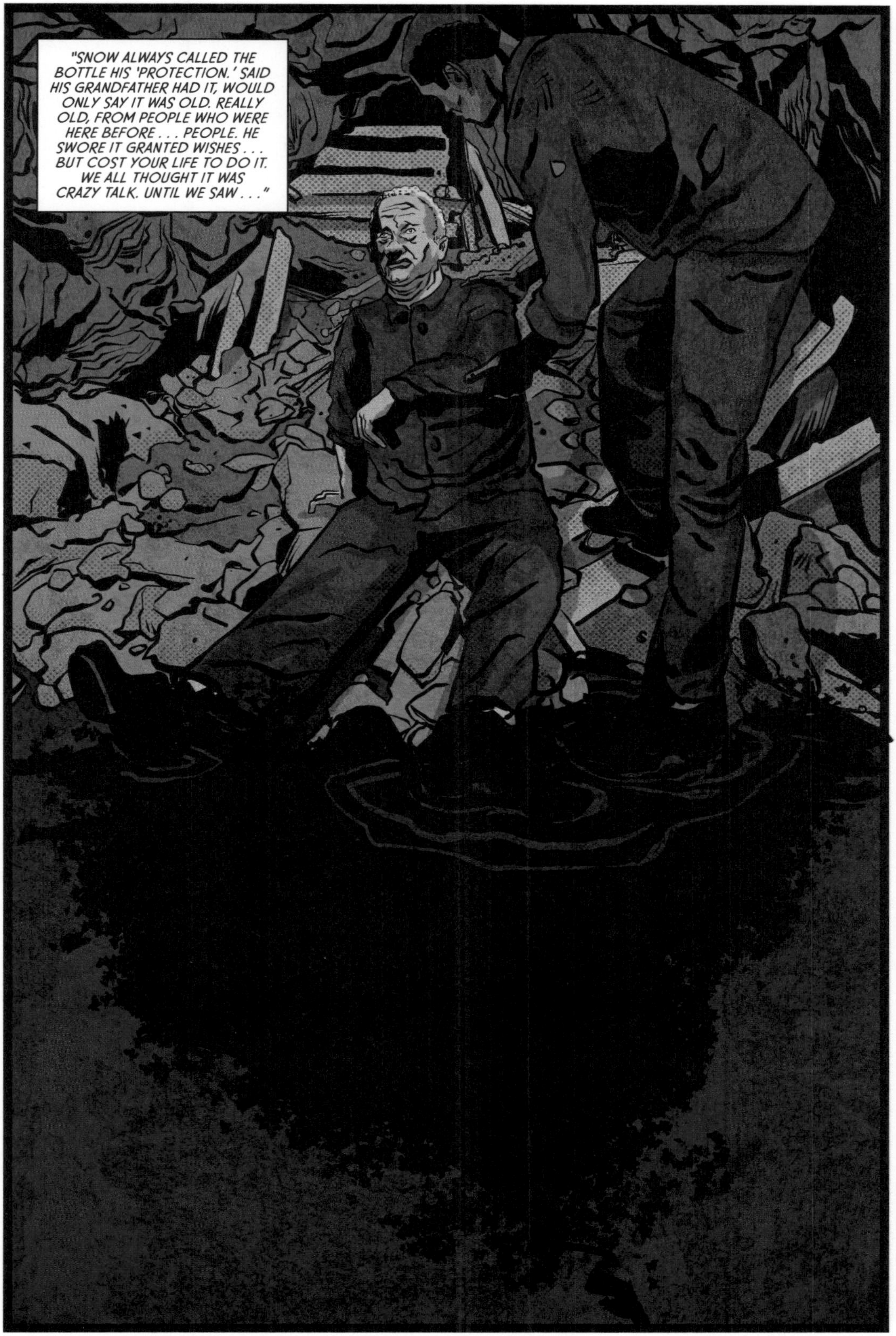
"SNOW ALWAYS CALLED THE BOTTLE HIS 'PROTECTION.' SAID HIS GRANDFATHER HAD IT, WOULD ONLY SAY IT WAS OLD. REALLY OLD, FROM PEOPLE WHO WERE HERE BEFORE . . . PEOPLE. HE SWORE IT GRANTED WISHES . . . BUT COST YOUR LIFE TO DO IT. WE ALL THOUGHT IT WAS CRAZY TALK. UNTIL WE SAW . . ."

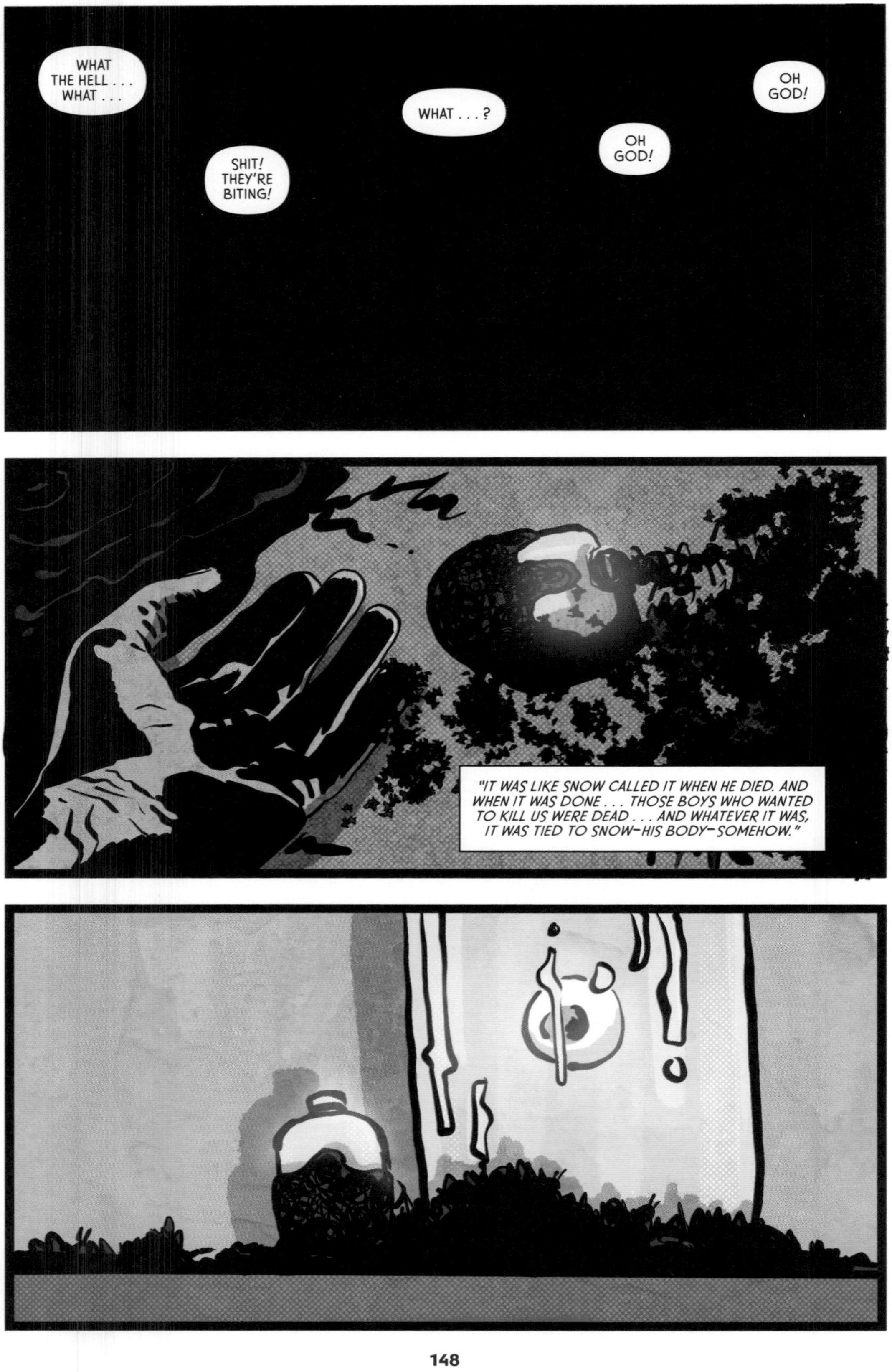

WHAT THE HELL . . . WHAT . . .
SHIT! THEY'RE BITING!
WHAT . . . ?
OH GOD!
OH GOD!
"IT WAS LIKE SNOW CALLED IT WHEN HE DIED. AND WHEN IT WAS DONE . . . THOSE BOYS WHO WANTED TO KILL US WERE DEAD . . . AND WHATEVER IT WAS, IT WAS TIED TO SNOW—HIS BODY—SOMEHOW."

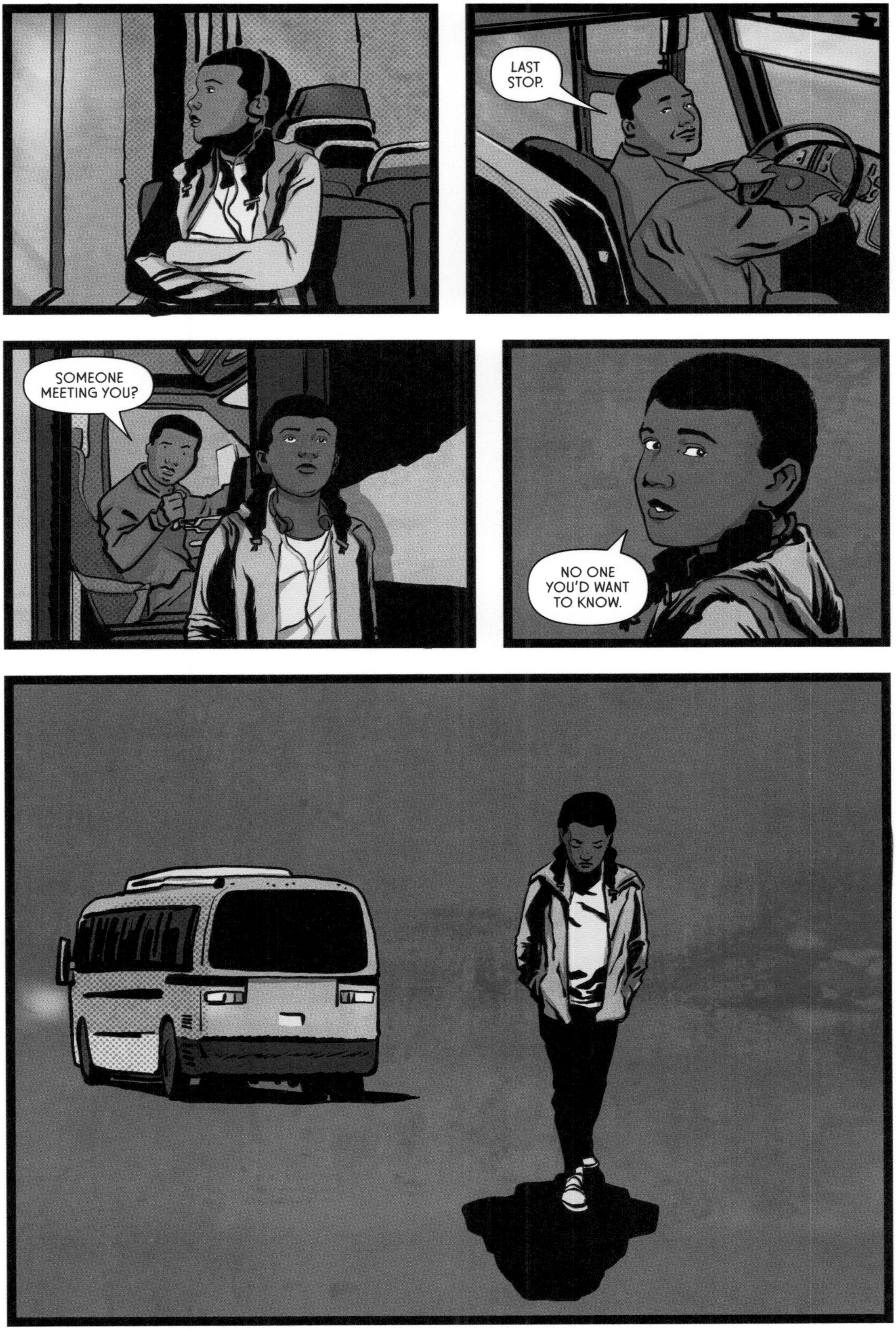
LAST STOP.
SOMEONE MEETING YOU?
NO ONE YOU'D WANT TO KNOW.

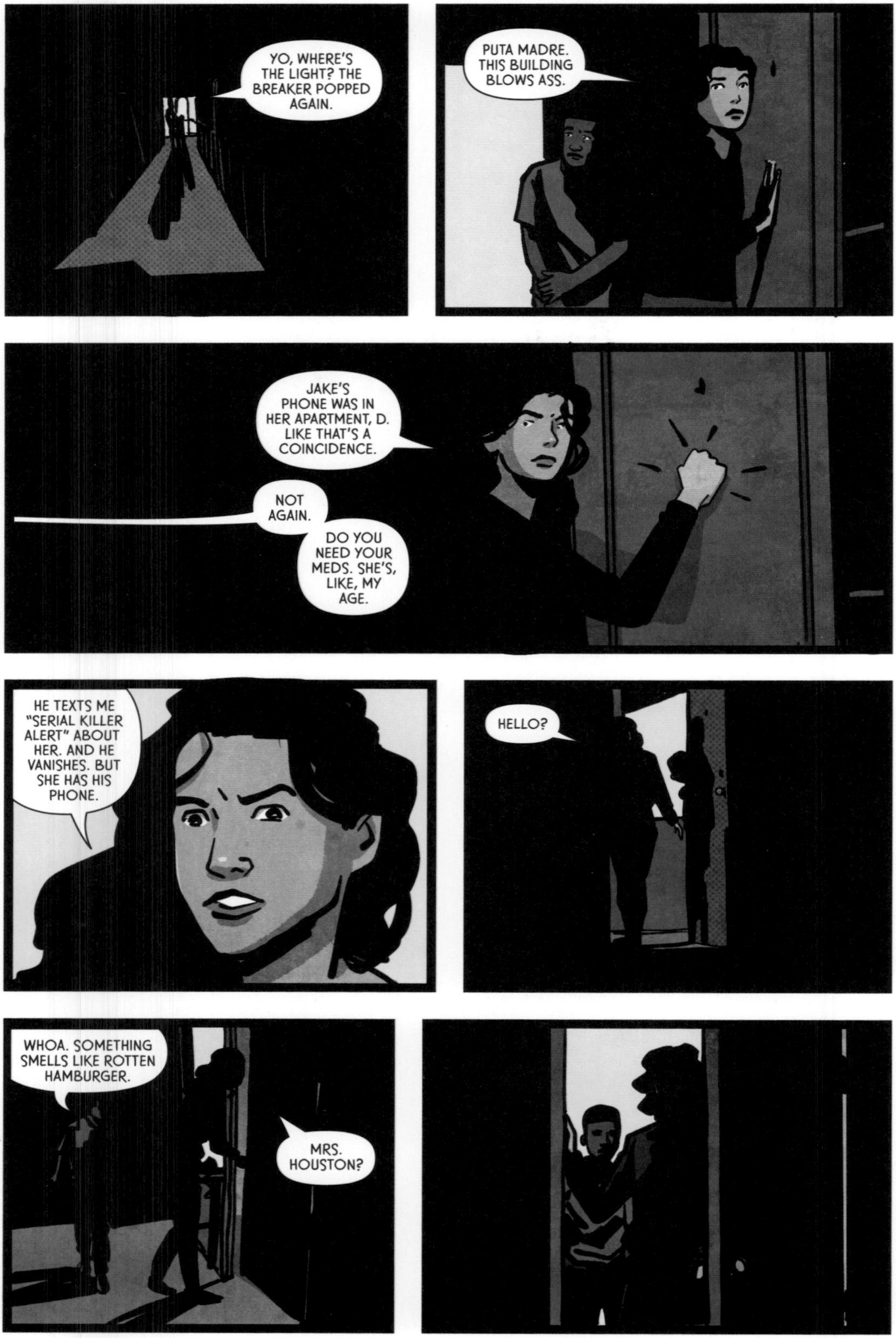
YO, WHERE'S THE LIGHT? THE BREAKER POPPED AGAIN.
PUTA MADRE. THIS BUILDING BLOWS ASS.
JAKE'S PHONE WAS IN HER APARTMENT, D. LIKE THAT'S A COINCIDENCE.
NOT AGAIN.
DO YOU NEED YOUR MEDS. SHE'S, LIKE, MY AGE.
HE TEXTS ME "SERIAL KILLER ALERT" ABOUT HER. AND HE VANISHES. BUT SHE HAS HIS PHONE.
HELLO?
WHOA. SOMETHING SMELLS LIKE ROTTEN HAMBURGER.
MRS. HOUSTON?

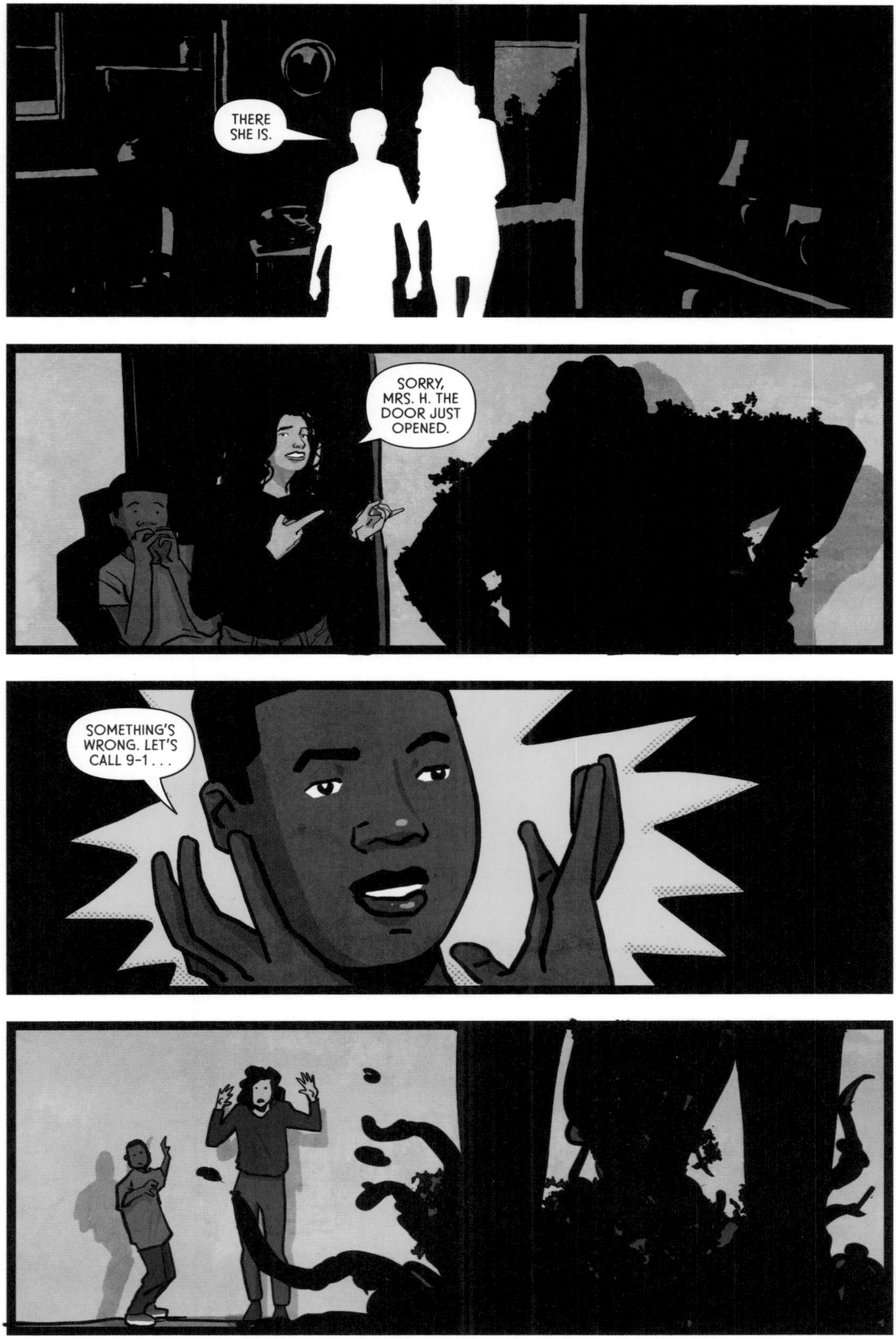
THERE SHE IS.
SORRY, MRS. H. THE DOOR JUST OPENED.
SOMETHING'S WRONG. LET'S CALL 9-1 . . .

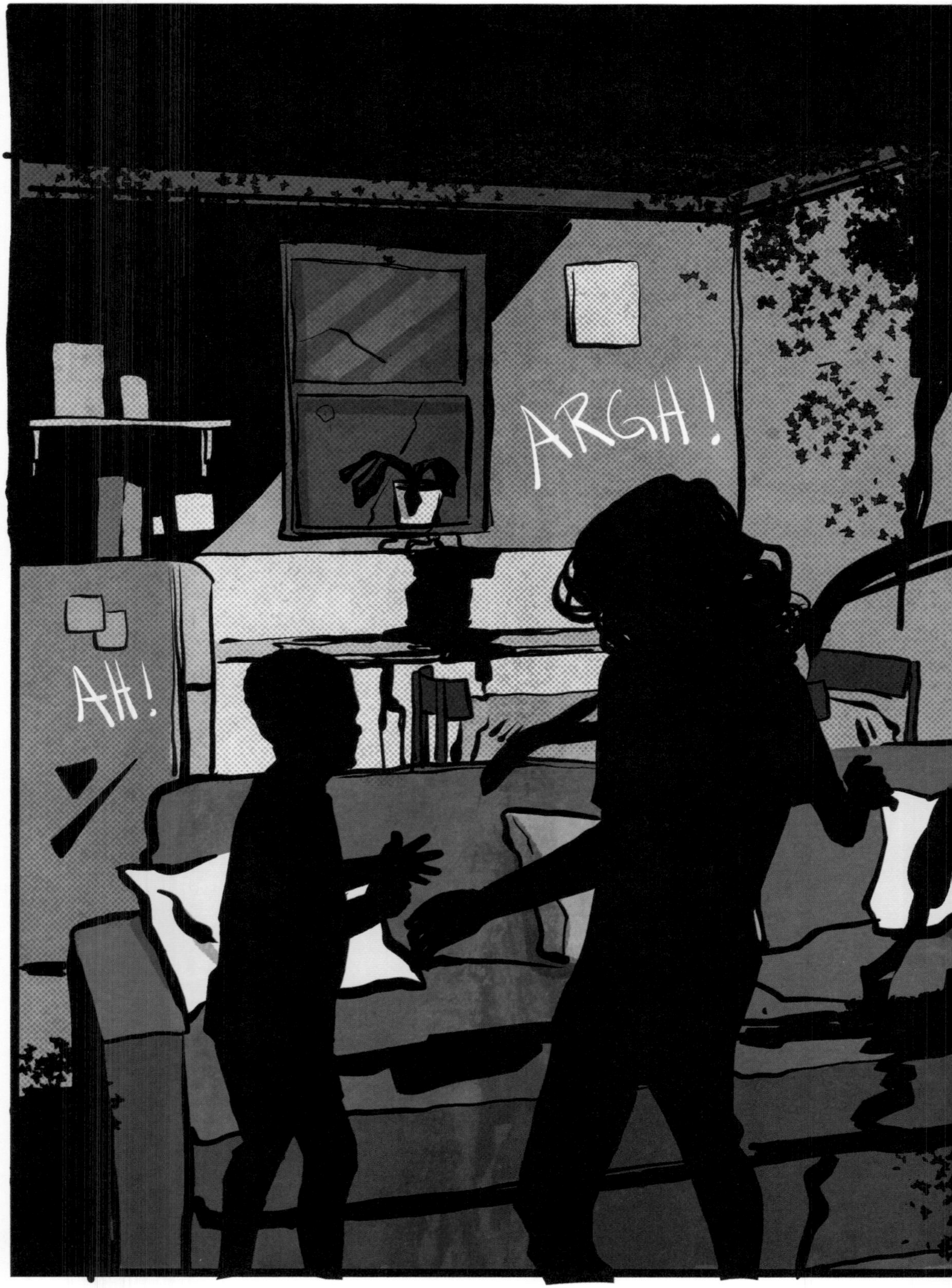
AH!
ARGH!

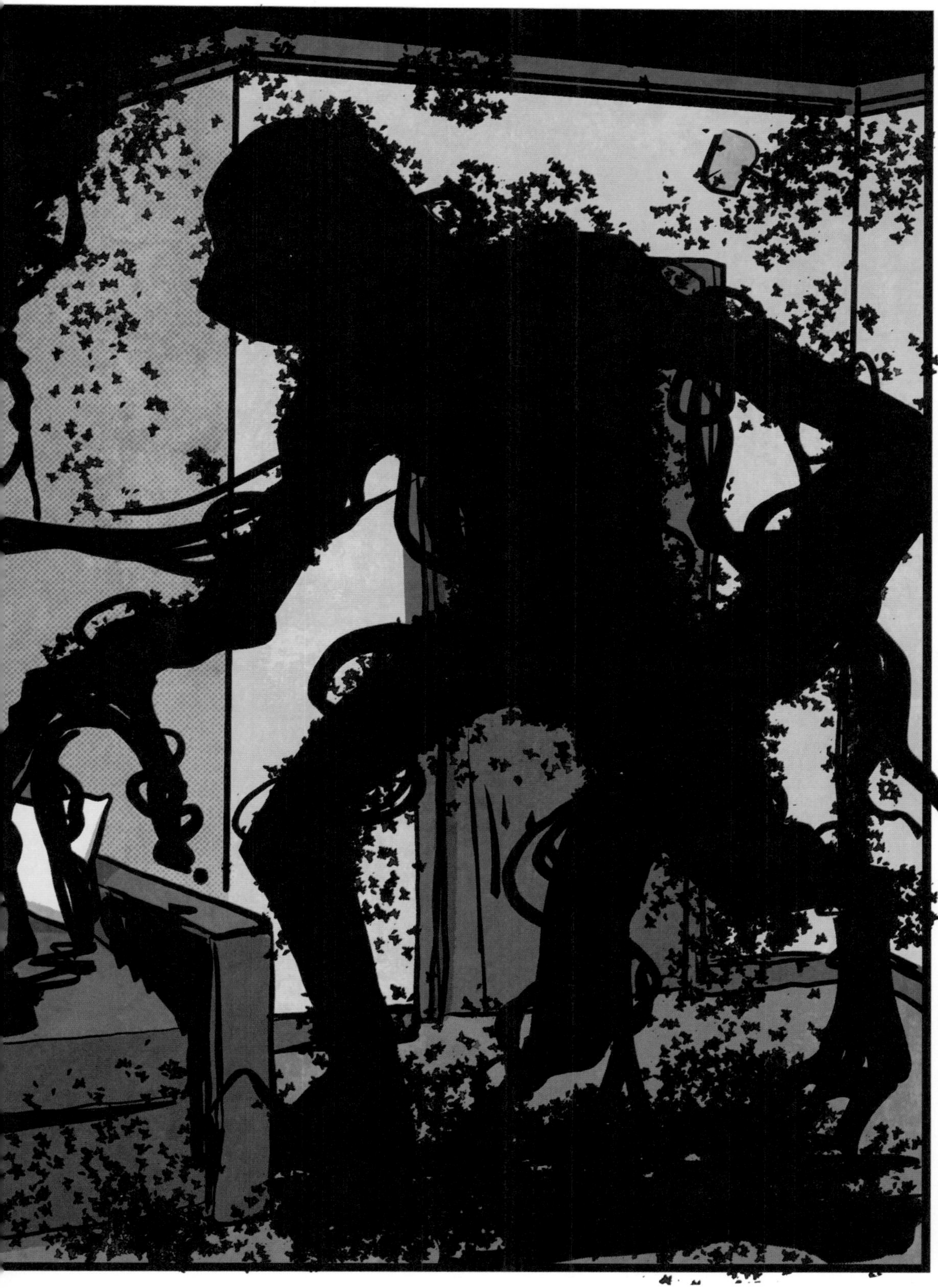

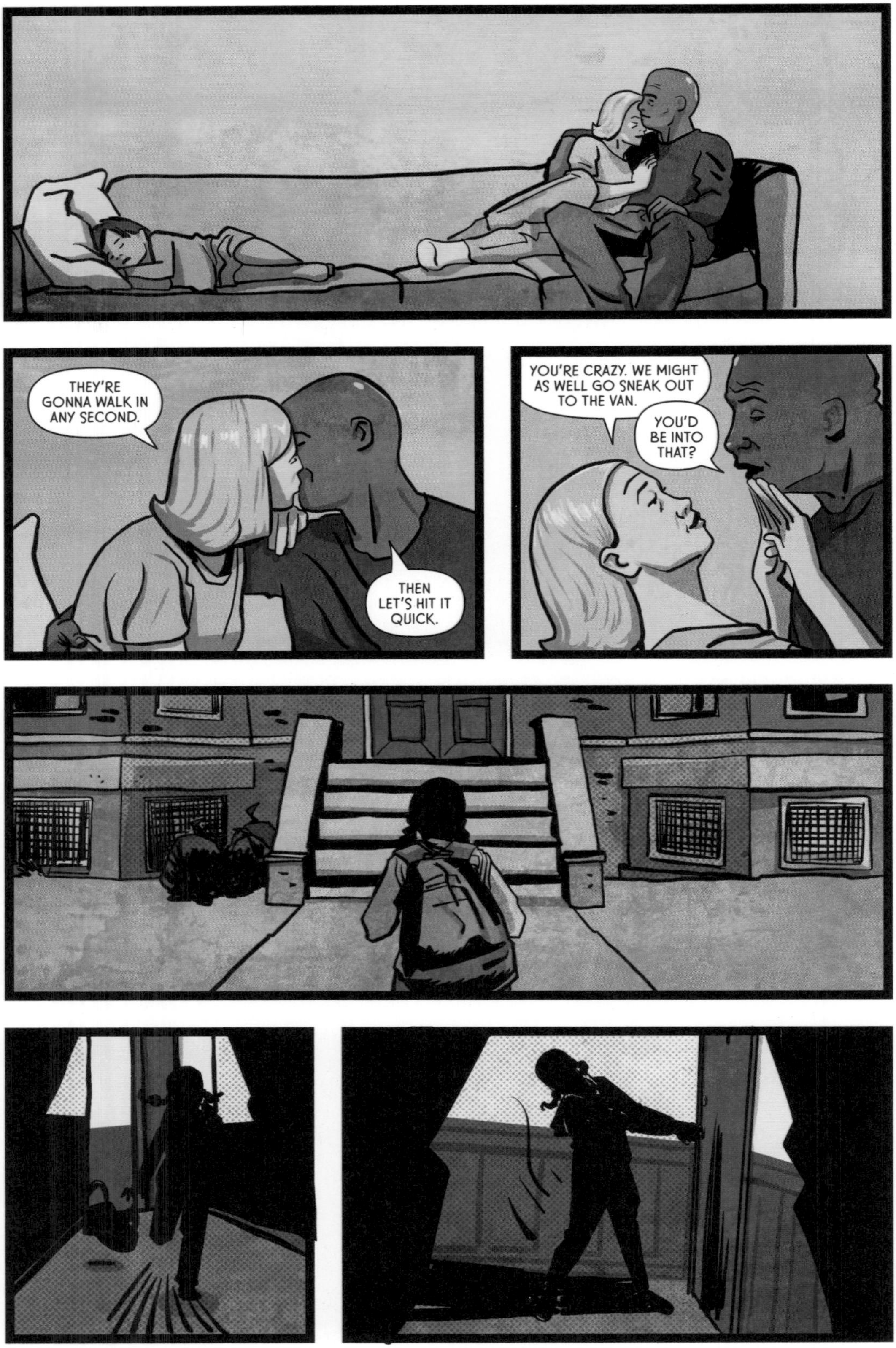
THEY'RE GONNA WALK IN ANY SECOND.
THEN LET'S HIT IT QUICK.
YOU'RE CRAZY. WE MIGHT AS WELL GO SNEAK OUT TO THE VAN.
YOU'D BE INTO THAT?

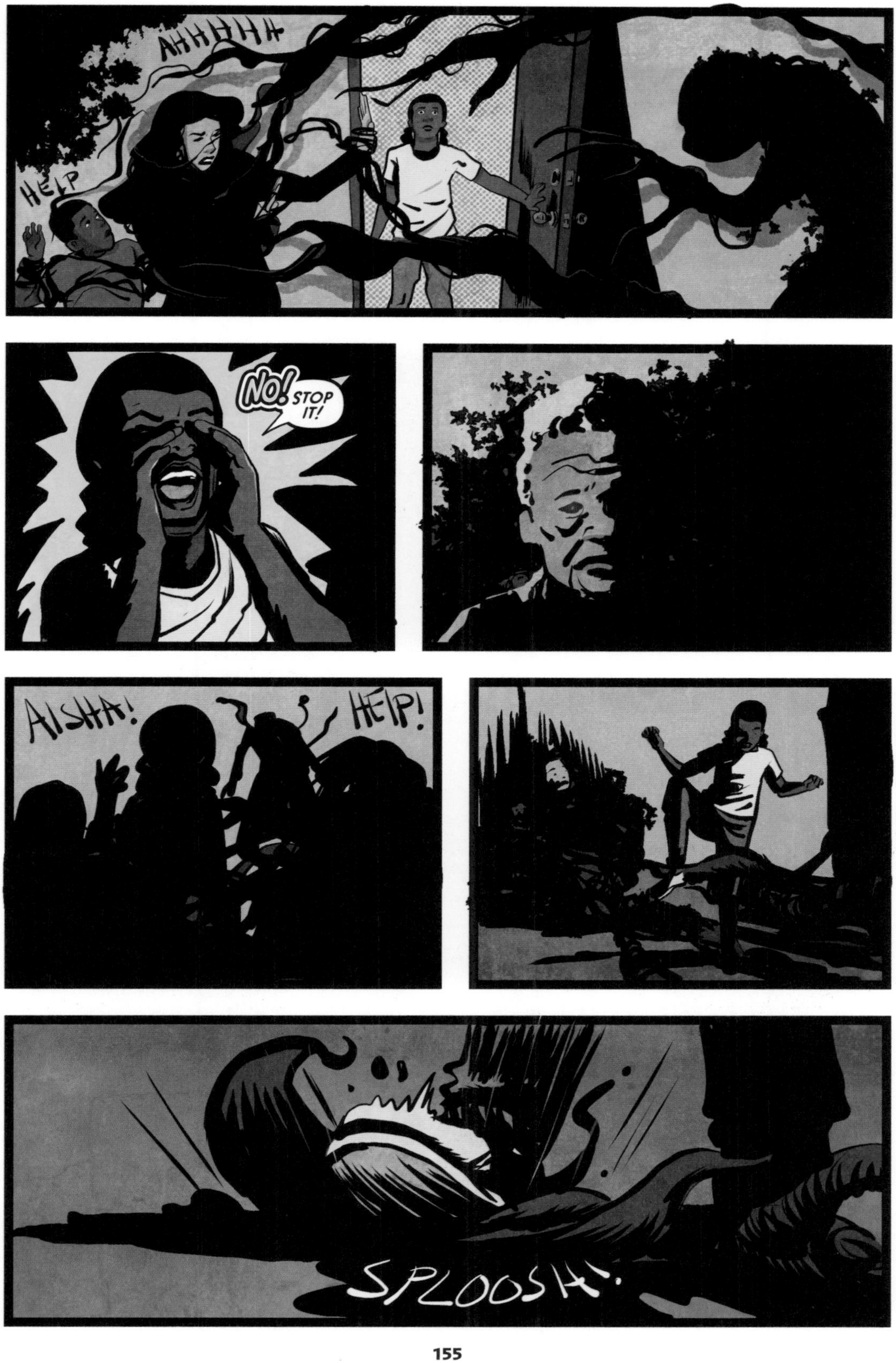
AHHHHH
HELP
NO! STOP IT!
AISHA!
HELP!
SPLOOSH!

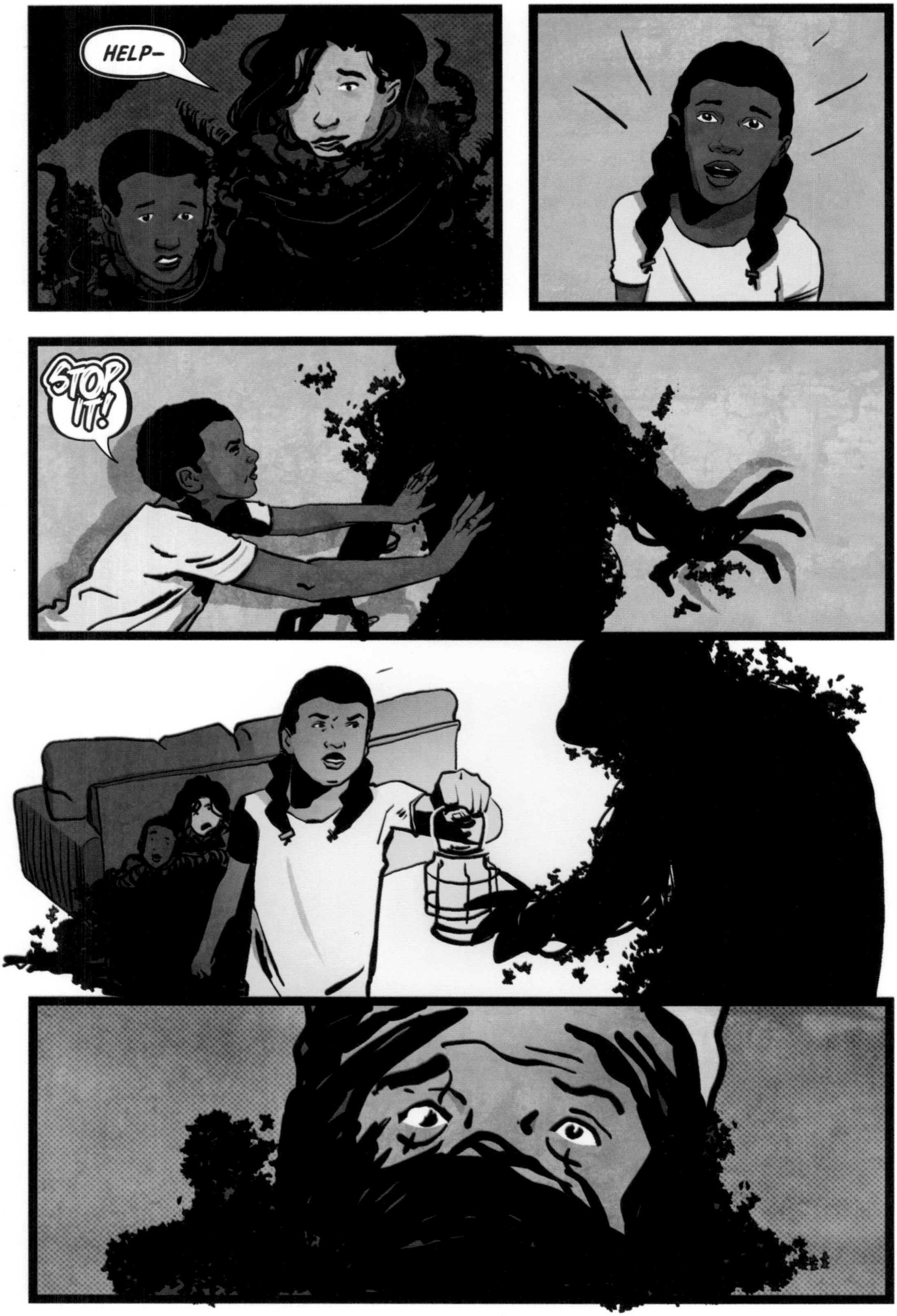
HELP-
STOP IT!

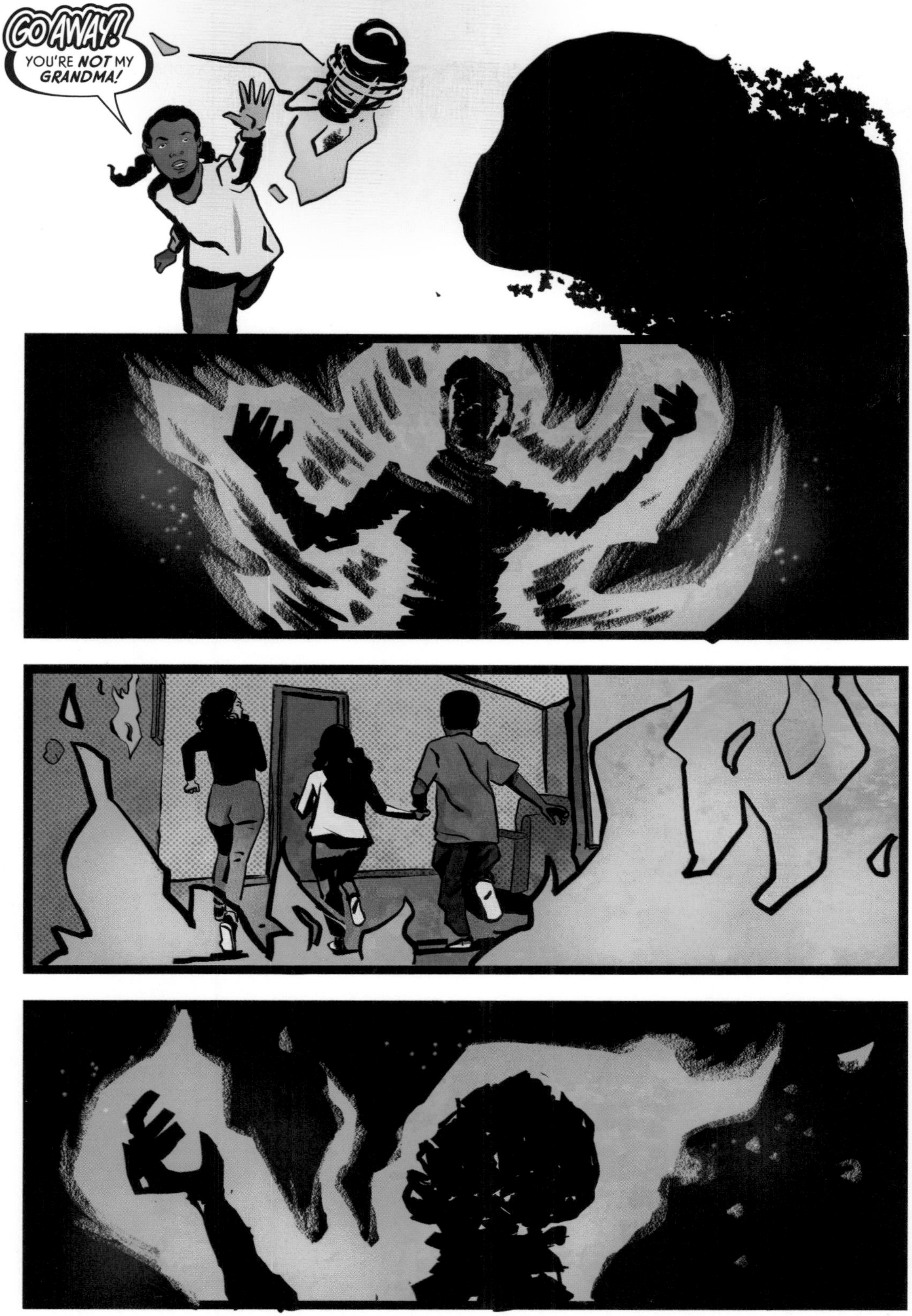
GO AWAY!!
YOU'RE **NOT** MY **GRANDMA!**

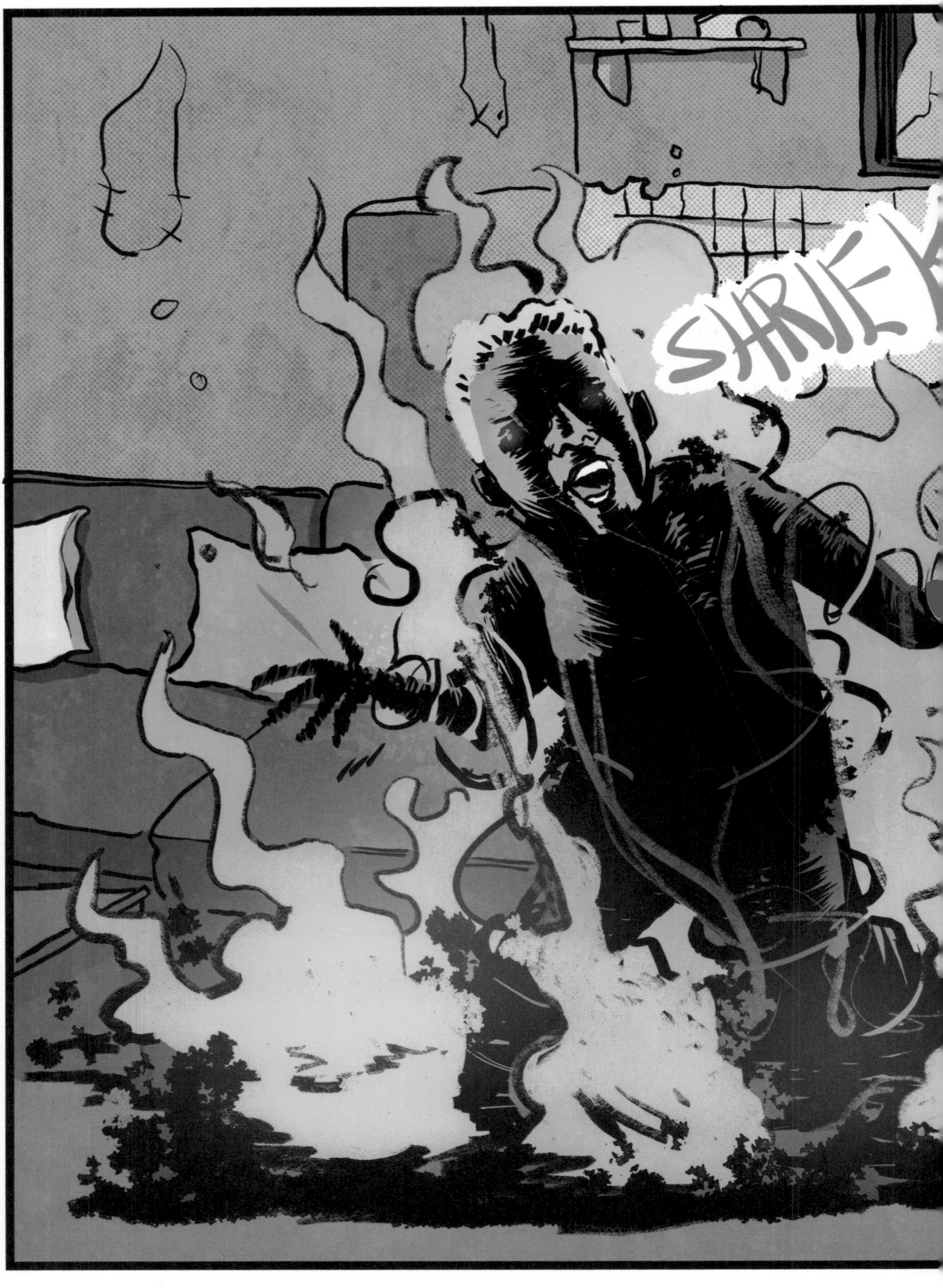
SHRIE

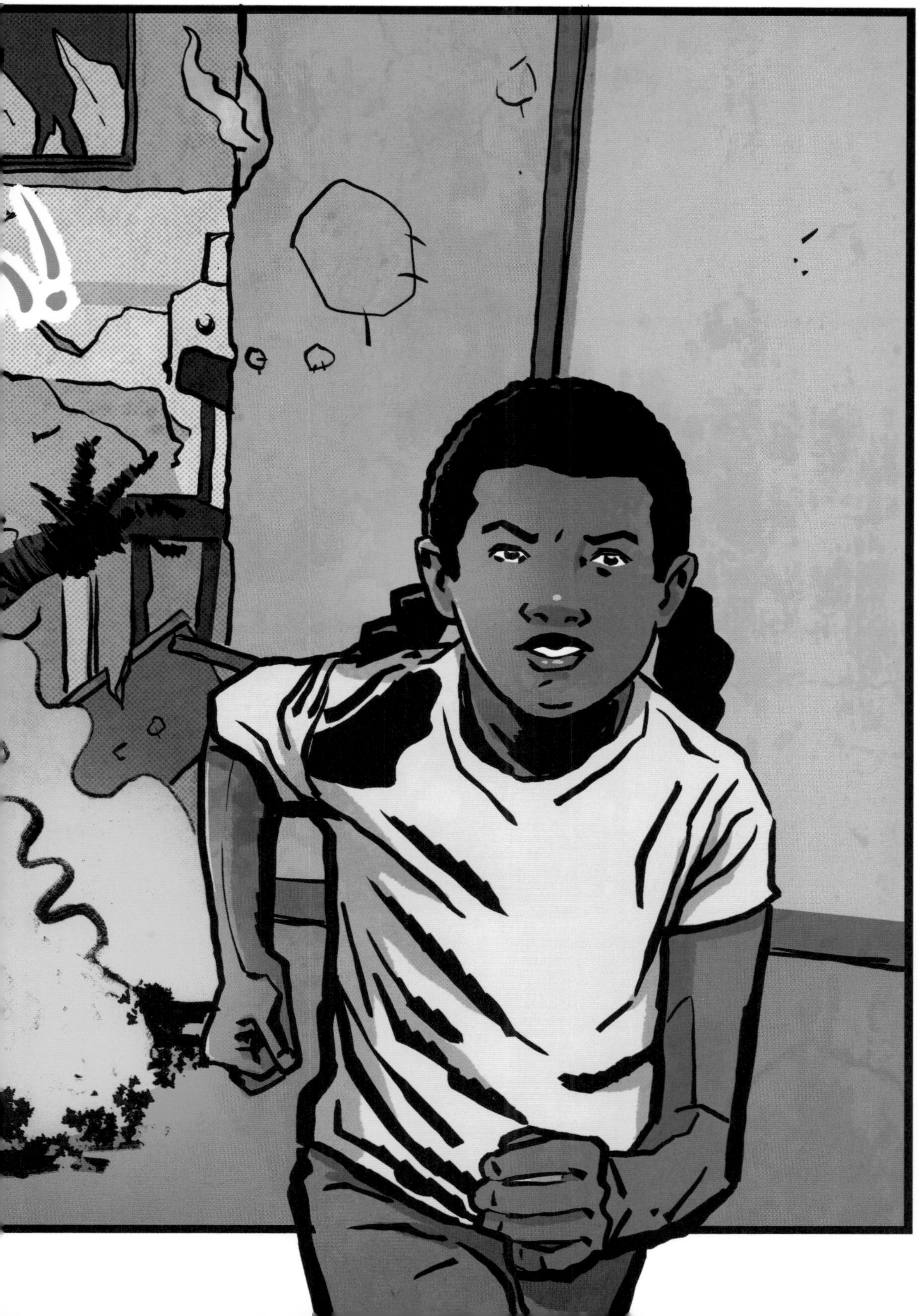

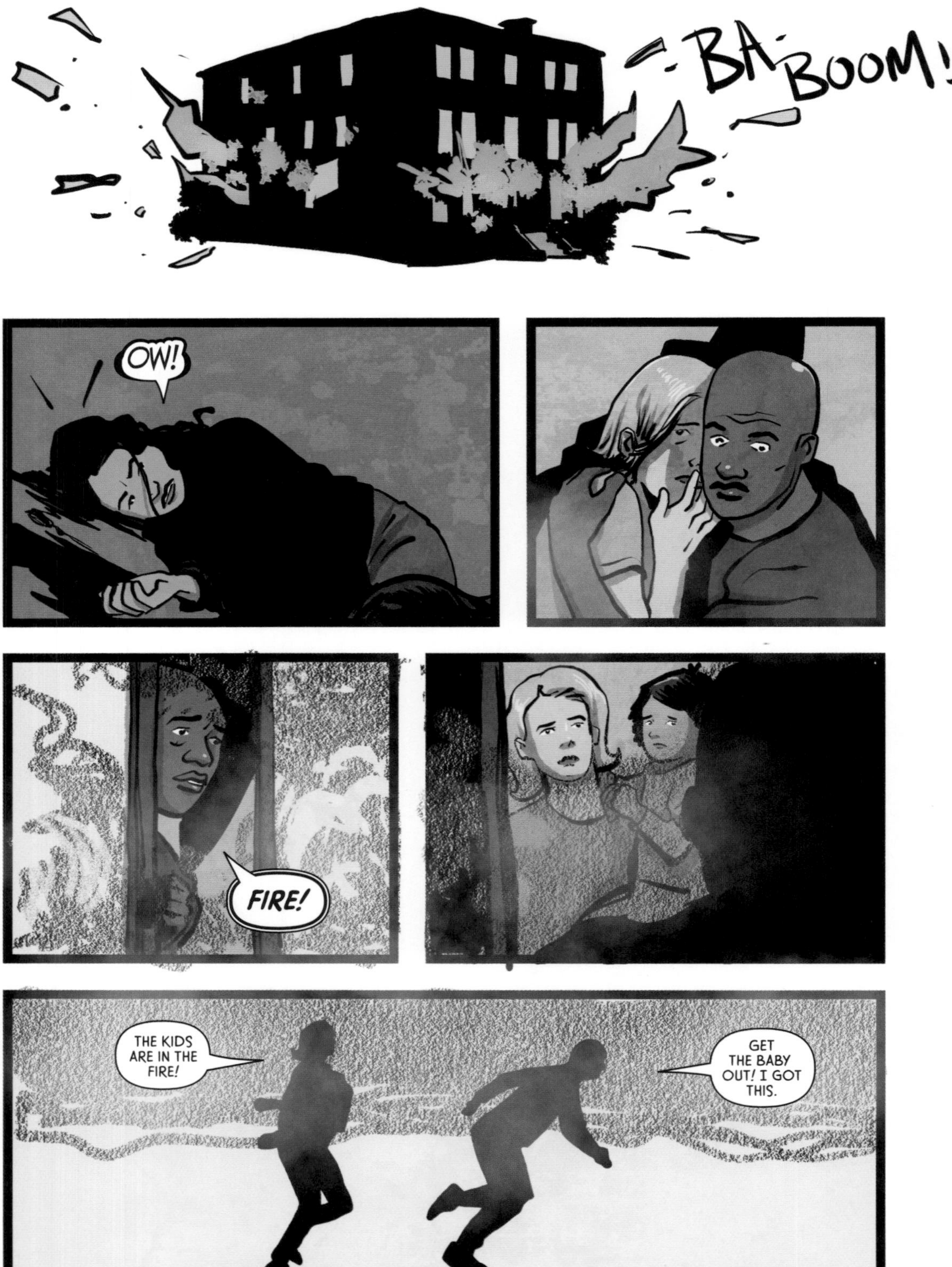
BA-BOOM!
OW!
FIRE!
THE KIDS ARE IN THE FIRE!
GET THE BABY OUT! I GOT THIS.

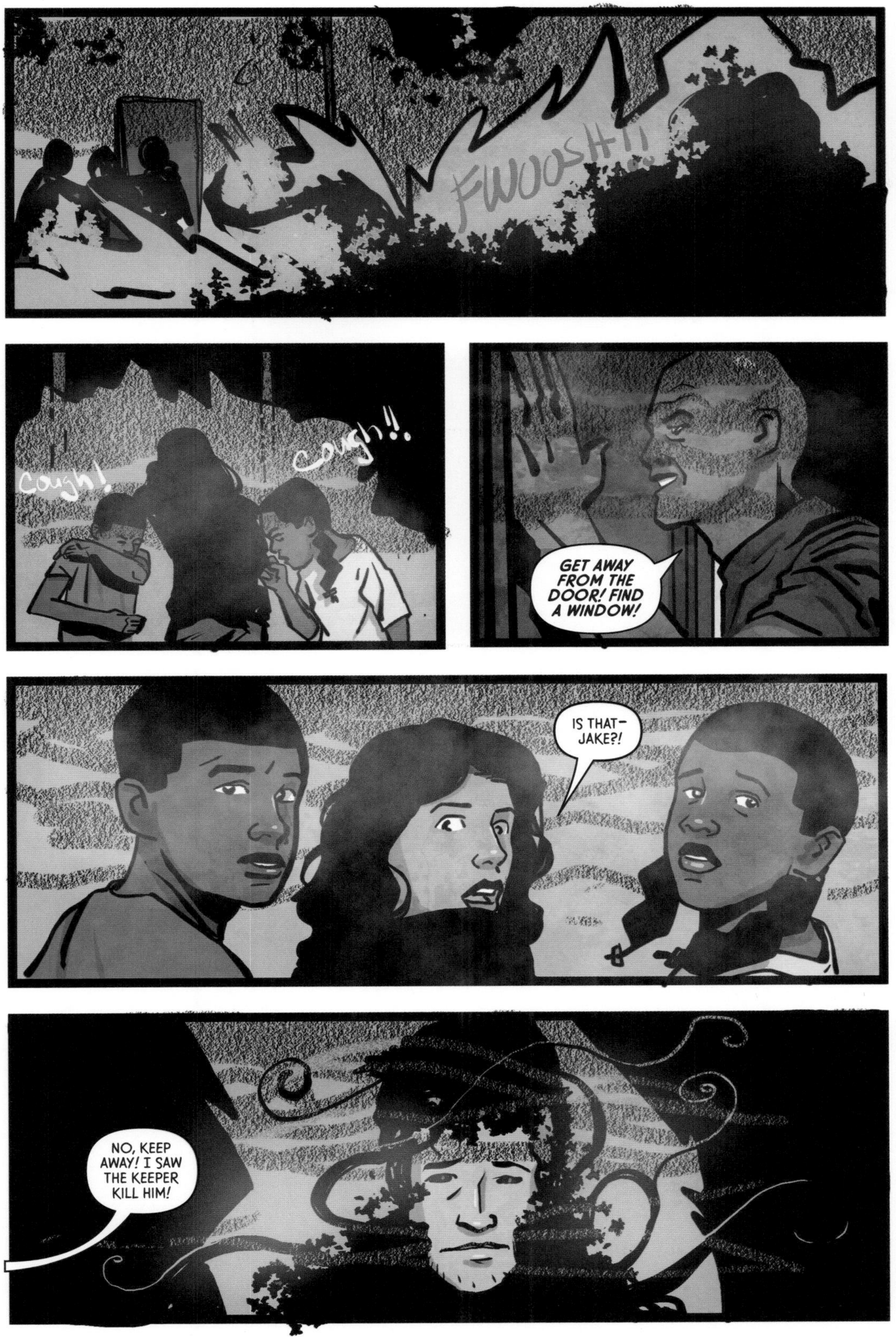
FWOOSH!!
COUGH!
COUGH!!
GET AWAY FROM THE DOOR! FIND A WINDOW!
IS THAT— JAKE?!
NO, KEEP AWAY! I SAW THE KEEPER KILL HIM!

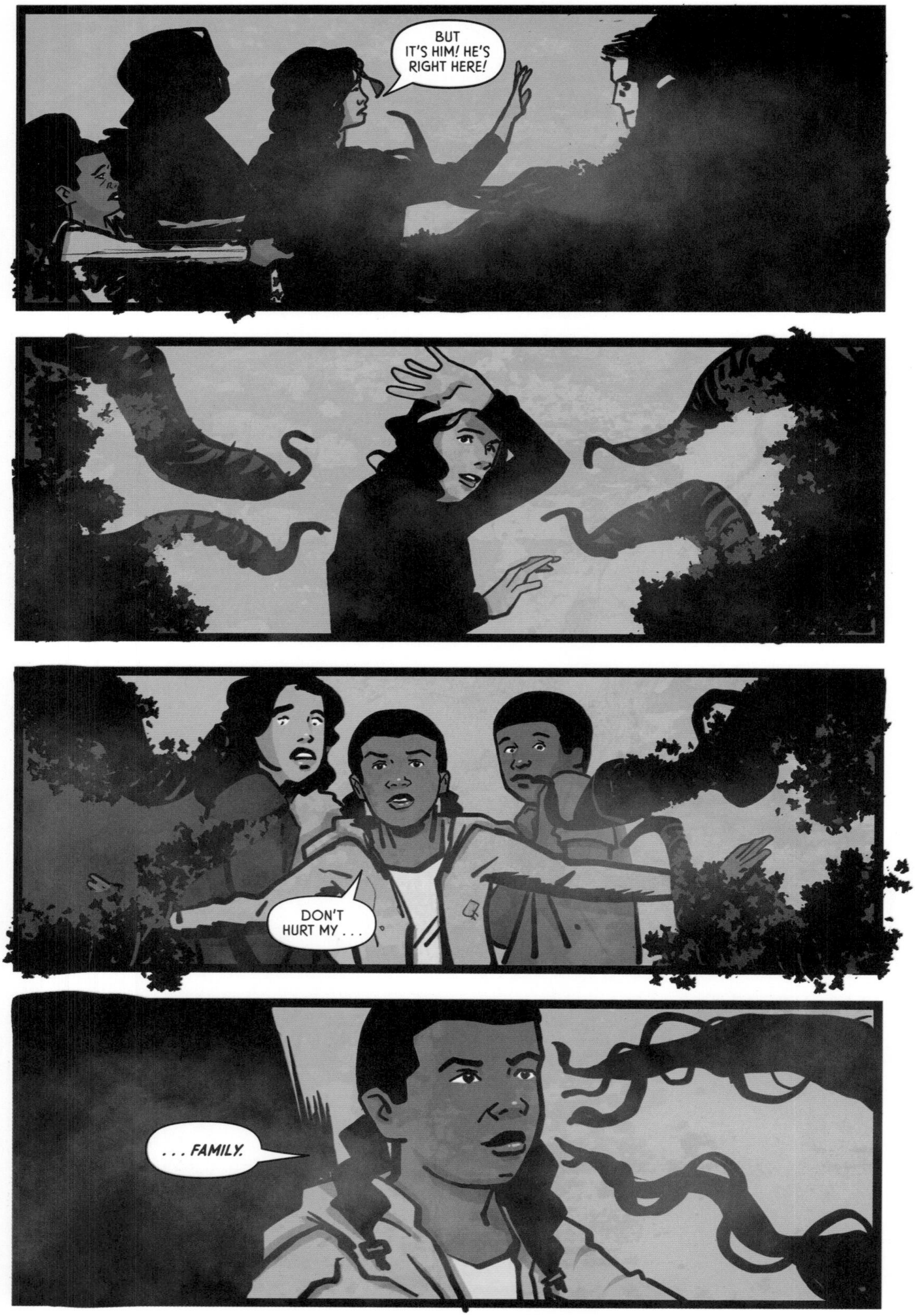
BUT IT'S HIM! HE'S RIGHT HERE!
DON'T HURT MY . . .
. . . FAMILY.

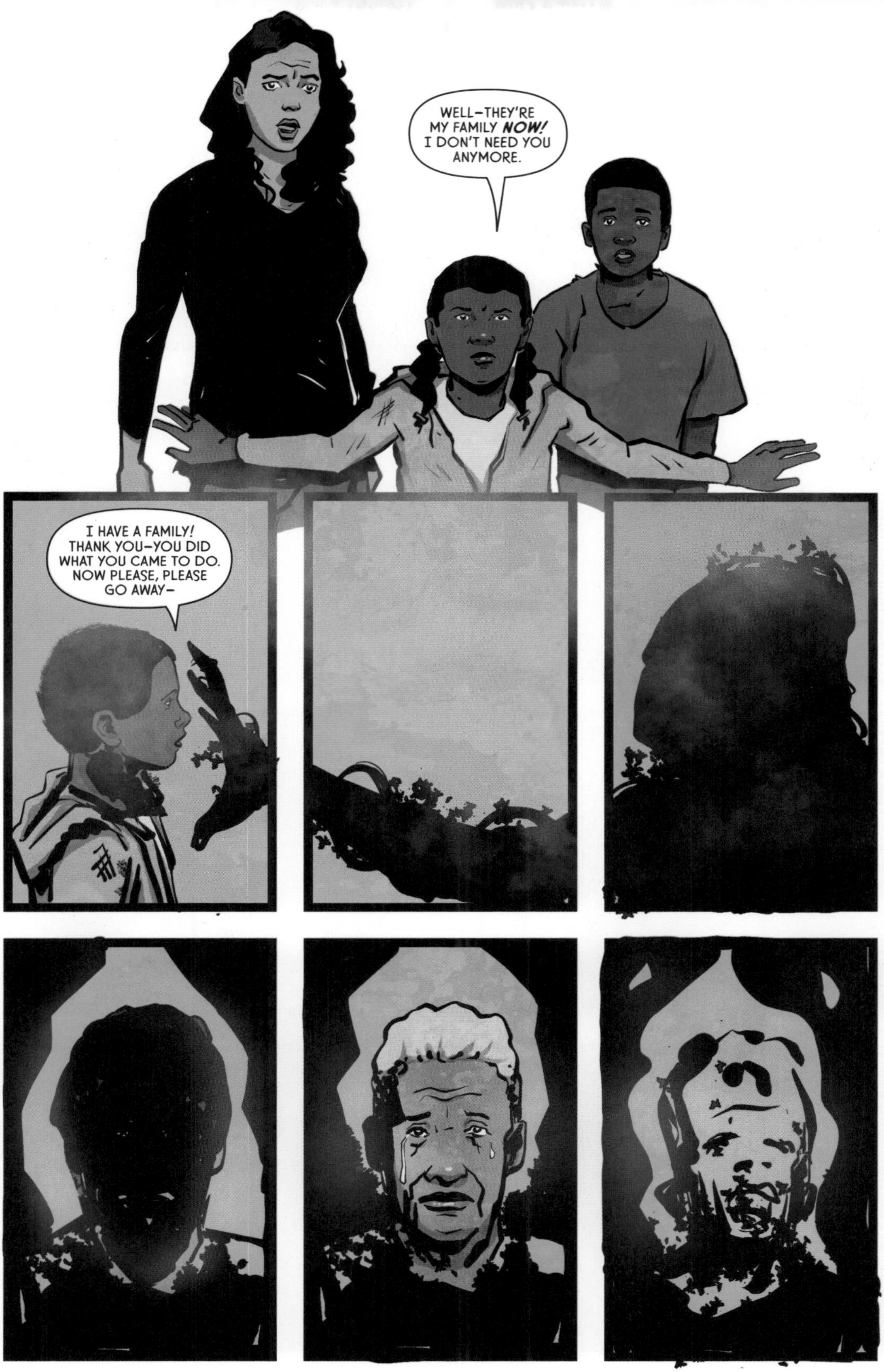
WELL—THEY'RE MY FAMILY **NOW!** I DON'T NEED YOU ANYMORE.
I HAVE A FAMILY! THANK YOU—YOU DID WHAT YOU CAME TO DO. NOW PLEASE, PLEASE GO AWAY—

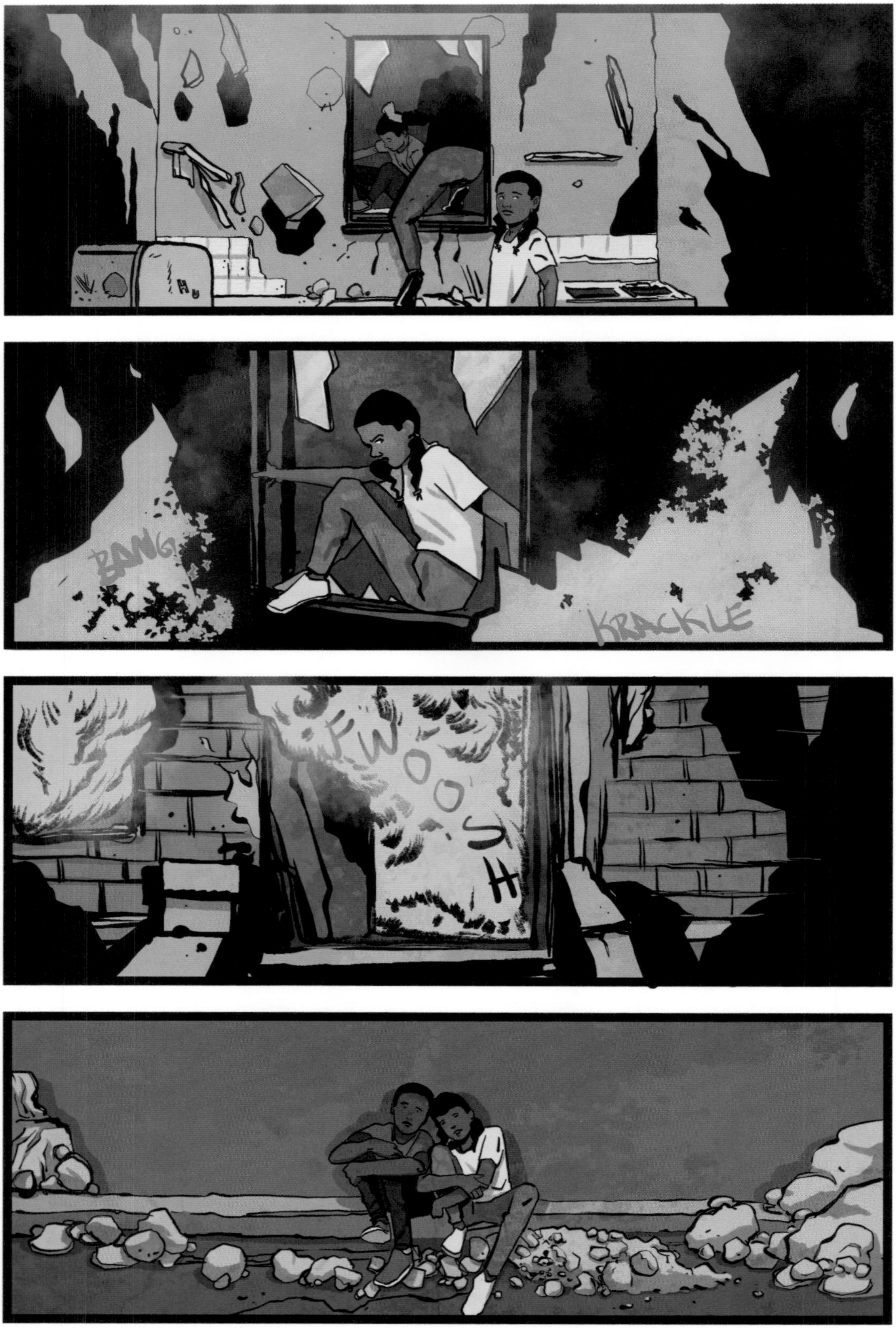
BANG!
KRACKLE
FWOOSH

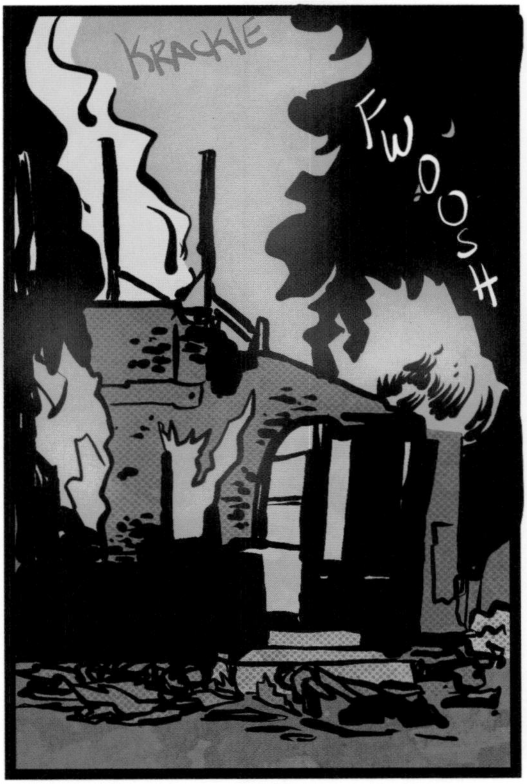
KRACKLE
FWOOSH
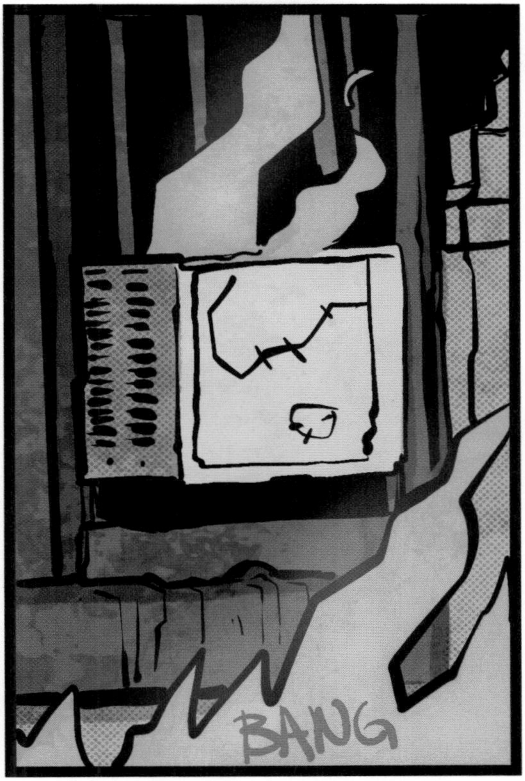
BANG
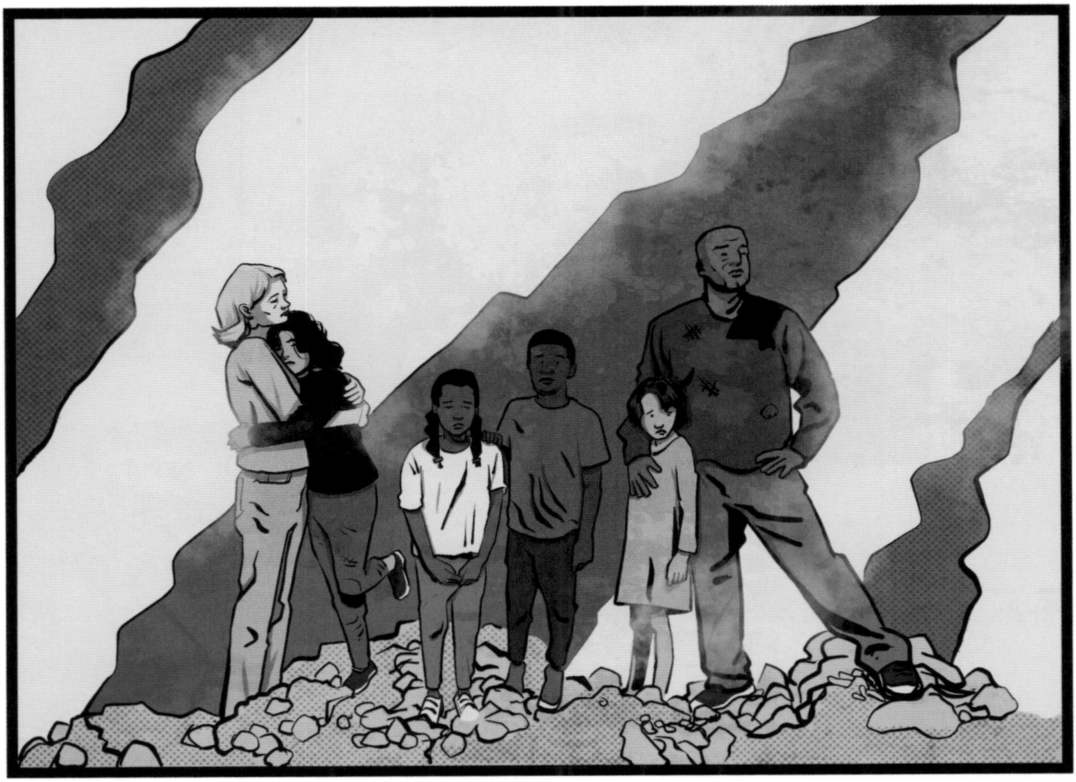

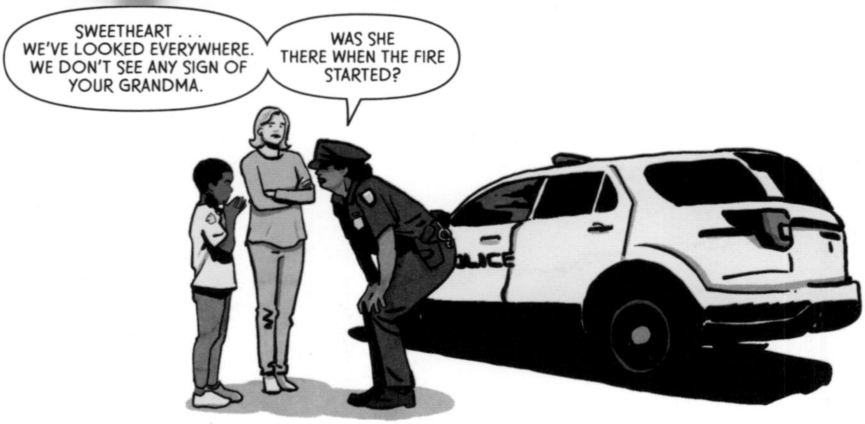
SWEETHEART . . . WE'VE LOOKED EVERYWHERE. WE DON'T SEE ANY SIGN OF YOUR GRANDMA.
WAS SHE THERE WHEN THE FIRE STARTED?
POLICE

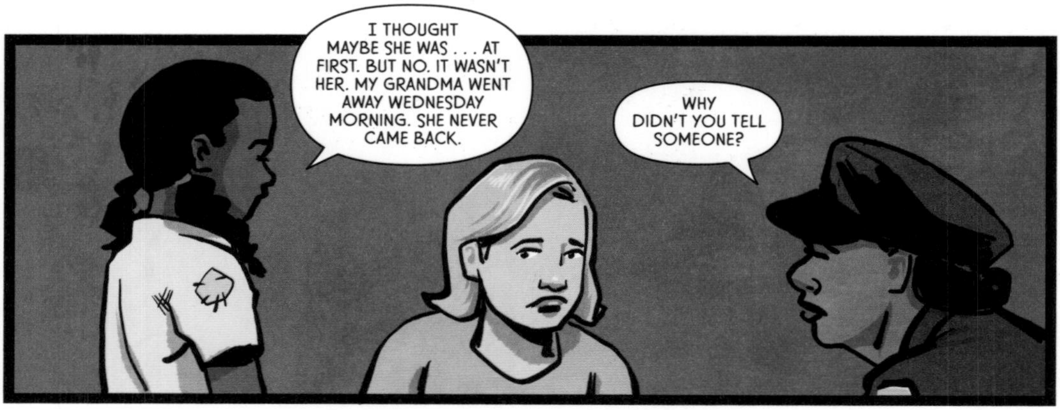
I THOUGHT MAYBE SHE WAS . . . AT FIRST. BUT NO. IT WASN'T HER. MY GRANDMA WENT AWAY WEDNESDAY MORNING. SHE NEVER CAME BACK.
WHY DIDN'T YOU TELL SOMEONE?

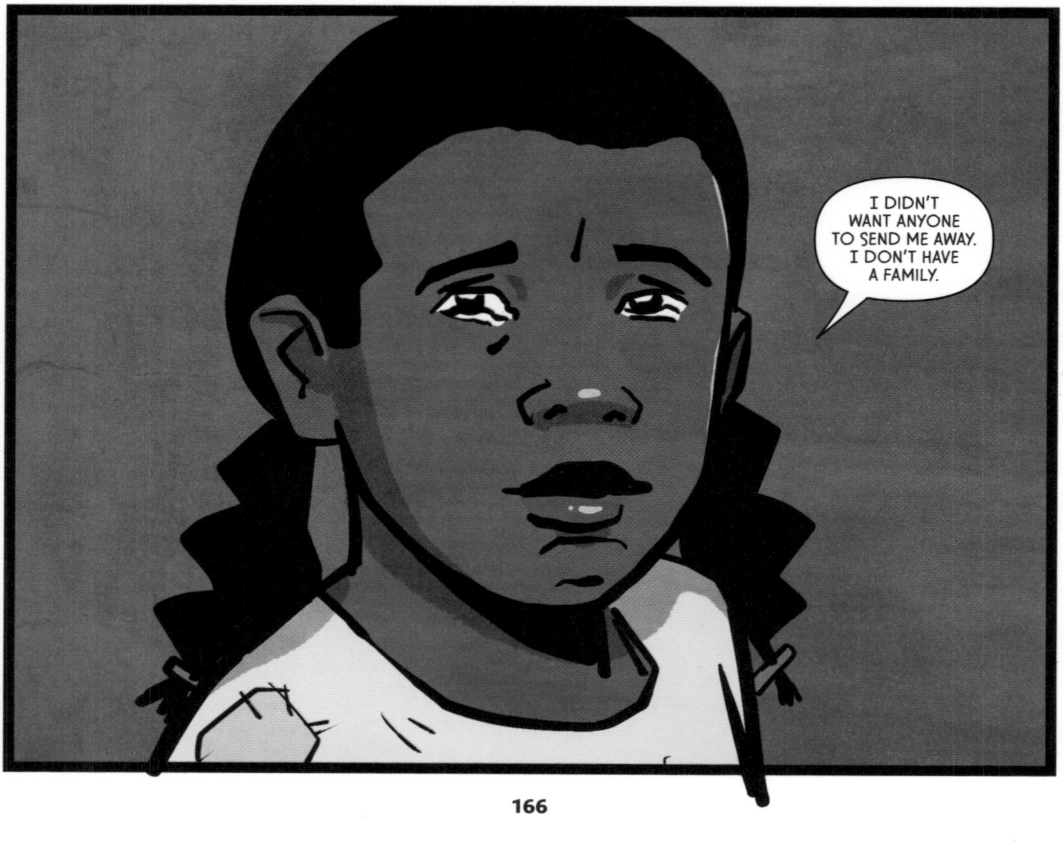
I DIDN'T WANT ANYONE TO SEND ME AWAY. I DON'T HAVE A FAMILY.

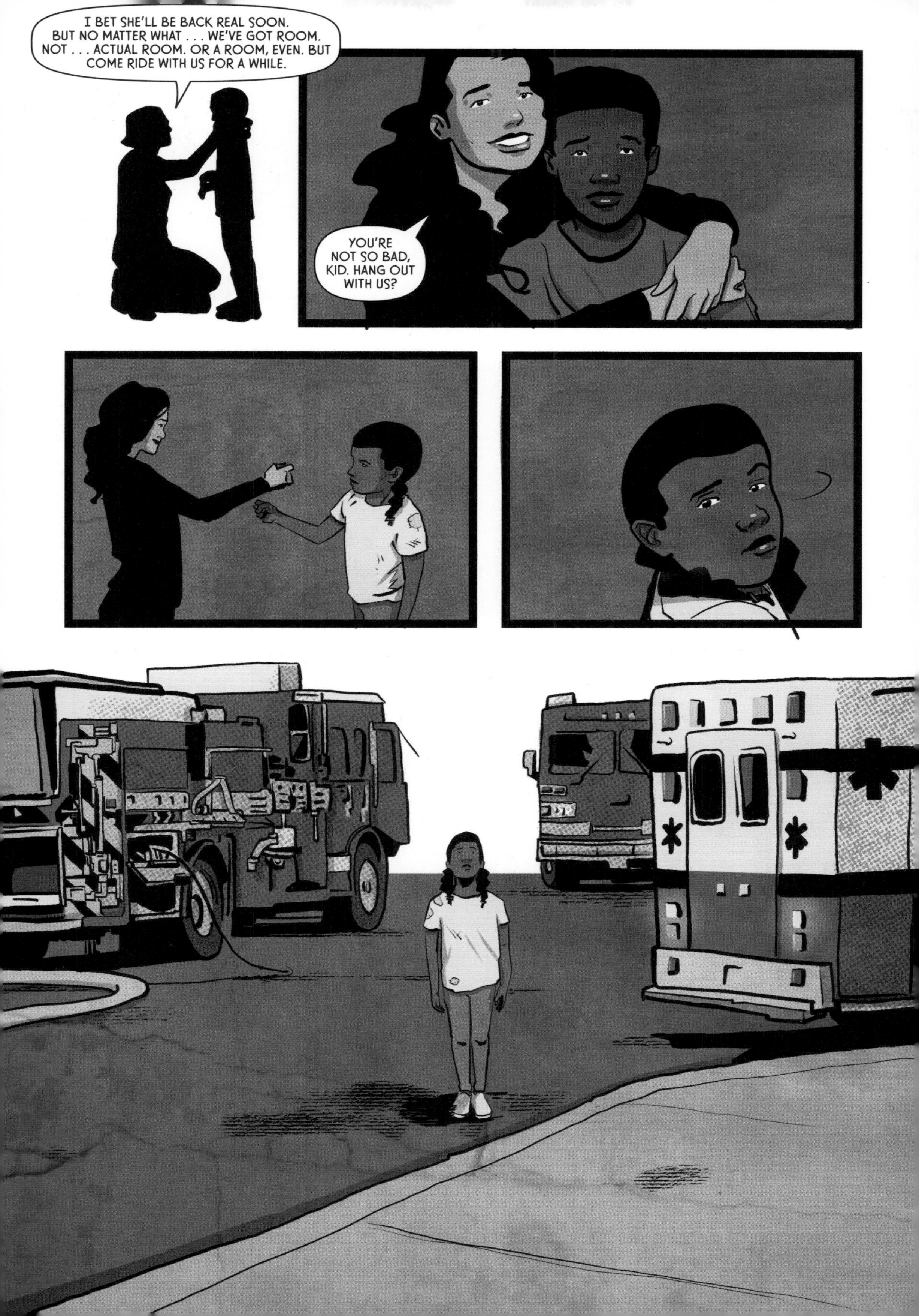
I BET SHE'LL BE BACK REAL SOON. BUT NO MATTER WHAT . . . WE'VE GOT ROOM. NOT . . . ACTUAL ROOM. OR A ROOM, EVEN. BUT COME RIDE WITH US FOR A WHILE.
YOU'RE NOT SO BAD, KID. HANG OUT WITH US?

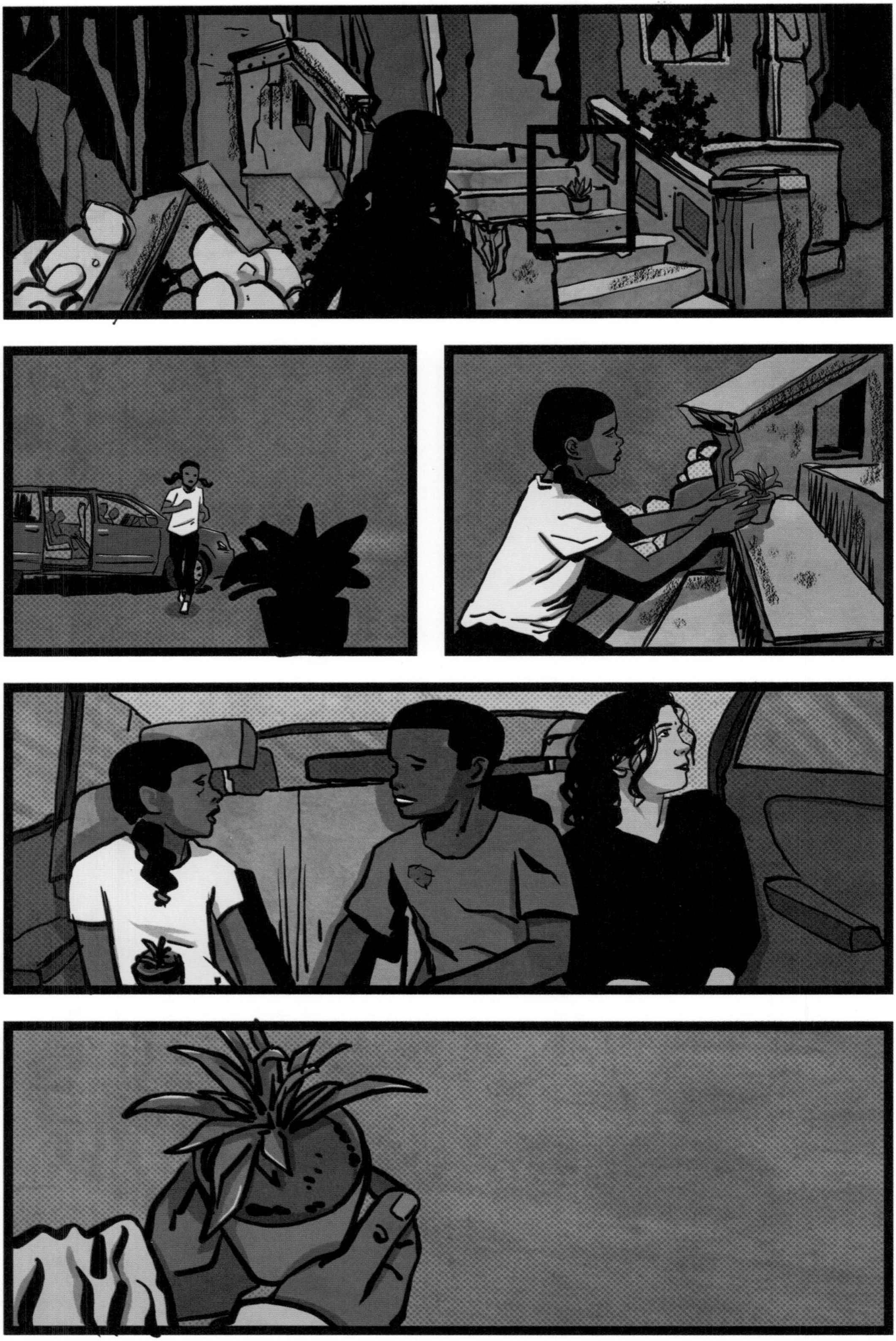

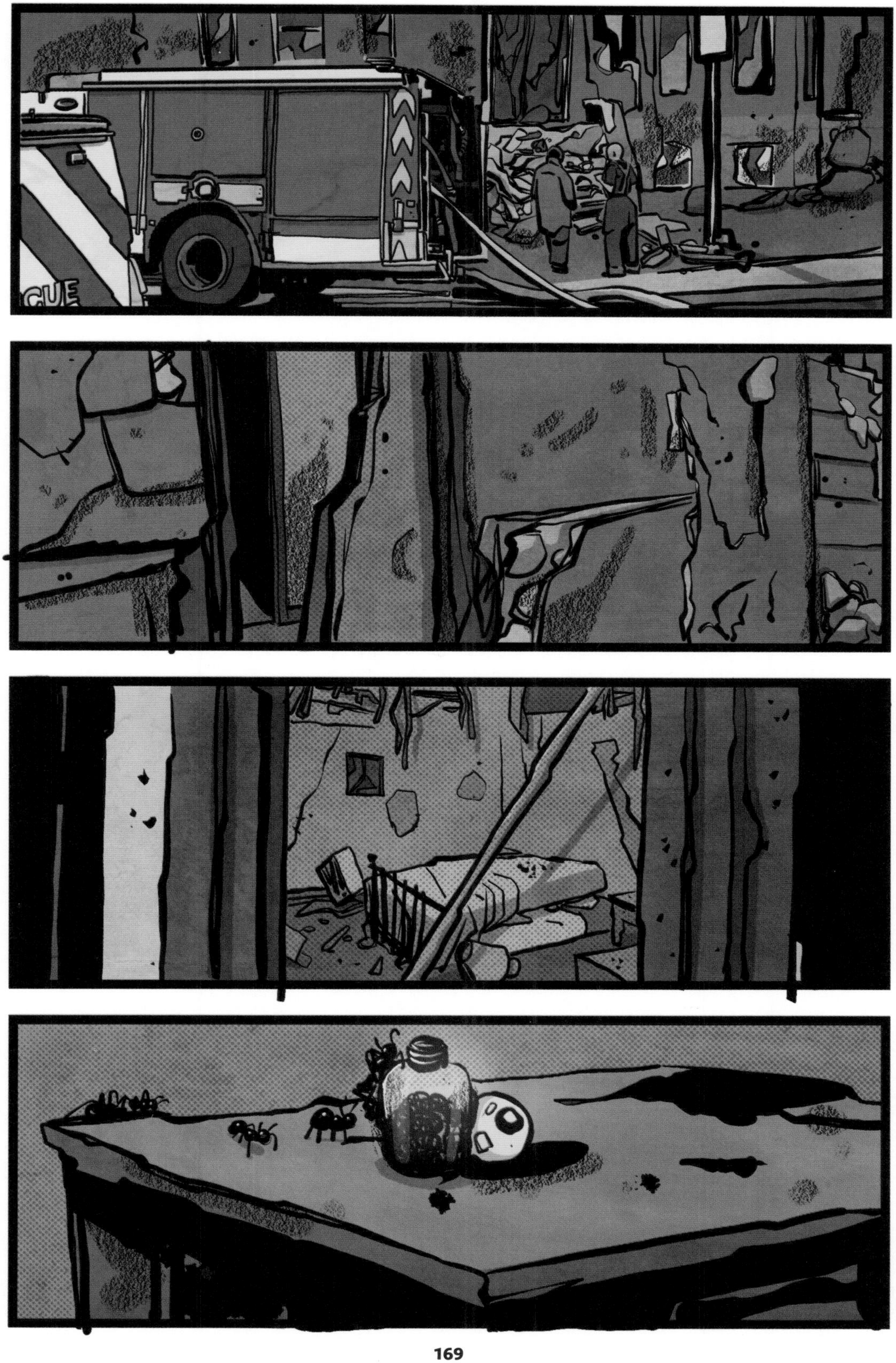
CUE

ACKNOWLEDGMENTS

For us, the story of *The Keeper* is one of disappointment turned into triumph, and we're so grateful for the team that made this happen.

Tananarive had an idea for a feature script about a young girl whose grandmother conjured a Keeper to protect her after she was dead—in part inspired by an incident when she was a young girl and spent the night in a room with her Great-Grandmother Lydia, who had emphysema and was using an oxygen machine. It was an early lesson on mortality and aging that stuck with her. We wrote the script. A favorite director said he "loved it" and wanted to put it into film development—but the studio where he had his deal passed. It was a real gut punch.

But along the way, we had shown the treatment to John Jennings for feedback. Not only did John like the treatment, but he also said he thought it would be a great graphic novel as a part of his exciting new speculative fiction imprint, Megascope—and he paired us with standout artist Marco Finnegan to bring it to life. Marco was like the director and cinematographer in his fantastic choices in adapting the script to this graphic novel.

So, our deepest thanks to John Jennings and Megascope, our amazing illustrator Marco Finnegan, Charlotte Greenbaum, Lauren White-Jackson, Andrea Miller, Marie Oishi, Angelica Busanet, and the rest of the Abrams ComicArts team.

This is our first joint graphic novel, and it is truly a dream come true.

—SB and TD

First of all, I have to thank John and Charlotte for thinking of me when it came time to find an artist for this book; your faith in me through the making of this book is huge and I appreciate your guidance, friendship, and support. Extra-special thanks to Tananarive and Steve for letting me play in their world and trusting me with their toys. Thanks to the whole *Keeper* team: Alexandria for making my art look so good with your amazing colors, Andy for all the tech support, and Lauren for keeping us all sane and on the same page!

Thanks to agent extraordinaire Dara Hyde for guiding me and having my back all the time.

Thanks to my boys Justin, Dylan, and Colton for pitching in for photo references even when you had other things to do.

Most of all I want to thank my beautiful wife, Lisa, for her invaluable support and love. I wouldn't be making these books if it weren't for you believing in me.

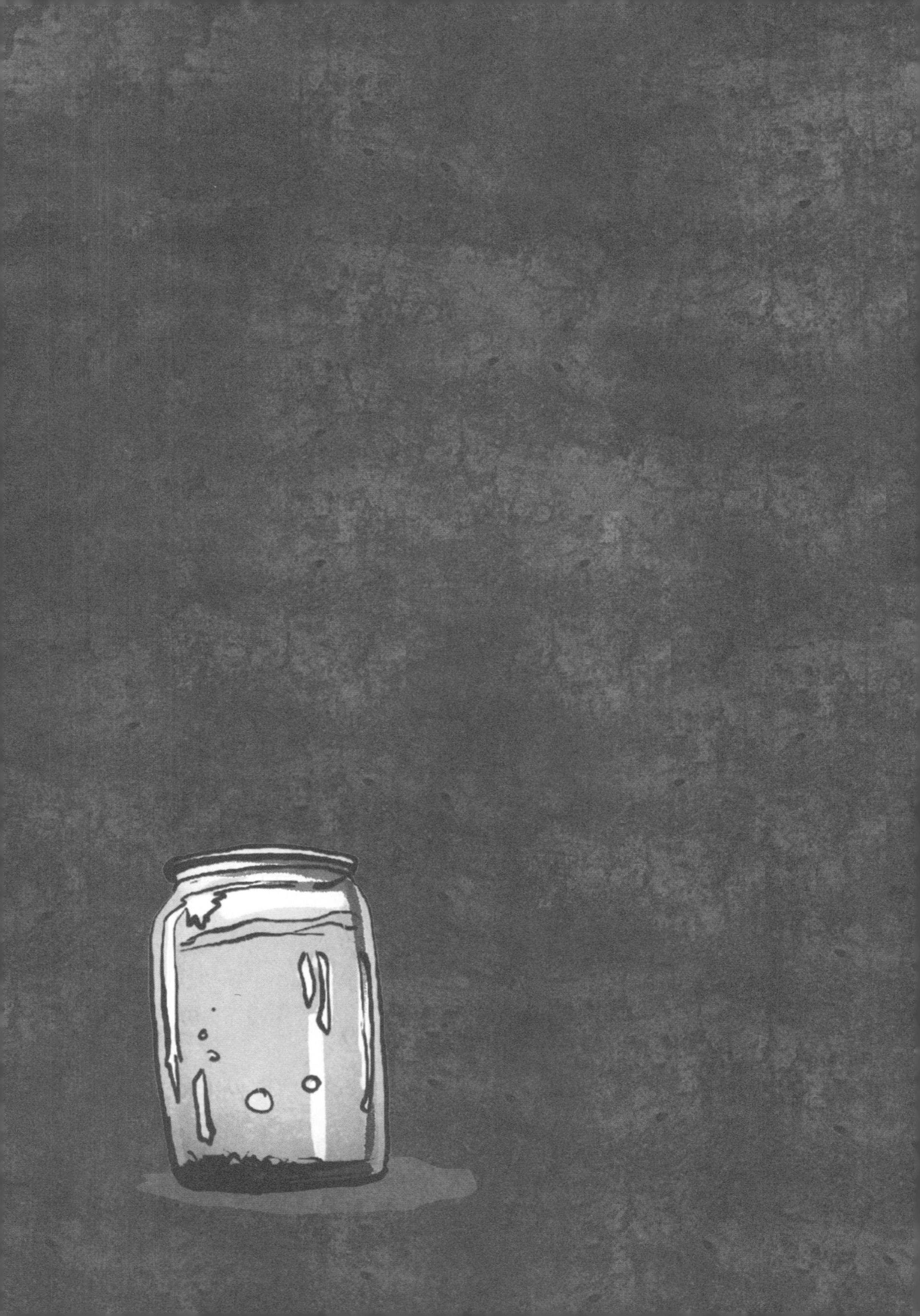